Fugitive Slaves and Spaces of Freedom in North America

Southern Dissent

UNIVERSITY PRESS OF FLORIDA

Florida A&M University, Tallahassee
Florida Atlantic University, Boca Raton
Florida Gulf Coast University, Ft. Myers
Florida International University, Miami
Florida State University, Tallahassee
New College of Florida, Sarasota
University of Central Florida, Orlando
University of Florida, Gainesville
University of North Florida, Jacksonville
University of South Florida, Tampa
University of West Florida, Pensacola

FUGITIVE SLAVES AND SPACES OF FREEDOM IN NORTH AMERICA

EDITED BY

DAMIAN ALAN PARGAS

Foreword by Stanley Harrold and Randall M. Miller

University Press of Florida
Gainesville · Tallahassee · Tampa · Boca Raton
Pensacola · Orlando · Miami · Jacksonville · Ft. Myers · Sarasota

Copyright 2018 by Damian Alan Pargas
All rights reserved
Published in the United States of America

First cloth printing, 2018
First paperback printing, 2020

25 24 23 22 21 20   6 5 4 3 2 1

Library of Congress Cataloging-in-Publication Data
Names: Pargas, Damian Alan, editor.
Title: Fugitive slaves and spaces of freedom in North America / edited by
    Damian Alan Pargas.
Other titles: Southern dissent.
Description: Gainesville : University Press of Florida, 2018. | Series:
    Southern dissent | Includes bibliographical references and index.
Identifiers: LCCN 2017060267 | ISBN 9780813056036 (cloth : alk. paper)
ISBN 9780813068367 (pbk.)
Subjects: LCSH: Fugitive slaves—United States. | Slavery—United
    States—History. | Slaves—Emancipation—United States.
Classification: LCC E450 .F957 2018 | DDC 973.7/115—dc23
LC record available at https://lccn.loc.gov/2017060267

The University Press of Florida is the scholarly publishing agency for the State University System of Florida, comprising Florida A&M University, Florida Atlantic University, Florida Gulf Coast University, Florida International University, Florida State University, New College of Florida, University of Central Florida, University of Florida, University of North Florida, University of South Florida, and University of West Florida.

University Press of Florida
2046 NE Waldo Road
Suite 2100
Gainesville, FL 32609
http://upress.ufl.edu

CONTENTS

List of Figures vii
List of Tables ix
Foreword xi

Introduction: Spaces of Freedom in North America 1
Damian Alan Pargas

1. Black Self-Emancipation, Gradual Emancipation, and the Underground Railroad in the Northern Colonies and States, 1763–1804 21
Graham Russell Gao Hodges

2. Revisiting "British Principle Talk": Antebellum Black Expectations and Racism in Early Ontario 34
Gordon S. Barker

3. The Underground Railroad in "Indian Country": Northwest Ohio, 1795–1843 70
Roy E. Finkenbine

4. After 1850: Reassessing the Impact of the Fugitive Slave Law 93
Matthew Pinsker

5. Seeking Freedom in the Midst of Slavery: Fugitive Slaves in the Antebellum South 116
Damian Alan Pargas

6. Illegal but Tolerated: Slave Refugees in Richmond, Virginia, 1800–1860 137
Viola Franziska Müller

7. Borderland Maroons 168
Sylviane A. Diouf

8. Advertising Maranda: Runaway Slaves in Texas, 1835–1865   197
   Kyle Ainsworth

9. "Design His Course to Mexico": The Fugitive Slave Experience in the Texas–Mexico Borderlands, 1850–1853   232
   Mekala Audain

10. Freedom Interrupted: Runaway Slaves and Insecure Borders in the Mexican Northeast   251
    James David Nichols

11. The U.S. Coastal Passage and Caribbean Spaces of Freedom   275
    Jeffrey R. Kerr-Ritchie

List of Contributors   317
Index   319

FIGURES

8.1. Newspaper advertisement submitted by Robert F. Millard of Nacogdoches, Texas   198

8.2. Newspaper notice for a horse captured from a runaway slave   202

TABLES

8.1. Runaway slave content in Texas documents, 1835–1865   203

8.2. Newspaper repetitions of Texas runaway slave advertisements   204

8.3. Days between when a runaway escaped and when the slave owner wrote the advertisement   206

8.4. Days between when a runaway escaped and when the advertisement was published in a newspaper   206

8.5. Frequency of slave flight attempts from Texas counties, 1835–1865   208

8.6. Presumed destination of fugitive slaves in Texas, 1835–1865   209

8.7. Escape attempts where the runaway slave stole a horse or mule   216

8A.1. Departure locations for fugitive slave escapes in Texas, 1835–1865   218

8A.2. Capture locations for fugitive slave captures in Texas, 1835–1865   220

11.1. Liberated captives from select U.S. coastal slavers in the Caribbean, 1826–1841   306

FOREWORD

So long as slavery existed in North America, people escaped from it. During the seventeenth century, when black chattel slavery replaced white indentured servitude as the predominant form of unfree labor in Britain's North American colonies (especially in the Chesapeake region and southward), slaves left their masters to seek freedom. Usually traveling on foot, they sought refuge in forests and swamps, in American Indian villages, in towns and cities, and in neighboring colonies. During the eighteenth century and thereafter, slaves escaped by sea as well as by land. Young men always predominated among fugitives. But women, children, and entire families fled bondage as well.

Such ventures were extremely risky. Fugitive slaves faced difficult journeys through unfamiliar landscapes. Finding food and shelter, as well as help and guidance, posed daunting difficulties. Masters hired "slave catchers" to run down and apprehend escapes. Masters also sought government support for recovering their "property" and inflicting punishments on those they recaptured. The Virginia colony, for example, in 1705 adopted a law that allowed masters to kill slaves who attempted to abscond. Nevertheless, escapes continued. During the American War for Independence, thousands of slaves left their masters. Many of them took refuge behind British lines. Some served in British armies. All of this led to the inclusion of a fugitive slave clause in the U.S. Constitution as adopted in 1789. Four years later Congress passed the first federal Fugitive Slave Act. It empowered masters or their agents to cross state lines in pursuit of escapees, capture them, and return them to slavery.

As escapes mounted during the nineteenth century, northern state legislatures passed "personal liberty" laws designed to protect free black residents from being kidnapped into slavery—and to make renditions of fugitive slaves more difficult. As a result, slave escape became a major political issue that divided the country, rivaling slavery expansion into western territories as a threat to the Union. When the Compromise of 1850 included a new, more stringent fugitive law that empowered U.S. marshals to aid masters in apprehending escapes and called on northerners to aid in taking up alleged fugitives, many black and white people physically resisted its enforcement. During the same period, many black people left the northern states for refuge in Canada.

As Damian Alan Pargas points out in his introduction to *Fugitive Slaves and Spaces of Freedom in North America*, the number of books and journal articles dealing with slave escapes has swelled during recent years. New studies of slave-escape networks, referred to collectively as the Underground Railroad, that emphasize northward escapes are prominent within this scholarship. But slave escapes into the Caribbean and Mexico have attracted increasing attention. There have also been studies of slaves who escaped their masters and remained in the South. Nearly all of these recent studies center on one region, era, and escape process.

In contrast, as a collection of eleven essays, *Fugitive Slaves and Spaces of Freedom in North America* provides a comprehensive and comparative view of the escape phenomenon. Also, as the term "spaces of freedom" suggests, the essays stress the degrees of freedom that escapees gained. They discuss legal freedom afforded former slaves who reached Canada or Mexico, limited freedom in the northern states of the United States, and precarious freedom in southern cities and such inaccessible places as Virginia's Great Dismal Swamp. Within this book's wide context, each essay has its own focus. But the overall accomplishment is a broad, up-to-date portrait of slaves' physical search for, and maintenance of, freedom stretching from the end of the French and Indian War to just before the start of the Civil War. Within that context, as the authors show, the slaves' efforts to find freedom were varied but constant. Their efforts contradicted proslavery arguments that the enslaved were content in their bondage. The diversity and multiple directions of slave escapes also led many northerners to consider their own interests in defending freedom and the right to be free. The collection is a welcome addition to the *Southern Dissent* series.

Stanley Harrold and Randall M. Miller
Series Editors

Introduction

Spaces of Freedom in North America

DAMIAN ALAN PARGAS

On the Fourth of July 1825, most white residents of Washington, D.C., celebrated the anniversary of their freedom and independence from Great Britain with parades, elaborate theater productions, and other amusements that included a "GRAND OLIO of Song, Dance, and Recitation" and "a GRAND SCROLL DANCE by the Corps de Ballet." At the same time, dozens of enslaved people from the surrounding farm districts of Maryland and Virginia were making their own attempts to secure freedom and independence from a life of bondage. The *Daily National Intelligencer* printed no less than ten runaway slave advertisements that day—some of them for groups and even entire families—a significant number for any single issue. The presumed whereabouts of the runaways ran the full gamut of possible destinations, illuminating the complicated geography of slavery and freedom that existed throughout the continent.

Some runaways, for example, were explicitly presumed to be disguising their visibility as slaves and attempting to pass for free, even while remaining within the slaveholding South. Indeed, three were supposedly posing as *whites*. Granderson, a twenty-three-year-old carpenter who was described as "remarkably white for a slave, and might be readily taken for a white man," had absconded with the intention "doubtless to pass as a free man" and practice his trade right in Washington. Two brothers named Rezin and Harry (eighteen and sixteen years old, respectively), who were also "of so bright a complexion, that they would hardly be taken for mulattoes," were likewise suspected of lurking about the city and passing for white. Even runaways with a dark complexion could hope to disguise their visibility as slaves in Washington, which in the antebellum period had a sizable free black population that at times outnumbered the slave population by as much as four to one. Tom, a local bondsman and a skilled wagoner, was presumed to be passing himself off as a free black in the city, where he would "probably offer his services." Others like him were described as having changed their names and run off "with forged papers" to live among the free blacks of the District.[1]

Predictably, a handful of freedom seekers had safer territory in mind. With the Pennsylvania border a mere sixty miles north of Washington as the crow flies, free soil seemed tantalizingly close to bondspeople living in the capital region. Daniel, Moses, and Scipio, all between the ages of twenty-five and thirty, were suspected of having "obtained [forged] passes" to travel "out of the States of Virginia, Maryland, and the District of Columbia" to a northern free state. Another bondsman named George was also thought to be making his way north, his master so baffled by the flight of his "most industrious and faithful field hand" that he concluded that his slave "must have been decoyed off" by somebody who had provided him with a false pass. To some runaways, however, even the northern states—where federal laws allowed for southern masters to reclaim their fugitive slaves and drag them back to the South—did not seem quite safe enough. One entire family consisting of an enslaved carpenter named Ben, his three daughters, and his son-in-law—all from Stafford County, Virginia—executed a daring attempt to leave the United States altogether and make for free territory elsewhere in the hemisphere. The group reportedly fled to Washington with forged free papers, having told friends that they intended to board a vessel bound for the Caribbean because they wanted "to go to St. Domingo," where slavery had not only been abolished but where the government also promised asylum and citizenship to all runaway slaves who reached its shores. Their secret plans had somehow become known to their master, but the other slaves who were advertised as missing on that Fourth of July slipped away more quietly and left no trace of their intentions or possible whereabouts; their masters presumed them to be either hiding out in Washington or making their way to a free state—it was anybody's guess.[2]

What is so striking about these advertisements is that the presumed destinations of the runaway slaves were so diverse. They included places where slavery had been abolished (such as the northern states and Haiti) *and* places where it still existed (such as Washington). From the perspective of enslaved people seeking to flee bondage in the antebellum South, in other words, freedom in one form or another could be found in a wide variety of geographical, political, and social settings. Freedom could be forged in the north, south, east, or west; it could be reached by crossing political borders or by remaining within the borders of the slaveholding territories; it could be attained by disguising one's true identity or by openly claiming asylum. Different destinations required different strategies of absconding, and no place constituted an *ideal* destination for runaway slaves, but, however imperfect, North America in the decades preceding the Civil War provided enslaved people with various spaces to which they could flee to try to escape slavery.

The essays in this volume examine the experiences of permanent runaway slaves—those who had no intention of returning to their masters—in various settings in North America during a period of important structural transitions. Throughout the Americas, the geography of slavery and freedom was radically and irrevocably transformed in the late eighteenth and early nineteenth centuries. For many African Americans, it was an age of emancipation. Whereas prior to the American Revolution human bondage was legally sanctioned and rarely questioned in every part of the hemisphere, the last quarter of the eighteenth century witnessed what Steven Hahn has called a "deepening crisis of slave regimes" as growing moral doubts about slaveholding among Quakers and Protestant evangelicals dovetailed with economic and intellectual challenges to the institution's perceived inefficiency, social undesirability, and political unsustainability among prominent thinkers in Europe and America.[3] Transatlantic discourses in the age of revolutions had a profound effect upon slavery in the New World, ultimately leading to the legal abolition of the transatlantic slave trade and of slavery itself in various parts of the Americas. Moreover, this period witnessed a spike in individual manumissions and self-purchase schemes by slaveholders who for ideological or financial reasons struggled with the idea of keeping some or all of their bondspeople enslaved for life, which resulted in the emergence or bolstering of free black communities *within* slaveholding territories (especially in urban areas). In short, significant numbers of black people in the Atlantic world legally exited slavery in the late eighteenth and early nineteenth centuries.[4]

Yet for countless other African Americans it was an age of what Dale Tomich has called "the second slavery," a period of intensification of slavery in regions such as the American South, Brazil, and Cuba. Indeed, the entrenchment of slavery, even as antislavery scored its first victories, constituted one of the great paradoxes of the Atlantic world. While some parts of the Americas saw their free black populations considerably augmented, others devolved into "freedom's mirror," as Ada Ferrer recently put it. For those still enslaved, the changing landscape of slavery and freedom provided new opportunities to escape and therefore gave rise to waves of asylum-based migration as droves of slave refugees crossed into geographic spaces and places that constituted sites of *formal freedom* (where slavery was abolished according to "free-soil" principles, such as Haiti) or *informal freedom* (regions within slaveholding territories, especially urban areas, where slaves attempted to escape by blending in with newly augmented free black populations).[5]

In North America, the geography of slavery and freedom that emerged in the late eighteenth and early nineteenth centuries was even more complicated as it included sites of formal, semiformal, and informal freedom for fugitive slaves. The northern United States, British Canada, and Mexico all abolished slavery between 1777 and 1834. Yet only in British Canada and Mexico did spaces of *formal freedom*—eventually—emerge on paper (although in practice the meanings and security of this freedom were contested in a multitude of ways). And even there the shift to free soil was protracted and wrought with inconsistencies. For example, the legislature of Upper Canada passed An Act to Prevent the Further Introduction of Slaves and to Limit the Term of Contracts for Servitude within this Province in 1793, nobly declaring it "unjust that a people who enjoy Freedom by Law should encourage the introduction of Slaves" and "highly expedient to abolish Slavery in this Province, so far as the same may gradually be done without violating private property." Yet the law fell short of fully abolishing slavery outright, merely decreeing that no new slaves could be imported or brought into the province and that children born to slave mothers would be freed at age twenty-five. According to the act, those already enslaved would remain so for life. Subsequent legislation hastened the transition to freedom in the province, and the dominion went to great lengths not to extradite fugitive slaves from the United States, but it would take until the final abolition of slavery throughout the British Empire in 1834 for bondage in all of Canada to end definitively. The development of an independence movement in early-nineteenth-century Mexico, meanwhile, also took place in a revolutionary atmosphere hostile to slavery, with the movement's founding document—Father Hidalgo's Grito de Dolores (1810)—explicitly calling for the eradication of bondage throughout New Spain. But there, too, the transition to freedom was a painfully slow and nonlinear process. Upon achieving independence in 1821, Mexico continued to experience political struggles between various pro- and antislavery factions, which brought about a series of confusing and often contradictory decrees regarding the legality of the institution, but the central government nevertheless ordered unequivocally in 1823 that all slave children under the age of fourteen be emancipated, and on September 15, 1829, President Vicente Guerrero formally abolished slavery outright, announcing in the simplest and most unambiguous terms possible: "Queda abolida la esclavitud en la República" ("Slavery in the Republic is abolished"), and "Son consiguiente libres los que hasta hoy se habian considerado como esclavos" ("Those who until today were considered slaves are hereafter free"). By the 1830s both Canada and Mexico had become spaces of unconditional formal freedom, where runaway slaves were theoretically safe from extradition and reenslavement, at least on paper. (In practice, illegal border raids in the Texas borderlands made recapture a possibility for fugitive slaves in northern Mexico).[6]

In the northern United States, state-level abolition—what scholars have dubbed the "First Emancipation"—was achieved through a complicated maze of constitutional clauses, court verdicts, and gradual emancipation acts. With the notable exceptions of Vermont and Massachusetts, most northern states abolished slavery in the same protracted manner that Canada and Mexico did, and, like both of those countries, most had to eventually pass subsequent legislation to definitively end the institution. The northern transition to free soil, which began with Vermont in 1777, was virtually set in stone by 1804, however, when all states and territories north of the Mason–Dixon line and Ohio River—including the federal Northwest Territory—had either prohibited slavery or enacted gradual abolition acts. By the early decades of the nineteenth century, slaves were all but absent in the North. Unlike in Canada and Mexico, however, northern legislation against slavery was theoretically curtailed by overarching federal fugitive slave laws—embedded in Article IV of the United States Constitution and reaffirmed in the Fugitive Slave Acts of 1793 and 1850—that upheld the rights of slaveholders to recover their runaway slaves. Although northern representatives to the federal government specifically supported federal fugitive slave laws (especially those of the Constitution and of 1793), ordinary citizens and local authorities often felt that federal laws forced them to accept slavery in their midst, and as the rift over slavery grew wider in the antebellum period many northern communities went to great lengths to prevent the recapture of runaway slaves. Indeed, most northern state legislatures attempted to safeguard the refugees within their jurisdictions by passing various "personal liberty laws" that required jury trials for fugitive slave cases and placed the burden of proof on slave catchers. After the deeply unpopular Fugitive Slave Law of 1850 some went so far as to prohibit state officials from complying with federal authorities in such instances, and Wisconsin even attempted to nullify the law altogether. Abolitionist organizations, meanwhile, made a point of harboring fugitive slaves and helping them to reach sites of formal freedom in Canada. These actions certainly helped to protect runaway slaves from reenslavement, but they were still a far cry from full legal immunity from extradition. Sites of freedom for fugitive slaves in the northern states therefore remained semiformal: refugees found themselves theoretically on free soil, but their claims to freedom from reenslavement remained precarious at best and often contested in the courts.[7]

Meanwhile, sites of informal freedom for fugitive slaves emerged within the slaveholding South itself after a wave of individual manumissions in the (post-)revolutionary and early federal periods—especially between 1790 and 1810—bolstered free black populations in countless towns and cities across the region, attracting innumerable runaways who attempted to escape their masters by getting lost in the crowd and passing for free. The same revolutionary climate that resulted in the abolition of slavery in the northern states also convinced many southern lawmakers to open the doors of freedom—if ever so slightly—for enslaved people by enacting legislation that greatly facilitated and even encouraged manumissions. Virginia's manumission law of 1782—passed in an era of not only revolutionary fervor but also declining tobacco productivity and a growing pessimism in the future of slavery—provides an illustrative case in point. While it did not abolish slavery itself (although abolition was proposed by some lawmakers), the Act to Authorize the Manumission of Slaves nevertheless simplified the freeing of bondspeople under the age of forty-five held by slaveholders of the revolutionary generation who wished to bestow this "privilege" upon their slaves. The act specified that "it shall hereafter be lawful for any person, by his or her last will and testament, or by any other instrument in writing . . . to emancipate and set free, his or her slaves, or any of them, who shall thereupon be entirely and fully discharged from the performance of any contract entered into during servitude, and enjoy as full freedom as if they had been particularly named and freed by this act."[8] Considering that Virginia was the largest slave state, and one where manumissions had theretofore been very difficult to get approval for (only the governor could approve a manumission request, and then only for "meritous service"), the act of 1782 certainly seemed to usher in a change in course. Although strongly opposed by many white residents and largely reversed in the early nineteenth century, it was a piece of legislation that more than a few Virginia slaveholders made use of in the three decades subsequent to its passage. Whereas before 1782 less than 1 percent of Virginia's African American population was free, by 1790 free blacks accounted for 4.2 percent of the total, and by 1810 they had reached 7.2 percent, surging in absolute numbers from 1,800 to 30,570 in less than thirty years. The number of free blacks living in the port town of Alexandria alone grew from 52 in 1790 to 1,168 in 1820—Richmond, Petersburg, and Norfolk showed proportionally similar trends.[9]

Throughout the Upper South more than 10 percent of African Americans were classified as free by 1810, many of them concentrated in cities such as Baltimore, Washington, and Richmond. In the Lower South the number of free blacks increased less dramatically—from 1.6 percent of the black population in 1790 to 3.9 percent in 1810—but enough to significantly augment the free black populations of places like Charleston, New Orleans, and countless smaller towns across the southern states. This wave of manumissions at the turn of the nineteenth century "provided the basis for the South's free black population in the antebellum period," as Peter Kolchin has argued, for after

1810—as the revolutionary fervor died out and the South became more openly committed to slavery—manumission became much more difficult, and relatively few slaves were freed.[10]

Indeed, in the South as a whole, the institution of slavery continued to grow at a feverish pace between the American Revolution and the Civil War, following the expansion of cotton into the southern interior and generating a lucrative domestic slave trade that washed almost a million American-born slaves from the Upper South and eastern seaboard to the Deep South, tearing families and communities apart in its wake. The more entrenched bondage became in the American South during the era of the second slavery, the more determined some slaves became to flee captivity altogether, enticed by the prospect of freedom in various geographical settings. The border regions of the North, Canada, and Mexico as well as urban free black communities within the South became the destinations of thousands of runaways. Various spaces and places throughout the continent teemed with freedom seekers looking to escape slavery.[11]

Running away from slavery was of course nothing new in antebellum America; the endemic slave flight that characterized black resistance in the age of the second slavery indeed built upon strategies of absconding that were originally established in the colonial period. Long before the first states moved to facilitate manumission or abolish slavery, enslaved people in North America tried to escape bondage whenever they were presented with opportunities to do so. Sites of formal freedom were absent, but sanctuary spaces and places did exist where daring refugees from bondage could (and did) attempt to carve out lives of informal and even semiformal freedom for themselves and their loved ones. Three strategies in particular were employed, all of which were extremely risky and only seldom successful on a long-term basis. Whatever their shortcomings, however, they established a culture of seeking, creating, and even forcing sanctuary spaces that would later more widely be employed—in a changed landscape of slavery and freedom—in the nineteenth century.

The first two strategies entailed fleeing to sites of informal freedom. First, runaway slaves practiced wilderness marronage, hiding out in forests, swamps, and other sparsely settled areas. The Great Dismal Swamp in southern Virginia alone was thought to harbor hundreds of runaway slaves, to the great consternation of local slaveholders and colonial authorities, who often enlisted the help of the state militia to raid maroon settlements and recover their human property. Colonial authorities up and down the Atlantic seaboard faced similar challenges, as wilderness areas, mountain ranges, and swamps from New York to South Carolina provided refuge for untold numbers of fugitives.[12] Second, runaway slaves in colonial America concealed themselves in urban areas or even attempted to pass for free in towns that already had free black populations, again clandestinely navigating sites of informal freedom. Ad hoc manumissions in the seventeenth and early eighteenth centuries had created small clusters of free black communities throughout the colonies, even in the southern colonies where manumissions were legally most circumscribed. Their numbers were tiny: on the eve of the Revolution, free blacks composed less than 5 percent of the entire black population in the colonies, but their communities nevertheless served as beacons of freedom to some daring runaway slaves.[13]

Finally, enslaved people in colonial America took advantage of temporary wartime situations and geopolitical conflicts to flee to their masters' enemies. More specifically, they sought asylum in Spanish Florida, with local indigenous communities, and—to enter the revolutionary era itself—behind British lines and in British-occupied territories during the American Revolution. In these sites of semiformal freedom, runaways clearly pressed for—and were often granted—protection from extradition and reenslavement, but there were no guarantees. The official status of slave refugees in such theaters of conflict was indeed usually conditional, ambiguous, and unclear. For example, Spanish Florida—itself a society with slaves—promised asylum to runaway slaves from the British colonies as early as 1687 upon the condition that the refugees convert to the "True Faith." But uncertainties regarding the correct interpretation of royal policy led to some runaways remaining enslaved or even being sold abroad. In a notorious example, Governor Antonio de Benavides sold a group of newly arrived fugitive slaves at public auction in 1725 because South Carolina slaveholders were threatening to come and reclaim them by force, and when he wrote to Spain to inquire if the slaves were entitled to sanctuary no reply was forthcoming.[14] Likewise, fleeing to Native American communities offered no guarantees of protection; some Native Americans willingly harbored runaway slaves in the colonial period, but others returned slaves to their masters or even killed them, depending on their relations with local white authorities. The Creek even signed a treaty with the governor of South Carolina in 1721 in which they promised to apprehend and return "any Negro or other Slave which shall run away from any English Settlements to our Nation."[15] And although the British famously granted freedom to runaway slaves who enlisted in the king's cause during the American Revolution—and subsequently evacuated thousands of African American refugees following capitulation—they were unable and unwilling to help all those who sought protection. As Sylvia Frey has argued, the British were never genuinely committed to liberation for slaves during the Revolution—their wartime policy constituted at best a "selective offer of freedom" that was designed to meet their specific manpower needs and help suppress the rebellion.[16]

In all of these cases freedom was (vaguely) promised to fugitive slaves purely as a matter of geopolitical expediency and not as a matter of ideological or moral principle. Even in Spanish Florida, where the policy of protecting slaves who ran away from the English colonies was publicly justified on religious and humanitarian grounds, the idea was mainly to attract a much-needed source of labor (both military and civil) and to populate the border with mortal enemies of the English colonists on the other side. What changed in the wake of the American Revolution, and in the age of revolutions more broadly, was a structural reordering of the geography of slavery and freedom that provided enslaved people who wished to permanently escape bondage with a greatly expanded realm of opportunities to do so. Crucially, this reordering was ideologically motivated and permanent, thereby greatly enhancing runaway slaves' chances of success. Colonial strategies of running away of course did not disappear—marronage continued to be employed by some, and the War of 1812 provided a repeat scenario of British promises of freedom and subsequent evacuations of slave refugees from the Chesapeake—but most enslaved people who sought to flee the antebellum South did so by exploiting the changing social and political landscape and fleeing to various spaces of freedom.[17]

The last few years have witnessed a surge in academic interest in the experiences of runaway slaves, with a number of recent publications garnering widespread acclaim among historians of American slavery. Much of this new scholarship focuses on the traditional northern routes to sites of formal and semiformal freedom (although they do not employ those terms) as well as the abolitionist networks that assisted fugitive slaves in those regions. Sydney Nathans' *To Free a Family* (2013) and Eric Foner's latest book *Gateway to Freedom* (2015) stand out in particular for their meticulous research on these themes. But historians are also intensifying their examination of runaway slaves who attempted to attain freedom by fleeing southward, including into Mexico and the British Caribbean. Scholars such as Andrew Torget, Sarah Cornell, James David Nichols, and Mekala Audain are pioneering new perspectives on how fugitive slaves pursued and navigated freedom in the Texas–Mexico borderlands, and Matthew Clavin's recent book *Aiming for Pensacola* (2015) constitutes a watershed in understanding how southern port towns served as "gateways to freedom" for runaway slaves who wished to undertake escape attempts to the Bahamas and elsewhere in the Caribbean.[18]

By contrast, runaway slaves who sought to escape bondage by living clandestine lives of informal freedom within the slaveholding South remain relatively understudied. Yet a handful of historians are not only revisiting this group but also beginning to challenge the traditional view that such fugitives consisted mainly of truants or outliers, as has often been argued in standard works such as John Hope Franklin and Loren Schweninger's *Runaway Slaves* (1999). Sylviane Diouf, for one, forcefully argues in her book *Slavery's Exiles* (2014) that many of the "borderland maroons" of the antebellum South were in fact permanent freedom seekers, and my own research has come to the same conclusion for runaways who attempted to pass for free in antebellum southern cities.[19]

What these pioneering studies collectively reveal is that slave flight in the age of the second slavery was a truly continental phenomenon. As various spaces of freedom opened up throughout North America, enslaved people in the antebellum South sought to escape slavery by fleeing in every possible direction. Time and space were intrinsically interlinked with the various flows of slave flight, with British Canada increasingly becoming a beacon of freedom with the passage of the 1850 Fugitive Slave Law in the United States, with Texas and Mexico attracting more and more runaways after Mexican abolition in the 1829, with southern cities concealing increasing numbers of fugitive slaves as urban free black populations grew ever larger and as the domestic slave trade increasingly wrought havoc on slave communities, and with northern border states such as Pennsylvania receiving disproportionate numbers of slave refugees as they completed their transition from slavery to freedom in the early nineteenth century. Not only did these spaces of freedom emerge at different times but the meanings of freedom within these spaces changed over time as well—the status of fugitive slaves in the northern United States was always vulnerable and made significantly more so after 1850, for example, while that of slave refugees in British Canada evolved in the opposite direction as the British became more devoted to abolition. This complicates our understanding of the geography of slavery and freedom in the period between the American Revolution and the outbreak of the U.S. Civil War. The need to "reroute" and reconceptualize the geography of freedom in America during the age of slavery, as Rachel Adams has argued, constitutes a poignant gap in the historiography and is long overdue.[20]

The innovative character of *Fugitive Slaves and Spaces of Freedom in North America* lies in two specific methodological elements. First, it offers a new typology for understanding the changing geography of slavery and freedom in North America. This volume is the first book on slave refugees in the Americas to make a conceptual distinction between spaces of formal, semiformal, and informal freedom. This typology does not pretend to be static or absolute but rather encourages scholars to rethink how various legal regimes affected the nature of slave flight in the era of the second slavery. The contributions in this volume examine themes such as slaves' motivations for choosing various sites of freedom, their status and the ways in which they navigated these types of freedom, the networks that assisted them, and the interconnectedness of different spaces of freedom. And, second, this volume is first of its kind to provide a truly continental perspective of fugitive slave migration in the antebellum period. It includes not only the latest scholarship on runaway slaves in the "traditional" North–South axis but also in the Mexican borderlands, urban environments within the South, and even the British Bahamas. As such, it moves away from narrower national and regional paradigms of analysis.

The volume is largely structured geographically, but it begins with a contribution by Graham Hodges that explores the extent, meaning, and impact of slave flight during the era of the American Revolution (up until the final northern abolition act of New Jersey in 1804). Hodges argues that black self-emancipation via flight—including individual actions but also the mass movements of the revolutionary Black Loyalists—was the single greatest method for enslaved people to gain freedom in this rapidly changing political landscape. Slave flight indeed affected American construction of slave laws during the revolutionary era.

The next three chapters, by Gordon Barker, Roy Finkenbine, and Matthew Pinsker, examine the legal complications and experiences of slave refugees in sites of both formal and semiformal freedom in the northern United States and Canada. Barker explores the meaning of freedom for fugitive slaves in Canada West by examining the legal framework relating to slavery and race that emerged in what is now modern-day Ontario. Changes in statutory law, jurisprudence, and British free-soil diplomacy are addressed in this chapter, revealing the evolution of Canada West as a safe haven from which fugitive slaves were largely protected from slave catchers or state-sanctioned extradition. Finkenbine argues that the "Indian Country" of northwestern Ohio—inhabited primarily by the Shawnee, Ottawa, and Wyandot—provided runaway slaves with a unique space of freedom where fugitives on the northbound routes were frequently assisted by Native American communities sympathetic to their plight. Pinsker's chapter reexamines the legal and sometimes violent contest between antislavery and proslavery forces regarding enforcement of the federal fugitive slave code in the urban North. It argues that recent scholarship on this subject has made clearer that northern vigilance committees were remarkably successful in pursuing various legal and political strategies on the ground, even in cities with strong antiblack, proslavery sentiment and even after passage of the draconian 1850 Fugitive Slave Act.

The next three chapters, by Damian Alan Pargas, Viola Müller, and Sylviane Diouf, explore the experiences of fugitive slaves who fled to sites of informal freedom by remaining within the slaveholding South during the era of the second slavery. The chapter by Pargas broadly examines the experiences of fugitive slaves who fled to southern cities between 1800 and 1860. It touches upon themes such as the motivations for fleeing to urban areas, the networks that facilitated such flight attempts, and the ways in which runaway slaves navigated sites of "informal freedom" after arrival in urban areas. Following up on Pargas' contribution, Müller zooms in on a specific case study and focuses on the residential and economic integration of runaway slaves within the bustling environment of antebellum Richmond, Virginia. Drawing from police registers, runaway slave ads, and court documents, Müller specifically reveals how fugitive slaves and free blacks intermingled in urban spaces, and how runaway slaves navigated informal freedom in ways similar to the migration experiences of today's undocumented immigrants. The contribution by Sylviane Diouf—drawn from her recent monograph *Slavery's Exiles*—examines the nature and prevalence of "borderland maroons" in the antebellum South: permanent enslaved runaways who created lives for themselves in the forests and swamps that bordered the plantations.

The next cluster of chapters, by Kyle Ainsworth, Mekala Audain, and James David Nichols, all focus on the Texas–Mexican borderlands as spaces of formal and informal freedom for fugitive slaves from the U.S. South. Drawing from the Texas Runaway Slave Project database, Ainsworth's chapter examines how runaways navigated the changing geography of slavery and freedom in that state in the antebellum period. It breaks new ground by placing Texas in the growing Atlantic historiography of runaway slaves and by considering the impact that horses had on the methods of flight in the southwestern borderlands. Audain broadly examines the process in which runaway slaves from Texas escaped to Mexico in the antebellum period. Specifically, she explores how enslaved people learned about freedom south of the border, the types of supplies they gathered for their escape attempts, and the ways in which Texas' vast landscape shaped their experiences. Her study argues that the routes that led fugitive slaves to freedom in Mexico were a part of a precarious southern Underground Railroad, but one that operated in the absence of formal networks or a well-organized abolitionist movement. Nichols, meanwhile, argues that Mexican spaces of legal formal freedom did not always provide runaway slaves with full protection from reenslavement in practice. Focusing on Tamaulipas, Mexico, as a case study, he reveals how U.S. American jurisprudence could continue to affect Mexican space formally and informally from the outside, greatly troubling Mexican sovereignty in the process and rendering the status of fugitive slaves there insecure in practice.

The volume ends with a fascinating chapter by Jeffrey Kerr-Ritchie, which examines the understudied maritime dimensions of the domestic slave trade as well as slave revolt at sea. Zooming in on the 1841 slave revolt aboard the *Creole*, whereby slaves destined for New Orleans steered to formal freedom in the British Bahamas and claimed asylum, Kerr-Ritchie focuses on south-to-south fugitive slave actions at sea in contrast to the more familiar narrative of south-to-north over the land. Moreover, its examination of the *Creole* revolt's international dimensions differs from antebellum sectional rivalry that usually frames the event.

In short, the contributions in this volume provide new continental perspectives on slave flight in very different spaces of freedom between the American Revolution and the U.S. Civil War, thereby revealing the differences and similarities between various beacons of freedom and in the process remapping the geography of slavery and freedom in North America in an age of important transitions.

NOTES

1. *Daily National Intelligencer*, July 4, 1825. Between 1820 and 1850 the free black population of Washington increased dramatically, from 1,696 in 1820 to 8,158 in 1850. That of nearby Baltimore—also a popular destination for runaway slaves—increased from 10,326 to 25,442, making it relatively easy for runaways to pass for free. See the Federal Population Census Schedules for 1820 and 1850, National Archives and Records Administration (hereafter, NARA), Washington, DC (microfilm). See also Julie Winch, *Between Slavery and Freedom: Free People of Color in America from Settlement to Civil War* (Lanham, Md.: Rowman and Littlefield, 2014), 85.

2. *Daily National Intelligencer*, July 4, 1825; see also Ada Ferrer, "Haiti, Free Soil, and Antislavery in the Revolutionary Atlantic," *American Historical Review* 117, no. 1 (February 2012): 40–66.

3. Steven Hahn, "Forging Freedom," in *The Routledge History of Slavery*, ed. Gad Heuman and Trevor Burnard, 298–99 (New York: Routledge, 2011).

4. Christopher Brown, *Moral Capital: The Foundations of British Abolitionism* (Chapel Hill: University of North Carolina Press, 2006); Seymour Drescher, *Capitalism and Antislavery: British Mobilization in Comparative Perspective* (New York: Oxford University Press, 1987); David Brion Davis, *The Problem of Slavery in the Age of Revolution* (New York: Oxford University Press, 1999); David Brion Davis, *The Problem of Slavery in the Age of Emancipation* (New York: Knopf, 2014); Robin Blackburn, *The American Crucible: Slavery, Emancipation and Human Rights* (London: Verso, 2011), 162–69; and Seymour Drescher, "Civil Society and Paths to Abolition," *Journal of Global Slavery* 1, no. 1 (April 2016): 44–71. For the emergence of "free soil" politics in the revolutionary Atlantic, see, for example, Ferrer, "Haiti, Free Soil, and Antislavery," 40–66. Ferrer more fully develops her comparison between sites of liberation and entrenchment of slavery

in her book *Freedom's Mirror: Cuba and Haiti in the Age of Revolution* (New York: Cambridge University Press, 2014). For more on the prevalence of manumissions in revolutionary North America, see Peter Kolchin, *American Slavery, 1619–1877* (New York: Hill & Wang, 2003), 80–85; Ira Berlin, *Generations of Captivity: A History of African-American Slaves* (Cambridge, Mass.: Harvard University Press, 2003), 119–23, 135–50; and Rosemary Brana-Shute and Randy J. Sparks, eds., *Paths to Freedom: Manumission in the Atlantic World* (Columbia: University of South Carolina Press, 2009).

5. For more on the "second slavery" in the Atlantic world, see Dale W. Tomich, "The 'Second Slavery': Bonded Labor and the Transformations of the Nineteenth-Century World Economy," in *Rethinking the Nineteenth Century: Contradictions and Movement*, ed. Francisco O. Ramírez, 103–17 (New York: Greenwood, 1988); Dale W. Tomich, *Through the Prism of Slavery: Labor, Capital, and World Economy* (Lanham, Md.: Rowman and Littlefield, 2004); Dale W. Tomich and Michael Zeuske, eds., "The Second Slavery: Mass Slavery, World Economy, and Comparative Microhistories, Part I" [special issue], *Review: A Journal of the Fernand Braudel Center* 31, no. 2 (2008); Anthony E. Kaye, "The Second Slavery: Modernity in the Nineteenth-Century South and the Atlantic World," *Journal of Southern History* 75, no. 3 (August 2009): 627–50; Javier Lavina and Michael Zeuske, eds., *The Second Slavery: Mass Slaveries and Modernity in the Americas and in the Atlantic Basin* (Berlin: Lit Verlag, 2014); and Ferrer, *Freedom's Mirror*, 10.

6. An Act to Prevent the further Introduction of Slaves and to limit the Term of Contracts for Servitude within this Province (July 9, 1793), in *A Collection of the Acts Passed in the Parliament of Great Britain, Particularly Applying to the Province of Upper-Canada, and of Such Ordinances of the Late Province of Quebec, as Have Force of Law Therein* (York: R. C. Horne, 1818), 30–32, 30 (quotes); Sigrid Nicole Gallant, "Perspectives on the Motives for the Migration of African Americans to and from Ontario, Canada: From the Abolition of Slavery in Canada to the Abolition of Slavery in the United States," *Journal of Negro History* 86 (Summer 2001): 392–93; Sean Kelley, "'Mexico in His Head': Slavery and the Texas–Mexico Border, 1810–1860," *Journal of Social History* 37 (Spring 2004): 711–15; Andrew Jonathan Torget, "Cotton Empire: Slavery and the Texas Borderlands, 1820–1837" (PhD diss., University of Virginia, 2009), 210–11; and *Decreto del gobierno—Abolición de la esclavitud* (September 15, 1829), in *Legislación mexicana; o colección completa de disposiciones legislativas expedidas desde la independencia de la República*, Manuel Dublán et al. (México: Imprenta de Comercio, 1876), vol. 2: 163 (quotes).

7. Gary Nash, *The Unknown American Revolution: The Unruly Birth of Democracy and the Struggle to Create America* (New York: Penguin, 2005), 157–65, 223–31, 320–38, 407–16; Berlin, *Generations of Captivity*, 119–23, 135–50, 159–244; Kolchin, *American Slavery*, 80–85; U.S. Congress, An Act Respecting Fugitives from Justice and Persons Escaping from the Service of their Masters (1793); U.S. Congress, An Act to Amend, and Supplementary to, the Act Entitled "An Act Respecting Fugitives from Justice and Persons Escaping from the Service of their Masters" (1850); Graham Russell Gao Hodges, *Root & Branch: African Americans*

in New York and East Jersey, 1613–1863 (Chapel Hill: University of North Carolina Press, 1999), 161–165; and Shane White, *Somewhat More Independent: The End of Slavery in New York, 1770–1810* (Athens: University of Georgia Press, 1991), 141–47.

8. An Act to Authorize the Manumission of Slaves (May 1782), in *The Statutes at Large; Being a Collection of All the Laws of Virginia from the First Session of Legislature, in the Year 1619*, vol. 11, ed. William Waller Hening (Richmond, Va.: George Cochran, 1823), 39.

9. Kolchin, *American Slavery*, 81; U.S. Population Census, 1790 and 1820, NARA; Eva Sheppard Wolf, *Race and Liberty in the New Nation: Emancipation in Virginia from the Revolution to Nat Turner's Rebellion* (Baton Rouge: Louisiana State University Press, 2006), 110–11; and Ted Maris-Wolf, *Family Bonds: Free Blacks and Re-enslavement Law in Antebellum Virginia* (Chapel Hill: University of North Carolina Press, 2015), 24–44.

10. Kolchin, *American Slavery*, 80–85, 81; see also Nash, *The Unknown American Revolution*, 157–65, 223–31, 320–38, 407–16; Berlin, *Generations of Captivity*, 119–23, 135–50, 159–244; Sean Condon, "The Slave Owner's Family and Manumission in the Post-Revolutionary Chesapeake Tidewater: Evidence from Anne Arundel County Wills, 1790–1820," in *Paths to Freedom: Manumission in the Atlantic World*, ed. Rosemary Brana-Shute and Randy J. Sparks, 339–62 (Columbia: University of South Carolina Press, 2009); and Ellen Eslinger, "Liberation in a Rural Context: The Valley of Virginia, 1800–1860," in *Paths to Freedom: Manumission in the Atlantic World*, ed. Rosemary Brana-Shute and Randy J. Sparks, 663–80 (Columbia: University of South Carolina Press, 2009).

11. There is a rich literature on the domestic slave trade and the extent to which it forcibly separated slave families in the antebellum period. See, for example, Michael Tadman, *Speculators and Slaves: Masters, Traders, and Slaves in the Old South* (Madison: University of Wisconsin Press, 1989), esp. 133–78; Walter Johnson, *Soul by Soul: Life Inside the Antebellum Slave Market* (Cambridge, Mass.: Harvard University Press, 1999); Steven Deyle, *Carry Me Back: The Domestic Slave Trade in American Life* (New York: Oxford University Press, 2005), 246–47; Robert H. Gudmestad, *A Troublesome Commerce: The Transformation of the Interstate Slave Trade* (Baton Rouge: Louisiana State University Press, 2003); and Damian Alan Pargas, *Slavery and Forced Migration in the Antebellum South* (New York: Cambridge University Press, 2014).

12. Herbert Aptheker, "Maroons within the Present Limits of the United States," *Journal of Negro History* 24 (April 1939): 167–84; Richard Price, *Maroon Societies: Rebel Slave Communities in the Americas* (Baltimore: Johns Hopkins University Press, 1973); Eugene D. Genovese, *From Rebellion to Revolution: Afro-American Slave Revolts in the Making of the Modern World* (Baton Rouge: Louisiana State University Press, 1979), 51–81; Gad Heuman, ed., *Out of the House of Bondage: Runaways, Resistance and Marronage in Africa and the New World* (London: Frank Cass, 1986); John Hope Franklin and Loren Schweninger, *Runaway Slaves: Rebels on the Plantation* (New York: Oxford University Press, 1999),

98–103; Timothy James Lockley, ed., *Maroon Communities in South Carolina: A Documentary Record* (Columbia: University of South Carolina Press, 2009); Sylviane A. Diouf, *Slavery's Exiles: The Story of the American Maroons* (New York: New York University Press, 2014); and Nathaniel Millett, "Defining Freedom in the Atlantic Borderlands of the Revolutionary Southeast," *Early American Studies* 5 (Fall 2007): 367–94.

13. Donald R. Wright, *African Americans in the Early Republic, 1789–1831* (Arlington Heights, Ill.: Harlan Davidson, 1993), 126; and Berlin, *Generations of Captivity*, 21–49. Manumission was severely circumscribed in the southern colonies. In 1691 Virginia required manumitted slaves to be transported out of the state at the master's cost, and in 1723 it forbade manumission except by approval of the governor, and then only for "meritous services." See Ariela Gross and Alejandro de la Fuente, "Slaves, Free Blacks, and Race in the Legal Regimes of Cuba, Louisiana, and Virginia: A Comparison," *North Carolina Law Review* 91 (2013): 1727–30; Edmund Morgan, *American Slavery, American Freedom: The Ordeal of Colonial Virginia* (New York: W. W. Norton, 1975), 154–55, 337; General Assembly of Virginia, "An Act for Suppressing Outlying Slaves (1691)," reprinted in *The Statutes at Large: Being a Collection of All Laws of Virginia, from the First Session of the Legislature, in the Year 1619*, vol. 3, ed. William Waller Hening, 86–88 (Philadelphia: R. & W. & G. Bartow, 1823); and Mariana L. R. Dantas, *Black Townsmen: Urban Slavery and Freedom in the Eighteenth-Century Americas* (New York: Palgrave Macmillan, 2008), 97–99.

14. Jane Landers, "'Giving Liberty to All': Spanish Florida as a Black Sanctuary, 1673–1790," in *La Florida: Five Hundred Years of Hispanic Presence*, ed. Rachel A. May and Viviana Diaz Balsera, 125–26 (Gainesville: University Press of Florida, 2014); Jane Landers, *Black Society in Spanish Florida* (Urbana: University of Illinois Press, 1999), 24–25; Peter Wood, *Black Majority: Negroes in Colonial South Carolina* (New York: Knopf, 1974), 239; Millett, "Defining Freedom," 367–94; and Larry E. Rivers, *Slavery in Florida: Territorial Days to Emancipation* (Gainesville: University Press of Florida, 2000), 4–5.

15. Wood, *Black Majority*, 260–261; see also Lockley, *Maroon Communities in South Carolina*, 132. Even in the northern colonies, such as New York, slaves often sought protection with Native American communities. See, for example, Richard E. Bond, "Ebb and Flow: Free Blacks and Urban Slavery in Eighteen-Century New York" (PhD diss., Johns Hopkins University, 2005), 242–43; and Eric Foner, *Gateway to Freedom: The Hidden History of the Underground Railroad* (New York: Norton, 2016), 30–32.

16. Sylvia R. Frey, "Between Slavery and Freedom: Virginia Blacks in the American Revolution," *Journal of Southern History* 49 (August 1983): 375–98, 387; see also Kolchin, *American Slavery*, 70–73; Benjamin Quarles, *The Negro in the American Revolution* (Chapel Hill: University of North Carolina Press, 1961); Sylvia Frey, *Water from the Rock: Black Resistance in a Revolutionary Age* (Princeton, N.J.: Princeton University Press, 1992); Douglas R. Egerton, *Death or Liberty: African Americans and Revolutionary America* (New York: Oxford University

Press, 2011); Nash, *The Unknown American Revolution*, 157–66, 163; and Alan Taylor, *The Internal Enemy: Slavery and War in Virginia, 1771–1832* (New York: W. W. Norton, 2014).

17. Landers, "'Giving Liberty to All,'" 125–26; Diouf, *Slavery's Exiles*; and Taylor, *Internal Enemy*, 245–74.

18. Some recent studies that examine runaway slaves in the northern United States and Canada include, for example, Sydney Nathans, *To Free a Family: The Journey of Mary Walker* (Cambridge, Mass.: Harvard University Press, 2012); Richard Blackett, *Making Freedom: The Underground Railroad and the Politics of Freedom* (Chapel Hill: University of North Carolina Press, 2013); Graham Russell Gao Hodges, *David Ruggles: A Radical Black Abolitionist and the Underground Railroad in New York City* (Chapel Hill: University of North Carolina Press, 2012); Karolyn Smardz Frost and Veta Smith Tucker, eds. *A Fluid Frontier: Slavery, Resistance and the Underground Railroad in the Detroit River Borderland* (Detroit: Wayne State University Press, 2016); Foner, *Gateway to Freedom*; Gordon Barker, *Fugitive Slaves and the Unfinished American Revolution: Eight Cases, 1848–1856* (Jefferson, N.C.: McFarland, 2013); and Steven Lubet, *Fugitive Justice: Runaways, Rescuers, and Slavery and Trial* (New York: Cambridge University Press, 2010). For new studies on fugitive slaves in Mexico, see, for example, Andrew J. Torget, *Seeds of Empire: Slavery, Cotton, and the Transformation of the Texas Borderlands, 1800–1850* (Chapel Hill: University of North Carolina Press, 2015); Sarah E. Cornell, "Citizens of Nowhere: Fugitive Slaves and Free African Americans in Mexico, 1833–1857," *Journal of American History* 100, no. 2 (2013): 351–74; Kelley, "Mexico in His Head," 709–23; James David Nichols, "The Line of Liberty: Runaway Slaves and Fugitive Peons in the Texas-Mexico Borderlands," *Western Historical Quarterly* 44, no. 4 (Winter 2013): 413–33; and Mekala Audain, "Mexican Canaan: Fugitive Slaves and Free Blacks on the American Frontier, 1804–1867" (PhD diss., Rutgers University, 2014). Matthew Clavin's recent work views Pensacola as a conduit for fugitive slaves fleeing southward into the Caribbean (especially the British Caribbean). Matthew J. Clavin, *Aiming for Pensacola: Fugitive Slaves in the Southern and Atlantic Frontier* (Cambridge, Mass.: Harvard University Press, 2015). For a brief overview of the diplomatic consequences of fugitive slaves in North America (only those who crossed international borders), see Jeffrey Kerr-Ritchie, "Fugitive Slaves across North America," in *Workers across the Americas: The Transnational Turn in Labor History* (Oxford Scholarship Online, 2011).

19. For brief treatment of truancy within the South, see, for example, Stephanie M. H. Camp, *Closer to Freedom: Enslaved Women and Everyday Resistance in the Plantation South* (Chapel Hill: University of North Carolina Press, 2004), 35–59; and Franklin and Schweninger, *Runaway Slaves*, 97–103, 124–48. Franklin and Schweninger argue that "few absconders [within the South] remained permanently at large." John Hope Franklin and Loren Schweninger, "The Quest for Freedom: Runaway Slaves and the Plantation South," in *Slavery, Resistance, Freedom*, ed. Ira Berlin, Scott Hancock, and G. S. Boritt, 21–39 (New York: Oxford

University Press, 2007), 25. For southern runaways as permanent freedom seekers, see, for example, Christopher Phillips, *Freedom's Port: The African American Community of Baltimore, 1790–1860* (Urbana: University of Illinois Press, 1997); Clavin, *Aiming for Pensacola*; Amani Marshall, "'They Will Endeavor to Pass for Free': Enslaved Runaways' Performances of Freedom in Antebellum South Carolina," *Slavery and Abolition* 31 (May 2010): 161–80; and Diouf, *Slavery's Exiles*.

20. Rachel Adams, *Continental Divides: Remapping the Cultures of North America* (Chicago: University of Chicago Press, 2009), 61–100.

1

Black Self-Emancipation, Gradual Emancipation, and the Underground Railroad in the Northern Colonies and States, 1763–1804

GRAHAM RUSSELL GAO HODGES

The remarkable self-emancipation of Black Loyalists in the revolutionary era—who fled to and fought for the British during the war itself, and later both openly campaigned to end slavery in the northern United States and protected fugitive slaves in their midst—should compel historians to reevaluate the starting point of the Underground Railroad. This chapter contends that black self-emancipation during and after the Revolution not only constituted an early strand of abolitionism but that it affected the end of slavery in the North just as much as white abolitionism and the mechanism of gradual emancipation did, as defected slaves from the Revolution subsequently became tireless activists in the struggle against bondage. In other words, Black Loyalists not only escaped slavery by fleeing to their enemies' masters during the war itself but also actively participated in the creation of spaces of freedom after the war had ended, both for themselves and for other slave refugees from the southern states. Black self-emancipation should be included in the saga of freedom-making in the revolutionary period, on par with gradual emancipation as well as individual religious and other philanthropic efforts.[1]

Historical scholarship until recently allotted credit for gradual abolition in the northern states to white philanthropists and free labor advocates, who, imbued with egalitarian concerns about the contradictions of the Revolution and holding evangelical and philosophical beliefs about the equality of humankind, successfully promoted gradual emancipation of enslaved peoples or took their own actions to liberate their bondspeople. This process began with the constitution of the breakaway province of Vermont in 1777 and culminated in the passage of gradual emancipation in New Jersey in 1804. Gradual emancipation could be excruciatingly slow, allowing for the continuance of human bondage in some states until the eve of the Civil War and encouraging such abuses as illicit sales of infant blacks to the southern states in the 1820s.[2]

Manisha Sinha's magisterial and encyclopedic study, *The Slave's Cause* (2016), however, has recently advanced new perspectives on black abolitionism that challenge earlier credit to white philanthropists and free labor advocates. Key to her book is the argument that "slave resistance, not bourgeois liberalism, laid at the heart of the abolition movement." She explains that "the enslaved inspired the formation of the first Quaker-dominated abolition and manumission societies," which were established in the early national period.[3] Sinha's work has importantly dislodged our views that Quaker antislavery ideology and actions were the only components of colonial abolitionism. By presenting various acts of resistance in the colonial and revolutionary periods, from self-emancipation to conspiracies and uprisings to the contributions of early black abolitionists, Sinha has stimulated a genuine shift in early American and abolitionist historiography. She shows that while the Quakers were often intermittent abolitionists, enslaved and free blacks were consistent in their attacks on slavery. Whereas the Philadelphia meeting debated cleansing their theology of the sin of slavery and, by 1755, insisted that all Friends abandon slaveholding, the New York meeting and the North Carolina Friends were much slower to get the message. Moreover, after the Revolution, although Friends dominated the Manumission Society, they were not, nor were their colonial and revolutionary forebears, interracial. Sinha argues that the movement was interracial, which one cannot say about the early Friends. Here, much of what Sinha discusses initially is widely understood, with references to white and black literary artists on the need for abolition and the obvious contradiction between American yelps for liberty from slave drivers. Sinha also discusses the black petition writers from Massachusetts who decried the hypocrisy of the Patriots. Her major contribution is to prescribe all positive acts of colonial black resistance as abolitionist.

Following Sinha, I contend that colonial and early national black resistance in the form of self-emancipation were forms of abolitionism. At times it was violent, a quality not recognized generally among abolitionists until the slave rescue cases of the 1850s and ultimately, of course, in John Brown's raid. Stanley Harrold's book *Border War* argues that violence characterized abolitionism from the 1820s onward.[4]

Even early abolitionism was not always pacific. In a society where blacks had no political or social rights, violence was often the only recourse. The most important examples of this tendency were the black conspiracies in New York City in 1712 and 1741 and the slave rebellion in Stono, South Carolina, in 1739. We can find even more ordinary abolitionists among the self-emancipated, or "runaways," as they are often termed. Running away singly or in groups (large and small, sometimes even interracial), the self-emancipated constituted a major refutation of slavery and an extensive property loss for masters, and, most importantly, it created psychological and physical freedom. Whether they "pretended to be free" or simply fled, these slavery survivors created their own liberty.[5]

This was most apparent in the Revolutionary War, during which opportunities to exit bondage by fleeing to (or collaborating with) one of the warring parties—especially the British—opened up. Reevaluations or rediscovery of Black Loyalists and Patriot military involvement in the American Revolution have now illuminated the extent of enslaved self-emancipation, either by self-purchase, negotiated release, or flight. Enslaved people in the northern states especially secured their freedom most commonly through flight.[6]

Extending her conflation of early black violent resistance and abolition, Sinha points to the rising of blacks summoned by Lord Dunmore in Virginia and the creation of the Ethiopian Regiments. Dunmore's proclamation eventually led to tens of thousands of American blacks becoming diaspora Black Loyalists. Evacuated by the British after the war, many eventually settled in Canada, the West Indies, London, Germany, and eventually Sierra Leone. Some became lifetime British soldiers and served as far away as Australia. Others stayed closer to home, serving with Native American groups in battles against the American Patriots in the 1780s and 1790s. Sinha's inclusion of the Black Loyalists and their Patriot counterparts as a story of resistance makes them inspirers of the abolitionist movement. In fact, if one looks closely at the Sierra Leone Black Loyalists, one can discern a republicanism much more radical than the Patriot version. As Maya Jasanoff reminds us, they were imbued with the spirit of 1783, in contrast to our evocation of 1776.[7]

There is now a fairly sizable literature on the Black Loyalists. Studies have demonstrated that the Black Loyalists were significant contributors to the British war effort and then, once the English honored commitments to freedom made during the war, circumnavigated the Black Atlantic and made a return diaspora to found the nation of Sierra Leone. As Cassandra Pybus has shown, some became lifetime soldiers for the British Empire and fought for the Crown in the Caribbean, India and Australia. In a remarkable account of one individual Black Loyalist, John Kizell migrated first to Nova Scotia, then to Sierra Leone, where he became a valiant opponent of the slave trade.[8]

The Black Loyalists, along with the black freedom fighters of other American wars, combined their individual dreams of freedom with national liberty. Later, white and black abolitionists believed that connecting African American contributions to the American Revolution would make other Americans recognize their overall value and equity in national society.[9] For example, the Black Loyalists in Sierra Leone were frequently in contact with free blacks in the northern cities of America in the first decades of the nineteenth century.[10]

Several influential works from the antebellum period are useful in creating an understanding of the role of black self-emancipation in revolutionary America. Eric Foner, in his recent book on the Underground Railroad, argues that all "fugitives" bring to mind the Underground Railroad.[11] Would this statement, applied to the 1840s, be true as well for the colonial and revolutionary periods? Who, then, would be the conductors? Other blacks, proletarian whites? The possibilities are endless. Two recent works on the Civil War offer theoretical pathways for understanding black movements before and during the American Revolution. Steven Hahn has argued that black participation in the Civil War should be considered the most sizable slave rebellion ever. Hahn contends that this rebellion was not hidden or something that must be teased out of archival sources but rather something "that stares us in the face."[12] Similarly, Chandra Manning, in her study of contraband camps during the Civil War, has shown the development of black freedom communities in the midst of war-torn turmoil.[13] Hahn also emphasizes the importance of black towns in the antebellum period that served as maroon communities. Other studies have pointed out that black towns were key depots on the Underground Railroad.[14]

Early examples of concerted, coordinated black efforts that were early harbingers of the Black Loyalists and, ultimately, the Underground Railroad occurred as Patriots began to separate from English rule. In November 1775, Virginia Crown governor Lord Dunmore proclaimed freedom for enslaved people in exchange for their military service to help put down the American revolt. Coincidentally, or perhaps responding to rapid streams of communication among enslaved blacks, Titus Corlies, about twenty-one years of age, near six feet high and wearing a gray homespun coat, brown breeches, and blue and white stockings, left his Quaker master, John Corlies of Shrewsbury, Monmouth County, New Jersey, apparently bound for Virginia where an Ethiopian Regiment was forming to help Dunmore subdue the rebellious Americans. Within two years, Titus returned to New Jersey. Now known as Colonel Tye, he led a "motley crew" of black and white guerilla warriors who raided Patriot homes, taking captives plus livestock, forage, food, and silver plate and selling all to the British garrison in New York City. Tye was so successful that Governor William Livingston of New Jersey was forced to impose martial law on Monmouth County. Before his death in 1780 from a wound that caused lockjaw, Tye terrorized Patriots on many occasions and took prominent local militiamen captive for the British.[15]

Tye was by no means the only enslaved black to act upon British calls for service. British general Sir Henry Clinton issued the Philipsburg Proclamation in 1779 that offered similar terms to blacks in the New York City region. Emboldened by these appeals and by the 1772 Somerset Decision in England that affirmed the concept of "free soil" in nations where human bondage was unlawful, American enslaved and free black men and women and their children used every opportunity to secure self-emancipation inside British lines. More than 3,000 gained safety in British-occupied wartime New York City. They arrived in New York City from all over the Atlantic Coast, with over 200 from Virginia alone, escaping from such noted slave owners as George Washington and Thomas Jefferson. Over 130 free and 535 self-emancipated blacks from New York and New Jersey chose to fight as Black Loyalists for the British against the Patriots. Home in 1780 to nearly 60,000 people, including several thousand blacks, Loyalist New York became the nation's first true free black community. Living in Lower Manhattan, free and self-emancipated blacks fought for the British army, serving as soldiers, spies, scouts, and personal servants.

Advertisements for capture of the self-emancipated reflected the attraction of the British calls to freedom. Pompy, who escaped in 1777, was "supposed to be in the Queen's Rangers or some other department." Two men and a woman "have entered his Majesty's service as wagon drivers, and their names on Commissary's books, but they are my property," wailed another master. Duke and Peter had likely "imposed himself upon the gentlemen of the [British] army." In early manifestation of a route commonly used by the self-emancipated in the antebellum period, Watt escaped from his master in Kent, Maryland, and made an effort to "get on board the British fleet when they were up Chesapeake Bay," and now "has either made for the Delaware Bay or the Jersies."[16]

The elements of black community were present. Black Loyalists worked as carters (a trade previously segregated to whites), carpenters, privateers, sailors, chimney sweeps, brewers and at innumerable other occupations. Blacks married, had families, created religious congregations, and formed themselves as paramilitary units.[17] New York City remained a beacon of freedom even as the war wound down. Reue Crosuier of Albany, New York, sought to recapture his self-emancipated man Bill, in early 1783. Crosuier believed that Bill was headed for New York City, as he had been taken "at the capture of Cornwallis," and hoped to leave with the English.[18] Nearly all advertisements in the revolutionary era emphasized warnings to masters of vessels not to allow the self-emancipated on board.

Revolutionary-era self-emancipators employed deception in their escapes from slavery, a method commonly used during the later era of the Underground Railroad. Revolutionary-era masters often accused fugitive slaves of deceit while acknowledging political and military destinations. Harry, advertised his former master, ran away with the British light infantry in early 1778; nine months later Robert Johnson of Salem, New Jersey, was still hoping to recapture him, though he acknowledged the former bondsman "may perhaps endeavor to pass for a free man." In the midst of the fierce winter of 1779–80, Toney, from Somerset County, New Jersey, was supposed to "go over to the enemy." Patriot masters were at times unclear whether the British forces or other "evil minded persons" enticed their bondspeople away. Such was the case with Robin, who called himself Levi and was "very modest in speech, has a sober look, and can frame a smooth story from rough materials."[19] Women ran away more frequently during the revolutionary conflict than before or after. Sarah, who changed her name to Rachel, self-extricated herself and her six-year-old son, Bob, from slavery, even as she was pregnant, and "passed herself as a free woman. She had a husband in the British army." Free women chose to join the English "black town" in New York City. Mary Thompson of Newark, her daughter Margaret and her three children, all born free, were part of the Black Brigade that was the last departing unit of the British forces leaving New York City on November 25, 1783.[20]

The New York region was hardly the only source of Black Loyalists. Many came from further afield to join the black town in lower New York City. In one of the first recordings of black freedom migration, joining local blacks were 352 black Virginians and many from Maryland, Pennsylvania, and Delaware. There was a sizable contingent from South Carolina that came to New York City late in the conflict. Adding wartime escapes enlarges the number of known black self-emancipators. Including the Revolutionary War (for which there is now ample work about black resistance and Crown assistance) substantially enlarges the scope of what is currently called the Underground Railroad. If we redefine the term to include support for fugitive slaves, then most of the Black Loyalist actions, involving by the most conservative estimates some 15,000 men, women, and children in a concentrated period of eight years, would certainly qualify. Including the Revolutionary War in such analyses also helps explain the fugitive slave clauses of the Constitution and the Fugitive Slave Act of 1793. It is then a short step to incorporate the 4,000-plus Virginians who escaped to British lines in the War of 1812, as Alan Taylor has fully documented in his recent book, *The Internal Enemy: Slavery and War in Virginia, 1772–1832*.[21]

The Black Loyalists were among the first and largest recorded examples of a freedom-seeking black migration. Ira Berlin's book on black migrations in American history charts the late-eighteenth-century international slave trade and the nineteenth-century internal slave trade that badly disrupted black families and created a huge wave of forced black migrants from the mid-Atlantic and Chesapeake states to the cotton states of the Southeast. There was a reverse migration as well of the self-emancipated. Beginning with the thousands of Black Loyalists and continuing via the Underground Railroad and the War of 1812, black migrants moved to spaces of formal and semiformal freedom, especially north to the free states and Canada, west into the Native American territories, and for decades south into Spanish Florida.[22]

A key aspect of the Underground Railroad and of gradual emancipation was the religious impulse. There is no doubt about the religious thrust of black community and migration methods among the Black Loyalists. Every scholar who has observed the Black Loyalists has remarked about the role of religious leaders, community organization, and eventually migration to Nova Scotia, Sierra Leone, and beyond. Ministers such as George Liele, David George, Thomas Peters, Boston King, and Stephen Bleuke are widely recognized for such combined leadership. Lesser known are such figures as Mark and Jenney, who fled from masters in Bergen County, New Jersey, in 1775. Mark was a "Negro Preacher." His wife, Jenney, had forged a pass so they could travel freely.[23]

At the same time, military organization was prominent among the Black Loyalists. Companies of Black Pioneers, Scouts, and the elite Black Brigade formed in Virginia and New York, continued throughout the war, traveled to Nova Scotia intact and there formed basic units of society. Black Pioneers felled trees, constructed rude huts, and plotted land. While the Black Loyalists overall encountered troublesome difficulties stemming from natural conditions and white racism, military units helped the new Afro–Nova Scotians maintain order. Stemming partly from the assignments made by white authorities, Black Loyalist towns soon emerged. Even after the Black Loyalists soured on life in Nova Scotia, they retained military units in addition to church membership to provide shape and structure to their journey.[24]

Crucially, black self-emancipation continued to have far-reaching political consequences after the war ended. The next focus of this chapter is on the period from the end of the American Revolution, through the passage of Fugitive Slave Act of 1793 (for which most northerners voted yea), to the legislation enabling gradual emancipation in New Jersey, the last northern state to pass such a motion, in 1804. The years after the American Revolution in New York and New Jersey were not kind to African Americans aspiring for freedom. Patriots resented blacks for their alliance to the British and openly asked why blacks should deserve liberation from slavery.

The debate over gradual emancipation, which lasted in New York until 1799 and 1804 in New Jersey, seems to be the most important part of a freedom narrative in the early national period. Make no mistake, blacks resisted slavery in the mid-Atlantic fiercely in the years before the gradual emancipation acts in New York and New Jersey. My research and that of Shane White has pointed out the significance of black flight and self-emancipation in New York and New Jersey. Black flight from rural New Jersey and New York State was the largest source of newcomers to New York City, creating an urban mass important to fill the nascent black churches and fraternal associations; populating a secular world of black street sellers, performers, tavern and boarding-house keepers; and sustaining a cadre of skilled blacks who could have participated in the Industrial Revolution, were it not for racism and Alexander Hamilton's famous plan to entice industrial workers from Europe.[25]

Blacks used self-emancipation to gain freedom during the debate over gradual emancipation. The Fugitive Slave Act of 1793, passed to assuage southern fears that the northern states would become sanctuaries for freedom-bound blacks, barely deterred mid-Atlantic blacks seeking to escape bondage. In the early years after the war, the British freedom message remained potent. One master advertised the flight of Scipio in May 1784 and complained that he had run way in 1776, had been returned forcibly to his master in 1783, and had escaped again. Brock, also known as Tom, was "probably lurking about New York City until he could get passage to Nova Scotia," in 1785.[26]

There were decided splits among mid-Atlantic Patriots over black self-emancipation. While slave owners universally wanted their escaped bondspeople returned to them, white philanthropists in New York and New Jersey provided protection to the self-emancipated from the southern states, protected the free papers of local blacks, and pushed suits against masters who reneged on promises of freedom. State legislators were unsure about what to do. As they debated gradual emancipation and many held membership in the New York and New Jersey manumission societies, they also opposed black self-emancipation. Federalists joined Republicans in efforts to gain compensation for the value lost when Black Loyalists departed for Nova Scotia and beyond. Every New York and New Jersey legislator but one voted in favor of the Act. Shane White counted over 1,200 self-emancipations between 1770 and 1800, of which over one-third took place between 1796 and 1800. Neither the Fugitive Slave Act nor the progress toward New York's Gradual Emancipation Act of 1799 convinced freedom-minded blacks that white reforms were sufficient. Once self-emancipated, individual blacks celebrated by changing their names to Thomas Paine, Royal Cromwell, and New Year Evans.[27]

Sympathetic whites helped the cause, creating early examples of the Underground Railroad. Isaac Hopper of Philadelphia used legal legerdemain to help self-emancipated people secure their freedom. The New York Manumission Society tried unsuccessfully to convince newspaper owners to cease printing runaway slave advertisements. At the same time and place, blacks initiated their own plans and methods. Richard Allen and other black Methodists in Philadelphia helped Ona Judge, a personal handmaiden to Martha Washington, to escape to freedom in New England when the first president's wife determined to return her enslaved to Virginia. One may look to New York City, where several times between 1788 and 1818 black mobs struggled fiercely and successfully to stop kidnappers from stealing people to enslave them in the southern states. These manifestations of the fusion of abolitionism and what became the Underground Railroad were characterized by interracial cooperation and a mixture of legal slight, pacifism, and occasional violence. Taken together, these actions and numbers of self-emancipated spread over nine decades make the movement a powerful, unacknowledged force in American history.[28]

In sum, even this brief survey indicates that there were exceptional similarities between the self-emancipated of the colonial, revolutionary, early national, and antebellum periods. Their methods of gaining freedom often dovetailed, either acting solely or with the help of others. In the antebellum period, we call such actions the Underground Railroad.

For the earlier periods, a new notion might be called freedom-making. Once we connect these strands, in what Vincent Harding long ago called a river of resistance, then we will have a more complete understanding of how enslaved African Americans made their own freedoms throughout the continent.[29]

NOTES

1. Richard Blackett, *Making Freedom: The Underground Railroad and the Politics of Slavery* (Chapel Hill: University of North Carolina Press, 2013).

2. The classic work on gradual emancipation is Arthur Zilversmit, *The First Emancipation: The Abolition of Slavery in the North* (Chicago: University of Chicago Press, 1967). See also William M. Wiecek, *The Sources of Antislavery Constitutionalism in America, 1760–1848* (Ithaca, N.Y.: Cornell University Press, 1977); and David Gellman, *Emancipating New York: The Politics of Slavery and Freedom, 1777–1827* (Baton Rouge: Louisiana State University Press, 2008).

3. Manisha Sinha, *The Slave's Cause: A History of Abolition* (New Haven: Yale University Press, 2016), 2.

4. Stanley Harrold, *Border War: Fighting over Slavery before the Civil War* (Chapel Hill: University of North Carolina Press, 2010).

5. Sinha, *The Slave's Cause*, 51–53.

6. Shane White, *Somewhat More Independent: The End of Slavery in New York City, 1770–1810* (Athens: University of Georgia, 1990), 127; Graham Russell Gao Hodges, *Root & Branch: African Americans in New York and East Jersey, 1613–1863* (Chapel Hill: University of North Carolina Press, 1999); Alan Gilbert, *Black Patriots and Loyalists: Fighting for Emancipation in the War of Independence* (Chicago: University of Chicago Press, 2012); and Antonio Bly, *Escaping Bondage: A Documentary History of Runaway Slaves in Eighteenth-Century New England, 1770–1789* (Lanham, Md.: Lexington Books, 2012).

7. Veta Smith Tucker, "Uncertain Freedom in Frontier Detroit," in *A Fluid Frontier: Slavery, Resistance and the Underground Railroad in the Detroit River Borderland*, ed. Karolyn Smardz Frost and Veta Smith Tucker, 27–43 (Detroit: Wayne State University Press, 2016); and Maya Jasanoff, *Liberty's Exiles: American Loyalists in the Revolutionary World* (New York: Knopf, 2011).

8. Key works include Hodges, *Root & Branch*, 138–61; Gilbert, *Black Patriots and Loyalists*, 1–15, 95–152; Cassandra Pybus, *Epic Journeys of Freedom: Runaway Slaves of the American Revolution and Their Global Quest for Liberty* (Boston: Beacon Press, 2007); Simon Schama, *Rough Crossings: The Slaves, the British, and the American Revolution* (New York: Harper, 2007); Gary B. Nash, *The Forgotten Fifth: African Americans in the Age of Revolution* (Cambridge: Cambridge University Press, 2006); Sylvia Frey, *Water from the Rock: Black Resistance in a Revolutionary Age* (Princeton, N.J.: Princeton University Press, 1992); and Jasanoff *Liberty's Exiles*.

9. For example, see William Cooper Nell, *The Colored Patriots of the American Revolution* (Boston: Robert F. Wallcut, 1855).

10. Hodges, *Root & Branch*, 189; and Kevin G. Lowther, *The African American Odyssey of John Kizell: A South Carolina Slave Returns to Fight the Slave Trade in his African Homeland* (Columbia: University of South Carolina Press, 2011).

11. Eric Foner, *Gateway to Freedom: The Hidden History of the Underground Railroad* (New York: W. W. Norton, 2014).

12. Steven Hahn, *The Political Worlds of Slavery and Freedom* (Cambridge, Mass.: Harvard University Press, 2009), 55–115.

13. Chandra Manning, *Troubled Refuge: Struggling for Refuge in the Civil War* (New York: Knopf, 2016).

14. Hahn, *Political Worlds of Slavery and Freedom*, 41–43; and Cheryl LaRoche, *Free Black Communities and the Underground Railroad: The Geography of Resistance* (Urbana: University of Illinois Press, 2013).

15. For an account of Tye, see my *Root & Branch*, 152–59.

16. *New-York Gazette and the Weekly Mercury*, June 2, 1777 (Pompy), June 9, 1777 (wagon drivers), August 4, 1777 (Duke), November 3, 1777 (Peter); and *New-Jersey Gazette*, June 23, 1779 (Watt).

17. Hodges, *Root & Branch*, 144–50; and Graham Russell Hodges ed., *The Black Loyalist Directory* (New York: Garland, 1996).

18. *Connecticut Courant*, June 3, 1783.

19. *New-Jersey Gazette*, September 23, 1778 (Harry), February 16, 1780 (Toney); and *New-Jersey Journal*, May 7, 1780 (Robin or Levi).

20. *New-Jersey Gazette*, October 28, 1778 (Rachel); for the Thompson family, see Hodges, *Black Loyalist Directory*, 212.

21. Alan Taylor, *The Internal Enemy: Slavery and War in Virginia, 1772–1832* (New York: W. W. Norton, 2013).

22. Ira Berlin, *The Making of African America: The Four Great Migrations* (New York: Viking, 2010), 99–152. See also Ira Berlin, *The Long Emancipation: The Demise of Slavery in the United States* (Cambridge, Mass.: Harvard University Press, 2015).

23. *New-York Journal, or the General Advertiser*, January 12, 1775; Hodges, *Root & Branch*, 147; Jasanoff, *Liberty's Exiles*, 267; Ellen Gibson Wilson, *The Loyal Blacks* (New York: Penguin, 1976); George W. St. G. Walker, *The Black Loyalists: The Search for a Promised Land in Nova Scotia and Sierra Leone, 1783–1870* (Toronto: University of Toronto Press, 1976); and Hodges, *The Black Loyalists Directory*, introduction.

24. Hodges, *Black Loyalist Directory*, xxiii; and Gilbert, *Black Patriots and Loyalists*, 210.

25. Hodges, *Root & Branch*, 161–65; White, *Somewhat More Independent*, 141–47. I expand upon the impact of Hamilton's plan in my new book, *Black New Jersey, 1664–to the Present* (New Brunswick, N.J.: Rutgers University Press, 2018).

26. Hodges, *Root & Branch*, 174; Wiecek, *Sources of Antislavery Constitutionalism*, 98–100; and David Waldstreicher, *Slavery's Constitution: From Revolution to Ratification* (New York: Hill & Wang, 2009), 88–99.

27. Hodges, *Root & Branch*, 174; White, *Somewhat More Independent*, 188–202; and Gellman, *Emancipating New York*, 136–37.

28. Fergus M. Bordewich, *Bound for Canaan: The Epic Story of the Underground Railroad, America's First Civil Rights Movement* (New York: Amistad, 2006), 46–64; Hodges, *Root & Branch*, 189; Nash, *Forgotten Fifth*, 61–66; and Gellman, *Emancipating New York*, 160–61.

29. Blackett, *Making Freedom*; and Vincent Harding, *There Is a River: The Black Struggle for Freedom in America* (New York: Harcourt, 1993).

2

Revisiting "British Principle Talk"

Antebellum Black Expectations
and Racism in Early Ontario

GORDON S. BARKER

In February 1861 the Reverend William Troy, the son of a free black woman and her enslaved husband, completed his only book-length work entitled *Hair-Breadth Escapes from Slavery to Freedom*.[1] With the help of Arthur Mursell, an English abolitionist living in Manchester, Troy published a collection of stories of fugitive slaves who sought places of freedom and followed the North Star to Canada. Though free, he too made the journey. Seeking to escape oppression as a free black in Virginia, he moved to Cincinnati in 1848, where he endured virulent race prejudice sanctioned by Ohio's infamous Black Laws. Determined to distance himself from racism and threats of being kidnapped into slavery, he moved to Windsor on the Canadian side of the Detroit River. After the American Civil War, Troy returned to Virginia, settling in Richmond among recently freed people. He played a "prominent role" in the city's black community during the challenging years of Reconstruction.[2]

When Troy moved to Canada in the early 1850s and founded Windsor's First Baptist Church, he joined several thousand African Americans in Britain's northern dominion. Like the fugitive slave preacher Alexander Hemsley, who sought refuge in St. Catharines and vowed to scourge his "American blood," Troy wanted to become a "regular Britisher."[3] Ministering to a congregation of fugitive slaves and free blacks, he was touched by their accounts of ordeals in bondage and arduous journeys northward. Telling their stories, Troy celebrated Canada as a Canaan where the hunted fugitive could find "protection by law for his liberty," sketching a space of formal freedom that provided unconditional asylum to runaway slaves and a safe haven to persecuted free blacks. Troy claimed that in Canada blacks could live "without the least social proscription" and enjoy "rights and immunities of the country without embarrassment."[4]

Troy's accounts built on Benjamin Drew's *The Refugee: or the Narratives of Fugitive Slaves in Canada*, published five years earlier. In that remarkable compendium, Drew suggested that, for blacks, Canada meant "Refuge for the Oppressed," whether the word was whispered in the big house, uttered in the quarters, shouted in the fields, or murmured in prayer. He traced such views to the gradual abolition bill that Lieutenant Governor John Graves Simcoe pushed through the colonial legislature in 1793, a year before Eli Whitney invented the cotton gin that transformed the American South into a cotton kingdom and fueled demand for slaves. Simcoe, a friend of William Wilberforce, "seized the opportunity" to prohibit the import of slaves and free the children of existing bondspeople at the age of twenty-five after William Vrooman, a Niagara slaveholder, ignited an antislavery groundswell when he sold his female slave Chloe Cooley into the American market. Reports that the former New York resident dragged her, "kicking and screaming," to the docks where he forced her onto a vessel leaving for the United States fanned abolitionist sentiment, allowing Simcoe to enact the law despite opposition from slaveholders on his executive council. Simcoe's Act to Limit Slavery served as the death knell of the hateful institution in early Ontario, ensuring it would die out within a generation. By 1800, court decisions "rendered slavery virtually untenable" in the neighboring province of Quebec as well.[5]

During the early nineteenth century, colonial officials strengthened Canada's safe-haven status by refusing to extradite runaways, sometimes even when they were charged as felons. As more fugitive slaves arrived after the War of 1812, American slaveholders demanded their extradition. Despite improving Anglo-American relations following the signing of the Treaty of Ghent on Christmas Eve in 1814, Canadian authorities rejected Washington's requests for an extradition agreement on fugitive slaves. In 1819 American officials were particularly disturbed when Canadians adopted a stance consistent with Lord

Mansfield's landmark opinion in *Somerset v. Stewart* (1772), a decision that had been generally interpreted as ending slavery in England.[6] Responding to persistent demands from James Monroe's administration for an extradition treaty, Chief Justice John Beverley Robinson issued an opinion declaring that Canada had "adopted the Law of England as the rule of decision in all questions relative to property and civil rights, and [personal] freedom." He said, "Whatever may have been the condition of these Negroes in the Country to which they formerly belonged, here they are free."[7] The new lieutenant governor, Sir Peregrine Maitland, endorsed Robinson's position and confessed privately that he hoped more "runaway slaves might find sanctuary" in Canada. Seeking to encourage loyal settlers and appear as a good humanitarian, Maitland also set aside lands between Lake Simcoe and Lake Huron's Penetanguishene Bay to be granted to black veterans of the War of 1812; he quickly signed orders-in-council providing for grants to four blacks—Charles Faulkner, Samuel Edmonds, Solomon Albert, and Jonathan Butler.[8]

The diplomatic stalemate on extradition between the United States and Britain continued in the 1820s.[9] After American secretary of state Henry Clay and U.S. ambassador to Britain Albert Gallatin again sought a treaty, Lord Aberdeen issued a terse refusal from London in 1828, saying "the law of Parliament gave freedom to every slave who effected his landing upon British ground."[10] Aberdeen's statement, five years before Parliament approved imperial emancipation with the Slavery Abolition Act, is best understood in the broader context of the rise of the British antislavery movement and its impact upon public opinion. Aberdeen's remarks reflected post-*Somerset* romanticizing of "a perennially free Britain" rooted in Mansfield's famous reference to slavery as "so odious" as to be immoral.[11] In rendering his decision in *Somerset v. Stewart*, Mansfield did not comment on the legality of slavery in the colonies; he "merely maintained that slaves brought to England could not be forcibly removed from the Island without habeas corpus review."[12] But abolitionists and slavery apologists immediately advanced revisionist interpretations of his decision that informed slavery debates on both sides of the Atlantic. Their exaggerations implied that the "principle sprung fresh, and beautiful, and perfect from the mind of Lord Mansfield . . . [that] by the common law, a slave, of whatever country or color, the moment he was on English ground, became free."[13] Slaveholders raised the specter of abolitionism taking hold everywhere in America. Members of Virginia's House of Burgesses were obsessed with what they viewed as British intentions "to offer Freedom to our Slaves"; Arthur Lee, studying in London, piqued such fear in letters to his brothers.[14] Lord Dunmore's proclamation in November 1775 offering freedom to slaves who joined British ranks and Sir Henry Clinton's proclamation four years later in Philipsburg seemed to confirm planters' worst fears.

For their part, William Wilberforce, Granville Sharp, Thomas Clarkson, Olaudah Equiano, and other London abolitionists chose to disregard the chief justice's reference to the authority of local law and transformed the "limited scope of Mansfield's ruling into broad effusions." They argued that England was a model with "freedom in the respiration of its air, and in the very contact of its soil!"[15] They stressed Mansfield's implied embrace of natural law in his remarks on slavery's immorality, downplaying his reasoning that positive law could sanction slavery. Sharp wanted the application of *Somerset* to the colonies and urged Lord North "to abolish immediately both the trade and the slavery of the human species in all the British dominions." Clarkson spoke of the "glorious result of the trial," declaring that "as soon as ever any slave set foot upon English territory, he became free."[16] George Thompson joined the chorus, stressing "the right of human beings to liberty"; he also disregarded Mansfield's inferences on positive law as he called for an end to American slavery.[17] In Eric Foner's words, *Somerset* birthed the "freedom principle."[18]

In the mid-1820s, abolitionists embellished *Somerset* revisionism with scriptural arguments from Elizabeth Heyrick's pamphlet entitled *Immediate, Not Gradual Abolition*. She branded slavery as "a sin to be forsaken immediately," and her "fierce moral clarity" fit perfectly with *Somerset* effusions, creating a more potent British abolitionism rooted in both the Bible and law, which underpinned the final push for imperial emancipation.[19] Heyrick's views offset angst about possible negative impacts of West Indian abolitionism on British economic growth.[20] Her doctrines informed a generation of militants that included leading African Americans who credited her with delivering the final blow that struck down slavery in the Empire. "Justice . . . smote the monster in the height of his power; link after link fell from the massive chain, and *eight hundred thousand human beings sprung into life again*," said James Forten Jr. "It was . . . [Heyrick] who prompted Justice to the work."[21]

Thompson took Heyrick's message to the antislavery lecture circuit in America. "By keeping a Slave, a man invades the proprietary right of the Eternal Lord of All," declared Thompson, labeling slavery "treason" against the Creator.[22] Such interpretations informed William Lloyd Garrison's New England immediatism, Theodore Dwight Weld's antislavery teachings in the Midwest, and John Rankin's letters from Ripley, Ohio, documenting the "sinfulness of slaveholding."[23] Thompson spoke to women's organizations, igniting activists who, like Heyrick, were often "bolder" and very effective in mobilizing grassroots antislavery support.[24] After he lectured to the Philadelphia Female Anti-Slavery Society in 1835, Sarah Forten remarked that "never has there been such an awakening of consciences."[25] British-inspired radical abolitionism had exposed slavery as a "type of authority forbidden by God"; slaveholders interposed themselves between the Creator and His earthly beings, sinfully "contending against divine sovereignty."[26] These arguments struck a responsive chord among African Americans, set the stage for the Higher Law critique of slavery that took hold in late antebellum America, and raised blacks' expectations about the liberties and formal freedom available to them on British soil.

In the early 1830s, *Somerset* effusion, Heyrick-informed immediatism, British treaties with European nations to end the transatlantic slave trade, and Royal Navy seizures of slave ships on the high seas ignited "British principle talk" among African Americans to an extent unseen since the heady days when Parliament banned the slave trade in 1807.[27] At that time, the Reverend Absalom Jones of St. Thomas's Episcopal Church in Philadelphia praised the British, saying, "We pray, O God, for all our friends and benefactors in Great Britain." In New York City's African Methodist Episcopal Church, the Reverend George Lawrence thundered from the pulpit that "the name of a Sharp, a Pitt, and a Fox . . . shall ever dwell with delight on our memories."[28] Pitt and Fox were instrumental politically in making sure the legislation outlawing British participation in the international slave trade passed. This is more evidence of British principle talk among African Americans.

On the eve of imperial emancipation, John Russworm and Samuel Cornish, editors of New York's *Freedom's Journal*, took British principle talk to a wider audience. They returned to Mansfield's decision and lauded his remarks on natural law, stressing that he ensured "the cause of liberty was no longer to be tried on the ground of a mere special indictment." Mansfield, they said, had enshrined "the broad principle of the essential and constitutional right of every man in England to the liberty of his person."[29] The black editors celebrated the "free and religious [English] nation" that looked "the dreadful evil [slavery] in the face."[30] Returning from Britain, the African American orator Charles Lenox Remond also glorified everything British, comparing the lack of prejudice he encountered during his trip to the racism he endured daily in America. "In the course of nineteen months' travelling in England, Ireland, and Scotland," Remond stated, "I was received, treated and recognized, in public and private society, without any regard to my complexion."[31]

David Walker, perhaps the most outspoken black abolitionist in America on the eve of imperial emancipation, also engaged in British principle talk, notably in his *Appeal, in Four Articles*, which shocked pacifist abolitionists and threw slaveholders "into paroxysms of rage" but stirred many African Americans.[32] Walker echoed Heyrick, as he called on blacks to deliver themselves from "wretched, abject and servile slavery" and declared that America "is as much ours as it is the whites." "God Almighty is the sole proprietor or master of the WHOLE human family," wrote Walker, asserting that earthly beings were to serve Him alone. He denounced slaveholders claiming human property and "drag[ging] our mothers, our fathers, our wives, our children and ourselves, around the world in chains and handcuffs." After Walker's sudden death, his disciples, including Boston's Maria W. Stewart and New York City's Underground Railroad conductor David Ruggles, carried on his message. Railing against the abuse of slave women and slaveholders' destruction of slave marriages, Ruggles declared that "slave laws utterly nullify the Supreme Lawgiver—'What God hath joined together, let not man put asunder.'" As Walker's *Appeal* gained popularity, his views fueled British principle talk. He recognized the British as "the best friends the coloured people have." Alluding to *Somerset* and British leadership in halting the transatlantic slave trade, Walker stated the British have "done one hundred times more for the melioration of our condition, than all the other nations of the earth put together." He told blacks to "respect the English"; they were African Americans' "greatest benefactors."³³ His words seemed to ring true when Cincinnati blacks published a letter from Upper Canada's lieutenant governor, Sir John Colborne, to James C. Brown, a black Ohioan, saying, "Tell the Republicans on your side of the line that we do not know men by their colour. If you come to us, you will be entitled to all the privileges of the rest of His Majesty's subjects."³⁴

In *Hair-Breadth Escapes*, Troy joined passionately in this British principle talk, arguing that the British upheld black freedom and enshrined "justice which has been so long delayed."³⁵ So too did many other leading blacks, including Martin Delany. In *Blake; or, The Huts of America*, Delany memorialized "the colossal stature of the Lord Chief Justice when standing up declaring . . . that by the force of British intelligence, the purity of their morals, the splendour of their magnanimity, and the aegis of the Magna Charta, the moment the foot of a slave touched British soil, he stood erect, disenthralled in the dignity of a freeman."³⁶ For Delany, *Somerset* signaled black freedom, making the "universal language of people of color"—as a black subscriber to *The Liberator* put it—"God Bless Great Britain."³⁷

After the abolition of slavery in the empire, black celebrations of Emancipation Day on August 1 sustained British principle talk. In 1839 Jehu Jones described the Reverend William Miller's Emancipation Day praise of Queen Victoria. "I was highly gratified," wrote Jones in the *Colored American*, "with his [Miller's] performance; his prayer [for the Queen] was fervent and sublime." Jones went on to emphasize to blacks that on the "soil of her Britannic Majesty, Queen Victoria . . . you become a man, [and] every American disability falls at your feet."³⁸ On Emancipation Day in 1854, Toronto blacks praised "Her Most Gracious Majesty, Queen Victoria," pledging their loyalty on "the anniversary of our *death* to *Slavery*, and our *birth* to *Freedom*." They exclaimed, "With what feelings, or what words can we adequately express our gratitude to England for such a boon?"³⁹

Fugitive slave crises also fueled British principle talk, especially when slaves gained their freedom on British soil. Sir John Colborne's refusal to extradite Thornton and Ruthie Blackburn, fugitive slaves who sought asylum in Canada after their freedom struggle sparked the Detroit uprising of 1833, confirmed early Ontario's status as a safe haven and space of formal freedom. In 1835 the rescue of the Stanfords, a fugitive slave family seized by slavecatchers in St. Catharines, sent another powerful message to slaveholders. Canadian blacks pursued the Stanfords' kidnappers and, after a pitched battle near Buffalo that William Wells Brown described as "one of the most fearful fights for freedom," they returned the family to Canada, and colonial authorities indicted two Canadians who had participated in the kidnapping.[40]

The rescue of Solomon Moseby, a Kentucky runaway who escaped using his master's horse and reached Niagara-on-the-Lake in 1837, also drew much attention. Discovering Moseby's whereabouts, his master pressured Washington to demand his extradition on charges of horse stealing. In light of the alleged theft, Canadian officials felt obliged to act in the interest of upholding law and order. After Moseby's arrest, however, a black preacher named Herbert Holmes led "two hundred determined black men," supported by their wives, in the daring rescue of the captured runaway. Although Holmes was killed in the affray, the rescuers spirited Moseby to Montreal, where he boarded a ship for England. When Americans demanded that Holmes' accomplices be indicted, Canadian authorities refused to charge them.[41]

Most important, however, was the Jesse Happy extradition drama. It erupted about the same time as the Moseby crisis even though Happy arrived in early Ontario four years before. The resolution of the Happy controversy basically defined Canada's fugitive slave extradition policy for the rest of the antebellum era. Happy had also absconded from Kentucky using his master's horse but had left it at the border to avoid being charged as a felon and wrote to his master to tell him where he could find the animal. Although Happy fled in 1833, his case only surfaced in 1837 when Lexington prosecutors charged him with horse stealing and Governor James Clark asked the State Department to demand his return. When Washington requested he be sent back, Upper Canada's lieutenant governor, Sir Francis Bond Head, convened an inquiry under the leadership of John Beverley Robinson. Skeptical about Kentucky's four-year delay in pressing charges and knowing that extradition would condemn Happy to life in bondage even if he was acquitted of horse stealing, the Canadian chief justice advised against sending Happy back. Bond Head concurred but referred the case to London for review. Abolitionists and proslavery advocates on both sides of the Atlantic waited anxiously.

Examining the file, Colonial Secretary Lord Glenelg concluded that "no positive rule [existed] either in the British Statute Book or in the Law of Nations, requiring or forbidding the restitution of such Criminals [as fugitive slaves]." He advised that henceforth extradition decisions should be made on a case-by-case basis.[42] Foreign Secretary Lord Palmerston also reviewed the dossier. He considered that Happy had not "taken the horse with theft in mind" and declared that even if he had, his re-enslavement for life, if returned, would be "such as our principles of jurisdiction compell [sic] us to regard as indefensible and disproportionate to the crime."[43] The Law Officers of the Crown, a group that included Mansfield's biographer, John Campbell, were also against extraditing Happy. They reasoned that "what took place was not Horse Stealing according to the Laws of Upper Canada, but merely an unauthorized use of a Horse, without any intention of appropriating it."[44] They recommended that alleged runaways should only be surrendered if they committed acts that were crimes in Canada. They noted that because slavery was illegal in Canada, "flight from slavery did not constitute a crime."[45] Abolitionists on both sides of the Atlantic rejoiced. African Americans and Canada's new black residents were especially pleased.

During this same period, Canadian blacks also celebrated Britain's recognition of black troops' contributions to putting down the Canadian Rebellion of 1837. Addressing the legislature, Bond Head paid "striking tribute" to the Coloured Corps, saying blacks were the "foremost to defend the glorious institutions of Great Britain."[46] South of the border, African Americans evinced pride in their brethren's military feats, particularly since blacks were not permitted to bear arms in state militias. The *Colored American* reported that "great confidence is reposed in this regiment [Coloured Corps] . . . in consequence of their acknowledged loyalty to the British Crown."[47] Reverend Jermain W. Loguen praised the "desperate valor" blacks had shown in defending Navy Island, a strategically important British possession in the Niagara River.[48]

It was in this context that the *Colored American* celebrated Britain's "pinnacle of greatness and [the] glory she holds in the scale of nations." The newspaper suggested Canada was as "salubrious and fertile as any other country under the sun" and predicted that "the time is not distant when hundreds of thousands of our brethren will reside there."[49] Blacks were further encouraged by British resistance to Secretary of State Daniel Webster's demand for a fugitive slave extradition agreement during the negotiations leading up to the Treaty of Washington in 1842. As discussions got under way, Lord Ashburton "repudiate[d] any proposal to surrender up a person charged with the mere offence of escaping from Slavery." Then, in November 1841, before the treaty was sealed, the *Creole* crisis confirmed the safe haven status of "her Majesty's dominions" and led to African Americans and their abolitionist allies lionizing the British. In the *Creole* affair, slaves being transported to New Orleans took control of the slave ship and landed it in the Bahamas after killing two crew members.[50] British officials refused to surrender the alleged murderers, asserting "the intent and object of the slaves was not that of plunder on the High Seas"; the officials indicated the mutinous slaves had acted "with the sole object of compelling the crew to take them . . . to some Port where they might obtain their Freedom." British law, they said, recognized natural rights to freedom; self-theft was a defense of the right to liberty.[51]

* * *

When juxtaposed against slavery's horrors, British principle talk increased early Ontario's appeal and heightened African Americans' expectations about the quality of life north of the border. For fugitive slaves, flight to Canada was a way to escape slavery's oppression—regardless of whether they journeyed with the intent of permanent migration or merely for sojourning. Some runaways fled with little or no planning, desperately attempting to avoid an imminent horror. For free blacks, moving to Canada reduced risks of being kidnapped and sold into slavery. Typically, however, most blacks traveled to Britain's northern dominion for several reasons that, taken together, give special meaning to the North Star. British principle talk informed them that if they were enslaved, their "shackles were struck off" on Canadian soil;[52] if they were free, they could not be claimed as property because by "the laws of Englishmen" they stood as persons.[53] As Hemsley put it, "a man was a man by [English] law."[54] In New York's St. Philip's Church, the Reverend Peter Williams thanked "God, in his good providence" for having "opened up" such a sanctuary as "the neighboring British province." For American blacks, it was a most "convenient asylum."[55]

In addition to printed texts, speeches, and sermons, song played an instrumental role in British principle talk by transmitting and popularizing messages of black freedom in Canada. In *Hair-Breadth Escapes*,

Troy published one of antebellum blacks' favorite verses celebrating the Canadian Canaan:

> I heard our Queen Victoria say—
> If we would forsake
> Our native land and slavery,
> And come across the lake—
> That she was standing on the shore
> With arms extended wide,
> To give us all a peaceful home
> Beyond the rolling tide
> Farewell, old master,
> That's enough for me;
> I'm just in sight of Canada,
> Where coloured men are free.[56]

Another very popular Underground Railroad ballad underscored the protection of fugitive slaves under British law:

> I stand as a freeman along the northern shore of Old Erie, the freshwater sea
> And it cheers my very soul to behold the billows roll
> And to know as a man I am free
> Old Master and mistress, don't come after me,
> For I won't be a slave any more;
> I'm under British law safe beside the lion's paw
> And he'll growl if you come near me sure.[57]

Revered in many ways, the North Star shone brightly for black Americans. As an adolescent enslaved on William Brent's plantation near Falmouth, Virginia, Anthony Burns heard of black liberty in the North Country from older slaves telling stories at night in the quarters. Such tales "kindled a fire in his young breast that never went out."[58] James Smith, another fugitive slave from Virginia, remembered feeling threatened by slave hunters in the Free States. He came to believe that Canada was the "only place . . . where he could rest in any degree of safety." He decided to take refuge "under the 'Union Jack'" and moved to Amherstburg on the north shore of Lake Erie.[59]

Nineteenth-century narratives suggest that specific situations that blacks confronted, juxtaposed against British principle talk, often spurred flight to Canada. Elisha Valentine fled to Ontario from North Carolina, a distance of nearly one thousand miles through unknown country, to avoid punishment "for striking the overseer." Another North Carolina runaway named Hopkins sought refuge north of the border because his master encouraged "bucking," which entailed the binding of a slave's hands and feet while also placing "his arms over the knees, and shoving a strong stick between the arms and knees, thus rendering the slave entirely helpless" for whipping. Hearing that his master had ordered the overseer to buck him, Hopkins fled. Robert Blackburn escaped from Virginia because he could not endure another flogging for "insubordination." He set out on a "perilous" twelve-hundred-mile journey that took him to Baltimore; Philadelphia; New York City; Cincinnati; Sandusky, Ohio; Detroit; and, finally, Amherstburg fourteenth months later.[60] John Holmes absconded to London, Ontario, escaping a master who believed "a man must be whipped, else he wouldn't know he was a *nigger*." The lashing of Dan Josiah Lockhart's wife and children prompted his flight to St. Catharines. He could not countenance such abuse and told Drew, "I don't want any man to meddle with my wife."[61] He fled alone and then wrote to his wife to have her follow with some of their children when he reached Pittsburgh but there is no evidence that she did or that they were ever reunited. He initially escaped to Pittsburgh but had to leave there for Canada when slave hunters found him.

Fears of being sold to the Deep South also sparked flight, especially as King Cotton swept the lower states and traders profited by shipping human cargo down the river. In 1844 the Lexington firm of Hughes & Downing enjoyed a 60 percent return selling Kentucky slaves in Natchez, Mississippi.[62] William Johnson endured "a great deal of affliction" as a slave but confessed that "the fear of being sold South had more influence than any other thing" on his flight. Benedict Duncan lived and suffered twenty-eight years in Maryland slavery. When his master experienced hard times, however, Duncan decided to flee to Toronto because of his "fear of being sold" to the Deep South.[63]

Fugitive slaves often fled to avoid separation from loved ones, usually spouses or children. The "spectacular story" of the Crafts who escaped from Georgia, with the light-skinned Ellen disguised as an ailing young male planter and William pretending to be his personal servant, reflected the couple's determination to protect their relationship.[64] After they arrived in Britain, their transatlantic correspondence and staging of a mock slave auction at the Crystal Palace revealed the horrors of slavery to a global audience and boosted British principle talk on both sides of the Atlantic. Also motivated by a desire not to lose loved ones, a Kentucky fugitive slave known only as Mother Monroe led the largest family escape from Boone County. Hearing that her master planned to sell her children, Monroe stole across the Ohio River in 1856 with her son and ten daughters, aged six to nineteen years. They later crossed the Detroit River narrows and landed in Windsor "on British soil" in earshot of their angry master yelling "Stop! Stop!" from the American shore.[65]

For African Americans, the Fugitive Slave Law of 1850 underscored the divergence between American policy and liberty under the lion's paw, thus contributing to British principle talk, which boosted the numbers of blacks seeking sanctuary in Canada. The law encouraged free black kidnapping because it prohibited alleged fugitive slaves from testifying and paid slave commissioners a higher fee if they ruled in favor of the master. After its enactment, "a Baptist church in Buffalo lost 130 members; another in Rochester reported losing 112 of its 114 worshippers; in Detroit, some 80 members of the city's black Baptist church were reported to have left in haste for Canada."[66] Theodore Parker estimated that "400 persons of color" departed from the Boston area.[67] James Smith, a Virginia runaway, told Troy that, although he had settled and lived comfortably in Pittsburgh, he left for Canada when President Millard Fillmore signed the bill into law because "slave catchers filled the city."[68] Charles Peyton Lucas, also from the Old Dominion, said he decided to "go to Canada" even if it meant leaving Geneva, New York, where he had prospered for ten years.[69] Nelson Moss left Pennsylvania, and Philip Younger fled Alabama, also "in consequence of the passage of the Fugitive Slave Bill."[70] Some blacks moved to avoid incarceration under the law; Samuel Ringgold Ward and Jermain W. Loguen, key actors in Syracuse's "Jerry Rescue," hastened to Canada.

Reports of free access to education, a priority for blacks who had been deprived of schooling in the South, resonated deeply among African Americans. Troy recalled that as a child he had been forced to "hide his books" so that his teacher would not suffer a "fine or imprisonment." He cited the Virginia law of 1849 that stated, "Every assemblage of [N]egroes for the purpose of instruction in reading or writing shall be an unlawful assembly." He remembered studying "with tears" in his eyes.[71] William Grose, a fugitive slave from Virginia, was determined that his children would have schooling that he had never enjoyed. He settled in St. Catharines hoping to give them "a good education." Henry and Martha Gowens escaped from Alabama to ensure their children's instruction. Martha said, "I have five smart children . . . [and] I mean they shall have a good education." Wealthier black Americans too considered Canada an ideal place for learning. John H. Rapier sent two of his sons to the Buxton Mission School, which by the mid-1850s had become renowned throughout America.[72]

British principle talk's celebration of blacks' political and legal equality in Canada especially inspired free blacks struggling with prejudice. Troy, along with many other antebellum African Americans, believed that the "precious rights denied in the United States—the right to vote, the right to serve on juries, equal protection under the law—were theirs in Canada."[73] Henry Bibb, the fugitive slave editor of the *Voice of the Fugitive*, told African Americans that in Canada they could serve on juries and cast votes. He claimed, "the vote of the colored man is as mighty as that of a white man."[74] Mary Ann Shadd, editor of the *Provincial Freeman* and a strong advocate of integration, denounced "Yankeedom with [its] disenfranchisement and oppression" by comparing it to Canada's "impartial laws and . . . no distinctions of color."[75] Many early Ontario blacks contrasted their ability to bear arms in the Canadian Coloured Corps with their exclusion from military service in America. Bibb also stressed independence arising from land ownership that blacks could enjoy in Britain's northern dominion. He spoke of the availability of prime agricultural land at low prices, reporting that fertile farmland around Windsor could be purchased for as little as $9 per acre and forested land near Sandwich for as little as $7 per acre. He advised black migrants not to "stop short of Canada," where he contended they could "improve their moral, mental and political condition" as independent owners of property.[76]

Finally, Troy placed special emphasis on Canada's reputation for religious liberty. He recalled that in Virginia he became "more dissatisfied with regard to [his] own condition in the church" as he was constantly reminded of his inferior status. "When I went into the chapel, however early, even if a hundred seats were empty," wrote Troy, "I could not occupy one of them."[77] He remembered having to sit in the colored people's gallery. Williamson Pease fled to Hamilton, Ontario, resenting his Tennessee master's declaration that it was "perfect nonsense to have a preacher for niggers." For most blacks, Canada was a place where Negro pews did not exist and blacks had the freedom to establish their own churches if they so desired. In Toronto, Drew reported that there were "three churches exclusively belonging to the colored people—a Baptist and two Methodist churches."[78]

* * *

If British principle talk raised African Americans' expectations about the attractiveness of black life on the Queen's northern soil, their experiences after arriving exposed a very different reality—one that shattered Canada's image as an ideal safe haven and later contributed to a huge reverse migration that began in 1863. In less than a decade, perhaps some three-quarters of early Ontario's blacks returned to the United States, leaving an Afro-Ontarian population of less than fifteen thousand in 1871. Although usual explanations of this exodus stress blacks' desires to reunite with kin, reexamining the historical evidence reveals the importance of two main considerations. First, many blacks who crossed the border did not seek permanent homes in Canada, and, second, after their arrival, many experienced levels of prejudice they never expected. Indeed, Canada fell so short of its idyllic portrayal in British principle talk that even successful blacks who had family north of the border returned to the United States. For many antebellum blacks, freedom in Canada came to mean more struggles against discrimination; they felt alienated in a strange landscape. If Canadian whites supported black liberty, they also made it clear they did not want blacks to live in their neighborhoods, have sexual relations with or marry their children, attend their schools, worship in their pews, compete for their jobs, sit on their juries, vote in their elections, or represent them in their parliaments. As Robin Winks pointed out in his seminal study of the black experience in Canada, white racism typically crushed blacks' political aspirations. The only black ever to be elected to public office in early Ontario was Mary Ann Shadd's father, Abraham D. Shadd, who won a seat on the Raleigh Town Council in 1859. It was not until 1968, when Lincoln Alexander entered the Canadian Parliament, that a black Ontarian was elected to the House of Commons.[79] Simply put, "caught between formal legal equality and deeply entrenched societal and economic inequality," antebellum blacks in Canada confronted a frustrating paradox.[80] They were formally free, neither enslaved nor threatened with slavery, but they were stigmatized as an unwanted minority and deprived of fundamental rights enjoyed by the Queen's other Canadian subjects.

It is thus perhaps not surprising that when American slavery ended, most early Ontario black residents felt that they had little reason to stay; many headed south, becoming "transmigrants" searching for better lives and responding to the promises of Radical Reconstruction. With America's mid-nineteenth-century black population exceeding several million, returning blacks could also feel some safety in numbers, which was more appealing than remaining an unwanted minority in a hostile land.[81] Further, many blacks shared David Walker's view that America was just as much their country as it was the country of the whites; for more than two hundred years, it had been "enriched" with the "blood and tears" of their ancestors.[82] Such sentiments would have been especially strong among blacks who had not planned to reside permanently in Canada. Narratives provided by Troy and Drew, as well as the return of such prominent blacks as Harriet Tubman, Samuel Ringgold Ward, Jermain W. Loguen, and John Rapier, prove that although blacks celebrated Canadian free soil, many did not evince a "deep commitment" to it.[83] Troy too is an example; his scourging of his American blood did not last long; he returned to Virginia, preached in Richmond, engaged in social uplift, cared for the elderly, and in 1876 encouraged the Virginia Assembly to pass "An Act to Incorporate the Aged Home Association."[84]

Some blacks who traveled to Canada revealed mixed emotions strikingly similar to those of truants who slipped away from plantations built by their forebears and often still lived on by loved ones but from which they had to escape—at least temporarily—to avoid impending horrors such as being lashed, raped, or sold to a trader. Watching from the fringes, truants waited, hoping for conditions on the plantation to change. Likewise, many antebellum blacks in Canada waited on America's borderlands and prayed for change in their homeland, acting principally as sojourners. Their decisions to return were probably hastened by the unexpectedly adverse conditions they endured in the host country. During Samuel Gridley Howe's tour of Ontario in 1863, a fugitive slave couple told him of harsh realities they faced in Canada. The husband stressed that he and his wife had moved north only to escape slavery and indicated that they did not plan to stay. He said that he would be happy to return "as soon as he could be free" in the United States; his wife complained that "prejudice was 'a heap' stronger in Canada than it was at home." Shortly after this exchange, a white farmer confirmed racism in the Ontario countryside when he told the Boston philanthropist that "blacks were the worst people [a]round."[85]

Even a self-avowed "Britisher" like Hemsley confessed that his thoughts constantly reverted to his homeland, and he hoped that "something might happen" to enable his return. Mother Monroe was thankful for her family having "narrowly escaped" separation, but she acknowledged feeling an emptiness in Canada where "she had no friends but her children."[86] Nancy Howard declared that she had been forced to "come here [to Canada]" to avoid slavery, but she stressed that she had ended up "lower to the ground."[87] Although involved in ministering to fugitive slaves in St. Catharines and schooling black children, Loguen admitted to being a sojourner when he penned an open letter to New York's governor, Washington Hunt. He referred to himself as a "Christian minister in exile" and said that he hoped to return to Syracuse—a city from which he had been "driven."[88] As black sojourners looked southward, deceptions associated with prejudice and institutionalized racism north of the border weighed heavily upon them.

Writing to Henry Bibb, Samuel Ringgold Ward described the "Canadian Negro hate" that he endured on the *St. Lawrence*, a steamship that transported the Queen's mail on the Great Lakes. "The *St. Lawrence*, under the patronage of the British Government, and sailing upon British waters, with a British subject for a captain, compels a black man to take deck passage—or none," lamented Ward. He thought "the boast of Englishmen, of their freedom from social negrophobia [sic] . . . about as empty as the Yankee boast of democracy."[89]

Similar to racist Americans, many Canadians viewed blacks as "inherently inferior," frequently mocking them as they discriminated against them.[90] Traveling on a Lake Ontario steamer, the white merchant Charles Kadwell described a black passenger and his wife saying that "he was completely *à la nigger*; rings on his fingers & in ears, superfluous in breast pin & watch guard, & with respect to clothing appeared lately let loose from the hands of Master Snip." Sarcastically, he added that "the man had the vanity to consider himself, *a colored gentleman*," and he derided the couple's affection for each other by saying they seemed to "lub" each other.[91] In Toronto, similar to many American cities, minstrel shows were a rage during the antebellum period. When, in 1841, Wilson Ruffin Abbott and forty-five other blacks petitioned city hall to prohibit such ridiculing of blacks, the mayor bowed to white racism and rejected their demand.[92] After Benjamin Lundy visited early Ontario, he concluded that Canadian whites "retain all the prejudices" existing in the United States.[93] Racism certainly prevailed among whites in the countryside. Many, including Thomas Connor from the small town of Elora near Guelph, "complained that the number of blacks immigrating to Canada West was on the rise." Even attitudes of missionaries like Fidelia Coburn who often denounced slavery and racism, which she said "chills them [blacks] to the heart," believed in white superiority.[94] Not surprisingly, prejudiced Canadian whites began to organize politically to keep blacks from moving into their neighborhoods. As early as 1830, some early Ontario politicians opposed "the settlement of Negroes"; in 1832 whites circulated a petition seeking to ban "the settlement of more [N]egroes."[95]

Blacks frequently felt hostility as soon as they set foot on Canadian soil—particularly those who crossed the Detroit River to Windsor, Colchester, and Amherstburg, where racism flourished. Whites in these towns deemed black migrants "not pleasing" and often branded them "thievish and otherwise immoral," saying they were "unwelcome intruders" who would "foster serious racial tension."[96] Such hostility helped to quash the new arrivals' "hopes and dreams for better lives and equal rights."[97] By 1835, with in-migration swelling after imperial emancipation, whites in the southwestern corridor between Windsor and London protested more vigorously, denouncing "the very numerous & troublesome black population coming into this District from the Slave States."[98] By the 1850s, Windsor whites even sought to check any efforts by Detroit's legendary Underground Railroad conductor George DeBaptiste "to purchase town lots" upon which blacks could settle.[99]

Blacks resented such mounting racism. A correspondent for the *Colored American* reported that African Americans who migrated to Canada were disillusioned by the prejudice of white Canadians, which they found "just as strong" as that they endured south of the border.

After visiting Canada, the correspondent concluded that prejudice in the northern dominion actually weighed "more heavily on the colored man." Most disturbing was his view that white Canadians were "afraid of emancipation" because they feared it would cause a flood of blacks to "empty into Canada." He contended that Canadians were "prejudiced to Emancipation, and the emancipated."[100] John W. Lindsay, a St. Catharines black, complained that the "colored people of Canada have no chance for advancement . . . [and] are barred out from everything."[101] He thought Canadians were more prejudiced than southern slaveholders. So too did the black pastor Lewis Chambers; he said that racism in early Ontario was "worse than it is in the states."[102]

Although British principle talk frequently described Canadian cities as sanctuaries for runaways, most urban centers had their share of racists. In Hamilton, Member of Parliament Isaac Buchanan confessed that if a referendum were held on whether blacks should be allowed to stay in the city, "the people would vote against having the [N]egroes remain here." In Toronto, businessman William Davies complained that he had to deal with blacks "next door." Writing to his brother, he said that in Canada's Queen City whites bumped into "Free Niggers . . . at every step."[103] George Brown, editor of Toronto's *Globe and Mail*, believed that prejudice was "stronger in Canada" than in the United States. It affected Toronto's blacks in a variety of ways, including in relegating them to Negro pews in churches. Initially, Toronto's black Wesleyans "worshipped with whites," but by 1838 they established their own church on Richmond Street and selected their own black pastor, the Reverend Stephen Dutton, to distance themselves from discrimination.[104] In St. Catharines, blacks worshiped in the Zion Baptist Church and in the British Methodist Episcopal Salem Chapel, avoiding racism such as that experienced by the Reverend Chambers, who had been stopped from attending a service in a white church by a sexton telling him, "We don't want niggers here." Despite being known as the City of Refuge and the home of Anthony Burns, Harriet Tubman, Jermain Loguen, and Alexander Hemsley, St. Catharines experienced racial tensions that often threatened the black minority with extreme violence. When the labor market declined after the completion of the Welland Canal, job competition between whites, particularly Irish immigrants, and blacks led to hostility that erupted into the devastating St. Catharines race riot of 1852. A mob attacked the Coloured Corps during drill practice and then leveled the mostly black St. Paul's Ward, scorching homes, destroying businesses, and sending frightened residents fleeing for their lives.[105]

Review of white reactions to black settlements confirms prejudice and reveals the extent to which it "disadvantage[d]" blacks as they tried to establish roots in early Ontario.[106] In Oro Township, the only "government-sponsored" black settlement in the province, racism was evident from the very beginning. Although Sir Peregrine Maitland's order-in-council called for veterans of the War of 1812 "to receive Grants from the Crown . . . of two hundred acres" on the Penetanguishene Road, the executive council "preferred not to extend the special 200-acre homesteads to Negro settlers" and made less attractive grants to colored veterans. Blacks received only one-hundred-acre grants, and they were restricted to Wilberforce Street on the county line behind the Penetanguishene Road, effectively segregating Ontario's first black settlement. A total of twenty-three one-hundred-acre "militia certificates" were accorded to blacks between 1819 and 1826. Most grantees were fugitive slaves or free blacks who had recently arrived in Canada.[107]

The Oro Settlement struggled during the 1820s, hampered also by administrative disorganization that especially hurt black homesteaders. Exact lots had not been "specified" on the orders-in-council and no on-the-ground surveys were commissioned prior to the grants. Indeed, the grantees only received what amounted to a location ticket, and they were left on their own to "locate" their land, clear acreage, and erect dwellings before they could apply for official title by paying a patent fee of five pounds—an expense that few fugitive slaves or free blacks could afford after having carved farms out of the wilderness.[108] The result was that by 1827 only eight black grantees held clear title to their lands in Oro. Other blacks were essentially squatters who found themselves increasingly vulnerable as circumstances changed and increasing numbers of whites coveted the lands that they worked.[109]

When early Ontario's commissioner of Crown lands Peter Robinson, the chief justice's brother, moved to Oro, conditions for blacks deteriorated further, even as the numbers of blacks increased with the arrival of refugees from the Cincinnati race riot of 1829. By 1830 about 150 blacks had moved to Oro, seeking to build new lives but lacking many of the skills needed to survive on the frontier. They also had little support except for spiritual guidance from Ari Raymond, a white pastor, and his wife. These Oro blacks cleared land, harvested timber, and planted subsistence crops, but, without title to their lands, most remained "illegal squatters." When Robinson developed a new colonization plan tailored to white settlers who subsequently poured into the area, surveyed homesteads, and purchased patents from the Crown Lands Office, the black pioneers were evicted and lost any improvements they had made to the land. Officials' unwillingness to assist them seems best explained by their desire to curry favor with whites, who were often racist and felt "repugnance to [blacks] forming communities near them." By 1831 the black settlement in Oro began to decline. The colored population moved elsewhere, and whites seemed glad to see the experiment in black freedom fail. Robinson mused that if the Oro settlement had flourished, it might have encouraged "a greater number of blacks coming into the area"—something he thought would have alarmed most whites.[110] Mary Gapper, a white who liked her black neighbors, complained that "some of our wise members ... have resolved that the negro [sic] settlement is likely to disturb our neighborhood."[111] It was against this background that legislators debated resolutions stating that "the sudden introduction of a mass of Black Population ... is a matter dangerous to the peace and comfort of inhabitants." Blacks were, as the *African Repository and Colonial Journal* reported, "unwelcome intruders." Members of the Assembly of Upper Canada worried that it might be "necessary to prevent or check [black settlement] by some prudent restrictions." They concluded that the large numbers of blacks entering the province was "a just cause of alarm for the peace and security."[112]

After the Cincinnati race riot, Israel Lewis and Thomas Cresap led some two hundred blacks to another destination—the village of Lucan, where they established the Wilberforce Settlement. The first settlers arrived in 1829, and three years later some thirty-two families worked two thousand acres with "two hundred head of cattle, pigs and horses besides a grist mill, a saw mill, two schools and two Churches."[113] Austin Steward, a grocer from Rochester, New York, and the Reverend Benjamin Paul gave the settlement new leadership. They sought to establish a manual labor college to enhance skills of blacks. With the future looking promising, they sent Nathaniel Paul, Benjamin Paul's son, to Britain to raise funds.

Similar to Oro, however, the settlement quickly encountered opposition from neighboring whites, notably when the residents' early success seemed to suggest it might be "the first of perhaps many planned Negro communities." But the colony also soon suffered from division between its leaders. Steward and the settlement's board of managers charged Lewis with corruption and Nathaniel Paul with the misuse of funds after he returned from Britain having spent most of the money he collected to cover his personal expenses. By 1836 Wilberforce teetered on the edge of collapse. An embittered Nathaniel Paul left for Albany and Steward returned to Rochester. Racist whites took the opportunity to justify their prejudice, declaring "Negroes were incapable of planning," and observers described the Wilberforce inhabitants as impoverished and destitute.[114] The Reverend William Proudfoot of London reported that new arrivals lived in shanties. "The dwellings of the [N]egroes," he wrote, "[are] wretched, badly built and very small." His picture differed from the images of "comfortable log buildings" and "crops [that] smile ... upon the labor of our hands" that Steward and Paul had published in *The Liberator* in 1831.[115] The settlement continued to be plagued by controversy, legal disputes, and white prejudice. By 1842 Wilberforce "had become virtually non-existent and many of its original settlers had scattered."[116]

Still another group of Cincinnati blacks made their way to Woolwich Township near the Queen's Bush Clergy Reserves. Led by Paola Brown, these black Ohioans initially squatted near the site of the modern-day city of Kitchener-Waterloo, establishing the Colbornesburg Settlement, named in honor of Sir John Colborne. It proved to be short-lived, as land-hungry white settlers began to push the Ohio refugees off their lands by 1833 and into the nearby Clergy Reserves where the blacks founded the Queen's Bush Settlement on parts of Wellesley Township in Waterloo County and Peel Township in Wellington County. By 1840 more than one hundred black families had "settled illegally as squatters" in the district. They worked farms of up to one hundred acres that benefited from the area's fertile soil, and the region soon became widely known as "good wheat country."[117]

In early 1842, however, these black families again faced changing circumstances, and the changes were not for the better. In response to higher immigration from the British Isles, the government decided to survey lands in the Clergy Reserves with a view to raising revenues by selling homesteads to white settlers entering the Queen's Bush. Surveyors, followed by land agents ready to strike deals, arrived. Unable to pay inflated land prices, the Queen's Bush blacks united to request special consideration. In 1842 they wrote to Member of Parliament James Durand, apologizing for their "boldness of squatting in the Queen's Bush" but explaining that because they had only recently taken refuge in Canada, they could not afford to buy the lands that they had been improving. They asked Durand to "do the best for us you can." Receiving no response, they petitioned Lieutenant Governor Sir Charles Metcalfe, noting that they had endured the "horrors of slavery"; they were still very "poor"; and they had "no means of purchasing land." They "humbly pray[ed] that your Lordship will take our case into consideration and if agreeable to your Lordship's humanity to make us a grant of land." Metcalfe did not embrace their cause, and soon afterward Fidelia Coburn, founder of the Mount Hope School for black children, described a flood of white settlers arriving and intent on acquiring land.[118] She said these whites were "very much opposed" to blacks residing in the area. Targets of racism and lacking funds to acquire their homesteads, the Queen's Bush blacks were forced to move, abandoning improvements they had made to excellent wheat lands. Some again petitioned Lord Elgin in 1847 and in 1850 to "entreat their case into [his] humane consideration," but it was to no avail. The black population dwindled, and Coburn's Mount Hope School became a common school from which black children could be excluded.[119]

A review of the Dawn Settlement also confirms the existence of prejudice that undermined black expectations fueled by British principle talk. Founded by the Lane Seminary rebel Hiram Wilson and the legendary fugitive slave Josiah Henson, Dawn included a manual school known as the British-American Institute, which had been conceived because of whites' "insurmountable prejudices" and desires to keep blacks out of their schools. The all-black settlement was situated on two hundred acres of prime land adjacent to the Sydenham River, and it numbered about five hundred persons when the manual school opened in 1842. But Henson also embarked on the construction of a brickyard, a saw mill, and a gristmill that ran the institute's debt to more than $7,500 by 1849 and set the stage for the collapse of another experiment in black freedom.[120] In addition to excessive debts, "unclear aims," and "poor management," the actions of Hiram Wilson—and later those of John Scoble, who was appointed to oversee the institute—contributed to the Dawn's decline.[121]

Amid allegations of mismanagement and corruption, Wilson moved to St. Catharines, and a board of trustees took control of the institute's affairs. Henson traveled to England in search of funds to cover the substantial debt, but his trip marked the beginning of the end. Henson solicited $1,500 and visited Prince Albert's Crystal Palace where, along with William and Ellen Craft, he spoke against slavery; nevertheless, rumors surfaced that he was "an imposter, obtaining money under false pretences." The British and Foreign Antislavery Society immediately launched an inquiry and, although Henson was cleared, the society sent its secretary, John Scoble, to manage the institute. Scoble's racism and haughty demeanor ensured Dawn's demise as his behavior alienated black homesteaders. Meeting at Dresden in 1852, they complained that "the conduct of Scoble . . . was distasteful to the people of this community."[122] As the institute veered toward bankruptcy, it also became the target of whites who disdained black colonists' alleged "dependence", which they said cost "a great deal of money."[123] When Henson sought additional funds to keep the institute going, whites labeled him a beggar. Leading blacks also distanced themselves from Henson. For example, Mary Ann Shadd, the black editor of the *Provincial Freeman*, thought Henson had "lowered white Canadian opinion of fugitives and reinforced the belief that blacks were improvident."[124]

If the Dawn Settlement sparked racial tensions, the strident racism ignited by William King's Elgin Association, eventually the most successful all-black settlement and home of the famous Buxton Mission School, was even more striking. King founded the settlement to emancipate slaves he acquired through his wife, the daughter and heiress of a wealthy Louisiana planter. Hostility surfaced from the moment he purchased some four thousand acres in Raleigh Township near Chatham in 1849. In his autobiography, King remembered that "when it was known I intended to settle a colony of coloured persons in [Raleigh] Township, my popularity fell rapidly."[125] That was an understatement. Indeed, upon hearing of the proposed settlement, the racist politician Edwin Larwill immediately sought to quash King's project, declaring that the black community would be "highly deleterious to the morals and social conditions of the present and future [white] inhabitants of this district."[126] He claimed "there is but one feeling, and that is of disgust and hatred, that they [the Negroes] should be allowed to settle in any township where there is a white settlement." Larwill contended that "a colony of vicious blacks would be prejudicial to every interest of society" because it would result in race-mixing, hinder diplomatic relations with the United States, cause social and political disorder, and "discourage 'better stock' European immigrants."[127] By August 1849 Larwill, whose "tactics and speech were," as Robin Winks points out, "like many southern American senators," boasted more than four hundred signatures on a petition to stop the Elgin Settlement.[128] Ordinary whites, as well as many of the so-called better sorts, rallied at meetings and wrote to newspapers. Some, like J. Thompson of Galt, sent letters directly to King, seeking to convince him that blacks "steal" and "are lazy."[129]

Larwill and his allies spewed "pseudo-scientific doctrines supporting Negrophobic theories" of such writers as Dr. John Van Evrie. Meeting at the Royal Exchange Hotel in Chatham, they proclaimed that "the difference [between whites and blacks] . . . was such as could not be successfully overcome." They argued that natural law sanctioned segregation. They reasoned that "nature . . . has divided the same great family into distinct species, for good and wise purposes," and they called on Canadians to follow "her dictates and obey her laws." These whites declared that "it is with alarm we witness the fast increasing . . . settlement amongst us of the African race," claiming also that it could only have a "poisonous effect upon the moral and social habits of a community."[130] Larwill exploited ordinary whites' fears of job competition with blacks and predicted that blacks would also gain political influence. "Imagine our Legislative Halls studded, and our principal Departments managed by, these Ebony men," he proclaimed, stressing also that "it would be impossible to keep them out of the smaller elective offices. With black Councillors, [and] School Trustees," he added "The Genious [sic] of our Institutions would be destroyed."[131] Larwill wanted legislation banning land sales to blacks, implementing poll taxes for black voters, requiring security bonds for new arrivals, and introducing restrictions to prevent blacks from holding public offices. The racist rallying cry became, "Let us not countenance their [blacks'] further introduction among us."[132] Early Ontario's Western District

Council supported such proposals, but fortunately the Canadian legislature never acted upon them, thus allowing the Elgin Settlement to be established and become "home to some 1200 people" by the mid-1850s.[133]

* * *

Regardless of where early Ontario's blacks settled, they wanted their children to have access to education. Perhaps in no other aspect of life did the racism of Canadian whites take a greater toll—and it did so on several generations of black children. After David Johnson and his family crossed the Detroit River, Johnson lamented that "we have a great amount of prejudice to contend with." He complained that even after having paid school taxes, "our children are not permitted to attend the common schools." He scorned white fears of race-mixing, noting that they justified excluding blacks from schools by arguing "if the coloured and white children were allowed to go to school together, the white children would, according to the natural order of things, marry among some of the coloured families."[134] Such prejudice left many black children without any instruction at all and, as early as 1828, blacks united to protest discrimination against their children. In that year, Maitland received a petition from some two hundred blacks in the Ancaster-Hamilton area asserting that "the greatest disadvantage" they experienced was "the want of means of educating their children."[135] Rather than diminishing, exclusion of black children grew as prejudice mounted with more blacks arriving after imperial emancipation. Further, when the Canadian government responded to demands from early Ontario's Roman Catholic minority to establish separate schools, whites used the legislation to block black children from common schools by contending separate schools were established for racial minorities as well.

In 1843 Hamilton blacks, still enduring discrimination, petitioned Sir Charles Metcalfe for redress of their children's exclusion from schools. "We the people of colour in the Town of Hamilton have a right to inform your Excellency of the treatment that we have to undergo," they wrote, stressing that they paid school taxes, but their children were denied access to common schools. They said that when they came to Canada, they had expected that "under the British flag" they would not "be known" by their skin color.[136] About the same time as this crisis erupted, Amherstburg blacks also filed a complaint with Superintendent of Education Egerton Ryerson protesting that local school trustees had directed the common school teacher "not to let the colored children come to school." Investigating the situation, Ryerson found that a majority of Amherstburg whites opposed the "admission of the colored children." Sadly, Amherstburg was no exception in early Ontario. In most school districts west of Toronto, including Windsor, Sandwich, Chatham, London, and even St. Catharines, black children were excluded from common schools. Reports indicated that in London "if any colored child enters a school, the white children are withdrawn."[137]

Such mistreatment left early Ontario blacks with no alternative but to turn to the courts, which they did. In 1852, when school trustees refused Dennis Hill's son entry to the nearby common school and told him to send the child to a school four miles away, he protested vigorously. After the exclusion of his second son in 1855 and a failed appeal to Ryerson in which he stated that his son had been excluded "for no other crime than my skin is a few shades darker than some of my neighbors," Hill filed a suit upon which Chief Justice John Beverley Robinson rendered a truly infamous decision that effectively served to institutionalize racism.[138] In *Dennis Hill v. School Trustees of Camden*, he ruled that "the separate schools for coloured people were authorized ... out of defence to the prejudice of the white population." He then ordered Hill's sons to attend the distant separate school, sanctioning school segregation and subjecting black children in early Ontario to attend what sadly were often "unsatisfactory institutions" that typically provided "inferior education."[139]

In another 1855 opinion, Robinson decided in favor of a black plaintiff, but the latter's complaint revealed the extremes to which whites sometimes went to exclude black students from attending the same schools as their children. In *Solomon Washington v. School Trustees of Charlottesville*, a black farmer contested his son's exclusion from the local common school "owing to his color" and challenged trustees who gerrymandered his farm out of the school district to justify refusing to enroll his child. With no separate school nearby, Washington's son was deprived of instruction. In this case, Robinson recognized the trustees' bad faith and ruled that "colored people are not to be excluded from the ordinary school, if there be no separate school established."

But early Ontario blacks continued to fight against their race-based exclusion from common schools for another decade, even as the Civil War raged south of the border. In 1864, in *George Stewart v. Sandwich Trustees*, the province's new chief justice, William Draper, decided in favor of the black plaintiff who demanded that his daughter, Lively Stewart, be admitted to Sandwich's common school. Draper's decision, however, was heavily imbued with prevailing Canadian racism and disappointed Ontario's black residents as it failed to put blacks and whites on the same footing. Although Draper claimed to support equal access to education for blacks and ordered that Lively be admitted to the common school, he did so only because there was no separate school nearby. He refused to guarantee blacks unrestricted access to common schools, stating only that "coloured people are not to be excluded from the ordinary common schools if there be no separate school established and in operation for their use."[140]

As Draper failed to limit the impact of prejudice on black children, conditions south of the border changed dramatically. With Major General William Tecumseh Sherman sweeping through the South and taking Atlanta, Lincoln Republicans poised to win reelection, and the Wade-Davis Bill calling for new radicalism in reconstructing the South, early Ontario blacks weighed their alternatives. Black valor in the Union Army also seemed to have helped pave the way for new guarantees in America. In 1863 Dr. A. T. Jones, a black pastor in London, Ontario, perhaps best foresaw the consequences of white Canadian prejudice against black schoolchildren. He noted that "instead of leaving these children to grow up with that love for the country and the Queen," the racism they endured in their youth would distance them from Canada. Jones warned that "the day will come when you will hear them saying, 'this is the country that disenfranchises us, and deprives us of our rights.'" That day, the black pastor predicted, would come when the "war is decided."[141]

For many early Ontario blacks, the day did come. British principle talk had raised expectations but, in the final analysis, had only yielded empty promises. It was in these circumstances that the return migration began with some 2,500 black Canadians putting their lives on the line for the Union forces in the most casualty-ridden struggle the American republic had ever experienced. A trickle turned into a flood, and most blacks in the province embraced David Walker's message that America was just as much the country of the blacks as it was the country of the whites. After Fort Wagner, Milliken's Bend, Fort Pillow, and numerous other battles, American soil had been further enriched with African American blood and tears—and black Ontarians were still treated as unwanted intruders.[142]

NOTES

1. William Troy, *Hair-Breadth Escapes from Slavery to Freedom* (Chapel Hill: University of North Carolina Press, 2000).

2. Peter J. Rachleff, *Black Labor in Richmond, 1865–1890* (Urbana: University of Illinois Press, 1989), 57.

3. By 1853, Troy was leading small prayer meetings. The original First Baptist Church building was erected in 1858. See the African Canadian Community website, http://www.windsor-communities.com/african-religion-firstbaptist.php, accessed October 22, 2015. Benjamin Drew, *The North-Side View of Slavery. The Refugee: or, the Narratives of Fugitive Slaves in Canada* (Boston: John P. Jewett and Company, 1856), 39. As he was being returned South, Hemsley was freed on a ruling by Justice Theodore Frelinghuysen of the New Jersey Supreme Court after Justice Joseph C. Hornblower approved a writ of habeas corpus requested by antislavery militants wanting to stop his return to bondage. Debate on the numbers of fugitive slaves and free blacks entering Canada prior to the Civil War continues. For commentary, see Michael Wayne, "The Black Population of Canada West on the Eve of the American Civil War: A Reassessment Based on the Manuscript of the Census of 1861," *Histoire sociale / Social History* 28, no. 56 (November 1995): 467; and Matthew Furrow, "Samuel Gridley Howe, the Black Population of Canada West, and the Racial Ideology of the 'Blueprint for Radical Reconstruction,'" *Journal of American History* 97, no. 2 (September 2010): esp. 349–58.

4. *Colored American*, June 22, 1839. See also "Editorial by Henry Bibb," December 3, 1851, reprinted in *The Black Abolitionist Papers*, vol. 2, *Canada, 1830–1865*, ed. C. Peter Ripley (Chapel Hill: University of North Carolina Press, 1986), 200.

5. Drew, *North-Side View*, 17; and Gordon S. Barker, *The Imperfect Revolution: Anthony Burns and the Landscape of Race in Antebellum America* (Kent: Kent State University Press, 2010), 90. Robin W. Winks notes that at least six members of the colonial legislature owned slaves as did three members of the executive council—Peter Russell, Richard Cartwright, and James Baby. See Robin W. Winks, *The Blacks in Canada: A History* (Montreal: McGill-Queen's University Press, 1997), 97, 102.

6. James Oliver Horton and Lois E. Horton, *Slavery and the Making of America* (New York: Oxford University Press, 2005), 56–57.

7. William Renwick Riddell, "The Fugitive Slave in Upper Canada," *Journal of Negro History* 5, no. 3 (July 1920): 344.

8. Daniel G. Hill, *The Freedom-Seekers: Blacks in Early Canada* (Toronto: Stoddart, 1992), 18–19.

9. Gary E. French, *Men of Colour: An Historical Account of the Black Settlement on Wilberforce Street and in Oro Township, Simcoe County, Ontario, 1819–1949* (Orillia, Ont.: Dyment-Stubley Printers, 1978), 13–18.

10. Winks, *The Blacks in Canada*, 102.

11. Edlie L. Wong, *Neither Fugitive nor Free: Atlantic Slavery, Freedom Suits, and the Legal Culture of Travel* (New York: New York University Press, 2009), 12 (first quote); and *Somerset v. Stewart* (1772) accessed at http://www.commonlii.org/int/cases/EngR/1772/57.pdf on October 18, 2015 (second quote).

12. Justin Buckley Dyer, "After the Revolution: Somerset and the Antislavery Tradition in Anglo-American Constitutional Development," accessed at https://politicalscience.missouri.edu/sites/default/files/people-files/dyer_somerset.pdf on October 18, 2015. For the interpretation of the *Somerset* case as prohibiting slavery in England, see Horton and Horton, *Slavery and the Making of America*, 56–57.

13. Wong, *Neither Fugitive nor Free*, 12.

14. Woody Holton, *Forced Founders: Indians, Debtors, Slaves, and the Making of the American Revolution in Virginia* (Chapel Hill: University of North Carolina Press, 1999), 140–41.

15. Wong, *Neither Fugitive nor Free*, 21.

16. Thomas Clarkson, *The History of the Rise, Progress, and Accomplishment of the Abolition of the Slave-Trade by the British Parliament* (London: Longman, Hurst, Rees, and Orme, 1808), 79 and 77.

17. *Speech of George Thompson, Esq., M.P., Delivered at the Anti-Slavery Meeting, Broadmead, Bristol, September 4th, 1851* (Examiner Office, 1851), 9. It is remarkable that abolitionist effusions continued unabated even after Lord Stowell ruled in The *King v. Allan* (1827), also known as the *Case of the Slave Grace*. Stowell rejected Grace's argument that she "had been divested of her status as a slave when she moved to England," even though he upheld the *Somerset* "notion of a right to freedom by virtue of a residence in England." He reasoned that "residence in England conveys only the character so designated during the time of that residence" and considered that Grace had returned voluntarily to slavery, thus forfeiting the right of freedom that she acquired during residence on free soil. Dismayed by Stowell's dismissal of Mansfield's strictures on morality as *obiter dictum*, abolitionists stressed Grace's natural right to liberty.

18. Eric Foner, *Gateway to Freedom: The Hidden History of the Underground Railroad* (New York: W. W. Norton, 2015), 38.

19. Elizabeth Heyrick, *Immediate, Not Gradual Abolition* (Philadelphia: Philadelphia A. S. Society, 1837), 3; and Adam Hochschild, *Bury the Chains: Prophets*

and Rebels in the Fight to Free an Empire's Slaves (Boston: Houghton Mifflin, 2005), 324.

20. For a summary of the economic impact of the abolition in the West Indies on the British economy, see Kenneth Morgan, *Slavery, Atlantic Trade and the British Economy, 1660–1800* (Cambridge: Cambridge University Press, 2000), 50–54.

21. James Forten Jr., *Speech Delivered before the Philadelphia Female Anti-Slavery Society, Philadelphia, Pennsylvania, 14 April, 1836*, reprinted in Ripley, *Black Abolitionist Papers*, 2:154.

22. *Speech of George Thompson, Esq., M.P., Delivered at the Anti-Slavery Meeting, Broadmead, Bristol, September 4th, 1851*, accessed at https://archive.org/details/speechofgeorgethoothom.

23. *Liberator*, June 18, 1836.

24. Hochschild, *Bury the Chains*, 327.

25. Letter of Sarah L. Forten to Elizabeth H. Whittier reprinted in Ripley, *Black Abolitionist Papers*, 2:142.

26. Lewis Perry, *Radical Abolitionism: Anarchy and the Government of God in Antislavery Thought* (Ithaca, N.Y.: Cornell University Press, 1973), xi.

27. I coin the term "British principle talk" on the basis of the references by African Americans, including the Reverend William Troy, to British principles related to the liberties enjoyed by the Queen's subjects during the antebellum period. It should also be noted that when Troy spoke of British principles, he referred to the lack of prejudice as well as freedoms sanctioned by law. See Troy, *Hair-Breadth Escapes*, 9.

28. Absalom Jones, "A Thanksgiving Sermon, Preached January 1, 1808, In St. Thomas's, or the African Episcopal Church, Philadelphia: On Account of the Abolition of the African Slave Trade, on that Day, By the Congress of the United States," in Dorothy Porter, ed., *Early Negro Writing 1760–1837* (Boston: Beacon Press, 1971), 341.

29. *Freedom's Journal*, November 30, 1827.

30. Wong, *Neither Fugitive nor Free*, 21; and *Freedom's Journal*, March 7, 1828.

31. "Testimony by Charles Lenox Remond Delivered at the Massachusetts State House, Boston, Massachusetts, 10 February 1842," reprinted in *Black Abolitionist Papers*, vol. 3, ed. C. Peter Ripley, The United States, 1830–1846 (Chapel Hill: University of North Carolina Press), 370.

32. Herbert Aptheker, *"One Continual Cry" David Walker's Appeal to the Colored Citizens of the World (1829–1830): Its Setting & Its Meaning* (New York: Humanities Press, 1965), 1–2.

33. David Walker, *Appeal, in Four Articles; Together with a Preamble to the Coloured Citizens of the World, but in Particular, and Very Expressly to Those of the United States* (Boston: David Walker, 1830), 14–15, 62, 47; and David Ruggles, *The Abrogation of the Seventh Commandment by the American Churches* (New York: David Ruggles, 1835). On Ruggles' practical radical abolitionism, see Graham Russell Gao Hodges, *David Ruggles: A Radical Black Abolitionist and the*

Underground Railroad in New York City (Chapel Hill: University of North Carolina Press, 2010), esp. 63–154.

34. French, *Men of Colour*, 21; see also Winks, *The Blacks in Canada*, 156–57.

35. Troy, *Hair-Breadth Escapes*, 9.

36. Martin R. Delany, *Blake; or, The Huts of America* (Boston: Beacon, 1970), 263.

37. *Liberator*, April 4, 1835.

38. *Colored American*, September 14, 1839.

39. "Address to the Queen Presented by George Dupont Wells at the Government Grounds, Toronto, Canada West, 1 August 1854," reprinted in Ripley, *Black Abolitionist Papers*, 2:295.

40. *Blacks in the Niagara Peninsula*, St. Catharines Public Library Special Collections, St. Catharines, Ontario. On the Thornton and Ruthie Blackburn drama, see Karolyn Smardz Frost, *I've Got a Home in Glory Land: A Lost Tale of the Underground Railroad* (New York: Farrar, Straus and Giroux, 2007).

41. Janet Carnochan, "A Slave Rescue in Niagara Sixty Years Ago," (paper delivered to the Canadian Institute, Lundy's Lane Historical Society, and the Niagara Historical Society, 1897), 12, in *Blacks in the Niagara Peninsula*. See also Jason Howard Silverman, "Unwelcome Guests: American Fugitive Slaves in Canada, 1830–1860" (PhD diss., University of Kentucky, 1981), 38–41.

42. J. Mackenzie Leask, "Jesse Happy: A Fugitive from Kentucky," *Ontario History* 54 (1962): 87–106.

43. Alexander L. Murray, "The Extradition of Fugitive Slaves from Canada: A Re-evaluation," *Canadian Historical Review* 43 (1962): 298–314.

44. William Renwick Riddell, "The Fugitive Slave in Upper Canada," *Journal of Negro History* 5 (1920): 3, 52–53. See also Leask, "Jesse Happy," 87–106.

45. Barker, *Imperfect Revolution*, 97; and Murray, "Extradition of Fugitive Slaves," 298–314. Nelson Hackett, a fugitive slave from Arkansas arrested as a felon for having stolen the gold watch, beaver overcoat, saddle, and horse of Alfred Wallace, his master, was the only runaway extradited to the United States after the Jesse Happy affair. See Ripley, *Black Abolitionist Papers*, 2:399–401. On the eve of the Civil War, Canadian authorities liberated John Anderson, a fugitive slave accused of having murdered his master's neighbor. See Barker, *Imperfect Revolution*, 99.

46. Ernest Green, "Upper Canada's Black Defenders," *Ontario Historical Society Papers and Records* 27 (1931): 370–73.

47. *Colored American*, September 24, 1839.

48. J. W. Loguen, *The Rev. J. W. Loguen as a Slave and as a Freeman: A Narrative of Real Life* (Chapel Hill: University of North Carolina Press, 1999), 344. See also Fred Landon, "Canadian Negroes and the Rebellion of 1837," *Journal of Negro History* 7, no. 4 (1922): 377–79.

49. *Colored American*, January 22, 1839.

50. Murray, "Extradition of Fugitive Slaves," 306.

51. *Colored American*, December 1, 1838; and Murray, "Extradition of Fugitive Slaves," 304.

52. Drew, *North-Side View*, 38.

53. Wong, *Neither Fugitive nor Free*, 19.

54. Drew, *North-Side View*, 38.

55. Reverend Peter Williams, "A Discourse Delivered in St. Philip's Church, for the Benefit of the Coloured Community of Wilberforce, in Upper Canada, on the Fourth of July, 1830," in *Early Negro Writing 1760–1837*, ed. Dorothy Porter (Boston: Beacon Press, 1971), 296–99.

56. Troy, *Hair-Breadth Escapes*, 59.

57. Quoted in Barker, *Imperfect Revolution*, 87.

58. Charles Emery Stevens, *Anthony Burns: A History* (Boston: John P. Jewett, 1856), 154–55.

59. Troy, *Hair-Breadth Escapes*, 20.

60. Troy, *Hair-Breadth Escapes*, 15, 33, and 52–59.

61. Drew, *North-Side View*, 165, 46–49.

62. J. Winston Coleman Jr., "Lexington's Slave Dealers and Their Southern Trade," reprint from *The Filson Club History Quarterly* 12, no. 1 (January 1938): 1–28.

63. Drew, *North-Side View*, 29, 110.

64. *Liberator*, September 27, 1850; see also Gordon S. Barker, *Fugitive Slaves and the Unfinished American Revolution, Eight Cases, !848–1856* (Jefferson, N.C.: McFarland Publishers, 2013), 21–36.

65. Troy, *Hair-Breadth Escapes*, 39–42.

66. Fred Landon, "The Negro Migration to Canada after the Passing of the Fugitive Slave Act," *Journal of Negro History* 5, no.1 (1920): 22–24.

67. Albert Reville, *The Life and Writings of Theodore Parker* (London: Simpkin, Marshall, 1865), 117.

68. Troy, *Hair-Breadth Escapes*, 20.

69. Drew, *North-Side View*, 109; see also 153.

70. Drew, *North-Side View*, 250.

71. Troy, *Hair-Breadth Escapes*, 1–4.

72. Drew, *North-Side View*, 87 and 145. On the blacks' beliefs in the importance of education and the Buxton Mission School, see, Donald George Simpson, "Negroes in Ontario from Early Times to 1870" (PhD diss., University of Western Ontario, 1971), 26; and Richard M. Reid, *African Canadians in Union Blue: Volunteering for the Cause in the Civil War* (Vancouver: University of British Columbia Press, 2014), 30.

73. Ripley, *Black Abolitionist Papers*, 2:6.

74. *Voice of the Fugitive*, March 12, 1851.

75. Ripley, *Black Abolitionist Papers*, 2:7.

76. *Voice of the Fugitive*, March 12, 1851; April 9, 1851; and October 22, 1851; land prices from January 15, 1852, and June 18, 1852.

77. Troy, *Hair-Breadth Escapes*, 5.

78. Drew, *North-Side View*, 131 and 94.

79. See Winks, *The Blacks in Canada*, 215. Jason Howard Silverman also stresses the impact of Canadian white race prejudice. See Silverman, "Unwelcome Guests."

80. Barrington Walker, *Race on Trial: Black Defendants in Ontario's Criminal Courts, 1858* (Toronto: Osgoode Society for Canadian Legal History / University of Toronto Press, 2010), 3.

81. Nina Glick Schiller, *Nations Unbound: Transnational Projects, Postcolonial Predicaments and Demoralized Nation-States* (New York: Gordon and Breach, 1994).

82. Walker, *Appeal*, 73.

83. Reid, *African Canadians in Union Blue*, 20.

84. *Acts and Joint Resolutions passed by the Assembly of the State of Virginia at the Session of 1875–76* (Richmond: R. F. Walker Superintendent Public Printing, 1876), 54.

85. Samuel Gridley Howe, *The Refugees from Slavery in Canada West: Report to the Freedmen's Inquiry* (Boston: Wright & Potter, 1864), 68.

86. Drew, *North-Side View*, 39.

87. Drew, *North-Side View*, 51; see also Troy, *Hair-Breadth Escapes*, 42.

88. *St. Catharines Journal*, January 22, 1852.

89. Ripley, *Black Abolitionist Papers*, 2:177–79.

90. Simpson, "Negroes in Ontario," 31.

91. Quoted in Frank Mackey, *Done with Slavery: The Black Fact in Montreal 1760–1840* (Montreal: McGill-Queen's University Press, 2010), 179.

92. On the minstrel show controversy in Toronto, see Adrienne Shadd, Afua Cooper, and Karolyn Smardz Frost, *The Underground Railroad: Next Stop, Toronto* (Toronto: Natural Heritage Books, 2002), 51.

93. Merton L. Dillon, *Benjamin Lundy and the Struggle for Negro Freedom* (Urbana: University of Illinois Press, 1966), 172.

94. Linda Brown-Kubisch, *The Queen's Bush Settlement: Black Pioneers, 1839–1865* (Toronto: Dundurn Press, 2004), 126 and 70.

95. French, *Men of Colour*, 28–29.

96. Fred Landon, "Amherstburg, Terminus of the Underground Railroad," *Journal of Negro History* 10, no. 1 (1925): 6.

97. Silverman, "Unwanted Guests," 18 and 35.

98. Simpson, "Negroes in Ontario," 31.

99. Winks, *The Blacks in Canada*, 208.

100. *Colored American*, November 18, 1837.

101. Silverman, "Unwelcome Guests," 91.

102. Silverman, "Unwelcome Guests," 91.

103. Howe, *Refugees from Slavery*, 42–45.

104. William Sherwood Fox, ed., *Letters of William Davies, Toronto, 1854–1861* (Toronto: University of Toronto Press, 1945), 484–96; see also Shadd, Cooper, and Frost, *Underground Railroad*, 29.

105. Howe, *Refugees from Slavery*, 45. On St. Catharines race relations see, Barker, *Imperfect Revolution*, 107–116.

106. Howe, *Refugees from Slavery*, 54. See also Landon, "Amherstburg, Terminus of the Underground Railroad," 6.

107. French, *Men of Colour*, 12–14. French stresses that Oro was the only government-sponsored settlement.

108. French, *Men of Colour*, 2.

109. A. C. Robbins traces the Buxton families of John Morris and John Smith to the early Oro settlement. See Arlie C. Robbins, *Legacy to Buxton* (North Buxton, Ont.: A. C. Robbins, 2013), 37.

110. Silverman, "Unwelcome Guests," 19–24.

111. French, *Men of Colour*, 35.

112. *African Repository and Colonial Journal* 6 (1831): 28.

113. Robbins, *Legacy to Buxton*, 26.

114. Winks, *The Blacks in Canada*, 157.

115. Silverman, "Unwelcome Guests," 28; see also *Liberator*, September 17, 1831.

116. Robbins, *Legacy to Buxton*, 26.

117. Brown-Kubisch, *The Queen's Bush Settlement*, 31; and Drew, *North-Side View*, 190.

118. Brown-Kubisch, *The Queen's Bush Settlement*, 238. On Coburn and the Mount Hope School, see Winks, *The Blacks in Canada*, 224; and the Ontario Heritage Plaque for Queen's Bush accessible at http://www.ontarioplaques.com/Plaques/Plaque_Wellington31.html.

119. Brown-Kubisch, *The Queen's Bush Settlement*, 69, 129.

120. Josiah Henson, *Uncle Tom's Story of His Life: An Autobiography of the Rev. Josiah Henson* (Chapel Hill: University of North Carolina, 2000), 127–29.

121. Winks, *The Blacks in Canada*, 195.

122. Silverman, "Unwelcome Guests," 63.

123. Howe, *Refugees from Slavery*, 69–70. For Josiah Henson's recollections of this crisis, see Henson, *Uncle Tom's Story*, 133.

124. *Provincial Freeman*, May 2, 1857.

125. William King, *Autobiography of Rev. William King, Written at Intervals During Last Three Years of His Life*. Accessed online at Archives Canada, 76, www.collectionscanada.gc.ca.

126. To the Legislative Assembly of the Province of Canada in Parliament assembled, February 19, 1849, R4402-0-1-E, William King Collection, Library and Archives Canada, Ontario, Canada, http://www.collectionscanada.gc.ca/etoile-du-nord/033005-119.01-e.php?&fond_id_nbr=1&m_t_nbr=3&fond_seq=1_3_14&sk=11&s=3c&&PHPSESSID=j6cn76ponpmcop4ccgf1u6fmco.

127. Silverman, "Unwelcome Guests," 77; and Landon, "Amherstburg," 6 (second quotation).

128. Winks, *The Blacks in Canada*, 214.

129. J. Thompson to Reverend William King, March 29, 1849. Accessed online at Archives Canada.

130. *Kent Advertiser*, August 23, 1849. On John Van Evrie, see George M. Fredrickson, *The Black Image in the White Mind: The Debate on Afro-American Character and Destiny 1817–1914* (Middletown, Conn.: Wesleyan University Press, 1971), 92.

131. Silverman, "Unwelcome Guests," 75–77.

132. Victor Ullman, Look to the North Star: A Life of William King (Boston: Beacon Press, 1969), 115.

133. Afua Cooper, "Overview of the North Star Collections," accessed at Collections Canada, https://www.collectionscanada.gc.ca/northern-star/033005-1000-e.html.

134. Troy, *Hair-Breadth Escapes*, 26.

135. William Renwick Riddell, "A Petition, Discovered by the Honourable William Renwick Riddell, Justice of Appeal, Ontario, Canada," *Journal of Negro History* 15, no. 1 (1930): 115–16.

136. Ripley, *Black Abolitionist Papers*, 2:97.

137. Silverman, "Unwelcome Guests," 173–76.

138. Silverman, "Unwelcome Guests," 182.

139. Simpson, "Negroes in Ontario," 496; and Claudette Knight, "Black Parents Speak: Education in Mid-Nineteenth-Century Canada West," *Ontario History* 89 (1997): 278.

140. Knight, "Black Parents Speak," 281–82.

141. Howe, *Refugees from Slavery*, 51–52.

142. See Walker, *Appeal*, 79 and 9. For an excellent analysis of Afro-Canadian contributions to the Union war effort, see Reid, *African Canadians in Union Blue*.

3

The Underground Railroad in "Indian Country"

Northwest Ohio, 1795–1843

ROY E. FINKENBINE

During the summer of 1803 John Reed, a fugitive slave from Kentucky, turned up on the streets of Detroit. About the same time, a runaway slave advertisement by his master, one Colonel Grant, also reached the city. It promised a substantial reward. Daniel Ransom, an agent of Reed's owner, also reached the city. Authorities soon placed Reed in a jail cell. Fortunately, some among the local populace sought to protect him from being returned to bondage in the South, even if that meant buying his service as an indentured servant. Solomon Sibley, a local jurist and a member of the territorial council, wrote Grant to inquire about buying the runaway's freedom (or indenture). Sibley explained that it would be difficult to hold Reed in the city as a slave and further suggested that Grant should sell Reed at a low price, "rather than run the risk of taking him home through the Indian country."[1]

To most people in the eastern portion of the Old Northwest at the time of Reed's escape, "Indian Country" referred to the northwest quarter of the newly admitted state of Ohio. Five out of every six residents of the region were Native Americans. Although a few settlers, traders, and missionaries entered the region in the early nineteenth century, only 400 or so whites lived there by the outbreak of the War of 1812, nearly all of them along the north bank of the Maumee River or in white enclaves at the sites of Perrysburg and Lower Sandusky (contemporary Fremont). An earlier count from 1800 also listed some 139 blacks in the region. Meanwhile, an estimated 3,000 Native Americans lived in northwest Ohio at the outbreak of the War of 1812. They lived primarily in Ottawa villages along the Maumee River and on Blanchard's Fork more than forty miles to the south, in Shawnee villages near the headwaters of the Great Miami River, and in Wyandot villages along the Sandusky River, together with a few Delaware and Seneca and other Six Nations peoples who had recently migrated to the Sandusky River valley. Although maps of the era, such as Alexander Bourne's 1815 map of Ohio, often represented the region as an "empty quarter," devoid of population, the federal government formally recognized it as "Indian Country"—an area of tribal sovereignty. It constituted a political and cultural "middle ground" of sorts between white settlements in southeastern Michigan Territory to the north and in the other three quarters of Ohio to the south and east.[2]

Just eight years before Reed's escape, in 1795, the U.S. government and Ohio's Native American tribes had signed the Treaty of Greenville, officially acknowledging the area to be "Indian Country." The agreement established a line that ran from Fort Recovery near the midpoint of the state's current western boundary southeastward to nearby Fort Loramie, then slightly northeastward to Fort Laurens on the Tuscarawas River, continuing down the Tuscarawas and Cuyahoga Rivers to Lake Erie. All lands north and west of the line were recognized as Indian Country. The treaty granted Native Americans in the area tribal sovereignty, as well as $20,000 in presents, plus an annual payment to the tribe of $9,500. It also permitted the federal government the right to create a few enclaves north and west of the line for forts and trading posts and guaranteed the protection of the federal government against further incursions into Native American land. It further recognized a right of passage for Americans—white and black—moving through the territory on its rivers and trails. The treaty formally opened the lands south and east of the line to white settlers, who quickly flowed into the Ohio country by way of the Great Miami, Scioto, Muskingum, and other rivers. By 1803 Ohio had reached a population of more than 230,000 and easily achieved statehood.[3]

A major factor in allowing northwest Ohio to remain Indian Country in the early nineteenth century was the presence of the Great Black Swamp, a substantial wetlands area that covered much of the region.

Lying mostly to the south of the Maumee River, the swamp covered some 1,500 square miles and all or part of twelve contemporary counties. It was broken only by occasional sand ridges and rock outcroppings that provided the lone dry land within its confines. The swamp proved a major impediment to settlement and travel. Native Americans generally established their villages outside of or on the periphery of the swamp, entering it only on hunting expeditions or trading missions. Early travelers regularly commented on the region's impassibility. When Moravian missionary David Zeisberger crossed the swamp in 1791, he wrote in his journal of the many miles "where no bit of dry land was to be seen, and the horses at every step wading in the marsh up to their knees." But it was not just the unrelenting wetlands that made the region unattractive. In one of the earliest recorded impressions of the area, mapmaker Lewis Evans observed in his *Geographical, Historical, Political, Philosophical and Mechanical Essays* (1755) that "the stinging of Flies and divers other Insects but particularly Muskeetose in this Country are like to rival the Seven Plagues of Egypt." The presence of the Great Black Swamp, together with its relative impassibility and intolerable environment, limited white settlement in northwest Ohio for several decades.[4]

Although white settlement in northwest Ohio continued to be sparse until the 1830s, federal officials negotiated a series of treaties during the early nineteenth century that somewhat limited tribal sovereignty in the region. In the Treaty of Detroit (1807), the Ottawa gave up their claim to their territory north of the Maumee River except for a series of designated reservations. That established a precedent. The Treaty of Brownstown (1808) gave the United States the right to build two roads—both 120 feet wide—one from the Maumee River to Lower Sandusky (contemporary Fremont), the other from Lower Sandusky to the Greenville Treaty Line. The biggest change, however, came with the Treaty of the Foot of the Rapids (1817), which placed the remaining Native Americans in the region into specific reserves in exchange for additional annual payments, although they retained the right to continue to hunt and travel on the surrendered land. Another treaty the following year expanded the size of a few of these reservations. Northwest Ohio's reservations held an estimated Native American population of 2,200 by 1830. About 500 Shawnee occupied three large reservations near the headwaters of the Great Miami River at Wapakoneta, Hog Creek, and Lewistown. They shared the latter with some 200 Seneca. More than 300 Seneca and other Six Nations peoples inhabited a reservation near Lower Sandusky on the Sandusky River. Upstream from that was the eight-thousand-acre Wyandot Grand Reserve and its more than 500 souls centered at Upper Sandusky. Just to the south of that was a small reserve at Captain Pipe's Village, where less than 100 Delaware lived. The 1817 and 1818 treaties also expanded the Ottawa reservations in the Maumee River valley and established two new ones—one at the confluence of the Auglaize and Maumee Rivers, the other on Blanchard's Fork. All told, nearly 500 Ottawa lived in these reserves. Even with the limitations created by the reservation system, the white presence remained small. The 1820 census counted only 1,781 whites in the region, mostly in the Maumee River valley or in the white settlements at Perrysburg (at Fort Meigs) and Lower Sandusky. Ten years later census enumerators still counted fewer than 3,000 whites. There were probably 200–300 blacks living there as well. Nevertheless, for all practical purposes, most of the region still remained Indian Country.[5]

Congressional passage of the Indian Removal Act of 1830 eventually ended northwest Ohio's status as Indian Country. Over the next several years, thousands of Native Americans were escorted by federal officials to reservations west of the Mississippi in what is now Kansas. The Delaware and the Seneca at Lewistown left in 1831. The Shawnee, the remaining Seneca, and the Ottawa at the confluence of the Auglaize and Maumee Rivers tearfully abandoned their villages one year later. Seeing their options closing quickly, the bulk of the Ottawa went westward in 1837 and 1839. The Wyandot resisted removal for more than a decade, finally agreeing to leave their ancestral lands in 1842. One year later, they underwent a slow, painful exodus to their new, far less verdant reservation. As Native Americans moved out, white settlers flooded in; 38,916 of them were counted in the 1840 census of northwest Ohio.[6] For Native Americans in the region, this episode constituted another "Trail of Tears." For the hundreds of fugitive slaves like John Reed, who had passed through the region over the course of nearly a half century, it ended an important example of biracial cooperation between African American freedom seekers and Native Americans in their own version of what would come to called the Underground Railroad.

ENCOUNTERS ON THE TRAIL

The Indian Country of northwest Ohio lay astride the main routes used by fugitive slaves escaping from Kentucky, western Virginia, or beyond to the relative safety of Detroit or crossing into Upper Canada (contemporary Ontario) by way of the Detroit River borderland or the western half of Lake Erie. The majority of runaways passing through the region viewed it as a series of way stations, often receiving food, shelter, and other assistance in the Native American villages they encountered along the way; a minority, however, viewed these villages as spaces of freedom or terminuses in their own right, temporarily or permanently sojourning there or in the two white enclaves in the Maumee or Sandusky River valleys.

The first fugitive slaves to voluntarily migrate northward to or through Indian Country came in the final decades of the eighteenth century. The earliest to pass through may have been an unnamed runaway from Kentucky who reached Detroit in 1790. Sensing an opportunity, he entered into "a very lucrative trade" with a Wyandot he had encountered during his escape. Buying whiskey, gunpowder, blankets, and other necessities on credit in Detroit, they transported these goods "into the interior" of northwest Ohio, exchanging them for furs and hides in Native American villages at a profit of 1,000 percent. Their territory reached as far south as the Shawnee villages just above the Greenville Treaty Line.[7]

Two pieces of legislation enacted in 1793 greatly increased the number of fugitive slaves coming into Indian Country. The Fugitive Slave Act of 1793, approved by the U.S. Congress, permitted slave owners or their agents to seek and recover runaways anywhere in the new nation, including the so-called free states and territories north of the Ohio River. The 1793 Antislavery Act in Upper Canada also placed that province on the road to emancipation. Reacting to these laws, small numbers of runaway slaves began to choose Canada—usually by way of the Detroit River borderland or the western half of Lake Erie (after the emergence of steamboat traffic there in 1818)—as a destination in the years that followed. In a runaway slave advertisement published in 1798 in the *Kentucky Gazette*, for example, slave owner Peter LeGrand surmised that his slave Abraham was headed "to Detroit, where he was well acquainted." Five years later, the Kentucky fugitive Reed arrived in Detroit, as did a trickle of others. After the War of 1812, soldiers returning to their homes in Kentucky and western Virginia broadly circulated news about the land of freedom to the north. In mid-1819, John Beverly Robinson, Upper Canada's attorney general, made it clear to American officials that colonial authorities in the province would oppose any efforts to extradite fugitive slaves. "Whatever may have been the condition of the Negroes in the [United States]," he opined, "here they are free—For the enjoyment of all civil rights . . . and among them the right to personal freedom."[8] As word of Canadian freedom spread through the slave communities of the upper South, growing numbers of fugitive slaves headed northward across the Ohio River and into Indian Country.[9]

How many fugitive slaves came into Indian Country between 1795 and 1843? Although that is difficult to determine with precision, we can arrive at a reasonable estimate. The numbers were relatively small during the first two decades—perhaps 300 or so over this period—but they increased dramatically after the War of 1812. Reports from Upper Canada indicate that the first major wave of fugitive slaves to arrive in the province came between 1817 and 1822. The work of the late J. Blaine Hudson provides a more exacting estimate for the last three decades. He created a database of runaway slave advertisements posted or published in the Ohio River borderland during the antebellum years. These became the basis of the findings in his *Fugitive Slaves and the Underground Railroad in the Kentucky Borderland* (2002). Extrapolating from these advertisements, he estimated that an average of about five hundred fugitive slaves escaped each year from or through Kentucky between 1810 and 1829. Beginning in 1830 the annual number of fugitives was closer to 1,100. If these numbers are correct, some 24,300 slaves escaped across the Ohio River from Kentucky between 1810 and 1843. A high percentage of these crossed the river between Madison, Indiana, in the west and Adams County, Ohio (east of Ripley), in the east, then headed north into Indian Country. If only a third of Hudson's estimate followed this path, we can assume that more than 8,000 fugitive slaves came into Indian Country prior to final Indian removal.[10]

Fugitive slaves usually traversed the Indian Country of northwest Ohio by following one of four established trails through the region. Many runaways coming into the region by way of the Great Miami

River valley first reached the eight Shawnee villages (later the three Shawnee reservations at Wapakoneta, Hog Creek, and Lewistown) near the headwaters of that river. Although written documentation is scarce, extensive oral tradition makes clear that "the Shawnee towns were a sanctuary for the blacks who came up here." In these villages, fugitive slaves found safety, sustenance, shelter, and sources of information about the way northward. There is evidence that runaway slaves began fleeing to Ohio Shawnee towns as early as the era of the American Revolution. A case in point is Caesar, a Kentucky fugitive who escaped to Chillicothe in 1774 and was adopted by the Shawnee. He married a mixed-race Shawnee woman named Sally and fathered two children, known to history as "Sally's white son" and "Sally's black son" due to their difference in hue. The latter is still listed as "Sally's black son" in the roll of Shawnee migrants removed from Wapakoneta to the Kansas frontier in 1832. This is an early example from Ohio's Indian Country of what historian William Loren Katz labels "Black Indians."[11]

After leaving the Shawnee villages, some fugitive slaves made their way northwestward on the Auglaize Trail. This allowed freedom seekers to circumvent the worst of the Great Black Swamp. The Auglaize Trail meandered some sixty miles until it reached the Maumee River. It followed the Auglaize River most of the way, ending at the confluence, where the Auglaize emptied into the Maumee. An Ottawa village lay there in the vicinity of Fort Defiance. From that point, runaways often followed the Maumee downstream toward Perrysburg, receiving assistance in the several Ottawa villages along the river's north bank.[12]

Even more heavily traveled was a trail that is rarely mentioned by scholars but frequently appears in the county histories of northwest Ohio and the reminiscences of early white traders, such as Dresden Howard. Pioneering Underground Railroad historian Wilbur H. Siebert simply referred to it as "the west line." The trail went some thirty-five miles northeastward from the Shawnee reservation at Wapakoneta to the Ottawa village of Lower Tawa Town (contemporary Ottawa, Ohio) on Blanchard's Fork. Inhabitants of the latter town kept a lamp burning in the log council house at the center of the community that could allegedly be seen by approaching travelers (including escaped slaves) for a distance of five miles. Upon leaving the village, the trail continued another thirty-five miles northeastward to the Howard's trading post at Grand Rapids, Ohio, on the Maumee River. Across the river, runaway slaves were welcomed enthusiastically at Kinjeino's Town, an Ottawa village. The trail then followed the Maumee downstream until it intersected with Hull's Trace at Perrysburg. In September 1821 Ohio Indian Agent John Johnston cut a state road through the forest following the existing trail.[13] The road passed directly through the heart of the Great Black Swamp, but it dramatically lessened the distance for fugitive slaves passing through Indian Country.

To the east of the Shawnee villages, fugitive slaves frequently traversed Indian Country on an old Shawnee trail known as the Bullskin Trace. Running from the Ohio River to Detroit, it followed a path used by the Shawnee and other Native Americans to bring salt northward from the salt licks of Kentucky. By the early nineteenth century, it had also become an important conduit for runaways from Kentucky or beyond who were heading toward Canada. With conflict against Britain pending in 1812, and the need for rapid movement of men and supplies, General William Hull and his army cut a log road northward along the trail from Urbana (south of the Greenville Treaty Line) to the Maumee River at Perrysburg, then on to Detroit. Renamed Hull's Trace, it was barely more than a wagon track wide. Although it still made for difficult travel, it was far more passable in rainy weather or through the vast wetlands of the Great Black Swamp than had previously been the case. Furthermore, it offered direction northward through the "thick and almost trackless forest" for a growing number of runaway slaves.[14]

Fugitive slaves entering the easternmost part of Indian Country usually did so by traveling the Scioto Trail. It had been the "Great Highway" of the Shawnee in the eighteenth century, carrying them back and forth between their hunting grounds in Kentucky and their fishing grounds at Sandusky Bay and Lake Erie. A few of those runaways came northeastward from the Shawnee villages; many more followed the Scioto River northward from eastern Kentucky, or trekked overland from western Virginia. The trail followed the Scioto River northward until nearing Columbus, then followed the Olentangy River further northward, finally going overland until entering the Sandusky River valley near the Wyandot village of Upper Sandusky. Fugitive slaves then continued to follow the trail downstream until reaching Lower Sandusky, passing the Seneca reservation along the way. From there they could go westward to the rapids of the Maumee or northward to Sandusky Bay; either choice offered a way to Canada. During the War of 1812, this trail was a major route for the movement of soldiers and supplies. The part of the trail running through Indian Country was then renamed Harrison's Trail.[15]

Often fugitive slaves headed into the interior of Indian Country with little more than a few directions from friendly whites or free blacks that they encountered south of the Greenville Treaty Line, or from those who welcomed them at the Shawnee villages or reservations just north of it. As a result, many of them simply followed a trail or road northward until they encountered other friendly souls. Edward McCartney, a mixed-race trader along the Maumee River, remembered that when Native Americans encountered runaway slaves wandering on the trails or roads, they usually accompanied them further along to one of their villages or to a trading post. Often these freedom seekers merely indicated that they were heading "north toward Canada."[16]

Fugitive slaves were not the only ones who traveled the trails and roads of Indian Country, however. Slave catchers did too. With federal fugitive slave laws in effect, runaways' freedom was never secure, and they sometimes faced the danger of recapture while passing through the region. Many of these slave catchers were hired by masters in Kentucky and western Virginia to track their wayward slaves into Indian Country, even to portals to Upper Canada like Sandusky, Ohio, or Detroit and Brownstown, Michigan. These hired slave hunters regularly rode the trails and roads of northwest Ohio following the War of 1812. This included forays into the two white enclaves at Perrysburg and Lower Sandusky. Other slave hunters included settlers who occasionally sought the rewards for capturing a likely fugitive. A few were southerners who settled in key locations along the trails and roads of the region. Isaac Richardson, a Kentuckian, established a homestead near where Hull's Trace crossed the Maumee River valley. This offered him a prime vantage point from which to look for escaped slaves coming north on all of the major trails and roads. Although these routes placed runaways at risk, the runaways usually found safety among the Native Americans they encountered. Slave catchers rarely entered Native American villages and reservations.[17]

Fugitive slave escapes through Indian Country can be illustrated by looking at three such flights between 1818 and 1830 that were assisted by Native Americans. One involved a lone runaway—David Barrett. A second was taken by a family—that of Josiah Henson. A third was made by a party of at least twenty-one blacks from Richmond, Indiana, to save fugitive slave family members from slave catchers.

David Barrett was the eighteen-year-old slave of James Graves, a tavern keeper near Lexington, Kentucky, when he decided to seek his freedom in the autumn of 1818. Late coming home from a "frolic," he feared that he would be whipped. He stole his master's horse and headed up the Maysville Road. Upon reaching the Ohio River, he stole a canoe and paddled across, reaching the other shore just to the east of Ripley. Stealing another horse, he determined to take "a ride through Ohio," but let him go to confuse possible trackers on his trail. Aided by a few friendly whites and free blacks along the way, he walked east toward the Scioto River, and then followed the Scioto Trail northward toward Indian Country. One white man even accompanied him part of the way toward Columbus. Barrett decided to travel the roads during the daytime and sleep in nearby fields or woods at night. This visibility brought unwanted attention from whites, some of whom tried to capture him for the reward.

After passing by Columbus, Barrett veered away from the Scioto River, following the trail along the Olentangy River (then called the Whetstone) toward the Wyandot village of Upper Sandusky. Upon reaching the treeless Sandusky Plains, he was captured by slave catchers who intended on taking him southward toward Kentucky. Employing some deceit, he escaped again and continued up the Scioto Trail toward Lower Sandusky. On the way he hid for two days in an "old Indian camp"—probably on the Seneca reservation—before friendly whites concealed him in their own home for another five. Upon reaching Lower Sandusky, he found the nucleus of a small black community there who befriended him. He was also assisted by white tavern keeper Israel Harrington. When "two Kentuckians . . . who had been to Detroit hunting for runaway slaves" arrived in the village, Harrington deceived them by claiming that Barrett was his long-time indentured servant. Once they left, Barrett continued on without incident to the Maumee River valley and up to Amherstburg, Upper Canada.[18]

Josiah Henson was a forty-one-year-old slave in Daviess County, Kentucky, on the Ohio River, when he, his wife, Nancy, and their four children fled from bondage in mid-September 1830. A loyal slave to that point, he felt betrayed when his master, Isaac Riley, cheated him out of money he had paid him toward the purchase of his freedom.

After making preparations by laying aside provisions and sewing a knapsack in which to carry the two youngest children, they slipped away under cover of darkness and crossed to freedom with the help of a fellow slave, who rowed them across the river. After wandering for two weeks in southern Indiana, they reached Cincinnati, where they received aid and directions from Underground Railroad activists, who carried them by wagon some thirty miles northward. From that point they struck out toward Hull's Trace, traveling by night and resting by day until they entered Indian Country. When they reached the upper Scioto River, they recognized the road, in part, by the large sycamore and elm "that marked its beginning" that had been described to them.

The Henson family then headed northward on the trace. They traveled the entire first day without seeing anyone and with precious little food left to sustain them. They slept fitfully that night, hungry, weary, and frightened by the howling of unseen wolves. On the second day the wayfarers found walking on the log road tiring and troublesome. At one point, Nancy tripped on the logs, injured herself, and fainted. Rest and "a little dried beef" restored her energy somewhat, and they continued on. By midafternoon they encountered a party of three or four Native Americans—probably Ottawa—coming in their direction. They welcomed the Hensons into their village, fed them, and placed them in "a comfortable wigwam" for the night. The next day, several of their newfound friends accompanied them for some distance, eventually pointing out to them the route to Lake Erie. On the fourth day in Indian Country the family of fugitive slaves reached Sandusky, where they convinced a friendly ship's captain to carry them across the lake. When they reached Black Rock, New York (now part of Buffalo), he put them on a ferry to Upper Canada and paid their passage. They arrived in the land of freedom to the north on October 28, 1830. Henson soon became a leader in the fugitive slave community in the province.[19]

Sometimes African Americans already living in the free states felt the need to flee into and through Indian Country as well. Federal fugitive slave laws made free blacks especially vulnerable to kidnapping and sale in the South; many chose to flee beyond the borders of the United States. This was the case with a group living in Richmond, Indiana. A small community of free blacks and runaway slaves had formed in the village, and many of them worked for the Quaker migrants who had moved there from North Carolina in the early years of the nineteenth century. By the early 1820s slave catchers from Kentucky sometimes made their way to Richmond and recaptured several runaways. On occasion, they even captured a free black person. In most cases, local Quakers were able to track them and free the captive before their captors recrossed the Ohio River. Eventually, Richmond Quakers convinced these local blacks to make an exodus to Canada. Guided by Quaker Underground Railroad activists John Charles and Frederick Hoover, a party of twenty-one free blacks and fugitive slaves, including the families of Isom and Saby Thurman, James and Sarah Slaughter, and Robert and Nancy Hopkins, set out with horses, mules, and wagons on October 8, 1825, on a ten-day journey through the wilderness of northeastern Indiana, northwest Ohio, and southeastern Michigan. It would take them some 260 miles.

It took the party more than three days to reach Fort Wayne. Even though the Miami and Pottawatomi sometimes took payments from Kentucky slave owners to return runaways, they let these groups proceed through their lands unmolested out of respect for the Quakers. At Fort Wayne they headed northeastward down the Maumee River and into northwest Ohio. Hoover recorded that they stopped along the river and sang songs of praise to God for their safe passage to that point. Upon reaching Fort Defiance, they forded the river and passed through the series of Ottawa villages along its north bank, receiving food, shelter, and respite for themselves and their animals. Upon reaching Hull's Trace, they turned north toward Michigan Territory, reaching Upper Canada in another three days.[20]

These three examples represent the variety of fugitive slave escapes made through the Indian Country of northwest Ohio, between 1795 and 1843. Hundreds, perhaps thousands, more made similar treks, often receiving aid and comfort from the Native Americans they encountered on the trails and roads on which they traveled. For runaways passing through this region prior to Indian removal, Native Americans performed the Underground Railroad role played by white and black settlers in many other parts of the United States.

SOJOURNERS

Although the majority of fugitive slaves who reached Indian Country merely passed through the region on their way to Detroit or Upper

Canada, others sought to sojourn among the Native Americans there. Some became temporary sojourners in the Ottawa villages up and down the Maumee River valley. Others became permanent sojourners in places like Negro Town on the Wyandot Grand Reserve in the Sandusky River valley. A few settled in the primarily white enclaves of Perrysburg or Lower Sandusky or at established farmsteads in the vicinity of Native American villages and reservations.

Some fugitive slaves who reached the Ottawa villages along the north bank of the Maumee River chose a temporary sojourn of up to year or more among their newfound Native American friends. A few decided to remain longer. Whatever their stay, these runaways felt welcomed by their Native American hosts, who shared their meals of hominy, venison, other wild game, and wild honey. They also shared their wigwams. In reality, this was an exchange between guests and hosts, as the Ottawa expected freedom seekers living among them to contribute in a variety of ways for the benefit of the entire community. Some fugitives brought skills like metalworking or literacy. Others may have carried new seeds with them that enriched the community's diet. All could labor in the vast fields of corn alongside these towns, which provided a major staple of their diet. In villages like Kinjeino's Town, which saw its population halved in the decade of the 1820s, fugitive slaves—mostly male—also could enrich and continue the community's bloodlines. According to local Indian descendant Savannah Lee Eicher, there was "lots of mixing" between freedom seekers and the Ottawa in the Maumee River valley. Edward Gunn, the son of an early white trader at Damascus on the river, said that "he had often seen Negroes climb out of the tents of Indians early in the morning." Long after Indian removal, evidence of this exchange continued in the bodies of those born as a result of sexual relations between Ottawa and fugitives.[21]

Once a year in the spring, the Ottawa—sometimes with the assistance of white traders, such as Charles Gunn of Damascus or Edward and Dredsen Howard at Grand Rapids—would travel to Amherstburg, Upper Canada, to receive their annual payment from the British for fighting on their side in the War of 1812. This payment was in the form of goods, such as blankets, old army tents, and the like. On occasion, they traveled overland. Often, however, they went downstream in canoes to Lake Erie, then along its western banks and up the Detroit River until reaching their destination. When they made this annual trek, they took with them fugitive slaves who had spent all or part of the previous year in Ottawa villages along the Maumee. At least one time, the Howards and their Native American allies had to win a gun battle against Isaac Richardson and other slave catchers to get their fugitive friends safely out of the area. Upon reaching the Detroit River borderland, these runaways then joined the growing community of black refugees settling on the Canadian shore.[22]

Other fugitive slaves chose to become permanent sojourners in Indian Country. The best examples were those who populated Negro Town in the Wyandot Grand Reserve along the Upper Sandusky River. There is some disagreement about the settlement's origins. Writing in her *Atlas of Great Lakes Indian History*, Helen Hornbeck Tanner indicates that it dates back to the American Revolution. But it was more likely established near the beginning of the nineteenth century. Moravian missionary sources mention its existence in 1808. There are multiple accounts by American soldiers passing through during the War of 1812. Future Michigan governor William Woodbridge left a record of his observations when he passed through Negro Town in 1815. Suggesting a degree of cultural blending between the African Americans and Native Americans who lived in the area, he noted that his party "found 6 or 7 families of negroes dressed like Indians but who live much better. They have handsome cornfield[s] & much stock. . . . One Indian family also resides there."[23] Seven years earlier, Moravian missionary Abraham Luckenbach noted that the settlement "contains six or seven Negro families which already for a long time lived amongst the Indians and accepted their way of life."[24] Other sources indicate that a high rate of intermarriage occurred between the black settlers at Negro Town and the residents of the Wyandot village of Upper Sandusky six miles to the south.[25]

When federal officials inventoried Negro Town at the time of Wyandot removal in 1843, they found eight scattered farmsteads in the settlement, most in flourishing condition, with fields of wheat, corn, and oats, and extensive fruit orchards. Negro Town, then, was not a town in the traditional sense. It was an "associative settlement"—a clustering of adjacent farms whose residents shared a history, a sense of community, and a set of common social concerns, in this case related to slavery and race. This was typical of African American farming settlements throughout the Old Northwest. As Steven Hahn has observed in *The*

Political Worlds of Slavery and Freedom, such settlements "develop[ed] around early or sponsored groups of fugitives."[26] Negro Town differed only in that the members of the sponsoring group, rather than being residents of Quaker or free black settlements nearby, were the Wyandot inhabitants of the Grand Reserve who provided patronage and protection for the fugitive slaves that came their way.[27]

From its earliest days, Negro Town became a haven for fugitive slaves making their way north from Kentucky on the Scioto Trail. And the inhabitants of the settlement consistently aided and protected them. Although slave catchers also traveled that route, runaways apparently felt safe once they reached the community; one white traveler who passed through there in 1824 recorded that he had observed four fugitives wading and loudly laughing in a nearby stream during the day in clear eyeshot of the trail. An occasional runaway chose to remain in the settlement, but most moved on with assistance from the residents of the black settlement. By the early 1820s, they seem to have developed with mixed-race farmer Joseph Janey a localized Underground Railroad network about ten miles to the north of Negro Town. Escaped slaves who made it to Negro Town were eventually sent on to Janey's farm, where they often stayed overnight on their way to their ultimate goal of reaching Lake Erie at Sandusky or heading toward the Detroit River borderland. One antiquarian, who accumulated local reminiscences about Janey's exploits, claimed that his "shrewdness, courage, strong arm, and rifle thwarted many a slave catcher in his efforts to regain negro slaves escaping from Kentucky, for the route by the Sandusky River, near to which Janey lived, was one of the favored of the underground railroads."[28] Evidence also suggests that the name of Negro Town was known among the slaves south of the Ohio River.[29]

Positioned as it was within the Indian Country of northwest Ohio, Negro Town may be considered a maroon community of sorts to which fugitive slaves from Kentucky could escape to a permanent site of semiformal freedom and safety within the confines of the free states. As Hahn notes, such settlements "came to resemble maroons, not simply because they included substantial numbers of fugitives but also because of the way in which they developed in relation to the larger world around them."[30] In the case of Negro Town, however, it was not just the relative isolation that allowed it to approximate the maroon communities of the South that developed in swamps, in mountainous areas, and along the frontier. It was also the protection of the Wyandot. As noted earlier, slave catchers rarely invaded the sovereignty of Native American reservations in northwest Ohio, including the Wyandot Grand Reserve.[31]

In addition to sojourning in Ottawa and Wyandot villages and reservations, some fugitive slaves who entered Indian Country sought to reside in the largely white enclaves of Perrysburg or Lower Sandusky. The latter had a small African American community by the time David Barrett came there in 1818, mostly consisting of runaways who "sought safety living together."[32] A similar population started to develop in Perrysburg about the same time. When Kentucky runaway Henry Bibb reached the village in 1837, he "found quite a settlement of colored people, many of whom were fugitive slaves." Although he initially intended to travel on to Upper Canada, "they took me in and persuaded me to spend the winter in Perrysburgh, where I could get employment and go to Canada the next spring."[33] Virginia fugitive Henry Goings found a similar welcome when he reached the settlement three years later. Bibb and Goings were merely two among many runaways who decided to remain for a time in the village.[34] As a result, slave catchers occasionally came there in the 1820s and 1830s, looking for human prey. Fortunately for the fugitives involved, they generally found that they were in a relatively protective environment. Examples of Perrysburg residents—black and white—using force and trickery to rescue fugitive slaves from the clutches of slave catchers can be found as early as 1820.[35]

Fugitive slaves also sojourned in the several black farming settlements that developed in the region—like the one that emerged in the shadow of Negro Town, just a few miles north of the Wyandot Grand Reserve. Daniel Whetsel and Samuel Grimes were apparently free blacks from Virginia who bought 154 acres in the early 1820s in southern Seneca County. Their adjoining properties soon became the basis of a community built around their own large families. Runaways from the slave states also found their way there. Although slave catchers occasionally threatened this community, Whetsel and Grimes seem to have effectively protected their fugitive guests. Between 1830 and 1860, this community averaged thirty-six inhabitants, although it sometimes swelled to more than fifty persons—the additional ones probably being runaways. Eventually a burial ground, church, and log school were constructed. Underground Railroad historians cite these two black farmers as "conductors" in the effort to aid and protect fugitive slaves.[36]

A DIFFERENT SPACE OF FREEDOM

Fugitive slaves who arrived in northwest Ohio after 1843 encountered a very different space of freedom. It was no longer Indian Country. The vast majority of the Wyandot, Ottawa, Shawnee, Seneca, and Delaware now lived west of the Mississippi River. Only a tiny remnant remained behind, often masking their ethnicity or living in isolated hamlets. Some sought to pass themselves off as white; others melded into African American communities.[37] Runaways passing through this region could no longer look to Native Americans for aid and protection.

Those fugitive slaves who had settled in northwest Ohio during the preceding decades chose a variety of different paths following Indian removal. A few accompanied Native Americans on their forced migration from northwest Ohio to the Kansas frontier. Evidence shows that the blacks who accompanied the Wyandot westward, as well as the Wyandot themselves, continued to assist escaped slaves in their new home. Other runaways left for Canada. Levi Foster, a leader in Perrysburg's black community, moved to Amherstburg in the wake of Ottawa removal. Most blacks who had settled in northwest Ohio when it was Indian Country, however, remained even when it wasn't. Some stayed in the small black communities in settlements like Perrysburg and Lower Sandusky, partially for camaraderie and for the relative safety they provided. Others continued in rural neighborhoods like the one created by the Whetsel and Grimes families in Seneca County because a quarter century of farming and family life had given them a deep feeling for the place. When the Wyandot left, the residents of Negro Town dispersed into the surrounding countryside, many squatting on land between their old community and Tiffin. Generations of local residents would remember that area's main route as Niggertown Road. The 1850 census showed 249 African Americans living between Lower Sandusky and the former Wyandot Grand Reserve. Some lived in Lower Sandusky or in the new black community emerging in Tiffin in Seneca County; others farmed the fertile lands in those vicinities. Another 157 lived in Perrysburg or in or near the new urban center of Toledo immediately to the north. They also continued to aid freedom seekers passing through the region.[38]

A new group of settlers also began to assist the fugitive slaves passing through the region. White pioneers, many of them from New England and upstate New York, flooded into the former Native American homelands. Farmsteads, fields, and towns replaced interminable forest and Native American villages. Some of these new settlers, motivated by religion and reform sentiment, began to perform key roles on what was coming to be called the Underground Railroad. In many cases this occurred along the same routes and in the same or similar locations as Native American villages and reservations in an earlier time.[39]

Even before 1843, however, the Indian Country of northwest Ohio had been a different space of freedom. Although northwest Ohio was a space of semiformal freedom between 1795 and 1843, like the rest of the free states and territories north of the Mason–Dixon line, it remained a place apart. On the one hand, the region was subject to the Fugitive Slave Act of 1793, which made the situation of fugitive slaves legally precarious there. On the other hand, the presence of tribal sovereignty, the hesitancy of slave catchers to enter Native American villages and reservations, the extensive wilderness and relative difficulty of travel, and the absence of meaningful local and county governments in many areas greatly curtailed efforts to locate and capture fugitive slaves in Indian Country. Furthermore, Native Americans in the so-called free states above the Ohio River differed dramatically in their response to the matter of fugitive slaves coming into their midst from those Native Americans who lived within the confines of the slave states below the river. Prior to 1795, the few runaway slaves that made it to Native American towns in the Ohio country sometimes found welcome. After that date, however, the growing number of freedom seekers reaching Native American villages in northwest Ohio usually found safety, sustenance, shelter, and sources of information about the way northward. Those found wandering on the trails or roads by Native American hunting or trading parties were often fed, offered accommodations for the night, and accompanied further along the route the next day. On occasion runaways were provided temporary or permanent sojourn within their villages or reservations. Such hospitality was not limited to the Native Americans of northwest Ohio, however. In the early nineteenth century, the Wyandot communities at Brownstown and Monguagon in southeastern Michigan regularly assisted escaped slaves heading northward to Detroit. Similarly, when General William Henry Harrison and his army attacked Miami towns in northeastern Indiana during the War of 1812, he found a number of runaway slaves within their confines and reported that "countless other Indians and runaways fled."[40] Further east, Native Americans on the Atlantic coast aided numerous slave escapes as late as the 1850s, even by sea.[41]

Native American assistance to freedom seekers in northwest Ohio likely emerged from a variety of factors. As fugitive slaves began to regularly enter their villages or reservations and share their stories of bondage, they came to be seen as fellow victims of oppression. Historian Arwin Smallwood has noted that "as slavery spread and the cruelty of slavery became known among Native Americans, many began to sympathize with Africans and despise the institution of slavery. Many Indian nations began to harbor runaway slaves."[42] These views were probably reinforced by Native American interactions with the few non–Native American neighbors they had in northwest Ohio. Missionary work by Quakers among the Shawnee, by Methodists among the Wyandot, and by Presbyterians among the Ottawa in the early nineteenth century strengthened existing Native American views about slavery and the importance of aiding and protecting fugitive slaves, as did the presence of a few sympathetic white and mixed-race traders like Charles Gunn, the Howards, and Edward McCartney. Furthermore, as the population of Native American villages declined in the early nineteenth century, Native Americans probably also found it valuable to welcome freedom seekers, who brought additional skills, knowledge, and bloodlines into their villages, just as white captives and captives from other tribes had done a century earlier.[43]

South of the Ohio River, the attitudes and actions of Native Americans toward runaways differed greatly. Although southern freedom seekers had sometimes found welcome in Native American towns during the eighteenth century, by the beginning of the nineteenth century this hospitality had disappeared. During the antebellum years, most escaped slaves reaching Native American villages were re-enslaved or returned to their owners for the reward. Many southern Native American tribes held slaves themselves in that era, even after their removal west of the Mississippi River in the 1830s. As historian Christina Snyder has noted, in the South, "bondage in Indian Country mirrored the slavery practiced by their white neighbors."[44]

Since Wilbur H. Siebert pioneered the history of the Underground Railroad some twelve decades ago, it has often been envisioned as largely an enterprise in which charitable whites, primarily of the Quaker persuasion, aided and protected mostly anonymous fugitive slaves. The recent work of Keith Griffler and Cheryl LaRoche has provided a partial corrective, demonstrating the important role played by free black communities north of the Ohio River and highlighting that the work was at least a biracial effort. Recognizing their significance, Griffler has labeled these communities the "front line of freedom." But the story is an even broader one. The role played by Native Americans in the free states at various times and places, especially in northwest Ohio between 1795 and 1843, when it was known as Indian Country, demonstrates that the endeavor was a triracial enterprise. I once defined the work of the Underground Railroad as providing runaways with food, clothing, shelter, medical care, protection, assistance if they choose to stay in a place, and direction (and possible accompaniment) if they chose to go on.[45] Residents of the Native American villages and reservations of northwest Ohio did all that over the course of nearly a half century, earning the gratitude and respect of hundreds, if not thousands of fugitive slaves who came their way. It is important that their contributions be acknowledged in Underground Railroad studies.

NOTES

1. Tiya Miles, *The Dawn of Detroit: A Chronicle of Slavery and Freedom in the City of the Straits* (New York: New Press, 2017), 152–53.

2. Martin R. Katz, "The Black Swamp: A Study in Historical Geography," *Annals of the Association of American Geographers* 45 (March 1955): 4–7; James D. Rodabaugh, "The Negro in Ohio," *Journal of Negro History* 31 (January 1946): 9; Helen Hornbeck Tanner, ed., *Atlas of Great Lakes Indian History* (Norman: University of Oklahoma Press, 1987), 96, 98–99, 101; and Alexander Bourne, "A Map of the State of Ohio from Actual Survey" (Philadelphia, 1815), David Rumsey Historical Map Collection (www.davidrumsey.com).

3. R. Douglas Hurt, *The Ohio Frontier: Crucible of the Old Northwest, 1720–1830* (Bloomington: Indiana University Press, 1996), 120–42.

4. Katz, "Black Swamp," 1–4; see also Ardath Danford, *The Perrysburg Story, 1816–1966* (Perrysburg, Ohio: Sesquicentennial Publishing Committee, 1966), 9.

5. Mary Stockwell, *The Other Trail of Tears: The Removal of the Ohio Indians*

(Yardley, Penn.: Westholme Publishing, 2014), 61–87; Tanner, *Atlas*, 136; Katz, "Black Swamp," 9, 13; and Frank U. Quillin, *The Color Line in Ohio: A History of Race Prejudice in a Typical Northern State* (Ann Arbor, Mich.: George Wahr, 1913), 27. The 1830 census counted 115 blacks in northwest Ohio, but other evidence suggests that they were significantly undercounted in the Maumee River valley and on the Wyandot Grand Reserve.

6. Stockwell, *Other Trail of Tears*, 196–320; John P. Bowes, *Land too Good for Indians: Northern Indian Removal* (Norman: University of Oklahoma Press, 2016), 112–48; and Katz, "Black Swamp," 13.

7. Joseph Pitts, *Incidents of Border Life* (Chambersburg, Penn.: G. Hills, 1839), 414; and Kenneth W. Porter, "Negroes and the Fur Trade," *Minnesota History* 15 (December 1934): 424.

8. Sharon A. Roger Hepburn, *Crossing the Border: A Free Black Community in Canada* (Urbana: University of Illinois Press, 2007), 19–20.

9. Jacqueline L. Tobin, *From Midnight to Dawn: The Last Tracks of the Underground Railroad* (New York: Doubleday, 2007), 5–6; *Kentucky Gazette*, April 1, 1798; and Henry Wilson, *The Rise and Fall of the Slave Power in America* (Boston: James Osgood & Co., 1872), 2:63.

10. Daniel G. Hill, *The Freedom Seekers: Blacks in Early Canada* (Agincourt, Ont.: Book Society of Canada Limited, 1981), 48; and J. Blaine Hudson, *Fugitive Slaves and the Underground Railroad in the Kentucky Borderland* (Jefferson, N.C.: McFarland, 2002), 127, 162.

11. Mark F. McPherson, *Looking for Lisette: In Quest of an American Original* (Detroit: Mage Press, 2001), 283; Randall Buchman, telephone interview by author, August 20, 2015; Don Greene, *Shawnee Heritage I: Shawnee Genealogy and Family History* (n.p., 2008), 57, 268–69; Daniel Dunihue Diary, September 7, 1832, Conner Prairie (Ind.) Interactive History Park; and William Loren Katz, *Black Indians: A Hidden Heritage* (New York: Atheneum, 1986).

12. Frank N. Wilcox, *Ohio's Indian Trails*, ed. William A. McGill (Kent, Ohio: Kent State University Press, 2015), 120–21.

13. George D. Kinder, "Putnam County," in *A History of Northwest Ohio*, ed. Nevin Otto Winter (Chicago: Lewis Publishing Company, 1917), 1:542; D. W. H. Howard to W. H. Siebert, August 22, 1894, Wilbur H. Siebert Collection, Ohio Historical Society; Wilbur H. Siebert, *Mysteries of Ohio's Underground Railroad* (Columbus, Ohio: Long's College Book Company, 1951), 22–243; and Alan Borer, "John Johnston: From Wapakoneta to Fort Meigs," *Salmagundi* (blog), October 15, 2009, http://aborer1962.blogspot.com/2009/10/john-johnston-from-wapakoneta-to-fort.html.

14. Rosalie Yoakam, "Centuries-Old Road from the Ohio River to Michigan Still in Use Today," *Dayton Daily News*, June 2, 2011; Joan Baxter, "One of the Earliest Roads: Bullskin Trace," *Xenia* (Ohio) *Daily Gazette*, May 20, 2016; and Katz, "Black Swamp," 7.

15. Wilcox, *Ohio's Indian Trails*, 69–74.

16. Genevieve Eicher, interview with Charlotte Wangrin, April 2003, Henry County Historical Society, Napoleon, Ohio.

17. "Narrative of David Barrett," *Anti-Slavery Record* (July 1837), 10–11; and D. W. H. Howard to W. H. Siebert, August 22, 1894.

18. "Narrative of David Barrett," 1–11.

19. Josiah Henson, *The Life of Josiah Henson, Formerly a Slave* (Boston: A. D. Phelps, 1849), 45–55.

20. Andrew White Young, *History of Wayne County, Indiana, from Its First Settlement to the Present Time* (Cincinnati: R. Clarke & Co., 1872), 643; Frederick Hoover Journal (typescript), pp. 63–68, Frederick Hoover Collection, Earlham College; and "The Underground Railroad of Northwest Ohio," http://www.rootsweb.ancestry.com/~ohfulton/UNDERGROUNDRAILROADORNWOHIO.htm.

21. D. W. H. Howard Papers, File E, McClaren Collection, Fulton County Historical Society, Wauseon, Ohio; Lewis Cass Aldrich, *History of Henry and Fulton Counties, Ohio* (Syracuse: D. Mason & Co., 1888), 27; Savannah Lee Eicher, personal interview with author, October 9, 2016; Genevieve Eicher interview; and *Wood County Sentinel* (Bowling Green, Ohio), January 11, 1906.

22. Genevieve Eicher interview; and D. W. H. Howard to W. H. Siebert, August 22, 1894.

23. Woodbridge, quoted in Tanner, *Atlas*, 101.

24. MissInd 157.11 Travel Diary of Abraham Luckenbach, August 29, 1808, Moravian Archives, Bethlehem, Penn.

25. Milo M. Quaife, ed., "From Marietta to Detroit in 1815," *Northwest Ohio Quarterly* 14 (October 1942): 144.

26. Steven Hahn, *The Political Worlds of Slavery and Freedom* (Cambridge, Mass.: Harvard University Press, 2009), 33.

27. Lonny L. Honsberger, *A Book of Diagrams and Index of Indian Landholders on the Wyandot Reservation, Wyandot County, Ohio, at Time of Cession* (Upper Sandusky, Ohio: n.p., 1989), nos. 72, 82, 102, 152, 163–64; and Hahn, *Political Worlds*, 30–31.

28. Frank Dildine, "When Escaping Slaves Were Hunted Like Beasts of the Forest," Tiffin (Ohio) *Daily Tribune and Herald*, January 5, 1920.

29. C. C. Baldwin, "Indian Narrative of Judge Hugh Welch of Green Springs, Seneca and Sandusky Counties, Ohio," *Western Reserve and Northern Ohio Historical Society*, Tract No. 50 (November 1879), 108; and Dildine, "When Escaping Slaves Were Hunted," January 5, 1920, January 12, 1920, January 14, 1920.

30. Hahn, *Political Worlds*, 30.

31. Hahn, *Political Worlds*, 21–40; Randal Buchman interview.

32. "Fremont, Ohio," *Ohio History Central*, http://www.ohiohistorycentral.org/w/Fremont,_Ohio.

33. Henry Bibb, *Narrative of the Life and Adventures of Henry Bibb, an American Slave, Written by Himself* (New York: Published by the author, 1849), 55.

34. Henry Goings, *Rambles of a Runaway Slave from Southern Slavery*, ed. Calvin Schermerhorn, Michael Plunkett, and Edward Gaynor (Charlottesville: University of Virginia Press, 2012), 47.

35. *Commemorative Historical and Biographical Record of Wood County, Ohio: Its Past and Present* (Chicago, 1897), 368–369; and J. W. Scott to Adam Beatty, February 23, 1835, Hoole Special Collections, University of Alabama Libraries.

36. Tricia Valentine, "Revelations from the Underground: A New Perspective on the Underground Railroad in Seneca County," *ZigZag* (March–April 1999): 3–8.

37. Savannah Lee Eicher interview.

38. Steve Collins and Dorothy Collins, "Quindaro Underground Railroad: A Unique Ethnic Unity in America's Past," *Kansas City Kansas Community College E-Journal* 1 (October 2007): n.p., http://www.kckcc.edu/docs/default-source/ejournal/archives/volume-1-fall-2007/quindaro-underground-railroad-a-unique-ethnic-unity-in-america's-past.pdf; "Levi Foster," *Breaking the Chains*, Harriet Tubman Institute, York University, breakingthechains.tubmaninstitute.ca/levi_foster; Goings, *Rambles of a Runaway Slave*, 50–55; "Fremont, Ohio," *Ohio History Central*; Valentine, "Revelations from the Underground," 3–8; Myron Bruce Barnes, *Seneca Sentinel Bicentennial Sketches* (Tiffin, Ohio: Seneca County Museum, 1976), 35–36; and Quillin, *Color Line in Ohio*, 74.

39. Ohio Underground Railroad Association, *Freedom Seekers: Ohio and the Underground Railroad* (Columbus: Friends of Freedom, 2004), 91–104.

40. Gene Allen Smith, *The Slave's Gamble: Choosing Sides in the War of 1812* (New York: Palgrave Macmillan, 2013), 40.

41. Stanley Harrold, *Border War: Fighting over Slavery before the Civil War* (Chapel Hill: University of North Carolina Press, 2010), 25; Tanner, *Atlas*, 101–2; and Natalie Joy, "Finding Refuge in the Wigwam: Native Americans and the Underground Railroad" (unpublished manuscript in the author's possession).

42. Arwin D. Smallwood, "A History of African and Native American Relations from 1502 to 1900," *Negro History Bulletin* 62 (April–September 1999): 22.

43. Stockwell, *Other Trail of Tears*, 102–114; and Savannah Lee Eicher interview.

44. Christina Snyder, *Slavery in Indian Country: The Changing Face of Captivity in Early America* (Cambridge, Mass.: Harvard University Press, 2010), 201; see also 194–96.

45. Wilbur H. Siebert, *The Underground Railroad from Slavery to Freedom* (New York: Macmillan, 1898); Keith P. Griffler, *Front Line of Freedom: African Americans and the Underground Railroad in the Ohio Valley* (Lexington: University Press of Kentucky, 2004); and Cheryl J. LaRoche, *Free Black Communities and the Underground Railroad: The Geography of Resistance* (Urbana: University of Illinois Press, 2014). The definition I refer to is in Roy E. Finkenbine, "A Community Vigilant and Organized: The Colored Vigilance Committee of Detroit," in *A Fluid Frontier: Slavery, Resistance, and the Underground Railroad in the Detroit River Borderland*, ed. Karolyn Smardz Frost and Veta Smith Tucker (Detroit: Wayne State University Press, 2016), 157.

4

After 1850

Reassessing the Impact of the Fugitive Slave Law

MATTHEW PINSKER

The 1850 Fugitive Slave Law might well be the worst piece of legislation in American history. Abolitionists began denouncing its draconian provisions even before final passage, while the controversial measure continued to provoke waves of anxiety among free African Americans for years afterward. Yet the sporadic enforcement of the statute in the decade before the Civil War also provoked howls of complaints from proslavery southerners. By 1861 the fire-eaters in the Deep South appeared even unhappier than northern antislavery forces about the troubled *status quo*. Secessionists angrily dismissed the federal fugitive slave code, in the words of the Georgia secession declaration, as "a dead letter."[1]

Somehow this troubled by-product of what had once been a grand national compromise seemed to inspire almost equal measures of panic and contempt. Such a political and legal mess, however, provokes an underappreciated challenge for modern-day historians. Was the 1850 Fugitive Slave Law more of a draconian measure or a dead letter? Unlike polarized contemporaries, scholars and teachers cannot have it both ways. Moreover, how does choosing sides in this particular interpretive battle affect our understanding about sectionalism and the contested state of "semiformal freedom" in the antebellum North?

The best way to answer such questions would be with a careful dissection of the 1850 fugitive law and its actual impact on runaways, but such an exercise is surprisingly difficult. How many cases were there?

What were the outcomes? How often did resistance occur? None of these basic issues yield simple answers, certainly not ones that have been properly quantified. There have been good, landmark academic studies, such as Stanley W. Campbell's *The Slave-Catchers* (1970) or John Hope Franklin and Loren Schweninger's *Runaway Slaves* (1999), but these scholars were often forced to rely on incomplete data, and sometimes they were guilty of employing vaguely defined terms. The result has been a series of misunderstandings that permeate modern discussions of the subject.[2]

Consider the oft-cited total of 332 fugitive cases in the decade before the Civil War—a figure derived from Campbell's groundbreaking work. This number, which he acknowledged at that time was tentative, refers to individuals, not cases, and involves not only federal tribunals authorized under the 1850 law but also recaption (or kidnapping) episodes outside of the law itself that were reported sporadically in antebellum newspapers and collected into pamphlet form by abolitionists like Samuel J. May. A close study of the appendix in *The Slave-Catchers* reveals that Campbell actually identified only about 125 rendition hearings held by U.S. fugitive slave commissioners between 1850 and 1861.

That nuance has been lost over the years, but it changes assessments of the law's impact. There were critical differences between the process of fugitive slave rendition and the common-law doctrine of recaption. The word "recaption" does not even appear in Campbell's book because he uses the less technical phrase "returned without due process" instead. Yet for the majority of slaveholders, the preferred solution to the fugitive crisis had always been the precise idea of recaption, or the principle of simply taking back one's mobile property (such as farm animals) whenever it got lost or wandered away. American slaveholders considered recaption to be an essential element of their right to human property. Abolitionists disagreed and called it kidnapping.[3]

Once students begin to appreciate the more careful distinctions among these types of fugitive slave cases, then patterns emerge which shed greater light on the practical meaning of the 1850 law. There can be little argument that it was a spectacular failure in its actual operations. Although never quite a "dead letter," even an antislavery radical like Salmon P. Chase was admitting in private by 1859 (to Abraham Lincoln, no less) that the statute had become "almost absolutely useless as a practical measure of reclamation."[4] Even when the law worked, which it did on more than a few tragic occasions straight through the Civil War, it never really functioned as its framers had intended. Moreover, the exploding bitterness over the sporadic high-profile attempts at federal rendition also had a dramatic and positive impact on what Frederick Douglass sardonically labeled the "upper-ground railroad."[5] Black-led vigilance committees in the North spearheaded this defiant movement, but the coalition mobilized over the 1850s to frustrate all types of fugitive recapture was broad-based, multiracial, and—to a surprising degree—successful.

At its core, this resistance was about the free-soil principle and the evolving politics of sectionalism. Underground Railroad agents captivated public attention (both then and now), but it was the deliberate, persistent work of northern antislavery lawyers and politicians that ultimately exposed the crippling paradox embedded in the heart of the fugitive crisis, and which southern fire-eaters never conceded—that American federalism included a presumption of personal liberty to free black residents on free soil. This was the sectional concession that had made state personal liberty statues and individual habeas corpus petitions seem legitimate to most northerners, despite their own obvious color prejudice. Yet this crucial factor has long been obscured by the draconian shadow of the Fugitive Slave Law's harsh reputation. It has become almost too easy to forget how much free soil really mattered even after the federal code had changed so drastically in 1850.

ORIGINS OF THE FUGITIVE SLAVE LAW

The first thing to understand about the Fugitive Slave Law is that it was not called the Fugitive Slave Law—at least not officially. When the 31st Congress finally passed the measure in September of 1850, the bill's title read: "An Act to Amend an Act Supplementary to the Act Entitled, 'An Act Respecting Fugitives from Justice and Persons Escaping from the Service of Their Masters.'"[6] That mouthful was not simply the result of the ordinary legalese of bill making. It was instead the by-product of a seventy-plus-year debate over whether or not freedom was national in America.

The original U.S. Constitution excluded the words "slave" and "slavery." Historians still argue over what that omission really meant, but few bother to point out that those same words were omitted from the 1793 and 1850 fugitive slave laws as well. The awkwardly phrased statutes employed terms such as "fugitives from labor" or "persons escaping from the service of their masters."[7] In other words, enslaved runaways were defined in the U.S. code as people even as federal law allowed southerners to treat them as property. This was about more than just semantics. From early in the process, federal framers had recognized that when it came to the subject of fugitive slaves, state laws mattered and that some states would presume people in their jurisdiction, regardless of color, to be free. Even the so-called fugitive slave clause in the 1787 Constitution might just as well be termed the "personal liberty clause" because it acknowledged both sides of that debate.

The clause prohibited states from allowing any "Person held to Service or Labour in one State" from being "discharged from such Service or Labour" within their own borders because of "any Law or Regulation therein." This is usually portrayed as a major proslavery concession designed to limit the reach of northern abolition laws.[8] However, the exact phrasing was the result of a true sectional compromise that involved more than just the promise of emancipation. Pierce Butler and Charles Pinckney of South Carolina had proposed late in the summer of 1787 that the new Constitution should specifically require that "fugitive slaves and servants to be delivered up like criminals." Skeptical northern delegates quickly objected that this rule would end up compelling state governors to handle slave-catching duties "at public expense." They also invoked the doctrine of recaption in what might be called an act of political jujitsu. The always-acerbic Roger Sherman of Connecticut observed archly that there was no need to invoke the procedures of criminal rendition for fugitive slaves because, under the logic of slavery, there was "no more propriety in the public seizing and surrendering [of] a slave or servant than a horse."[9]

The result was a fugitive slave clause that pointedly differed from the criminal extradition clause (Article IV, Section 2, Clause 2) by not naming the "executive Authority of the State" as the source for the interstate request but rather by authorizing the process to be triggered solely in these cases "on Claim of the Party." Yet to have a "Person held to Service or Labour" be "delivered up" to the "Party to whom such Service or Labour may be due" was also to acknowledge that there would be no further judicial process, as in state-regulated criminal rendition. For the freedom seeker, there would only be an immediate return to enslavement. Thus, any hearing over the status of an accused fugitive would have to occur in the state where he or she had fled. This was where habeas corpus principles came into play, and yet by remaining silent on whether or how they could be applied in rendition hearings, the fugitive slave clause implicitly endorsed the concept of allowing personal liberty for free blacks in free-soil states. This helps explain why the clause was ultimately situated in article 4, and not article 1, because it was first and foremost about comity, or the relations among states. In short, nothing in the fugitive slave clause prevented free states from protecting their own black residents from kidnapping or from presuming (at least at first) that any black person seized within their territory was free. That was a necessary and significant concession to advocates for the *Somerset* or freedom principle.[10]

That was at least how free states began interpreting the clause. Before the Constitution was even formally ratified, the Pennsylvania legislature had passed an amendment to its 1780 gradual abolition law, which capitalized on these comity provisions by offering concrete protections for its free black residents. Section 7 of the revised 1788 statute threatened the punishment of £100 for anyone convicted of taking free blacks outside of the state "by force or violence" or through seduction "with the design and intention of selling and disposing" them as "a slave, or servant."[11] Over the years, most other northern states followed with their own anti-kidnapping or personal liberty laws. In his landmark study *Free Men All* (1974), Thomas Morris cataloged seventy relevant statutes from the 1780s to the 1860s in fourteen different free states, but even that impressive list was not quite comprehensive. Morris overlooked examples such as the 1816 Indiana statute called "Act to Prevent Man-Stealing" and the original California state criminal statute adopted in 1850, which threatened imprisonment of up to ten years per victim for the kidnapping of "any man, woman or child, whether white, black or colored."[12]

Morris also excluded from his purview what have been traditionally reviled as antebellum black laws or black codes. These discriminatory statutes in states such as Illinois and Iowa were notorious for attempting to prohibit the immigration of free blacks and for otherwise codifying various forms of segregation. Yet, despite this relentless color prejudice, these same laws also usually conceded valuable personal liberty rights to free blacks. In Illinois, for example, where the black laws were so vicious in nature that Frederick Douglass once asked sarcastically if the "people of Illinois" were "the offspring of wolves and tigers," they still included serious punishments for the attempted kidnapping of free black residents.[13]

This context is essential for understanding the origins of both federal fugitive slave laws (1793 and 1850). These proslavery measures are best understood as rear-guard actions designed principally to appease slaveholders who felt threatened by the various personal liberty statutes or emerging vigilance (self-protection) societies that were being organized with increasing frequency across the free states to help guarantee the reality of personal liberty. Thus, the changes in federal code were not driven merely by the national power of slaveholders but rather by the deepening breakdown of comity. That was the direct impetus for the 1793 fugitive statute, for example, which developed out Virginia's refusal to extradite a cohort of men accused of kidnapping a free black resident of Pennsylvania under Section 7 of the 1788 Pennsylvania statute. Slaveholding interests in the Congress then used the dispute as leverage for obtaining a federal rendition law designed to help implement the fugitive slave clause. The subsequent statute was remarkably concise (less than seven hundred words), especially considering that it covered both fugitives from "justice" (Sections 1 and 2) and from "labor" (Sections 3 and 4). What was also revealing was that, unlike the sections for obstructing judicial rendition, the 1793 fugitive slave provisions did not threaten criminal penalties against anyone who might attempt to "rescue" or "harbor or conceal" runaway slaves but instead limited their legal jeopardy under federal law to civil fines.[14]

Somewhat more indirectly, that was also how the more notorious 1850 law emerged, as a delayed reaction to the Pennsylvania personal liberty regime. The story began in the aftermath of the Supreme Court ruling in *Prigg v. Pennsylvania* (1842), which had overturned Pennsylvania personal liberty provisions (enacted in both 1788 and 1826). That case was about the fate of a Maryland constable and slave catcher named Edward Prigg and a group of his associates who had been convicted in Pennsylvania of kidnapping Margaret Morgan, an alleged fugitive slave, and some of her free-born children. The controversial opinion from Justice Joseph Story addressed the escalating controversy over northern personal liberty statutes by prohibiting states from interfering with the manner in which fugitives were "delivered up" but also conceding that they had no constitutional obligation to support the process with their own judicial officers or police resources. Ignoring its placement in Article IV and the obvious comity issues at stake, Story asserted that the fugitive slave clause imposed the greatest responsibility for rendition on the federal government, not the states. The Massachusetts-born jurist also pointedly endorsed a doctrine of national recaption, claiming that "the owner of a slave is clothed with entire authority, in every State in the Union, to seize and recapture his slave whenever he can do it without any breach of the peace or any illegal violence."[15]

That complex decision only made things worse, however. The rest of that decade was punctuated with dramatic and often bitterly contested fugitive cases and an escalating sense of a national "border war," as historian Stanley Harrold has put it.[16] Vigilance committees in the North began openly touting their successes in evading the federal law. This was the moment—in the mid-1840s—when the "underground railroad" metaphor was truly born. This was also the period when several northern states fully committed to their strategy of state nullification. Massachusetts and its 1843 "Latimer Law" pioneered a new generation of personal liberty statutes for northern states that now followed Story's guidelines but only exacerbated the existing interstate problems by attempting to withdraw involvement in fugitive matters altogether. Without participation from northern state and local officials, the rendition process became impossible to enforce. In his opinion, Story had addressed this problem by putting the onus squarely on Congress. "If there are not now agencies enough to make the assertion of the right to fugitives convenient to their owners," he wrote, "Congress can multiply them."[17] This particular challenge from *Prigg* became the driving force behind the 1850 Fugitive Slave Law.

What thus made the 1850 law so unique in American history was its ambitious plan to employ a network of specially designated U.S. commissioners to oversee a more efficient national rendition system. The law did not create these commissioners or administrative law officials for the various U.S. Circuit Courts, as some historians mistakenly claim, but it did represent probably the greatest expansion of federal criminal law enforcement up to that point.[18] The 1850 statute had ten sections and was more than twice as long as the 1793 law. The first five sections detailed the concurrent jurisdiction and full authority of the commissioners to act in fugitive slave matters. Most notably, this authority also extended to "all good citizens" who were "commanded to aid and assist in the prompt and efficient execution of this law."[19]

Section 6 then explained the surprisingly elaborate judicial process for deciding fugitive slave cases. Of course, the procedures for these otherwise routine hearings needed to be spelled out in such excruciating detail because of the contested nature of the operations. Under this section, slaveholding claimants or their authorized agents had the option either of first obtaining arrest warrants from the commissioners or of seizing and bringing the alleged fugitives to the commissioners themselves. Then they were supposed to produce written evidence establishing both the identity and the enslaved status of the alleged fugitive in forms that were to be certified by some legitimate judicial authority from their home state. Any testimony from the runaways themselves was supposed to be prohibited. If a commissioner did issue a certificate of removal, then the verdict was also supposed to be final, not subject to interference or "molestation" from any other state or local judicial authority.

These last procedural matters were clearly designed to frustrate the personal liberty regime that had been spreading across the North. So were several of the remaining and highly controversial elements of the statute, which included much tougher penalties for aiding runaways and obstructing the law, and a suspicious set of extra fees provided to commissioners when ruling for claimants. Section 7 in the new statute provided for up to one thousand dollars in fines and up to six months in prison for any convicted aiders and abettors, in addition to civil liabilities now up to one thousand dollars per fugitive. It was Section 8 that offered the commissioners the inflammatory ten dollars for issuing a certificate of removal versus five dollars when denying the claim. The statute's framers defended this inequity (or bribe, as its critics declared) as being justified by the extra paperwork required for rendition. The ninth section went even further in acknowledging the difficult realities of runaway slave rendition across sectional lines, explicitly authorizing federal marshals to use whatever security force they deemed "necessary" in order to return fugitives safely. The final section circled back to suggest that slaveholders or their agents should originally file a record of any escaping "person held to service or labor" with their home court at the time of flight because later such certified documents would be "taken to be full and conclusive evidence" in any federal rendition hearing.

The whole process stunk in the eyes of the northern antislavery press. Everything about the new system seemed stacked in favor of slaveholders. The fact that the law had been bundled together with the admission of California as a free state and other measures as part of the Compromise of 1850 did little to appease public outrage in the North. To antislavery forces, these measures appeared to be not only bad policy but also practically anti-American in their blatant disregard for personal liberty and due process. That explains the relentless propaganda, fiery convention gatherings, dramatic political cartoons, heated denunciations, and the litany of dire predictions hurled at the infamous statute as illustrations of the draconian nature of the Fugitive Slave Law.

However, there is always a difference between rules in the statute books and realities on the ground. The question in this situation was not so much about what the hated law promised (or threatened) but what it actually delivered. Over the next fourteen years until its final repeal in June 1864, the Fugitive Slave Law remained at, or near, the center of the sectional debate. Even during the Civil War, controversies over the law's enforcement occupied significant public attention among Unionists, especially in the border states. But, as is so often the case, all of that heat did not generate much light. From the beginning, the text of the 1850 Fugitive Slave Law got reworked, misconstrued, and sometimes outright ignored by the very people charged with bringing it to life.

OPERATIONS OF THE FUGITIVE SLAVE LAW

Perhaps no northern city better illustrates the challenges of implementing the post-1850 fugitive slave procedures than Philadelphia. President Millard Fillmore had signed the measure into law on September 18, 1850. Just one month later, the city experienced its first case under the new regime. But, of course, the new U.S. commissioner was not yet in place, so it was Supreme Court justice Robert Grier, sitting as a U.S. circuit judge, who presided over the hearing on the second floor of what is now known as Independence Hall. Despite the statutory efforts to limit due process for the accused fugitives, both sides in this matter had attorneys present and each called witnesses. There was also a large, mostly antislavery crowd gathered outside. Inside the hearing room, the Pennsylvania-born jurist claimed that he "was disposed to give justice to the master as to the slave" but also added ominously for the slaveholding interests that "the master must prove his case to the very letter." Ultimately, Justice Grier ruled in favor of the accused fugitive, releasing him on a technicality borne out of the complicated and poorly followed procedures that had been detailed in the sixth section of the new law.[20]

Nor did things get much better for the so-called Slave Power once they finally got a real rendition from Philadelphia ordered up by the new commissioner, Edward Ingraham, after he had assumed his place in mid-December. Ingraham, a noted book collector and attorney, heard the case of Adam Gibson, who had been seized by ex-Philadelphia constable George F. Alberti and some of his deputies on December 21, 1850. These experienced slave catchers had arrested Gibson on the pretext that he was stealing chickens, but it was all a well-planned ruse. Instead, they hauled him over to the U.S. marshal at Independence Hall. Gibson had tried to resist, but the constables subdued him with a pistol, as angry crowds quickly gathered outside. What followed was not the kind of summary hearing that the statute's framers had envisioned. Somehow vigilance operatives had once again succeeding in mobilizing their network of antislavery lawyers, and within a couple of hours some of the city's toughest litigators were representing Gibson. They badgered the stunned novice commissioner with a variety of motions and convinced him to hear testimony from Gibson himself. None of this activity, however, swayed Ingraham, who ordered the fugitive sent back to his alleged owner in Elkton, Maryland. Yet, amazingly, the Maryland slaveholder refused to take custody of Gibson, acknowledging that the runaway slave he had been seeking was someone else.[21]

So the federal marshal in charge of the rendition prepared to bring Gibson back to Pennsylvania, presumably to free him, but while they were between trains in Delaware, the prisoner broke away and returned to Philadelphia by foot. He then received protection from local vigilance committee leader James G. Bias and appears to have been married within the next year and relocated with his wife, Sarah, and their growing family to the free black community in Timbuctoo, New Jersey, where he lived peacefully as a farm laborer until late into the nineteenth century.[22]

By contrast, Gibson's main nemesis, former constable Alberti, suffered a much different fate. In the spring of 1851 he went on trial in state court, along with one of his deputies, for kidnapping the free-born child of an alleged fugitive. The state judge was merciless in rendering his verdict, sentencing Alberti under the terms of Pennsylvania's revised (post-*Prigg*) 1847 personal liberty statute to a term of ten years of hard labor in prison and a one-thousand-dollar fine. Calling the kidnapping crime involving an infant to be a case "without a parallel in atrocity," the judge angrily declared "that the law of our State imposes it, and we will protect those colored persons *who are in a free land*."[23] Although Alberti eventually ended up receiving a pardon and serving less than two years in the penitentiary, it was still a remarkably revealing moment about the difference that free soil made in deciding matters of law and justice.

Naturally, not every fugitive case ended as well as the Gibson case for the northern antislavery forces. Stanley Campbell identifies about sixty individuals who were subject to the federal rendition process in that first year of operation under the new law. He believes fifty of those people were returned to the South and re-enslaved (although he mistakenly includes Gibson in this sad total), with another thirty or so taken in known recaption episodes.[24] But what absorbed public attention even more than the orderly renditions or the continuation of recaption customs were the handful of examples of dramatic rescue efforts. In 1851 three headline-grabbing episodes created particular shockwaves, especially in the South. The Shadrach case in Boston (February), the Christiana Riot in Lancaster County, Pennsylvania (September), and the Jerry rescue in Syracuse, NewYork (October), all involved successful efforts by northern vigilance committees and antislavery forces to impede the law. In total, six fugitives were rescued from federal custody by violent force, and one Maryland slaveholder was killed. Yet of the nearly seventy-five antislavery activists who were charged afterward in either state or federal courts, including thirty-eight men for committing treason at Christiana (still the largest treason indictment in U.S. history), only one was convicted.[25]

The Fillmore administration tried to not back down from what it perceived as an all-out assault on law and order. The Whig president responded by authorizing occasional deployments of military force (such as with the April 1851 extradition of Thomas Sims from Boston) and by naming aggressive new commissioners, such as Richard McAllister in Harrisburg. Both national parties (Whig and Democrat) also pointedly endorsed the Compromise of 1850 measures, including the Fugitive Slave Law, in their 1852 election platforms. Still, the bottom line for enforcement was gravely disappointing to southerners. Between 1852 and 1854, there only about two dozen rendition hearings across the country and although episodes of violent resistance were fewer and less sensational, they still occurred. Moreover, a careful look behind the rendition statistics revealed serious disparities in enforcement. One particularly aggressive commissioner, like McAllister in Harrisburg, could skew the meager numbers dramatically. The central Pennsylvania commissioner accounted for nearly 40 percent of all the fugitives formally sent back to the South under the statutory rendition process during his brief time in office.[26]

In his recent book, *Making Freedom* (2013), Richard Blackett paints a devastating portrait of the little-known McAllister, who was, by southern standards at least, the model northern fugitive slave commissioner. The Harrisburg attorney once boasted to federal officials that he had remanded more fugitives "than any other U.S. Com," a true statement when he made it but one that also seems to have been his undoing. Federal auditors began scrutinizing his bulging reimbursement requests with increasing hostility. One rendition effort from Harrisburg to Maryland cost more than $233. The aggressive tactics of his office also turned McAllister and his men into local pariahs. He was forced out as a church vestryman, and his top deputies lost their elections for constable. Within less than two years, by 1853, the beleaguered officer had enough. McAllister resigned as a slave commissioner and eventually relocated to the Kansas territory where he served as a Franklin Pierce administration appointee. The Harrisburg slave-hunting operation was never the same.[27]

Vigilance operatives could be even more intimidating and quite effective further away from the Mason–Dixon line, in heavily antislavery New England and the Old Northwest. In 1854 a deputy federal marshal was killed in Boston during an attempted rescue of fugitive Anthony Burns and yet nobody went to jail for that crime. The Burns case was successful by some proslavery standards—the fugitive was returned (temporarily) to Virginia—but this was also the last official rendition of any fugitive from the New England states in the years before the Civil

War.[28] It was a symbol of failure for any true southern fire-eater. There were a couple of other sporadic recaption episodes in New England but no more formal hearings after May 1854.[29]

The especially combustible state of affairs in that region was evident just shortly after the Burns rendition, when the arresting officer in the case, Asa Butman, experienced a form of mob retribution as he was pursuing a different fugitive in Worcester, Massachusetts. That city's vigilance committee quickly spread the word about the presence of a notorious "kidnapper" with a series of broadsides, and soon crowds began to attack him. Before long, vigilance operatives tried to shield Butman from harm, fearing more bloodshed, although their admonitions to the crowd were sometimes carefully phrased. "Boys, don't kill him—don't strike him—but abuse him as much as you can!" one agent reportedly cried out. Butman went into hiding after the riot and subsequently abandoned his slave-catching duties, although he remained employed as a constable in Boston long after the war.[30]

This was also the same year that abolitionist Sherman Booth and his allies in Wisconsin rescued fugitive Joshua Glover from federal custody in Milwaukee—a dramatic case that would eventually reach the Supreme Court as *Ableman v. Booth* in 1859. The Wisconsin Supreme Court tried to nullify the 1850 Fugitive Slave Law in this extended legal saga, an action that Chief Justice Roger Taney found astonishing. In this instance, he dismissed their states' rights maneuvers by observing in his 1859 opinion that the national government could not "have lasted a single year" if states like Wisconsin could obstruct enforcement of federal fugitive slave laws through their personal liberty statutes.[31]

Stanley Campbell takes note of these well-known episodes but records only nineteen successful rescue episodes in seven different northern states between 1850 and 1861. He therefore concludes that the statute was enforced far more often than it was resisted. That is a somewhat misleading insight, however. Campbell's figures do not include a resistance episode like the one in Worcester that intimidated constable Butman. Nor does the scholar address a wide range of physical and often-violent confrontations that "rescued" fugitives by generally preventing recapture efforts. By contrast, Lois Horton reports that she has identified through her newspaper research more than eighty episodes that she characterizes as "well publicized rescues and rescue attempts."[32] Here is also one area where digital databases offer even greater promise for expanding the scope of available information. Consider this previously unnoticed report from Abraham Lincoln's hometown newspaper in Springfield, Illinois, which appeared in August 1857 under the headline: "Attempt to Kidnap Free Negroes at Cairo." That story claimed "a large party of armed Missourians" had attacked the southern Illinois town on a recent Sunday morning, attempting to carry away local black residents as runaway slaves. According to the correspondent, some of Cairo's white citizens fought back against this unwarranted invasion, foiling the kidnapping, badly wounding one of the Missourians, and then arresting several of the others.[33]

Remember, this was not Thomas Wentworth Higginson's Boston but rather notoriously proslavery southern Illinois. The author of the state's hated black codes, John A. Logan, represented this region in the legislature. If any single piece of evidence can demonstrate the underappreciated extent of northern resistance to the Fugitive Slave Law during the 1850s, it might be this one, which was not counted in Campbell's tabulations but which future president Lincoln surely read about with considerable interest.

This forgotten episode in southern Illinois also underscores a regional shift that was occurring in the enforcement patterns under the new fugitive slave code. During the entire period between 1850 and 1861, almost 90 percent of the official rendition hearings took place in just five states: Illinois, Indiana, New York, Ohio, and Pennsylvania.[34] But if the Mason–Dixon line marked the main combat theater of the fugitive crisis during the first half of the decade, then it was the Ohio River that became the critical frontline of the battle in the second half of the 1850s. During the six years directly preceding the Civil War, there were only about eighty-one accused fugitives who appeared in front of a U.S. commissioner in any of the free states. Just over 20 percent of them were either rescued or released from custody. The remaining sixty-four individuals were sent back to slavery, but these cases were almost exclusively concentrated in Ohio. Between 1855 and 1861, nearly 75 percent of the official fugitive renditions taking place from within the free states occurred just across the very tense border between Kentucky and Ohio. These involved some of the most infamous and tragic events of the antebellum era, such as the Margaret Garner affair in 1856, where a mother killed her daughter in Cincinnati to avoid her rendition to Kentucky, or the Oberlin-Wellington rescue of 1858, where a group of die-hard abolitionists faced jail and potential martyrdom for rescuing a fugitive from federal custody.

Southerners paid careful attention to what was happening in Ohio. In June 1857 the *Charleston Mercury* featured an article about growing sectionalism under the headline "The Progress of Treason." The piece focused (without much irony) on the problem of northern nullification and reprinted angry excerpts from a Democratic newspaper in Cincinnati that had just recently blasted Ohio's governor, Salmon P. Chase, for his role in obstructing the 1850 Fugitive Slave Law. It accused him "and his abolition crew" of making "the equivalent to a declaration of war . . . against the United States Courts." Complaining about the varied state and local attempts to frustrate the rendition of a Kentucky fugitive named Addison White, the editorial was adamant that there had never been "a more outrageous case of resistance to the authority of the United States."[35] To begin, White had resisted his arrest with a gun. Then local residents helped rescue him with pitchforks and some deception. Frustrated, the federal marshals arrested several of these local operatives but soon found themselves threatened with their own arrests by an antislavery local sheriff and his men, whom they subsequently beat in violent fashion. But that did not end the story. Ohio law enforcement eventually managed to detain some of the federal marshals, creating a high stakes legal standoff. Today this case is largely forgotten, but at the time it was one of the more notable fugitive battles of the era. Moreover, the tense jurisdictional issues were not fully resolved until later that summer when Governor Chase and President James Buchanan met in secret in Washington to cut a deal that avoided any further escalation in hostilities between Ohio and the federal government.

The deal did not include any rendition for Addison White or any punishment for the local Underground Railroad operatives. Everybody, including the federal marshals, was released from jail, with all charges dropped. The only concession to slavery was that the residents of Mechanicsburg, Ohio, where White had been residing, agreed to help pay off his disgruntled owner by formally purchasing his freedom. Addison White later served in the Union army as part of the 54th Massachusetts and returned to life as a farmer in Ohio after the war. For Stanley Campbell, who includes a vivid series of details about this episode in his monograph, the bottom line was somehow that it had proven how well the new system worked. "While Addison White was rescued," he writes, "Southerners could not argue in this case that federal officers did not vigorously prosecute the violators of the Fugitive Slave Law."[36]

Such a conclusion almost defies belief. Nobody in Ohio faced any real consequences for defying federal authority in 1857. Proslavery southerners had long argued that resistance to the law was not only widespread across pockets of the North but also utterly unpunished, almost from the beginning of the system's operations. The problem as southerners saw it went far beyond just the lack of consequences for those involved in high-profile resistance episodes, like those seventy-five activists who largely escaped punishment in 1851. In fact, it is difficult to identify northern figures who got punished under Section 7 of the 1850 statute, whether by fines or imprisonment. One well-known civil penalty concerned the fate of Rush R. Sloane, an attorney in Sandusky, Ohio, who stood accused of obstructing a Kentucky claimant in 1852 whose three slaves had been released by the local mayor under intense pressure and threat of violence. Two years later, a federal jury did assess damages, and Sloane was compelled to pay over $3,000 with costs.[37] That was an exceptionally steep payout, however, and a rare one. Moreover, most fines and assessments got reduced after trial. One Missouri slaveholder spent three fruitless years at the beginning of the decade chasing after $2,900 promised to him in a jury award leveled against a group of antislavery Quakers from Salem, Iowa. As one local historian put it, the slaveholder finally gave up in disgust, having "never collected a dime."[38]

Criminal punishments were even less common than civil penalties. There were no more than a handful or two of convictions over the course of the entire antebellum decade, and some of them were purely symbolic. In what the *New York Herald* labeled a "singular slave case in Indiana," there was a "successful" prosecution of Benjamin Waterhouse in late 1854. He was convicted of obstructing the fugitive law with help from the testimony of former president Millard Fillmore's brother, but the jury returned a verdict of one-hour imprisonment (in the courtroom) with a fifty-dollar fine. "Such is the result of the first case tried in Indiana, under the 7th section of this Fugitive law," exclaimed the *Herald*. Another Illinois abolitionist, John Hossack, spent ten days in prison in Chicago in early 1860, but his sympathetic jailers allowed him out each night to dine with antislavery supporters.[39]

Even without the kind of harsh punishment in the North under federal law that southerners routinely meted out to their convicted "slave stealers" under their own state laws, there is still the fundamental question about the plight of the freedom seekers themselves once they reached northern soil. The majority of the few hundred runaways identified in Campbell's book were returned to enslavement, whether by rendition or recaption. That is a fact. But that is not nearly the whole story. Now that Eric Foner has rediscovered Sydney Howard Gay's "Record of Fugitives" covering the New York vigilance operations, with its documentation for over 200 individual runaways during the mid-1850s, there is basis for some important revisionism. The successful New York escape cases, combined with another 250 from the same period in the Boston vigilance records and more than 800 accounts in the Philadelphia vigilance materials preserved by William Still, suggests a hard, contemporary data set of about 1,250 successful covert escapes in the years following passage of the Fugitive Slave Law. But add to that baseline figure all of the successful escapes in other cities that were reported in the contemporary antislavery press and the total moves closer to a few thousand. In other words, it seems quite certain that runaways were at least ten times likelier to succeed than fail if they just made it across the Mason–Dixon line or the Ohio River during the years immediately before the Civil War.[40]

Context like this is essential for reinterpreting the threat of kidnapping and the patterns of free black migration after 1850. There is little doubt that the continued digitization of antebellum newspapers will uncover more episodes of both kidnapping and resistance from the 1850s, but it strains credulity to believe that thousands of cases went unreported in that highly polarized press. Fear of kidnapping may have intensified, but the reality on the ground was much different. The vigilance movement was obstructing rendition and frustrating recaption. While the passage of the Fugitive Slave Law undoubtedly sparked some mass removals of black church groups or small borderland communities, the majority of black residents in the North remained where they were, preferring to risk fight over flight.

This somewhat unconventional claim can be illustrated with a simple review of some key demographic figures. According to Michael Wayne's careful calculations on the 1861 Canadian census, there was only somewhere between 10,000 and 13,000 U.S.-born blacks living in Canada

West on the eve of the American Civil War out of total black population in that province (and thus effectively in all of Canada) that he estimates as between 17,000 and 23,000. Even if two-thirds of them had arrived during the 1850s (a very generous estimate), that likely range of 6,500 to 8,500 refugees over the span of a decade does not seem to match the hyperbole of free black "flight" (or a mass exodus of Canaan-bound runaways) following the passage of the Fugitive Slaw Law.[41] Compare, for example, those several thousand possible migrants to the 250,000 free blacks who remained in the antebellum North. Or look specifically at the gains in free black antebellum communities in northern border states like Ohio and Pennsylvania. In Ohio's case, there was an extraordinary overall 48 percent increase, from 25,000 black residents in 1850 to nearly 37,000 by 1860—and this despite the fact that Ohio was practically ground zero for Fugitive Slave Law enforcement in the North. In Pennsylvania, some key counties along the Mason–Dixon line did appear to lose small numbers of free black residents over the span of the decade (such as in Lancaster and York), but the most urban counties (like Philadelphia) made modest gains.[42] Ultimately, one cannot help but suspect that it was other economic factors, like the Panic of 1857, rather than the politics of the Fugitive Slave Law that was providing the main push–pull dynamic for antebellum black migration.

CONCLUSION

In February 1859 a story appeared in the *National Anti-Slavery Standard* that gleefully exposed the broken reality of the fugitive slave rendition system. The New York–based abolitionist newspaper (previously edited by Sydney Howard Gay) decided to break away from its reporting on an antislavery convention in Philadelphia to regale its readers with the views of George Alberti, the former slave catcher "whose name has been associated with almost every remarkable slave case that has occurred in Philadelphia for the last forty years." A correspondent had tracked down the sixty-nine-year-old man at his modest home in the south side of the city, interviewing him at length about his various encounters with runaway slaves. Alberti proudly showed off numerous scars, on his head, arms, and legs, claiming he had been shot at least sixteen times. They discussed his most sensational case, the one that resulted in his worst (but not his only) conviction in 1851. In fact, no

Underground Railroad agent in the North had ever faced such a severe punishment for a role in any fugitive episode. According to the *Standard*, it was because of such punishment and widespread resistance that Alberti had long since become a "historical" figure whose "occupation is gone." Alberti had been a leading slave catcher, perhaps the most notorious one in the entire North, and yet by 1859 abolitionists were willing to declare him a relic of a bygone era.[43]

That declaration of victory was perhaps premature, but it was not an isolated sentiment. A few months later, in the spring of 1859, as Republicans in Ohio were calling for a renewed national campaign to repeal the 1850 fugitive statute, Governor Chase expressed a similar view to Abraham Lincoln, a fellow antislavery politician whom he had not yet met in person. Lincoln had taken the initiative and quietly reached out to Chase in private correspondence because he feared that such calls for repeal would "explode" the 1860 Republican national convention. Always with an eye on the politics of the moment, Lincoln warned that the "cause of Republicanism" would be "hopeless in Illinois" under such radical public positions.[44]

Chase was not impressed by Lincoln's caution, assuring him that Republicans in Illinois would simply have to be "educated up to" the necessity of repealing the hated law, which the governor labeled as "unnecessarily harsh & severe" and yet also at the same time "almost absolutely useless as a practical measure of reclamation." Chase then offered a revealing insight for the benefit of Lincoln's calculating political mind. He pointed out that for "thousands who do not concur in our movement" and for what he asserted were "nearly all the leading minds of the South," there was also widespread agreement that the Fugitive Slave Law was "next to worthless as a practical measure." Then the legendary "Attorney General for Fugitive Slaves" tacked on a copy of some recent legal briefs filed by his state in notable fugitive cases and assured the Springfield attorney that he would be "very glad to have your views."[45]

Undaunted, Lincoln did soon share his legal views with Chase, which generally mirrored the position of Justice Story in the *Prigg* case (1842), but the purpose of his 1859 outreach was purely political. "My only object," Lincoln observed coolly, "was to impress [upon] you . . . that the introduction of a proposition for the repeal of the Fugitive Slave law, into the next Republican National convention, will explode the convention and the party."[46] For the always-pragmatic Lincoln, there seemed to be no point in arguing over a measure that everyone was acknowledging was either "absolutely useless" or "next to worthless."

The Republicans ended up following Lincoln's advice. Their 1860 platform mentioned nothing about repealing the Fugitive Slave Law. The party did denounce the Buchanan administration for its "attempted enforcement everywhere, on land and sea, through the intervention of Congress and of the Federal Courts of the extreme pretensions of a purely local interest," but beyond that vague statement, it did not go.[47] Still, secessionists understood those words as only further confirmation that a cornerstone of national compromise from 1850 had finally become little more than a "dead letter." As the Republicans prepared to take over the administration of the national government, the secession ordinances of several southern states complained bitterly about the history of noncompliance with the act. Ultimately, of course, Lincoln and Chase worked together during their wartime administration to curtail enforcement of the fugitive law and to help shepherd through its repeal by the Congress in spring 1864. By that point, both men and their party were fully committed to achieving the complete abolition of slavery through a constitutional amendment. What had always been so contested and so confused about the fate of American "fugitives from labor" was finally settled.

NOTES

1. Georgia declaration of secession, January 29, 1861, Yale Law School, Lillian Godman Law Library, The Avalon Project, http://avalon.law.yale.edu/19th_century/csa_geosec.asp.

2. Stanley W. Campbell, *The Slave Catchers: Enforcement of the Fugitive Slave Law, 1850–1860* (Chapel Hill: University of North Carolina Press, 1970); and John Hope Franklin and Loren Schweninger, *Runaway Slaves: Rebels on the Plantation* (New York: Oxford University Press, 1999).

3. On recaption, see Eric Foner, *Gateway to Freedom: The Hidden History of the Underground Railroad* (New York: W. W. Norton, 2015), 32.

4. Salmon P. Chase to Abraham Lincoln, June 13, 1859, Abraham Lincoln Papers, Library of Congress, Washington, D.C.

5. Frederick Douglass, *Narrative of the Life of Frederick Douglass: An American Slave* (Boston: Anti-Slavery Office, 1845), 101.

6. See full text of the 1793 statute under Acts of Congress, February 12, 1793, in *A Century of Lawmaking for a New Nation: U.S. Congressional Documents and*

Debates, 1774–1875, Annals of Congress, 2nd Congress, 2nd Session, American Memory Project, Library of Congress, http://memory.loc.gov/cgi-bin/ampage?collId=llac&fileName=003/llac003.db&recNum=702.

7. See full text of the 1850 statute, passed on September 18, 1850, Yale Law School, Lillian Godman Law Library, The Avalon Project, http://avalon.law.yale.edu/19th_century/fugitive.asp.

8. See David Waldstreicher, *Slavery's Constitution: From Revolution to Ratification* (New York: Hill and Wang, 2009).

9. From James Madison's notes on the Constitutional Convention, August 28, 1787, available at TeachingAmericanHistory.org, http://teachingamericanhistory.org/convention/debates/0828-2/.

10. Don E. Fehrenbacher with Ward M. McAfee, *The Slaveholding Republic: An Account of the United States Government's Relations to Slavery* (New York: Oxford University Press, 2001), 102.

11. Amended statute, March 29, 1788, available at "The President's House in Philadelphia," Independence Hall Association, http://www.ushistory.org/presidentshouse/history/amendment1788.php. Gary B. Nash and Jean R. Soderlund dismiss this now mostly forgotten amendment as offering little more than "meek provisions against kidnapping" in their seminal book *Freedom by Degrees: Emancipation in Pennsylvania and its Aftermath* (New York: Oxford University Press, 1991), 198, but they were analyzing its impact in the context of the kidnapping crisis that emerged along the Mason–Dixon line after 1800. The eventual failures of the law, however, should not mitigate the significance of its framers' intent. In 1788 Pennsylvania legislators took a pioneering stand for personal liberty.

12. Thomas D. Morris, *Free Men All: The Personal Liberty Laws of the North, 1780–1861* (Baltimore: Johns Hopkins University Press, 1974). For other relevant statutes in Indiana, California, and elsewhere, see John Codman Hurd, *The Law of Freedom and Bondage in the United States*, 2 vols. (Boston: Little, Brown, 1862).

13. Douglass in 1853 quoted in Matthew Norman, "The Other Lincoln–Douglas Debates: The Race Issue in Comparative Context," *Journal of the Abraham Lincoln Association* 31 (Winter 2010): 5.

14. Fehrenbacher and McAfee, *Slaveholding Republic*, 209–13.

15. *Prigg v. Pennsylvania*, 41 US 539 (1842), available at Justia, https://supreme.justia.com/cases/federal/us/41/539/.

16. Stanley Harrold, *Border War: Fighting over Slavery before the Civil War* (Chapel Hill: University of North Carolina Press, 2010).

17. *Prigg v. Pennsylvania*, 41 US 539 (1842).

18. Charles A. Lindquist, "The Origin and Development of the United States Commissioner System," *American Journal of Legal History* 14 (January 1970): 1–16.

19. 1850 fugitive statute, September 18, 1850.

20. "The First Fugitive Slave Case in Philadelphia," *Philadelphia Evening Bulletin*, October 18, 1850.

21. "Fugitive Slave Case," *Philadelphia Evening Bulletin*, December 21, 1850; and "Fugitive Slave Case," *Philadelphia Public Ledger*, December 23, 1850.

22. "Return of the Alleged Fugitive," *Philadelphia Public Ledger*, December 24, 1850. Adam Gibson, born in 1823 in Maryland, appears in the U.S. Census for Burlington County, New Jersey, with wife, Sarah, as late as 1880.

23. March 24, 1851, P. A. Browne, *A Review of the Trial, Conviction, and Sentence of George F. Alberti, for Kidnapping* [Philadelphia] 1851.

24. See Campbell, *The Slave-Catchers*, appendix.

25. Enoch Reed was convicted of resisting a federal officer in the Jerry rescue case and received a brief sentence that was likely to have been overturned, but he died while it was still on appeal. For details on the Jerry rescue, see Milton C. Sernett, *North Star Country: Upstate New York and the Crusade for African American Freedom* (Syracuse, N.Y.: Syracuse University Press, 2002), 143. For the Shadrach case, see Gary Collison, *Shadrach Minkins: From Fugitive Slave to Citizen* (Cambridge, Mass.: Harvard University Press, 1997). For the Christiana riot, see Thomas P. Slaughter, *Bloody Dawn: The Christiana Riot and Racial Violence in the Antebellum North* (New York: Oxford University Press, 1991).

26. Based on statistics derived from Campbell, *The Slave-Catchers*, appendix.

27. R. J. M. Blackett, *Making Freedom: The Underground Railroad and the Politics of Slavery* (Chapel Hill: University of North Carolina Press, 2013), 35–51.

28. Albert J. Von Frank, *The Trials of Anthony Burns: Freedom and Slavery in Emerson's Boston* (Cambridge, Mass.: Harvard University Press, 1998).

29. Campbell, *The Slave-Catchers*, appendix.

30. Von Frank, *Trials of Anthony Burns*, 305–6.

31. *Ableman v. Booth* 62 US 506 (1859), available at Cornell Law School, Legal Information Institute, https://www.law.cornell.edu/supremecourt/text/62/506. For details on the Glover rescue, see H. Robert Baker, *The Rescue of Joshua Glover: A Fugitive Slave, the Constitution, and the Coming of the Civil War* (Athens: Ohio University Press, 2006).

32. For reference to the eighty resistance episodes, see Lois E. Horton, "Kidnapping and Resistance: Antislavery Direct Action in the 1850s," in *Passages to Freedom: The Underground Railroad in History and Memory*, ed. David W. Blight (Washington, D.C.: Smithsonian Books; Cincinnati, Ohio: National Underground Railroad Freedom Center, 2006), 166. For Campbell's list, see table 12 in the appendix to Campbell, *Slave-Catchers*, 207.

33. Springfield *Illinois State Journal*, "Attempt to Kidnap Free Negroes at Cairo," August 1, 1857, p. 2, col. 3.

34. Statistics derived from Campbell, *The Slave-Catchers*, appendix.

35. *Cincinnati Enquirer* reprinted in "The Progress of Treason," *Charlestown Mercury*, June 17, 1857, p. 2, col. 1.

36. Campbell, *The Slave-Catchers*, 164.

37. Roberta Sue Alexander, *A Place of Recourse: A History of the U.S. District Court for the Southern District of Ohio, 1803–2003* (Athens: Ohio University Press, 2005), 40–42.

38. Lowell J. Soike, *Necessary Courage: Iowa's Underground Railroad in the Struggle Against Slavery* (Iowa City: University of Iowa Press, 2013), 46.

39. "Speech of John Hossack on the Fugitive Slave Law," 1860 broadside, available at Frontier to Heartland, Newberry Library, Chicago, Ill., http://publications.newberry.org/frontiertoheartland/items/show/245.

40. Foner, *Gateway*, 190–215; and Larry Gara, "William Still and the Underground Railroad," Pennsylvania History 28 (January 1961): 33–44. For Boston vigilance records, see the account books of Francis Jackson, Massachusetts Historical Society, digitized by students from Beverly High School, available at PrimaryResearch.org, http://primaryresearch.org/account-book-of-francis-jackson/. There was some overlap in cases from the Philadelphia, New York, and Boston records, but not enough to dilute the overall assessment that there are records to document "about" 1,250 documented successful escapes.

41. Michael Wayne, "The Black Population of Canada West on the Eve of the American Civil War: A Reassessment Based on the Manuscript Census of 1861," *Histoire Sociale/Social History* 28 (1995): 465–85.

42. Consult U.S. Census figures from 1850 to 1860.

43. "Interview with Alberti the Slave Catcher," *National Anti-Slavery Standard*, February 19, 1859, p. 2, col. 6.

44. To Salmon P. Chase, June 9, 1859, in Roy P. Basler, ed., *The Collected Works of Abraham Lincoln*, 8 vols. (New Brunswick, N.J.: Rutgers University Press, 1953), 3:384.

45. Salmon P. Chase to Abraham Lincoln, June 13, 1859, Abraham Lincoln Papers, Library of Congress.

46. To Salmon P. Chase, June 20, 1859, *Collected Works*, 3:386.

47. Republican Party Platform of 1860, adopted May 17, 1860, available at the American Presidency Project, http://www.presidency.ucsb.edu/ws/index.php?pid=29620.

5

Seeking Freedom in the Midst of Slavery

Fugitive Slaves in the Antebellum South

DAMIAN ALAN PARGAS

Moses Hutcherson, a "likely black fellow about twenty-three years old, five feet four or five inches high, neck somewhat long, and rather a prominent nose for a negro," decided in the spring of 1825 that he would no longer live in slavery. Surveying the possibilities to escape bondage from his farm on the Potomac River in southern Maryland, he concluded that the most logical course of action would be to flee to Pennsylvania, where slavery had been abolished. It was an option fraught with peril, of course. Despite the close proximity of the neighboring free state, flight attempts across the Mason–Dixon line were risky at best—Moses would have to traverse dozens of miles of slaveholding borderland undetected by heavily armed patrols and professional slave catchers. In case he would be stopped by anyone, he procured forged free papers under the false name of John Henry before starting off. Satisfied that his plan would work, he slipped away from his master's residence on April 1 and made for the North, but his hopes of reaching Pennsylvania were dashed when he was caught just north of Baltimore and thrown into jail. His master recovered him and dragged him back to the southern part of the state. Undaunted, Moses escaped again a month later. This time, however, he fled not to the "free" North but to the nearby slaveholding city of Washington, D.C., where he changed his name again and passed himself off as a free black. Indeed, the free black community of Washington helped him to conceal his true identity and assisted him in finding accommodations and employment. In the months that followed, Moses "served in many of the Taverns and Boarding Houses in [the] District" and remained harbored by "free negroes in [that] place," with whom he had come to have "considerable intercourse."[1]

Unlike thousands of his fellow bondsmen who escaped slavery by crossing state or international borders to parts of the continent where the institution had been abolished, Moses Hutcherson attempted to craft a life of freedom for himself by simply disguising his slave identity, living a clandestine life, and passing himself off as a free black *within* the slaveholding South. His story—and there are innumerable such cases in the history of the antebellum South—complicates our understanding of both the geography of slavery and freedom in North America and the opportunities for enslaved people to permanently escape bondage by fleeing the spaces and places in which they were held captive.

A number of historians have greatly contributed to our understanding of various aspects of slave flight in the antebellum period, with the seminal work by John Hope Franklin and Loren Schweninger, *Runaway Slaves: Rebels on the Plantation* (1999), standing out in particular for its broad and comprehensive analysis of the subject. Most scholarship on fugitive slaves has tended to focus on escape to sites of formal and semiformal freedom along the North–South axis, however, especially to the northern United States and Canada, and as such misses a broader understanding of the geography of slavery and freedom within North America. Other destinations for fugitive slaves have remained far less thoroughly explored by historians. Although briefly touched upon by Franklin and Schweninger, among others, the "southern underground railroad" that led fugitive slaves to Texas, Mexico, Spanish Florida, and even the Caribbean has only recently begun to receive more in-depth analysis from scholars. Few scholars have analyzed the experiences of slaves who sought informal forms of freedom by fleeing *within* the slaveholding states of the South. Those who have, moreover—Franklin and Schweninger, and Stephanie Camp, for example— have tended to underscore the temporary nature of such flight, characterizing runaways who remained in the slave territories as "truants" or "absentees" (temporary runaways or *petits marrons*) rather than permanent refugees from slavery (long-term migrants or *grand marrons*). Franklin and Schweninger describe the common act of fleeing to the forests that bordered southern plantations as "lying out," for example, and they interpret runaways who made for urban areas as "temporary sojourners" who experienced a "brief respite from bondage" or at best a "break . . . of longer duration" before being caught and sent back to their masters.[2]

A smattering of more recent works are beginning to challenge the view that fugitive slaves in the South only sought and experienced temporary interludes from slavery. Sylviane Diouf's revisionist study of antebellum America's "borderland maroons" specifically argues that many of these slaves "went to the Southern woods to *stay*."[3] Alan Taylor's research on runaway slaves in Virginia reveals how fugitives attempted to secure permanent freedom by actively seeking out the assistance of sympathetic British naval officers anchored in the Chesapeake Bay, especially during the War of 1812. And Matthew J. Clavin's work on fugitive slaves in antebellum Pensacola emphasizes the relative ease with which runaways in that seaport town were able to settle and find sustainable employment—although even they often attempted to flee onward to places where slavery had been abolished (especially the British Caribbean). Indeed, many southern cities—St. Louis, Baltimore, New Orleans—ultimately served as "gateways to freedom" for some daring runaways who sought to escape the South altogether, whether because of their proximity to free soil or because of the various transportation possibilities they offered. But runaway slave advertisements and court records consistently indicate that fugitive slaves who concealed themselves in towns and cities across the South often navigated urban areas not merely gateways to freedom in other parts of the hemisphere but as actual sites of freedom in their own right. In other words, they were permanent freedom seekers—at least by intent, and often by outcome—who made illegal yet quite earnest attempts to rebuild their lives in informal freedom rather than bolt for geographic spaces of formal freedom. Understanding why and how they did so is crucial for scholars' reconceptualization of these runaways as freedom seekers rather than mere truants, and for "rerouting" the geography of freedom in America during the age of slavery, as Rachel Adams recently called for.[4]

Taking a broad scope, this study contributes to the reinterpretation of fugitive slaves who remained in the South between 1800 and 1860 as permanent refugees from slavery. It touches upon themes such as the motivations that led slaves to flee within the South and the cooperation between free and enslaved blacks that enabled and facilitated their escape attempts and settlement processes. Most importantly, it highlights the experiences of runaways who, like Moses Hutcherson, escaped slavery by fleeing to sites of informal freedom rather than cross into geographic spaces of formal freedom.

Permanent refugees from slavery often ran away for reasons that were more structural than those that commonly motivated truancy or temporary flight. Impulsive decisions to temporarily flee the plantation and "lie out" were often sparked by significant abuse or the threat of corporal punishment, as stated above, although other factors also played a role. Franklin and Schweninger have even argued that the desire for a change of scenery underlay slave flight to urban environments. Young slaves in their teens and twenties found "the excitement and diversity" of urban environments "especially enticing," and "temporary sojourns" to southern cities were therefore frequent.[5] Slaves seeking to permanently escape within the South, however, were often more serious, less impulsive, and more calculated in their plans. When Mathy, "a griff aged about 38 years," and his wife, Litty, "black, aged about 35 years," ran away from a Louisiana plantation in the summer of 1845, they boarded a flatboat "on their way to South Alabama, where they were lately owned" and where they still had loved ones.[6] For Mathy and Litty, returning to family members from whom they had been forcibly separated was the prime motivation to flee. Indeed, enslaved people's commitment to family is essential to understanding why many bondspeople fled their plantations but remained within the borders of the slave South—fugitives within the South often fled with the intention of staying close or returning to loved ones still held in bondage. The threat or reality of forced separation was one of the most important motivations for permanent slave flight within the South.

In the era of the second slavery, when the Atlantic slave trade had been abolished and the domestic slave trade in the southern states flourished, forced separations increasingly wrought havoc on slave families. Eyewitnesses to the domestic slave trade consistently reported that family separations were common. Ethan Allen Andrews, a university professor charged with investigating the trade in 1835 and 1836, found that "family ties are often disregarded in this traffic." Visiting Franklin & Armfield's slave pen in Virginia in 1836, he discovered that "in almost every case, family ties have been broken in the purchase of these slaves." Another Alexandria slave trader assured Andrews that "he never separates families" upon sale (a lie intended to legitimize his business to the northerner) but admitted "that in purchasing them he is often compelled to do so, for that 'his business is to purchase, and he must take such as are in the market!'" When Andrews asked whether the traders often bought wives without their husbands, the reply was: "Yes, very often; and frequently, too, they sell me the mother while they keep her children. I have often known them to take away the infant from its mother's breast and keep it, while they sold her."[7] African Americans living in the supply regions of the interstate trade emphatically corroborated such charges, both during and after slavery. In 1854 James Redpath learned from a northern Virginia slave that the separation of slave families through deportation there was as "common as spring water runs."[8] Another bondsman from North Carolina reported after emancipation that in the region where he lived, the "breaking up of families and parting of children from their parents was common ... and one of the things that caused much bitterness among the slaves."[9]

Historical scholarship has confirmed that charges of forced separation through the interstate slave trade were no exaggeration. Family separation in fact made economic sense in the interregional trade. As Michael Tadman has argued, its very structure was "custom-built to maximize forcible separations."[10] As the antebellum slave trade was highly selective (in age, ability, and sex) according to the demands of specific markets, speculators usually preferred—even openly advised their agents—to purchase desirable slaves individually, tearing husbands from wives as well as children and young adults from their parents and younger siblings. A survey of New Orleans slave ship manifests confirms that most interstate migrants indeed arrived in the Deep South as individuals and not in family units. The brig *Tribune*, for example, a ship chartered by the infamous traders Franklin & Armfield in 1833, carried sixty-eight slaves from Alexandria and Norfolk, Virginia, to New Orleans, most of whom were in their teens and twenties, and only three of whom were in their thirties (the oldest was thirty-eight).

Of the ship's enslaved passengers, six young women were transported with one infant child each. The rest of the slaves in the customs manifest were listed individually, all with different surnames, implying that they were not related. Even when family members were deported together, they were often sold separately in the receiving societies because it was more profitable to do so. Scholars have estimated that forced separations probably destroyed one out of every three first marriages among slaves in the Upper South; at least half of all slave families in the region were ruptured through the deportation of either a spouse or child during the antebellum period. Local sales and the westward migration of slaveholders from the eastern seaboard to the southern interior, moreover, severed cross-plantation marriages as well as extended family bonds in countless slave communities.[11]

Flight became an important vehicle through which victims of forced migration attempted to either prevent separations or reunite bonds torn asunder. Prevention, especially, underlay innumerable escape attempts. Some fugitives who absconded within the South were slaves recently arrived at urban places of market to be disposed of but who fled in order to avoid removal. "Lucy M Downman's man [N]at absconded" upon arrival in Richmond in March 1834, for example, suspected of having disappeared among the city's large free black population. Nat's owner, from a neighboring county, "had Sent him to Richmond for Sale."[12] Likewise, a "Slave Traders man Henry Jackson" absconded in Richmond in 1834 to avoid being shipped south.[13] Other slaves fled when rumors of potential sale loomed. Fifty dollars reward was offered in North Carolina in 1822 for the apprehension of Jack, a "common mulatto, about 40 years of age," who took with him "his Wife and two Children." Fleeing to prevent a possible separation, the family was suspected of "lurking in Fayetteville, Newbern, or Washington, amongst the free negroes."[14] In 1835 a forty-five-year-old slave woman named Mary, from Charleston District in the South Carolina Low Country, disappeared among the free black population of Charleston when she was confronted with the prospect of moving over a hundred miles to the state capital. A runaway slave advertisement in the *Charleston Courier* openly claimed that "the cause of her running away was her dislike to be brought to Columbia."[15] And Joe, a forty-five-year-old Maryland slave from Charles County, "ran off immediately after the appraisement" of his master's estate, "knowing that he was to be sold in a few weeks." Joe was suspected of "lurking about the neighborhood of Bryan Town" and passing for free.[16]

For those who were unable to prevent forced removal, fleeing served as a vehicle to reconnect with loved ones lost through forced migration. A significant number of runaway slaves who stayed in the South were themselves forced migrants who had already been sold away from their home communities and who were fleeing in order to see their families again. Rather than flee to destinations where they could be legally free, they more often ran "home." Slaves who had been sold or removed locally (within the same state or region) were often in the best position to do this. Maria Hamilton, for example, a twenty-four-year-old slave from Alexandria, Virginia, who was sold into the countryside of Fairfax County, was suspected of having run either back to Alexandria, where she had a husband, or to neighboring Washington, where her sister and brother-in-law lived—"she may in all probability have gone there."[17] William Foley, another Virginia slave who ran away from his new master, was suspected of hiding out near "the residence of Mr. Cockerell of Fauquier [County], who owns his mother"[18] and from whom he had been sold away. The runaway Osborn, newly purchased by one William Davison of Winchester, Virginia, had "expressed a desire to visit his relations" across the border and down the Potomac River in his native Nanjemoy, Maryland, and was therefore suspected to be hiding out there.[19]

Remarkably, however, many fugitives who stayed within the South were victims of the interstate trade and traversed vast distances in order to be reunited with families forcibly left behind. As the domestic slave trade scattered black families across the southern states, slave refugees indeed played a prominent role in the "joining of places" (as historian Anthony Kaye dubbed it), creating networks that linked victims of forced migration with their home communities, even across state lines.[20] Southern newspapers from receiving societies are replete with illuminating examples. William, who fled his new plantation near Lexington, South Carolina, in 1830, was presumed to be "mak[ing] his way for North Carolina, as he was purchased . . . and brought from there."[21] A Virginia slave woman named Patsey absconded from her Georgia plantation and was suspected to have "endeavored to get back to Virginia," where she still had relations.[22] Interstate migrant Nicholas similarly left his South Carolina plantation in an attempt "to make his way to Maryland," where he was originally from.²³ Sally, a slave from the estate of George Mason in northern Virginia and purchased by an Alabama slaveholder, ran away "a few days" after arriving in the Deep South, suspected of making her way back home.²⁴ "Five Negro Men" from Maryland who had been sold to western Kentucky absconded together, suspected of having "endeavor[ed] to get to Cincinnati" (in a free state!) and "from thence to Baltimore."²⁵ In some cases slaves even ran to follow a loved one sold out of state. Dick, a thirty-seven-year-old slave from Kentucky, ran all the way to New Orleans and attempted to pass for free there to be with his wife, who was "living in that city" after being sold there.²⁶

Whatever the distances they traversed to be near loved ones, fugitive slaves who remained in the South were in constant danger of being discovered and sent back to their masters, unlike their counterparts who successfully reached geographic spaces of formal freedom such as Canada. Effectively going into hiding or at least concealing their identities to outsiders (especially whites) upon arrival, they depended on others to aid and assist them. Slave families and communities in rural districts provided fugitive slaves with the social networks necessary to sustain themselves for long periods of time without being caught. Refugees who remained in the southern countryside were almost always partly or wholly "harbored" by loved ones, sometimes within slave households but also often in the forests that bordered the plantations or farms where they were originally from, effectively becoming "borderland maroons" as Sylviane Diouf has argued. In February 1850, for example, a one-hundred-dollar reward was offered for "the arrest and conviction of the person who has harbored a slave contrary to law named MARGARET," who had been sold from her native Lake Providence to New Orleans and who was "supposed to be at or near Lake Providence," her old community, where she was suspected of hiding out near—and being kept hidden by—loved ones.²⁷ Southern newspapers are full of similar examples, but slave testimonies also regularly refer to cases of fugitive slaves in the woods being sustained by loved ones. Kitty, Ben, and Isaac, all three former slaves from the same plantation in Alabama, recalled in a 1910 interview that one bondswoman from their neighborhood "hid with her children in the woods" for a length of "two years," which Ben claimed was a "conservative" estimate. Living her life "in a precarious freedom," the fugitive slave woman reportedly created an underground shelter with a trap door "covered with leaves [so] no one could see it" and depended upon her family and friends, who often left food at the edge of the woods at dusk, to help feed her and her children. Only after the Civil War broke out two years subsequent to her escape were the woman and her family eventually able to procure "a freedom not of the swamp, but of the world."[28] Travelers' accounts and even court documents confirm that such cases were a regular occurrence in the South. Nanny, an "unmanageable" slave from North Carolina, ran away from the employer to which she was hired in 1851, "aided by her . . . husband," who was "well acquainted in much of the great Dismal Swamp." Her husband's assistance afforded Nanny "an easy opportunity" to escape to the wilderness indefinitely and avoid arrest.[29]

Such arrangements were desperate and often ad hoc by nature, and they were seldom intended to be permanent, even when they lasted years. Although they certainly did not constitute truancy (these fugitives were not intending to ever return to their masters), they often failed to provide sustainable long-lasting solutions to refugees' predicament. Most fugitives who were harbored by loved ones in the countryside can more accurately be perceived as runaways in transit—their final destinations were usually either sites of formal freedom (especially the northern states or Canada) or urban areas in the general vicinity of their home communities.[30]

Urban areas in the South provided slave refugees with spaces where they could realistically attempt to establish a permanent base for themselves in informal freedom—a freedom that did not exist on paper but that allowed them to escape bondage. Towns and cities provided refugees with relative anonymity due to the relatively large presence of free black communities. In public urban spaces runaways hoped to get lost in the crowd and largely conceal their slave status by pretending to be free blacks, often changing their names—one runaway to New Orleans, for example, was "familiar with the names Hildreth, Brown and Walker"—but more importantly changing their appearances.[31] As Amani Marshall has argued, successful procurement of informal freedom in southern cities required runaway slaves to assume "free identities," which they did by engaging in "intricate performances in which they exploited colour, dress, language, and employment skills to transcend lines of race and class."[32] For slave refugees, passing for free meant looking and acting free. Visibility was everything—erasing all markers of their slave identity was the key to navigating urban spaces undetected. Intriguingly, some light-skinned runaways attempted—sometimes successfully—to pass as white. One carpenter from North Carolina who ran away to Washington, D.C., was described as resembling "a white man . . . His eyes are blue, his hair very straight," saying he had run to the city "to pass as a free man."[33] But for most refugees in southern cities, assuming free identities entailed looking and acting like local free blacks. Indeed, upon arrival in urban areas, runaways' first order of business was often to procure the more fanciful clothing of the free black population to replace the ragged clothes that gave them away as country slaves. Sam, "an artful fellow" from eastern Maryland who had been sold to Kentucky, was presumed to have made his way all the way back to his native town "and will probably exchange his dress" to disguise his slave status.[34] One runaway slave who was suspected of lurking about Livingston, Alabama, was seen wearing "a black cashmere overcoat . . . and a silver huntsman's watch," no garb for a slave.[35]

Free blacks helped cloak the true identities of runaway slaves by harboring them in their homes or arranging for safe hiding places. Sometimes these were free family members. Tarlton, a twenty-four-year-old carpenter from Powhatan County, Virginia, ran away to Richmond in 1834 and was suspected of hiding out at the residence of one Stephen Green, "a free man who lives in Richmond [and] is the Father of Tarlton."[36] Other times the relations between the free black helpers and runaway slaves were less explicit. For example, Julia Johnson, from Staunton, Virginia, likewise ran away to Richmond, the police noting that "Isaac Adams free [was] Susp[ecte]d of decoying hir [sic] off" and arranging for her hiding place in the city.[37] Molly, who disappeared in the city of Alexandria, Virginia, was believed to be "connected with some evil disposed free negroes, and secreted by them."[38] James Lamar, who fled to New Orleans in 1845, was "harbored near the lower vegetable market, by a free black woman" who sold "victuals and coffee in said market."[39] Such was the extent of the assistance provided by free blacks that southern cities and states repeatedly passed legislation that threatened free black populations with heavy penalties for aiding and abetting runaway slaves. As historian William Link has found, Virginia free blacks ran great risks when they harbored runaway slaves. One free black man in Richmond was whipped in 1853 for allowing a fugitive slave to live in his cellar; a year later another Petersburg resident was brought before the mayor's court for harboring several runaways. In 1856 the General Assembly of Virginia specified that any free person "concerned in the escape of any slave" would receive a prison sentence of five to ten years and a public whipping.[40] The General Assembly of Mississippi passed a similar law in 1839, stating that any free black who helped a slave "to escape from his or her master or owner" would be found guilty of "feloniously stealing [said] slave or slaves."[41]

Southern towns and cities were also attractive destinations for slave refugees, providing them with opportunities to perform various occupations and earn money to sustain themselves indefinitely, to the great consternation of slaveholders throughout the South, who often explicitly warned white urban residents against employing their escaped slaves in the mistaken belief that they were free blacks. Skilled slaves were often in the best position to do so, as their services were in high demand in urban centers and their occupations often associated with economic activities usually performed by free blacks. Historian Larry Rivers recently argued in his study of slave resistance in antebellum Florida that an exceptionally high proportion of runaways in that state were skilled slaves, especially carpenters, blacksmiths, and river pilots. Runaway slave ads from other states confirm that skilled slaves tended to flee to urban areas within the South with remarkable frequency.[42] Examples from the Charleston newspapers are illuminating. In the summer of 1849, for example, a five-hundred-dollar reward was offered for the apprehension of four bondsmen from a plantation in Rowland Springs, Georgia, among them an artisan named Hercules. In the prime of his life—he was thirty years old—Hercules "had the peculiar brogue of low country negroes," having been raised in the South Carolina lowcountry and "bought from Charleston recently." The advertisement that announced his absence implicitly suspected him of having fled to Charleston, where he would have been able to remain in close contact with his home community in the lowcountry. Interestingly, the ad also explicitly specified that Hercules was "a Tinner by trade," presumably because his owner expected him to practice his trade upon arrival in the city.[43] Similarly, Ben Elliott, a twenty-five-year-old runaway originally from Charleston but sold to Augusta in 1833, had been missing for five months before his new master placed an advertisement in the *Charleston Courier* for his recapture. Ben was presumed to be hiding out with his mother in Charleston, a free woman "named Pheobe Elliott, who sells fruit in the market," and he had already been nearly caught several times passing himself off as a free black and "working about the wharves, and on board vessels, as a Stevedore or an Assistant."[44] Peter Youngblood fled his new Charleston residence for the town of Beaufort, "as he has a wife on Mrs. Hamilton's Plantation, in that neighborhood." An experienced boatman and a fisherman, he was suspected of being "employed in fishing in the neighborhood of that city."[45]

Female fugitive slaves in southern cities often succeeded in finding domestic employment in white households, their employers assuming that they were free blacks. "Fifty Dollars Reward" was offered "for the apprehension of TENAH, a female servant, who ran away from Barnwell Court House [South Carolina] on the 12th September" in 1830. Like many of her counterparts, Tenah had been separated from her loved ones when she was sold from a plantation near Charleston to Barnwell. The runaway slave ad that announced her flight stated that she was "brought to this city in June last, at a sale of the estate of Vancy's Negroes, and it is believed that she is harbored in Charleston by a free person," her husband being "a free man by the name of William Lewy, who lives in Goose Creek, and has been seen in her company at the person's house in which she is harbored." Tenah was suspected of illegally passing herself as a free black woman in order to gain employment, as her master "understood that she has been (perhaps unknowingly) employed by a white person as a washerwoman." Similarly, a slave woman named Milly was "Supposed to be in Richmond" where she had been hired in the household of one Fleming Griffiths; she fled and was suspected of hiring her services to another employer as a free woman.[46]

A significant portion of the enslaved population in any southern town or city consisted of hirelings, and hired slaves in turn made up a significant number of slave refugees in urban areas. Self-hire arrangements, whereby a slave was sent by his master to the city to hire himself, were common enough that some runaway slaves in the cities even attempted to disguise their identities by passing for hired slaves rather than free blacks. John Lewis, a Kentucky slave, ran away to Lexington with the intention of pretending "he has hired his own time."[47] Most tried to pass themselves off as free, however. Indeed, hired slaves' absence from their masters, their relative lack of supervision and freedom of movement, and their firsthand experience with urban labor markets placed them in an advantageous position to navigate southern cities disguised as free blacks. They knew the ropes, worked with and rubbed shoulders with free black populations, and were keen to trade in their "quasi-freedom" (as Jonathan Martin dubbed it) for freedom, albeit informal freedom.[48] For these runaways, the determination to live in freedom and the conviction that they deserved the fruits of their own labor were often more important motivations to flee bondage than family reunification. Henry, a refugee in New Orleans who had been "hired in this city as a drayman," absconded and found work for himself "in the shipping and about the levee," keeping his earnings for himself.[49] Urban hirelings also had the networks necessary to pull off a successful escape attempt. William Lee, a "smart, sensible, and very plausible fellow" as well as a "good wagoner" who had been hired in Fauquier Court House, Virginia, absconded and was suspected of hiring himself out around town as a free man. Lee had "extensive acquaintances" in the town in which he absconded, which facilitated his flight.[50] Another Virginia slave who went missing in 1825 "had been hired in Alexandria for some months past," her owner lamenting that "she is well known" there and would no doubt be aided in her flight.[51]

As stated above, the ability of fugitive slaves to abscond to and successfully earn a living in urban areas by passing themselves off as free blacks produced great consternation among slaveholders, who demanded that municipalities tighten police supervision of African Americans' economic activities in public spaces. City councils throughout the South explicitly complied with such demands, at least on paper. The city of Little Rock, Arkansas, for example, passed "an ordinance, concerning Slaves, and free Negroes and Mulattos" in January 1836 that declared, among other things, that "No person shall buy or receive from any slave any commodity whatever in this City, unless the said slave shall produce a written permit from his or her master, mistress or overseer."[52] Since free blacks could reasonably be suspected to be slaves until proven otherwise, this ordinance was implicitly intended to force white customers to ask black sellers for their papers before purchasing any wares from them, presumably in order to uncover fugitive slaves who were living illegally in the city. Similar ordinances were passed throughout the South, but in practice they were often poorly enforced, both by the authorities and by white customers.[53]

Southern municipalities largely failed in their attempts to distinguish between free blacks and runaway slaves in public spaces, despite strict legislation aimed at enhancing the visibility of both, such as requiring slaves to carry passes and free blacks to carry free certificates at all times. Fugitive slaves' precarious existence in the cities was indeed primarily based on the fact that they lacked formal papers to prove that they either had permission to reside in the city or that they were free. As illegals and noncitizens, the very public spaces that often provided them with anonymity could also produce dangerous encounters with whites that might reveal their true identities. Documentation—false documentation—was a great advantage for those who could procure it. Slaves who could read and write were in a position to forge their own passes or free papers, and many did. Frederick, a Georgia slave who was suspected of having run to Augusta in 1825, was presumed to be carrying "a forged pass with him, as he can read and write."[54] Ben, a Virginia slave who ran away with his three daughters to Washington, could "write a pretty good hand, and no doubt has copied the papers of some free man," his master even having "reason to believe he stole the Stafford County seal and attached the impression of it to his papers."[55] Most slaves were illiterate, however, and therefore depended on free blacks to provide them with the false documentation necessary to evade detection. Perhaps unsurprisingly, a black market in forged passes and facsimiles of free papers for runaway slaves—the antebellum equivalent of a fake passport for undocumented immigrants—flourished in urban areas, despite strict legislation against it. In Mississippi the General Assembly explicitly threatened "any free negro or mulatto who shall deliver or transfer to any slave the copy of the register of his or her freedom . . . with the intent to enable such slave to escape from his or her master" with a felony.[56] Every other southern state had similar legislation on the books, and by the eve of the Civil War even the sparsely settled southwestern territory of New Mexico threatened that "any person furnishing slaves free papers is liable to an imprisonment of not less than six months nor more than five years, and a fine of not less than $100 nor more than $1000."[57] Yet runaway slave ads reveal that forged papers were common anyway. Nancy, a "bright mulatto, aged about 25 years" and originally from the Natchez area of Mississippi, absconded from her new master in Plaquemines Parish, Louisiana, but had "lately been heard of in the neighborhood of Natchez with a forged pass."[58] Kitty, a Virginia slave suspected of having run to Washington, was advertised as "uncommonly artful, and no doubt will have free papers."[59] Amanda, from Monroe County, Georgia, fled to Augusta with "a pass given her" so that she could "attempt to pass as a free person."[60] David, "by profession a Methodist preacher" from Kentucky who ran to Lexington with his friend Charles, was understood to have "a forged pass."[61] And Will, a Virginia runaway, "probably has a pass or counterfeit papers of freedom."[62]

Such documents became increasingly necessary after the Nat Turner insurrection in 1831, when urban southerners became more vigilant in requiring free blacks to carry papers, and slaves to carry passes or badges, to prove that they resided in the city legally. Because assuming a false identity and a false legal status was so crucial to fugitives' lives in urban areas, those who failed to procure documents ran high risks of recapture. One slave owner from Columbia, South Carolina, advertised for his runaway slave named Mary, who fled back to her native Charleston in 1859, describing her as having "neither ticket nor badge, as required by the City Ordinance."[63] When recapture seemed imminent for those who were discovered without passes or papers, they often fled again, sometimes to geographic spaces where slavery had been abolished, a risky venture that was wrought with hazards. One slave couple named George and Jane, from Henrico County, Virginia, was recaptured in an escape attempt that illustrates the volatile existence of refugees in the cities. Having each fled the employers to which they were respectively hired in 1833, the two fugitives came together and made their way to neighboring Richmond. Upon arrival "George passed himself off as a freeman & hired himself as a cook on bord [sic] the schooner John Bendil," docked in the James River. When the captain of the ship eventually asked for George's free papers before departure, he "found that he was in fact a slave & not a freeman having a right to hire himself." Panicking, George fled, concealing himself on board a schooner bound for New York, where he was later discovered and arrested. Jane was also arrested, "making similar efforts to leave the state" and join her husband in the North.[64] As Matthew Clavin has argued, some southern cities indeed served as "gateways to freedom" for runaways who intended to seek freedom outside of the South from the outset; but many slaves who ultimately passed through such gateways (or attempted to do so) were in fact slaves who had initially attempted to create lives for themselves in informal freedom in towns and cities across the South but were forced to take flight again when they were detected.[65]

In conclusion, a thorough understanding of the geography of slavery and freedom on the North American continent in the antebellum period must include closer analysis of fugitive slaves who sought freedom by remaining within the slaveholding states. The actions of these runaways went far beyond mere truancy, as is often suggested in the literature. Fugitives to urban areas indeed clearly attempted to live their lives there indefinitely, and even maroons did not intend to return to their masters but were more often "in transit" to other sites of formal or informal freedom. Distinguishing between sites of formal freedom (where slavery had been abolished) and informal freedom (where fugitives attempted to live free illegally) as permanent destinations for runaway slaves is also crucial in understanding how slaves understood freedom (i.e., not always in political terms) and what their prime motivations for fleeing bondage were. Indeed, those who sought informal freedom clearly placed maintaining contact with loved ones still in bondage—even if it meant living illegally within the slave states—above the procurement of political or civil rights to freedom, which supports recent scholarship by historians such as Calvin Schermerhorn, who argued that slaves in the antebellum South almost always preferred "family over freedom"—at least freedom on paper.[66]

NOTES

1. *Daily National Intelligencer* (Washington, DC), July 4, 1825. For more on the Maryland–Pennsylvania borderland as a destination for fugitive slaves, see, for example, Richard S. Newman, "'Lucky to be born in Pennsylvania': Free Soil, Fugitive Slaves and the Making of Pennsylvania's Anti-Slavery Borderland," *Slavery & Abolition* 32, no. 3 (September 2011): 413–30.

2. John Hope Franklin and Loren Schweninger. *Runaway Slaves: Rebels on the Plantation* (New York: Oxford University Press, 1999). See also Paul Finkelman, ed., *Fugitive Slaves* (New York: Garland, 1989); Gordon Barker, *Fugitive Slaves and the Unfinished American Revolution: Eight Cases, 1848–1856* (Jefferson, N.C.: McFarland, 2013); Jason Silverman, *Unwelcome Guests: Canada West's Response to American Fugitive Slaves, 1800–1865* (Millwood, N.Y.: Associated Faculty Press, 1985); Sydney Nathans, *To Free a Family: The Journey of Mary Walker* (Cambridge, Mass.: Harvard University Press, 2013); Keith Griffer, *Front Line of Freedom: African Americans and the Forging of the Underground Railroad* (Lexington: University

of Kentucky Press, 2004); and Steven Lubet, *Fugitive Justice: Runaways, Rescuers, and Slavery and Trial* (New York: Cambridge University Press, 2010). For new studies on fugitive slaves in Mexico, see, for example, S. E. Cornell, "Citizens of Nowhere: Fugitive Slaves and Free African Americans in Mexico, 1833–1857," *Journal of American History* 100, no. 2 (2013): 351–74; Sean Kelley, "Mexico in His Head: Slavery and the Texas-Mexico Border, 1810–1860," *Journal of Social History* 37, no. 3 (2004): 709–23; and James David Nichols, "The Line of Liberty: Runaway Slaves and Fugitive Peons in the Texas–Mexico Borderlands," *Western Historical Quarterly* 44, no. 4 (Winter 2013): 413–33. Matthew Clavin's recent work views Pensacola as a conduit for fugitive slaves fleeing southward into the Caribbean (especially the British Caribbean). Matthew J. Clavin, *Aiming for Pensacola: Fugitive Slaves in the Southern and Atlantic Frontier* (Cambridge, Mass.: Harvard University Press, 2015). For a brief overview of the diplomatic consequences of fugitive slaves in North America (only those who crossed international borders), see Jeffrey Kerr-Ritchie, "Fugitive Slaves across North America," in *Workers across the Americas: The Transnational Turn in Labor History*, ed. Leon Fink (Oxford Scholarship Online, 2011).

3. Sylviane Diouf, *Slavery's Exiles: The Story of the American Maroons* (New York: New York University Press, 2014), 1.

4. Rachel Adams calls for a broader understanding of the geography of slavery and freedom in North America. See Rachel Adams, *Continental Divides: Remapping the Cultures of North America* (Chicago: University of Chicago Press, 2009), 61–100. For brief treatment of truancy within the South, especially in urban areas, see, for example, Stephanie M. H. Camp, *Closer to Freedom: Enslaved Women & Everyday Resistance in the Plantation South* (Chapel Hill: University of North Carolina Press, 2004), 35–59; and Franklin and Schweninger, *Runaway Slaves*, 97–103, 124–48. Franklin and Schweninger argued that "few absconders [within the South] remained permanently at large." See John Hope Franklin and Loren Schweninger, "The Quest for Freedom: Runaway Slaves and the Plantation South," in *Slavery, Resistance, Freedom*, ed. Ira Berlin, Scott Hancock, and G. S. Boritt, 21–39 (New York: Oxford University Press, 2007), 25. For southern runaways as permanent freedom seekers, see Christopher Phillips, *Freedom's Port: The African American Community of Baltimore, 1790–1860* (Urbana: University of Illinois Press, 1997); Clavin, *Aiming for Pensacola*; Amani Marshall, "'They Will Endeavor to Pass for Free': Enslaved Runaways' Performances of Freedom in Antebellum South Carolina," *Slavery and Abolition* 31 (May 2010): 161–80; and Alan Taylor, *The Internal Enemy: Slavery and War in Virginia, 1771–1832* (New York: W. W. Norton, 2014).

5. Franklin and Schweninger, *Runaway Slaves*, 126–27.

6. *The Times Picayune*, July 10, 1845.

7. Ethan Allen Andrews, *Slavery and the Domestic Slave Trade, in a Series of Letters Addressed to the Executive Committee of the American Union for the Relief and Improvement of the Colored Race* (1836; Freeport, N.Y.: Books for Libraries Press, 1971), 49, 137–39.

8. James Redpath, *The Roving Editor: Or, Talks with the Slaves in the Southern States* (1859; New York: Negro Universities Press, 1968), 199.

9. William Henry Singleton, *Recollections of My Slavery Days* (n.p., 1922), 2. There is a rich literature on the domestic slave trade and the extent to which sales, estate divisions, and long-term hiring forcibly separated slave families in the antebellum period. See, for example, Michael Tadman, *Speculators and Slaves: Masters, Traders, and Slaves in the Old South* (Madison: University of Wisconsin Press, 1989); Walter Johnson, *Soul by Soul: Life Inside the Antebellum Slave Market* (Cambridge, Mass.: Harvard University Press, 1999); Steven Deyle, *Carry Me Back: The Domestic Slave Trade in American Life* (New York: Oxford University Press, 2005); Robert H. Gudmestad, *A Troublesome Commerce: The Transformation of the Interstate Slave Trade* (Baton Rouge: Louisiana State University Press, 2003); Damian Alan Pargas, *Slavery and Forced Migration in the Antebellum South* (New York: Cambridge University Press, 2014).

10. Tadman, *Speculators and Slaves*, 141.

11. In the 1970s and 1980s the extent of family separations through interregional sale was the subject of considerable debate among historians, sparked by controversial conclusions drawn by Fogel and Engerman in *Time on the Cross* (1974), that the domestic slave trade accounted for only 2 percent of dissolved marriages among slaves living in the Upper South. Their calculations, however, have long since been refuted as a gross underestimate by historians such as Herbert Gutman and Michael Tadman, among others. See Robert William Fogel and Stanley L. Engerman, *Time on the Cross: The Economics of American Negro Slavery* (Boston: Little, Brown, 1974), 49; Herbert Gutman and Richard Sutch, "The Slave Family: Protected Agent of Capitalist Masters or Victim of the Slave Trade?" in *Reckoning with Slavery: A Critical Study in the Quantitative History of American Negro Slavery*, ed. Paul A. David, Herbert G. Gutman, Richard Sutch, Peter Temin, and Gavin Wright, 94–133 (New York: Oxford University Press, 1976); Herbert G. Gutman, *The Black Family in Slavery and Freedom, 1750–1925* (New York: Vintage, 1976), 144–52; Tadman, *Speculators and Slaves*, 133–78; Ira Berlin, *Generations of Captivity: A History of African-American Slaves* (Cambridge, Mass.: Harvard University Press, 2003), 169; Andrews, *Slavery and the Domestic Slave Trade*, 49–50; "Report and Manifest of the Cargo of Slaves on Board the Brig Tribune of New York," January 22, 1833, transcription at http://files.usgwarchives.net/va/shiplists/slavship.txt, consulted March 6, 2012; Gudmestad, *Troublesome Commerce*, 42; and Deyle, *Carry Me Back*, 246–47. Traders Franklin & Armfield, to their credit, began to purchase more slaves in family groups after 1834 in an effort to blunt criticism of the slave trade. Other traders, however, spread "fairy tales," claiming to keep families together when confronted with charges of inhumane practices by outsiders. See Gudmestad, *Troublesome Commerce*, 160–61. Such was the extent of family separation through interstate migration that it even began to affect families' ability to reproduce, especially in the Upper South. In the 1830s, when forced migration reached its peak, the natural growth rate among slaves fell to 24 percent after having risen in the previous decades. See Calvin

Schermerhorn, *Money over Mastery, Family over Freedom: Slavery in the Antebellum Upper South* (Baltimore: Johns Hopkins University Press, 2011), 14–15.

12. Daybook of the Richmond, Virginia Police Guard, March 12, 1834, University of Virginia, Alderman Library, Special Collections, Charlottesville, Va. (trans. by Leni Ashmore Sorensen).

13. Daybook of the Richmond, Virginia Police Guard, July 22, 1834.

14. *Raleigh Register and North Carolina Gazette*, April 26, 1822.

15. *Charleston Courier*, September 3, 1835.

16. Daybook of the Richmond, Virginia Police Guard, October 9, 1834.

17. *Alexandria Gazette*, August 7, 1826.

18. *Phenix Gazette*, September 16, 1826.

19. *Alexandria Advertiser and Commercial Intelligencer*, July 9, 1803.

20. Anthony E. Kaye, *Joining Places: Slave Neighborhoods in the Old South* (Chapel Hill: University of North Carolina Press, 2007).

21. *Charleston Courier*, November 2, 1830.

22. *Charleston Courier*, March 7, 1835.

23. *Charleston Courier*, October 29, 1830.

24. *Huntsville Democrat*, June 16, 1838.

25. *Reporter* (Lexington, Kentucky), December 2, 1809.

26. *Lexington Intelligencer*, July 7, 1838.

27. *Daily Picayune*, February 21, 1850.

28. John Blassingame, *Slave Testimony: Two Centuries of Letters, Speeches, Interviews, and Autobiographies* (Baton Rouge: Louisiana State University Press, 1977), 537–38.

29. "William Coppersmith and Elisha S. Nash to the Court of Pleas and Quarter Sessions, Pasquotank County, North Carolina, 1851," in *The Southern Debate over Slavery*, vol. 2: *Petitions to Southern County Courts, 175–1867*, ed. Loren Schweninger, 265–66 (Urbana: University of Illinois Press, 2008). See also Kaye, *Joining Places*, 129–35. Frederick Law Olmsted and William Howard Russell made similar observations regarding fugitive slaves in the Great Dismal Swamp during their travels through the South. See Frederick Law Olmsted, *A Journey in the Seaboard Slave States: With Remarks on Their Economy* (New York: Dix & Edwards, 1856), 159; and William Howard Russell, *My Diary North and South* (Boston: T. Burnham, 1863), 88–89.

30. For a detailed analysis of long-term or even semipermanent maroon communities in the American South, see Diouf, *Slavery's Exiles*.

31. *Daily Picayune*, March 3, 1850.

32. Marshall, "'They Will Endeavor to Pass for Free,'" 161.

33. *Daily National Intelligencer*, July 4, 1825.

34. *Frankfort Argus*, May 28, 1814.

35. *Mississippi and State Gazette*, September 5, 1851.

36. Daybook of the Richmond, Virginia Police Guard, March 14, 1834.

37. Daybook of the Richmond, Virginia Police Guard, September 28, 1834.

38. *Alexandria Advertiser and Commercial Intelligencer*, December 8, 1803.

39. *Daily Picayune*, November 2, 1845.

40. William A. Link, *Roots of Secession: Slavery and Politics in Antebellum Virginia* (Chapel Hill: University of North Carolina Press, 2005), 104–5.

41. T. J. Fox Alden and J. A. van Hoesen, *Digest of the Laws of Mississippi, Comprising All the Laws of a General Nature, Including the Acts of Session of 1839* (New York: Alexander Gould, 1839), 763. See also Ted Maris-Wolf, *Family Bonds: Free Blacks and Re-enslavement Law in Antebellum Virginia* (Chapel Hill: University of North Carolina Press, 2015).

42. Larry Eugene Rivers, *Rebels and Runaways: Slave Resistance in 19th-Century Florida* (Urbana: University of Illinois Press, 2012), 66–67. A study of runaway slave profiles in North Carolina comes to the same conclusion, with blacksmiths, carpenters, coopers, and shoemakers heavily overrepresented in runaways from that state. See Freddie L. Parker, "Runaway Slaves in North Carolina, 1775 to 1835" (Ph.D. diss., University of North Carolina, Chapel Hill, 1987), 197–99.

43. *Greenville Mountaineer*, August 17, 1849.

44. *Charleston Courier*, March 7, 1835.

45. *Charleston Courier*, September 28, 1830.

46. *Charleston Courier*, January 4, 1830.

47. *The Reporter* (Lexington, Kentucky), April 1, 1812.

48. Jonathan Martin, *Divided Mastery: Slave Hiring in the American South* (Cambridge, Mass.: Harvard University Press, 2004), 161–87. See also Franklin and Schweninger, *Runaway Slaves*, 134–45.

49. *Daily Picayune*, February 19, 1850.

50. *Daily National Intelligencer*, January 8, 1820.

51. *Daily National Intelligencer*, July 4, 1825.

52. *Arkansas Gazette*, January 12, 1836.

53. Gregg Kimball, *American City, Southern Place: A Cultural History of Antebellum Richmond* (Athens: University of Georgia Press, 2003), 124–58; Seth Rockman, *Scraping By: Wage Labor, Slavery, and Survival in Early Baltimore* (Baltimore: Johns Hopkins University Press, 2009), 52–53; James Campbell, *Slavery on Trial: Race, Class, and Criminal Justice in Antebellum Richmond, Virginia* (Gainesville: University Press of Florida), 146–85; and Thomas C. Buchanan, "Rascals on the Antebellum Mississippi: African American Steamboat Workers and the St. Louis Hanging of 1841," *Journal of Social History* 34 (Summer 2001): 797–817.

54. *Augusta Chronicle*, October 8, 1825.

55. *Daily National Intelligencer*, July 4, 1825.

56. Alden and Hoesen, *Digest of the Laws of Mississippi*, 763.

57. *Bangor (ME) Whig and Courier*, March 17, 1859.

58. *Times Picayune*, July 30, 1845.

59. *Alexandria Gazette*, January 1, 1822.

60. *Augusta Chronicle*, July 13, 1827.

61. *The Reporter* (Lexington, Kentucky), October 18, 1815.

62. *Daily National Intelligencer*, January 8, 1820. For more on cooperation between urban free blacks and slaves within the realm of resistance, see Kimball,

American City, Southern Place, 124–58; Rockman, *Scraping By*, 52–53; Campbell, *Slavery on Trial*, 146–85; and Buchanan, "Rascals on the Antebellum Mississippi," 797–817. William Link has found that the policing of documentation for free blacks and slaves in urban environments in Virginia was at best "sloppily maintained." See Link, *Roots of Secession*, 106.

63. *Charleston Courier*, January 1, 1859.

64. "Thomas Cowles to the County Court, Henrico County, Virginia, 1833," in *The Southern Debate over Slavery*, vol. 2: *Petitions to Southern County Courts, 175–1867*, ed. Loren Schweninger (Urbana: University of Illinois Press, 2008), 163.

65. Clavin, *Aiming for Pensacola*.

66. Schermerhorn, *Money over Mastery*.

6

Illegal but Tolerated

Slave Refugees in Richmond, Virginia, 1800–1860

VIOLA FRANZISKA MÜLLER

Throughout the antebellum period the southern states unleashed a firestorm of criticism and political furor on places like Spanish Florida, Mexico, Canada, and especially the northern United States because of their relatively open acceptance of slave refugees from the South.[1] Indignant slaveholders and impatient politicians continuously exercised pressure on bordering states and territories where slavery had been abolished or where runaway slaves regularly sought and found asylum, resulting in harsh diplomatic tensions that often led to (or at least greatly contributed to) far-reaching measures, including the incorporation of Florida in 1821, the annexation of Texas in 1845, and the Fugitive Slave Act of 1850, and of course the Civil War. Southern rhetoric directed at the northern states in particular was wrought with charges such as that northerners were on a "mad and mischievous crusade" that endangered the peace of the South by refusing to return runaways and even encouraging slave flight.[2] Southern orators in 1850 loudly proclaimed that "the South's losses in fugitive slaves amount to $22,000,000 in the last 40 years, and her annual losses amount to $550,000"—exorbitant figures for which the North was held directly responsible.[3]

Such outwardly directed accusations and attacks were somewhat ironic considering the vast numbers of runaway slaves who remained within the slaveholding South itself in the antebellum period, a phenomenon that was not only overshadowed by debates regarding slave flight to other regions at the time but has indeed continued to be marginalized by historians up to the present day. Because of the highly politicized and widely publicized nature of slave flight in the northern (and southern) borderlands, the historiography of slave flight in the antebellum period has tended to implicitly and explicitly depart from the assumption that fugitive slaves consisted mainly of runaways who fled slaveholding regions, crossed political borders, and arrived at places of free soil. The literature is heavily dominated by studies that examine slave flight from the southern to the northern states via the Underground Railroad, but in recent years scholars have also increasingly turned their attention to other border regions such as Mexico, continuing the free-soil approach.[4]

By contrast, the untold numbers of refugees from slavery who by intent and by outcome never migrated out of the slaveholding South have barely been the focus of in-depth historical inquiry, although they have certainly not gone completely unnoticed by leading scholars in the field. John Hope Franklin and Loren Schweninger observed that "most runaways remained in the South, few were aided by abolitionists or anyone else," and Peter Kolchin has argued that an "even larger number" than slaves who fled north stayed in the slaveholding states, "making their way to cities and merging with the free black population."[5] Some historians of antebellum cities with relatively large free black populations have argued that urban areas served as magnets for runaway slaves in the surrounding plantation districts but rarely made this the central focus of study. William Link, for one, found that in Richmond, Virginia, a "permanent runaway population blended with local African Americans."[6] His observation that these were *permanent* runaways is important as most scholars have tended to assume that fugitive slaves who stayed in the South were *truants* or temporary runaways. Franklin and Schweninger, for example, estimated that tens of thousands of fugitives headed to the towns and cities of the South in the antebellum decades in search for freedom and work, but they assumed that only a small fraction stayed for extended periods of time.[7] By dismissing the majority of southern fugitive slaves as truants, they stop short of in-depth analysis of the experiences of permanent freedom seekers in the southern states.[8]

Tying in with Damian Pargas' conceptualization of various "spaces of freedom" on the North American continent, slave flight within the

South reveals how runaway slaves sought and navigated spaces of informal freedom, where freedom from slavery was constructed in a clandestine manner that had no legal basis.[9] Such spaces of freedom complicate our understanding of what freedom meant to enslaved people. Kostas Vlassopoulos recently argued that essentialist understandings of slavery should be replaced by "an understanding of slavery as a temporally—and spatially—changing outcome of the entanglement of various processes," but I would argue that scholars should also approach freedom in the same way.[10] Freedom was, just like slavery, temporally and spatially changing and dependent on the interplay of a variety of processes, and spaces of freedom were not always limited to spaces where slavery had been abolished.

This study examines the experiences of runaway slaves in antebellum Richmond, Virginia, a city that served as a beacon of freedom for enslaved people throughout the central and southern parts of the state. What were the processes that made freedom for fugitive slaves in Virginia's capital possible? Why and how were slave refugees able to carve out living spaces for themselves? What were the consequences of their illegality? By whom were they employed, and how did city authorities deal with them? The contrasting attitudes toward, and the dealings with, fugitive slaves by various groups speaks volumes about how various interests and power relations clashed (and sometimes dovetailed) in the urban environment. This study specifically focuses on the solidarity that existed between free blacks (many of whom also resided illegally in the city) and fugitive slaves, which can partly be explained by their common experiences as vulnerable and undocumented residents.

Analyzing fugitive slaves in any southern city is no easy task because their strategy was precisely to remain invisible before the eyes of the authorities. Only those who failed in their endeavors occasionally left traces in the archives, especially in jail records, court cases, and newspaper articles. Runaway slave ads also provide valuable information on the presumed whereabouts of fugitive slaves, although they mostly represent the viewpoints of the masters. This study draws from these and other types of sources. Shedding light on the history of slave refugees in the South requires reading between the lines but is nevertheless crucial for understanding the agency of the enslaved and the choices they made to secure their own freedom from slavery, even under the most difficult and precarious circumstances. This contribution enlarges our understanding of a many-faced freedom in North America that can take place in a variety of small, dispersed localities, even within territories that theoretically do not envisage freedom for this particular group. The city of Richmond was one of these places.

SLAVE REFUGEES AND FREE AFRICAN AMERICANS

A perusal of records from antebellum Richmond reveals that permanent runaways from slavery in that city were numerous. From 1834 to 1844, some 935 black men and women were listed in the Daybook of the Richmond Police Guard as runaways for whom the police should be on the lookout. The majority were from nearby Virginia counties and from the city of Richmond itself. Fourteen were eventually reported as having voluntarily returned to their masters; 74 were reported as having been caught and delivered back. The rest—847 men and women—remained unaccounted for. Between 1841 and 1846 the city jail contained 215 black people who were incarcerated as runaways. Again, most had absconded from owners or employers in the surrounding region, especially counties of Chesterfield, Hanover, King William, Goochland, Caroline, and the city of Petersburg.[11] Besides police and jail records, Richmond newspapers carried daily runaway slave advertisements for fugitive slaves who were suspected to be hiding out in the city.

Runaway slaves gravitated to Richmond in the antebellum period because of the possibility for attaining anonymity there. The proximity of the Upper South to northern free soil might lead one to expect that most fugitive slaves from states like Virginia and Maryland would attempt to leave the slaveholding South altogether, and indeed slaveholders themselves often feared that their runaway slaves would make their way north, as runaway slave ads make abundantly clear. Yet in many cases factors such as family ties, employment prospects, a lack of contacts or networks in the northern states, or simple physical proximity made flight to a nearby urban center within the South a more promising endeavor. Such actions were common throughout the Upper South, and they often seemed so counterintuitive that they baffled slave owners. For example, Bill, an enslaved man from Frederick County, Virginia (now West Virginia), who was sold and moved to Hagerstown, Maryland, escaped from his new master and was apprehended in Jefferson County, (West) Virginia, where he was jailed. Evidently, he had been trying to make his way back *south*, even though in Hagerstown he was not six miles away from the Mason–Dixon line and the free soil of Pennsylvania. Similarly, a Virginia slave named Armstead left his owner, William Thompson, who was oblivious to his whereabouts and suspected him to be either dead or in one of the northern states. Eleven years later Armstead was jailed for murder outside of Richmond in Caroline County, claiming to authorities that he was a free man of color. Such practices were common enough that many slaveholders advertised their runaway slaves as having gone either to the North or to a nearby city, knowing that both were logical destinations for fugitives. "Jack, Commonly Known about town as Jack Gwathnay" with "teeth which are long and not close together and standing outward which makes his mouth as ugly as can be" decided to no longer serve his master, Thomas Crouch, in 1842. Crouch "feared he may try to leave the state by the way of Petersburg & City Point or he may have gone up the James River Canel." But he also admitted that "this is all conjecture" and "in all probability [Jack] may be lurking around Richmond or Rocketts," as he knew that many Virginia slaves managed to live in a state of de facto freedom there by getting lost in the crowd and hiding their identities.[12]

Richmond essentially formed a melting pot of black people of various statuses, slave and free, both legally and illegally residing in the city. Slave refugees there aimed at passing for free by blending in with the large African American population there, which composed a significant part of the city's population throughout the nineteenth century. Census data shows that by 1850 around 10,000 slaves and 2,400 free black people lived in the city, contrasting a white population of 15,300. This represented a spectacular growth of the black community in the antebellum period, which at all times counted for roughly half of the total population, sometimes more. In 1800 2,300 slaves, 600 free blacks, and 2,800 whites lived in the city; in 1830 there were 6,300 slaves, 2,000 free blacks, and 7,800 whites.[13] By the eve of the Civil War, however, Richmond's black population was so large that it was often remarked upon by visitors to the capital. Contemporary travelers like Frederick Law Olmsted and Robert Russell were astonished by the large numbers of black people they found roaming the streets in Virginia's capital city. Historians have often downplayed such observations by claiming that African Americans were simply more visible than whites in public urban spaces because of the distinct nature of their work, which was often performed on the streets and in public places.[14] But throughout the antebellum period the city's black population was large by any standard, and indeed it was almost certainly even greater than census data allowed for. A thriving, industrial city, Richmond's capacity to attract and absorb large numbers of runaway slaves from rural districts and unregistered free blacks (who resided in the city illegally) meant that its black population was undoubtedly much higher than the official census numbers. Municipal authorities themselves were often far from certain how many African Americans lived in the city, let alone what their exact status was. As early as 1820 Gov. Thomas Mann Randolph admitted in a speech to the House of Delegates that "the actual relation of numbers between the free citizens of the state, and that distinct and inferior race so unfortunately intermingled with them, must necessarily remain somewhat longer undetermined."[15] Any random African American whom one encountered on the streets of Richmond could theoretically be a legal resident (slave or free), a runaway slave, or a free black residing illegally in the city. At first glance it was usually impossible to tell.

The background of this confusion was a law passed by the Virginia legislature in 1806 that required that all newly emancipated slaves leave the state within twelve months.[16] Through its virtual unenforceability (many, if not most, emancipated slaves simply refused to leave) the ordinance created over a period of almost sixty years a significant illegal population of free black people throughout the state—legally emancipated but illegally residing in Virginia. The number of these illegal free African Americans presumably reached well into the thousands and must have stood in considerable contrast to the official census data.[17] The urban black communities that received and absorbed slave refugees heading to Richmond and other cities and towns in the state therefore comprised a complex, nontransparent composition of people of African descent with a variety of different legal statuses, illegal complications, and skin colors. The latter was important. Contrary to the Deep South, where in many places the free African American population was significantly lighter skinned than their enslaved counterparts (New Orleans and Charleston are good examples), Virginia free blacks appeared to white society to be a homogeneous mass, universally rejected and discriminated against on the basis of their race but also less transparent and more self-contained. Virginia was one of two states that attempted to officially define who was black and to distinguish blacks from mulattos, but over time all persons with any portion of African descent came to be regarded as black, by law and by custom, and by the antebellum period the free black population did not necessarily stand out for being lighter skinned.[18] This was an advantage for refugees from slavery who made their way to Richmond. However light or dark they were, they could easily attempt to pass for free without raising the suspicions of white residents.

In theory, there were three groups of free black Richmonders, or black Richmonders who passed for free: the elites (for instance, skilled craftsmen), the semi- and unskilled legal residents, and the undocumented.[19] The latter group encompassed large numbers of semi- and unskilled illegal freed people and slave refugees. In practice, it was hardly possible to distinguish between who was free, who was free but residing in the city illegally, and who was a runaway slave, so runaway slaves to Richmond were often successful at blending in with the free black population. Even when their owners knew they were in Richmond, it was often very difficult to find a runaway slave who had absconded to the city. After having absconded from Henrico County in 1848, for example, enslaved Nancy was "lurking in & about the City of Richmond," but although this information was known to her owner, he did not know "in what particular part of said city" she was hiding and was unable to find her.[20] Like many of her counterparts, Nancy literally camouflaged herself within the free black community of Richmond.

THE WHITE POPULATION

The law of 1806 that required emancipated slaves to leave the state was only one in a series of acts passed after the colonial period that increasingly tightened the legal and political situation of free African Americans. In order to understand how fugitive slaves and free blacks came to identify so strongly with each other in antebellum Richmond, it is important to examine the ways in which they were collectively treated by the white population.

In the wake of the American Revolution the most rigid laws concerning slavery and manumission actually seemed to be relaxed by Virginia's lawmakers. The revolutionary era had brought with it ideological changes that coincided with a flailing slave-based economy in the Upper South (due to extensive soil erosion through tobacco cultivation) and a reorientation of the economy away from plantation agriculture and toward mixed farming. Convinced that slavery was a dying institution, Virginia lawmakers eased manumission and self-purchasing schemes for slaves in their state, a move that was duplicated in other states as well, especially in the Upper South. But as the doors to freedom opened for significant numbers of Virginia slaves, the state's white population grew alarmed over the increasing numbers of free black people living among them, especially in the aftermath of the Haitian Revolution, which left many in fear and horror imagining what the black people they had held as slaves for so long might do to them. The General Assembly, largely composed of slaveholders, many of them huge estate owners, enacted a variety of laws to calm the panicked white population. Free blacks were compelled to carry freedom papers and to register their status, a measure that was designed to prevent slaves any possibility of passing as free.[21] The system turned from one of individual slave control (by slaveholders themselves) to one of social control of black people by white people.

By the beginning of the nineteenth century, African Americans had already become severely restricted in their movement. One of Gabriel Prosser's alleged coconspirators was witnessed to have complained that he could not visit his wife since it was very difficult for a black man to travel, adding that "the white people had turned so comical, a man can't go out of his house now but he is taken up to be hanged."[22] After the failed rebellion, the situation for black people predictably worsened. Citizens regularly demanded further restrictions on African Americans' freedom of movement, commerce, assembly, and education (especially the right to learn how to read and write).[23]

Such restrictions reflected a wider social reorganization that took place in Virginia in the aftermath of the American Revolution. Specifically, the traditional slaveholding aristocracy, an emerging slaveholding middle class, and poor whites came to converge on the need to severely restrict the free black population and prevent slave flight. The aristocracy of the large planters of the Tidewater and the Piedmont remained largely intact after Revolution. Possessing dozens and sometimes hundreds of enslaved people, these rich white men lamented the loss of a runaway slave but did not mourn it. For them, the bigger problem of slave flight was that fugitive slaves provided an incentive for other discontented slaves to follow their lead, which endangered the whole system of slavery, an institution that demanded the docility and compliance of those held in bondage. In order to protect their property and their slaveholding way of life, planters organized patrols to supervise rural areas and prevent slaves from absconding. Runaway slave Solomon Bayley recounted how, by the end of the eighteenth century, he escaped from a slave wagon while on his way to be sold: "When night came and I walked out of the bushes, I felt very awful. I set off to walk homewards, but soon was chased by dogs, at the same house where the man told the waggoner he had taken up a runaway three days before. . . . I got down to Richmond; but had liked to have been twice taken, for twice I was pursued by dogs."[24] Slave patrols constituted a constant threat to slave refugees, but planters had little interest in patrolling the roads themselves. Like other slaveholding states along the Atlantic seaboard, laws were enacted to have other (usually poor) white people do this job, which they did not always receive with enthusiasm. In 1825, for example, a group of eighty-three citizens from Lincoln County, North Carolina, "feeling it a greviance," complained at the General Assembly "that any person should be compelled to Ride or Serve as Patroler to guard Slaves who do not own any, nor wish to have any thing to do as respects the government or Discipline of the Negroes."[25] Such sentiments were no doubt shared by many white non-slaveholders in Virginia as well, at least those who had no direct stake in slavery. But even they feared emancipated blacks, and as the numbers of the latter grew dramatically, they almost universally felt vulnerable to economic competition from them; support for patrolling gradually grew as a result. White workers such as craftsmen and mechanics but also lower-ranked laborers also simultaneously (and desperately) tried to push their black competitors out of certain occupations, often submitting legislative petitions that were mostly unsuccessful.

The number of small slaveholders grew dramatically after the Revolution with the decline of primogeniture. Distributing property, and with it slave property, to a number of heirs instead of only the first-born male enlarged this social class while reducing the absolute wealth of every one of them. The result was a slaveholding middle class who suddenly shared the elite's efforts to keep the institution of slavery upright and to defend it against slave flight—and for small slaveholders, the loss of a slave *did* constitute a major financial loss. Wealthy families still determined politics, but by the midcentury the middle classes were doing their best to muscle in.[26] In sum, Virginia's plantation aristocracy, slaveholding middle class, and white working class converged on the need to prevent slave flight and curtail the rights (and presence) of free blacks.

NETWORKS AND SOLIDARITY

Such determination and hostility on the part of the white community did not deter runaways, however. Importantly, in this era the nature of slavery itself was changing in ways that ironically enhanced enslaved people's mobility and allowed them to create networks that could assist them in their flight attempts. The antebellum period as a whole corresponds with Dale Tomich's conceptualization of the era of the "second slavery," which saw a radical change in the living and working conditions of a considerable minority of enslaved people in the U.S. South.[27] Industrialization, urbanization, and the shift from tobacco to wheat production in Virginia allowed many slaveholders to hire out their surplus bondspeople in towns and cities in order to achieve additional gain. Having marginally existed in urban as well as in plantation slavery, hiring out became a central part of the former. Between 5 percent and 15 percent of enslaved laborers were hired out during the antebellum period in the South, with a peak toward the end of the era.[28] Hired slaves, particularly those with professional skills, enjoyed an increasing mobility and gained a wide geographical knowledge as well as personal and professional networks of interregional, interstate, and even international character.[29] Even enslaved men who were not hired out in the cities were often sent to town to run errands and market their masters' goods, allowing them to make contact with urban slaves and free blacks and to make plans for their escape. Thus, despite the severe restrictions placed on slaves and free blacks in the antebellum period, many slaves in the age of the second slavery ironically experienced increased mobility and were in a relatively advantageous position to make an informal bid for freedom in southern cities.

Upon arrival in Richmond, runaway slaves seem to have had clear ideas about where to go. At the beginning of the century, Richmond encompassed an area of roughly twenty-five city blocks centered on

Main Street and along the docks of the James River. In 1835 the city stretched forty-three blocks west to east and sixteen blocks from the north toward the river. Over the years it grew to be a "classic mid-Atlantic 'walking city,'" with an inner section occupied by industry and commerce. The James Falls to the southwest of the city powered the iron works and flour mills while tobacco manufacturers settled in the southeastern part.[30] In a city that was continuously changing and attracting new residents, visitors, commuters, and suppliers, it was relatively easy to hide, and slave refugees made use of their often extensive networks to do so.

For Richmond, runaway slave ads were often full of assumptions about fugitives being harbored by relatives who lived in the city. Masters knew about the family situations of their slaves, and white business partners and neighbors often did as well. They knew about their slaves' family ties in slavery and freedom, knew the names of relatives, and often even places and street names where runaways might try to hide. Precisely for this reason, the closest relatives were not always the best choice to seek permanent refuge with because masters would know where to look. James, whose owner knew that his mother lived at the cotton factory on the canal, believed him to be there in 1840, and he was caught two weeks later.[31] Over time more and more refugees appeared to prefer hiding out with free blacks, slave acquaintances, or other more distant knots in their networks. Professional networks became more relevant and may have over time even have outstripped the importance of kinship ties in providing refuge. These contacts clearly benefited from the hiring system. Industrialization needed a lot of flexible labor, which led to a high fluctuation of workers in Richmond manufactories. The result was a common intermingling among many laborers of various statuses, free and unfree. The owner of Lilytand, who ran away in Richmond in 1839, believed him to have "acquaintances working at almost every Tobacco factory in the place."[32] In the tobacco sector, the largely uncontrolled black work force created a pool of laborers with shared social and economic interests.

Besides specific acquaintances, in practice virtually the entire African American community functioned as a receiving society for runaway slaves in need. Indeed, Richmond's black population demonstrated remarkable solidarity across status lines, partly because they all shared many of the same fears and hardships. The illegal status of thousands of black Richmonders made all of them vulnerable and constituted a constant threat to their freedom. For free blacks illegally residing in the city, arrest and sentencing to slavery was a haunting possibility, and the prominent presence of the domestic slave trade in the city served as a visible reminder of the fate that could befall them. Forced apprenticeship could also be applied to their children, a condition that shockingly resembled slavery.[33] Consequently, the lives of free illegals and illegal refugees did not diverge as much as one might expect. When free illegals were arrested, they were often unable to pay their jail fees and ended up for years in a slavery-like condition.[34] When illegal refugees were detected, they were also sent back into slavery. The threat of slavery was ever-present to the enslaved, the free and the illegal alike. Family ties among Richmond's black population also transcended the boundaries of slavery and freedom, both legally and illegally, often even under the same roof.

The fragile nature of freedom worked as a connector within African American communities since the very meaning of freedom was framed within experiences of captivity or the threat thereof. Additionally, the strategies of social control that were implemented by whites in the early nineteenth century affected both free and enslaved black people similarly.[35] Since real upward social mobility was hardly achievable for any person of African descent in the Upper South, horizontal solidarities were strengthened as a consequence.[36] The shared legal and customary discriminations black people faced in so many parts of their daily lives and their exclusion from different spheres of society forced them to close ranks and construct their own society below the white society. By applying laws that were written for slaves to free black people as well, whites both excluded and consolidated them. By law and by custom, enslaved and free African American women and men were driven closer together, and social segregation was soon followed by spatial segregation.

Additionally, Enlightenment ideals, most visible in the American, French, and Haitian Revolutions, affected the attitudes of bondspeople toward their inhuman condition. Gradually African Americans came to see themselves as one race, which was to be united in the struggle against their oppressors. David Walker's *Appeal to the Coloured Citizens*, a pamphlet distributed throughout the American North and South, called for the unity of black people, challenged their alleged inferiority, and called for active resistance.[37] Walker was the first to publicly claim that free and unfree black people held common aspirations and in fact were one community. African Americans hardly needed to be convinced that slavery was a moral wrong, but they increasingly regarded it as their collective right to be free, including in antebellum Richmond.

SOCIAL INTEGRATION

In the early decades of the nineteenth century, white and black Richmonders lived mixed within the growing town. Most enslaved women and men either resided in the houses or apartments of their owners or stayed in outbuildings behind them. In Shockoe Creek, Bacon Bottom, and Jackson Ward, shacks popped up in narrow back alleys owned or rented by free blacks.[38] As the free black population grew, however, the residential pattern of the city began to transform. Although Elsa Barkley Brown and Gregg Kimball claim that residential segregation in antebellum Richmond did not assume the proportions of the twentieth century, developments in these directions are clearly recognizable long before the Civil War.[39] From the 1840s on, enslaved and free black city dwellers increasingly crowded together in the northwest and in Shockoe Creek close to the docks. Enslaved tobacco workers who were permitted (or forced) to secure their own boarding lived, for instance, in the African American neighborhood of Shockoe Bottom. Large numbers of them were in fact lodged by free blacks who, by renting out rooms, were able to earn some extra money to make ends meet. Estimations suggest that by 1860 almost half of all Richmond slaves were hired out, the majority of whom also resided separate from their masters. Increasingly, white people who could afford it moved away from the riverbank, where the iron industry blew thick smoke into the air that hung over the city like dark clouds, and up the hills into higher-lying neighborhoods. Most blacks and working-class whites came to live in industrial and low-lying areas, for instance in Oregon Hill, Rocketts, Fulton, Port Mayo, Mount Erin, or Butchertown (a neighborhood of Shockoe Valley).[40] Other blacks moved even further outside of Richmond's city limits. The western and eastern suburbs were not official parts of the city, and it is unlikely that the night watch ever went there, so these neighborhoods, too, attracted large numbers of fugitive slaves. For runaways from slavery, it was indeed easier to blend in with African American communities that lived rather isolated from whites. It provided them with additional anonymity and made detection by coincidence less likely, a condition that favored the building of refugee's social structures.

Segregation also extended into the spiritual sphere. The First African Baptist Church (FABC) was founded in 1841 as an African American branch of the mixed First Baptist Church, from which they were increasingly excluded by white congregants. The FABC was part of a variety of societies and organizations that African Americans in Richmond formed to give structure to their community separate from the white community. Among other things, they functioned as a form of social security—for instance, regarding poor relief—and also naturally provided a vehicle to growing interracial solidarity, autonomy, and eventually freedom.[41] Whites increasingly tried to demarcate themselves and the spaces they inhabited from blacks. Interaction between the two races was socially acceptable only on a master–servant basis, but otherwise they essentially occupied different worlds. To minimize contact between the lower classes especially, in 1846 it was even suggested to remove black people from the penitentiaries. Four years later the city jail followed these recommendations, announcing that "separate apartments ought to be provided for keeping the black + white prisoners + that they should not be kept together as present."[42]

The increasingly segregated spheres of black and white Richmonders might have been desirable for whites, but they were, ironically, even more beneficial for blacks. This allowed them to form their own parallel society, even with organizations and institutions that replaced official jurisdiction and provided safety nets for runaway slaves. As mentioned earlier, African American churches played a vital role in this regard when they assumed some of the functions of social control and mediation that usually fell to governmental authorities. The membership of the FABC grew from 2,100 in 1843 to 3,300 in 1860, and the construction of second, third, and forth African Baptist churches soon followed.[43] The members of the FABC consisted of both legally and illegally free women and men, slaves, and very likely also slave refugees. Several names of persons whose legal status seemed to have been unknown to the institution appear in the minute book of the church. In 1848, for example, one William Jackson passed away, reported as a free man with a question mark next to the word "free," suggesting that he was passing for free but had no papers to prove it, or that the church otherwise had cause to doubt that he was really free. The following year, the legal status column next to Maria Frances Myers' name, who was baptized that year, was simply left blank—church elders either did not ask whether she was a runaway slave or they did not wish to record such damning information in their register. The incomplete information in the church register is more than telling.[44] The boundaries between freedom and bondage were so blurry that not even an institution of trust, whose very existence stood for black resistance and community, knew about the legal status of many of its members. How, then, would city authorities know which black people they found on the streets were free and which were runaway slaves?

ECONOMIC INTEGRATION

It is altogether possible that Richmond municipal authorities essentially "tolerated"—if begrudgingly—the presence of runaway slaves in their city. What is certainly clear is that they generally failed to effectively enforce laws passed by the state of Virginia meant to keep free blacks and slaves separate, and to make slaves more visible to the authorities by requiring all black people to carry passes or free papers at all times. The most plausible reason for an unwritten policy of tolerance is simply that it would have been impossible and undesirable to round up all of the illegal black residents of the city. Not only were their numbers too large but, more importantly, Richmond's economy profited from black labor, and if black people who resided illegally in the city—free or slave—were to be eliminated, then the city's industries would have suffered a major blow.

At the crossroads between capitalist markets, burgeoning industry, and plantation slavery, Virginia's capital city indeed experienced significant economic growth in the antebellum period. Tobacconists and other industrial entrepreneurs were first and foremost businessmen who instrumented slavery as a form of labor.[45] Their concern was to gather sufficient workers to make their businesses run and to pay them as little as possible to gain the highest profits. They knowingly employed illegal black residents, and they did not pay attention to whether some of their employees were actually runaway slaves. It is likely that some might have taken advantage of the vulnerable situation of their illegal employees to exploit them even more. Others simply did not want to know, a situation similar to employers of undocumented migrant workers today. Accordingly, the job market was relatively beneficial for slave refugees who mixed with the free African American community and integrated into the lowest level of the city's labor force. Employment was relatively easy to come by—even if constant employment was, like freedom itself, insecure—and few people of color received wages above subsistence level.

The urban environment provided a variety of jobs for black men. In Richmond, skills in construction, shoemaking, carpentering, plastering, blacksmithing, and barbering were in especially high demand.[46] A slave refugee trained in one or more of these trades who could convincingly pass as a free man was usually able to find a relatively decent job in Richmond. "Mr Benjamin Wallers man Humphry runaway from Mr Thomas Mayberry of Rockbridge County whom he was hired to this year [1836]." Humphry, besides being a hired slave and a "good coarse Shoe maker" also had ties to freedom: "His wifes father lives in Richmond[,] a free man of colour name[d] Jonathan."[47] He possessed the skills to find employment, the experience of mobility as a hired slave, and the personal contacts to seek support. In many sectors labor was so highly in demand that employers did not seem to care where it came from or what the status of their workers was. In ironmaking, blacksmiths were constantly needed, for example.[48] Enslaved Billy must have had good chances to find employment when he escaped from his owner, Jeremiah Hoopers, from King William County in 1835. Having "a Scar on the Side of his neck produced by the cut of an ax & [being] a good Blacksmith by trade[,] said man is Suspected to be about Richmond."[49]

In most southern cities, African American women outnumbered men; Richmond was the great exception. Its economic focus on production and manufacturing attracted large numbers of free and enslaved men to the booming city. Significantly smaller numbers of female slave refugees appear in the official jail records of the city, which reflects the overall trend of more men fleeing slavery. Half of the black male work force worked in factories such as tobacco factories, paper mills, iron works, and flour production on the eve of the Civil War. In 1820 twenty tobacco factories operated in Richmond with some 760 employees. In 1850 nineteen factories employed more than 1,400 workers. Up until

1860, both numbers grew by almost three times. Although tobacco slaves—since the 1840s, mostly men—found themselves under constant surveillance in the factories, they were only regulated by the official slave laws before and after working time.[50] Unskilled black men, the majority of all runaway slaves, served as waiters and worked in white washing, stevedoring, and laboring as common day and factory workers, for which some even attempted to pass as hired slaves rather than free blacks.[51]

Besides tobacco factories, the coal pits (from where many slaves absconded) and railroad construction provided an opportunity for slave refugees and other illegals to find employment by the midcentury. Railroads, which were desperate for labor, were a dangerous occupation with a relatively high death toll, so slaveholders were discouraged from hiring their slaves out to them. For the construction companies, it was more efficient to employ free black and white workers because, in the event of accidental death, they did not have to reimburse any owners for loss of property. A black man "bearing the classic name of Quintus, to which had been added the appellation Terry . . . who has lived here for four years without a register, stated that he was employed by the Central Railroad Company" in 1860.[52] Whether Quintus was illegally in the state as a free black or was a slave refugee is unclear, but his case illustrates that it was perfectly possible for any group of illegals to find work even without showing any sort of register or freedom papers. Other bondspeople turned the tables on this strategy. An anonymous male slave was hired out in Richmond in 1854 and while working as a hired slave "actually pretended that he was a free man and made a contract as such with some man of Richmond County to hire himself to him for a few month" the year after.[53] This slave made provisions for a future escape attempt, pretending to be free. His long-term planning shows how difficult such an endeavor was and how thoroughly he prepared for it.

In line with general demographic trends of the fugitive community, runaway women gravitated to the city in lower numbers, but their presence was nevertheless important to the Richmond economy. Most tried to find work as domestic servants. The nature of domestic work was oppressive, with long hours of compulsory presence, but the wage was usually constant, and the work was not dependent on seasonal fluctuations.[54] Domestic servants, on the one hand, were more exposed to the risk of being detected due to their physical closeness to their (usually white) employers. This happened to Milly, who was "supposed to be in Richmond," where she had been hired in the household of one Fleming Griffiths. She fled and was suspected of hiring herself to another employer as a free woman.[55] One the other hand, the private sphere they worked in also provided them a certain degree of protection since their work was performed mostly behind closed doors rather than out in public spaces, and their employers were unlikely to turn them over to the authorities. Another large employment sector for many free and enslaved black women was laundry, a physically arduous but independent line of work. Finally, African American women in the city provided services for the working classes. Factory slaves received boarding money, for example, and women, free (even white women) and enslaved, provided all kinds of services to help them get through the week. They ran informal kitchens called "cook shops" and sublet lodging space to lower-class men and women at least since the 1840s in every part of the city. Others engaged in prostitution.[56]

In the city, black women were confronted with major hardships just to make ends meet. The racial division of the labor market was for them further aggravated by gender hierarchies that placed them in a doubly disadvantaged situation. This was a time when white Richmonders expressed grave concerns about the working and living conditions of poor white women, many of whom could barely make a living as seamstresses or laundresses.[57] If white women had such a difficult time, then one can only imagine the struggles that African American women—especially those who lived in the city illegally—faced. It was an arduous life. A mother without the financial support of a husband had to literally work round the clock to make ends meet for her family, and overwork took its toll on many women. Birth statistics reveal their precarious economic and health situation. Among city dwellers, free African Americans had the lowest relative number of children.[58] Despite such hardships, it was possible to survive, and many runaway slave women succeeded in creating lives of permanent freedom for themselves, however marginal or poor. "First rate Seamstress" Cicily Page was wanted by her owners from Williamsburg seven years after she had left them. She had successfully blended in with the free African American community in Richmond and was even thought to have two children.[59]

Many industrialists and other businessmen saw advantages in black work, and the demand for slaves in particular commonly exceeded the supply. In some phases of the economic cycle this was very noticeable. In January 1855 the annual hire for farm hands suddenly outran the hire for factory slaves, and many slave owners decided to shift their human capital to the countryside. Trends like this were conducive to slave refugees passing themselves off as hired slaves to gain employment in a tobacco factory or mill. Naturally, the labor market did not only react to macro developments, and work opportunities also depended on local customs. Around Christmas and well into January, manufacturers usually closed businesses, and free and enslaved workers were increasingly found on the streets, both celebrating their days off and negotiating their terms for the following year.[60] This was a welcome opportunity for slave refugees in Richmond to blend in with the black community and to establish important business connections.

DIVERGING INTERESTS

Even if antebellum Richmond employers implicitly accommodated runaway slaves by employing them without asking questions, municipal authorities did feel increasing pressure from the state and surrounding counties to tackle the fugitive slave problem, although they were generally incapable of locating or rounding up a vast majority of runaways. Here we see the diverging interests of Virginia's rural and urban elite regarding the matter played out. The capital city's political class was composed of merchants, industrialists, and financiers whose interests encompassed the promotion of the finance sector, industry, and infrastructure. As stated above, private industries benefited largely from cheap black labor, including that of runaway slaves, and the power structure was such that they exercised considerable influence on local political measures. (Individual businessmen also made use of political offices in order to ensure their business endeavors.[61]) The interests of the rural slaveholders and the urban slaveholding middle class, however, differed sharply from these local industrial interests, and by a certain point they could no longer be ignored by city authorities. Especially for small slaveholders, who ran manageable farms with just a few slaves, or urban masters with only one or two enslaved servants, the loss of a slave meant a significant financial reversal. As the class of small slaveholders grew, they obtained a louder voice in legislative bodies and demanded that slave flight be tackled. A slew of stricter laws were passed. To name just a few, legislators in the 1850s revamped their requirement for free blacks to always carry papers in public and for slaves to always carry a pass, with the intention to effectively distinguish between the two groups. They also outlawed the consumption of alcohol, self-hiring, and boarding out for slaves. Free blacks, who were seen as the prime facilitators of slave flight in the city, saw their right to assembly significantly curtailed and were subjected to a law that declared any gathering of more than five persons illegal.[62] One of the most draconian bills penalized the harboring of runaway slaves. Surprisingly, there was never any discussion about enacting a law that would have forbidden the employment of somebody else's slave without their consent—the urban industrial class presumably prevented any such policy.[63]

A great many of the ordinances that were supposed to protect slave property and prevent slave flight proved unenforceable, however, just like the manumission law of 1806. Blacks challenged the laws, but some whites also proved openly accommodating and supportive of the plight of black people, including runaways. A few whites' liberal attitudes formed an obstacle for the enforcement of certain laws, and the changing nature of slavery itself proved incompatible with these strict legal codes.[64] White opposition to the most draconian fugitive slave laws in Richmond alarmed the political elites, as they wished to keep white and black laborers pitted against each other. This was even more important as more and more poor immigrant laborers began to move to Richmond from Europe. Members of the lower classes theoretically shared common social and economic interests, and although their composition was complex and in nature heterogeneous, city authorities adopted measures to artificially drive the working classes apart.[65] Consorting among the lower classes was legislated against by prohibiting the maintenance of cook shops and grog shops that served liquor to African Americans and by encouraging residential segregation.[66]

Increasingly alarmed about the economic losses suffered as more and more enslaved people attempted to escape bondage, state authorities even enacted policies that were meant to make up for the loss by targeting free blacks to perform forced labor. Governor Randolph equated laborers with black people when he claimed in 1820 that "great loss is unavoidably sustained by individuals from the encouragement and facility given to secret pillage, by the numerous emancipated people of colour and their descendants every where to be found among us."[67] Different groups came up with different ideas to counteract the decrease of the population forcedly put to work for them. Citizens from Buckingham County communicated their fear of black people in 1831 and at the same time followed up on Thomas Jefferson's plan to continuously be able to exploit their labor. They petitioned to put newborns to industrious occupation until they came of proper age, and then deport them.[68] Those in power, however, had a more subtle plan. In a revealing study, Carey Latimore analyzed how legally manumitted but illegally (in the state) residing free African Americans and their offspring in Richmond were systematically tracked in times of labor shortage, jailed, and hired out for exceptionally low wages in order to pay off their jail fees.[69] The Society of Friends observed these procedures in 1844. It warned that free blacks without papers were regularly apprehended, jailed, and sold, and their children held in perpetual service. The society claimed that the punishment was disproportionate to the offence committed.[70] These political measures benefited the social group of small-scale slaveholders, small merchants, and middle-class craftsmen who either could not afford to buy or hire slaves or were disproportionally affected by slave flight. Such measures may have constituted a legal assault on the free black population of Richmond (and Virginia), but in practice, from the 1840s on, efforts by the city authorities to genuinely try to keep black people out of Richmond proved half-hearted at best and tended to spike during periods of acute fear or frustration among white residents.[71]

In 1851, for example, when the suffrage right was further extended to include white propertyless men, white society became more heterogeneous, and every group had to be given the impression that the political elite cared for its interests. Joseph Mayo was in 1853 the first popularly elected mayor of Richmond. Under his administration, free illegal blacks were systematically arrested, jailed, and sentenced to forced labor. Besides providing cheap labor for private and public employers, these show trials also demonstrated to the public that the mayor was acting against the large illegal free black population that constituted the economic threat to practically every social group that had the right to vote, except for the industrialists—who largely corresponded with the city's political elite.

A LIFE IN ILLEGALITY

Clandestine social life occurred in back alleys, shops, and taverns, often at night. Alcoholic beverages were consumed, and illegal card games like faro were played, mixing members of the lower classes of all ethnicities and legal statuses, including runaway slaves. These meeting points were usually located in alleys or were hidden venues altogether and naturally also included brothels. That these interethnic meeting places were an open secret becomes clear when reading that even Frederick Law Olmsted knew about them when he was just visiting the city for a short time. He wrote: "A great many low eating, and, I should think, drinking shops are frequented chiefly by the negroes. Dancing and other amusements are carried on in these at night."[72] William and Wellington Hawkins, members of the First African Baptist Church, were charged with visiting a "low house when dancing was going on," as were two other male members, in December 1857.[73] Taverns were not only a meeting point for men but also constituted places of networking for women. "Rebeca belonging to Jns Smith[,] Gingerbread Colour[,] tall and slim," was searched for by the Richmond police in November 1843. She had "been in the habit of washing in the back of the Bell Tavern" and it is very likely that there she established ties that benefited her attempt to escape bondage.[74]

Slave refugees sought shelter in all those places where black people were living and moved within all spaces where black people were moving. They worked in a variety of professions and occupations, lived within their communities, formed social ties, and went to church. They also married and were buried in black cemeteries. All these activities forced these self-emancipators to walk the streets and to sojourn in public places, which gave them a high visibility. Hence, slave refugees were often seen in market places, in the city center, near factories, at the river basin and on the docks, or at the bridge. In order to secure their fragile freedom, they had to be careful, had to assimilate, and had to look and act like they were free. Being members of a suppressed class, they faced serious social discrimination and economic exploitation, just like the free black population. Since free African Americans without registration were occasionally and, from the 1850s on, more systematically taken up, refugees from slavery sometimes ended up in the police guard's net as "by-catch." William Green was apprehended in 1841 and jailed for "going at large" and for "want of his free papers"; it later turned out that he was a runaway. The clandestine lives of refugees were thus theoretically always in jeopardy. As Latimore has pointed out, however, the local police kept track of parts of the undocumented free population to round them up any time they wanted, but it does not seem that slave refugees were similarly targeted in the same way.[75] Still, freedom remained fragile for both groups of illegals.

Although Richmond had a police guard and a night watch that operated during curfew hours, its small law enforcement units proved largely inefficient in a city whose population was over twenty thousand after 1840, almost half of whom were of African descent. Yet slaveholders constantly turned to the Richmond police to have them on the lookout for their missing slaves. And although some were apprehended, this happened on a much smaller scale than one might expect. Small slaveholders, the one group that should have complained about the ineffective legislative measures and the slack political and executive engagement, remained largely silent. Occasionally a master would lose his patience, like A. B. Shelton, whose runaway slave Armstead Meckins was not taken up, although "he has been seen every day since" he ran off in February 1844. To incentivize the police, Shelton offered a reward of ten dollars only if Meckins would be brought back within the remaining two weeks of the month. Otherwise he would only pay the legal fees.[76]

Masters usually applied private efforts, if any, to get their human property back. Some would invest in runaway slave advertisements that ran months or even years, while others tried to chase after their fugitives themselves. When two of William Cobbs' slaves, Tom and Ned, made their escape very much to their owner's surprise, Cobbs' manager asked him if he wanted to come from Lynchburg to Kanawha Salines to search for them himself.[77] Others formed joint ventures like the Society for the Prevention of the Absconding and Abduction of Slaves, active in Richmond and surrounding counties from 1833 into the 1840s. The efforts of the society, interestingly, focused on "the detection and recovery of such as shall have absconded or been abducted beyond the limits of the State," not on those who absconded within Virginia itself. Slave owners themselves volunteered for watches on the ward to detect possible fugitives in the act. Samuel S. Sanders did so in 1833, for example.[78] The owner of a tobacco factory, Sanders lost at least seven slaves between 1836 and 1843; three of them he suspected to be hiding in the Richmond, another one was seen in the city afterward.[79]

CONCLUSIONS

The exertion of the Society for the Prevention of the Absconding of Slaves was channeled toward the northern states. Measures to track down slave refugees in Richmond never went beyond the individual efforts of small slaveholders and were only slackly performed by the authorities. Middle-class slave owners were a powerless group compared to the large-scale slaveholding aristocrats, who constituted the highest political authorities in the state of Virginia, and the local elites, who were represented by the upcoming class of financiers, merchants, and industrialists. Toward the end of the antebellum era it seemed that middle-class entrepreneurs and small merchants were suited by the assignment of cheap laborers recruited from the undocumented black class. Their anger over the fugitive slave problem was directed at the North rather than at the runaways in their own state; in other words, they were distracted by what they perceived to be outsiders (i.e., northern abolitionists) enticing their slaves away to free soil to the extent that they underestimated how many slaves in fact sought refuge within the urban South itself.

Factory owners and other Richmond employers took advantage of illegal workers since they had a stake in a scattered working class and suffered from labor shortage most of the time. Unsurprisingly, those in power were the ones who gained most from this division, from the tolerance of the undocumented illegal black residents, and from the presence of slave refugees. But the latter also benefited from the situation. By hiring out their slaves and allowing them to live largely autonomously, many slave owners contributed their share to preparing their bondspeople for a life in freedom. Networks, knowledge, and mobility enabled them to taste freedom and to plan their escapes. Not all enslaved African Americans were equally conditioned to make it as refugees, and significant distinctions are recognizable concerning professional skills, gender, and family status. Cities like Richmond with a high grade of urbanization and increasing spatial segregation provided spaces unknown to slaveholders, or at least places they did not enter. There slave refugees could live in public. The uniquely high numbers of undocumented African American residents in Richmond, and in Virginia in general, gave them an advantage in blending in. Networks of free and enslaved relatives and acquaintances as well as economic services provided by lower-class blacks and whites made this possible.

Although the lives of laborers were arduous and slave refugees constantly faced the risk of unemployment and social and physical shortcomings due to their challenging socioeconomic conditions, the consequences of their illegal freedom resulted in lives that were not that different from the lives of free African Americans. They could find work but remained poor. Racism, economic discrimination, social exclusion, and the negation of political participation were realities their counterparts in the northern states were also exposed to. When freedom could be achieved in southern states in proximity to their loved ones, many freedom seekers opted for staying. Illegal freedom in the middle of slavery was possible. Just like Richmond, Virginia, there were other cities and towns in the antebellum southern states that were beacons of freedom for slave refugees. Their social experiences vary from place to place depending on legal frameworks, economic factors, and social developments. Economically thriving and demographically growing urban centers were the most welcoming places of refuge. The clandestine lives and strategies of success of these freedom seekers depended on them keeping a low profile, making them a largely invisible if important segment of antebellum Richmond's population.

NOTES

1. Labeling these people as slave refugees demarcates them from the judicially charged term "fugitives" (people who abscond from a righteous condition), which bears the connotation of desertion and reflects the perspective of the slave owners. "Refugees" underscores the urgency of their escape from a threatening condition and puts a focus on their social experiences as illegal residents.

2. *Journal of the House of Delegates of the Commonwealth of Virginia, Begun and Held at the Capitol, In the City of Richmond, on Monday, the Fifth Day of December, One Thousand Eight Hundred and Thirty-Six* (Richmond: Thomas Ritchie, 1836), 7–8, Library of Virginia (hereafter LVA), Richmond, Va.

3. Seth Barton, *The Randolph Epistles* (Washington, 1850), General Collections, Virginia Historical Society (hereafter VHS), Richmond, Va.

4. Leon Litwack, *North of Slavery: The Negro in the Free States, 1790–1860* (Chicago: University of Chicago Press, 1961); Daniel G. Hill, *Freedom Seekers: Blacks in Early Canada* (Toronto: Stodaart, 1992); Lerry Gara, *The Liberty Line:*

The Legend of the Underground Railroad (Lexington: University Press of Kentucky, 1996); Gordon Barker, *Fugitive Slaves and the Unfinished American Revolution: Eight Cases, 1848–1856* (Jefferson, N.C.: McFarland, 2013); Rosalie Schwartz, *Across de Rio to Freedom: U.S. Negroes in Mexico* (El Paso: Texas Western Press, 1975); Sarah E. Cornell, "Citizens of Nowhere: Fugitive Slaves and Free African Americans in Mexico, 1833–1857," *Journal of American History* 100, no. 2 (2013): 351–74; and Sean Kelley, "Mexico in His Head: Slavery and the Texas-Mexican Border, 1810–1860," *Journal of Social History* 37, no. 3 (2004): 709–23.

    5. John Hope Franklin and Loren Schweninger, *Runaway Slaves: Rebels on the Plantation* (Oxford: Oxford University Press, 1999), xiv; and Peter Kolchin, *American Slavery 1619–1877* (New York: Penguin Books, 1995), 158.

    6. William A. Link, *Roots of Secession: Slavery and Politics in Antebellum Virginia* (Chapel Hill: University of North Carolina Press, 2003), 106.

    7. Franklin and Schweninger, *Runaway Slaves*, 145–46. Other historians who take permanent urban refuge from slavery into account include Leonard Curry, *The Free Black in Urban America, 1800–1850: The Shadow of the Dream* (Chicago: University of Chicago Press, 1981), 4; David R. Goldfield, "Black Life in Old South Cities," in *Before Freedom Came: African-American Life in the Antebellum South*, ed. Edward D. C. Campbell Jr. and Kym S. Rice, (Richmond, Va.: Museum of the Confederacy, 1991), 140; Christopher Phillips, *Freedom's Port: The African American Community of Baltimore, 1790–1860* (Urbana: University of Illinois Press, 1997), 66–73; and Michael Zeuske, *Sklavereien, Emanzipationen und atlantische Weltgeschichte: Essays über Mikrogeschichten, Sklaven, Globalisierungen und Rassismus* (Leipzig: Leipziger Universitätsverlag, 2002), 146.

    8. Sylviane Diouf does account for permanent fugitives from slavery in the slaveholding South but focuses on those who sought freedom in wilderness areas choosing autonomy before integration into existing societies. Her approach therefore differs substantially. Sylviane Diouf, *Slavery's Exiles: The Story of the American Maroons* (New York: New York University Press, 2014).

    9. See chapter 5, by Damian Pargas, in the present volume, "Seeking Freedom in the Midst of Slavery: Fugitive Slaves in the South."

    10. Kostas Vlassopoulos, "Does Slavery Have a History? The Consequences of a Global Approach," *Journal of Global Slavery* 1, no. 1 (2016): 5.

    11. Daybook of the Richmond Police Guard, 1834–1844, Alderman Library, Special Collections, University of Virginia (hereafter UVA), transcribed by Leni Ashmore Sorensen (Ph.D. diss., College of William & Mary, 1996); and Richmond (Va.), City Sergeant, Section 1, Register, 1841–1846, VHS.

    12. *The Compiler*, February 24, 1835; Legislative Petitions, December 4, 1822, LVA, in Race and Slavery Petitions Project, Series 1, Legislative Petitions; and Daybook of the Richmond Police Guard, 1834–1844, August 8, 1842, UVA.

    13. The total population of the city grew to be 38,000 in 1860 with 62 percent native and foreign-born whites. J. D. B. De Bow, *Statistical View of the United States . . . Being a Compendium of the Seventh Census* (Washington, D.C.: Beverly

Tucker, 1854), 398–99; *Population of the United States in 1860: Compiled from the Original Returns of the Eighth Census* (Washington, D.C.: Government Printing Office, 1864), xiii, xxxii, in Gregg Kimball, *American City, Southern Place: A Cultural History of Antebellum Richmond* (Athens: University of Georgia Press, 2003), 31; and U.S. Bureau of the Census, Population, 1800–1860, in Midori Takagi, *"Rearing Wolves to Our Own Destruction": Slavery in Richmond, Virginia, 1782–1865* (Charlottesville: University Press of Virginia, 2002), 17.

14. Frederick Law Olmsted, *A Journey in the Seaboard Slave States; With Remarks on Their Economy* (New York: Dix and Edwards, 1856), 51; Robert Russell, *North America, Its Agriculture and Climate, Containing Observations on the Agriculture and Climate of Canada, the United States, and the Island of Cuba* (Edinburgh: Adam and Charles Black, 1857), 151; and Richard C. Wade, *Slavery in the Cities: The South 1820–1860* (New York: Oxford University Press, 1964), 16–17.

15. Executive Communications, The Speaker of the House of Delegates, December 4, 1820, LVA.

16. General Assembly, "An ACT to amend the several laws concerning slaves" (1806), transcribed from *The Statutes at Large of Virginia, from October Session 1792, to December Session 1806*, ed. Samuel Shepherd (Richmond: Samuel Shepherd, 1836), 252.

17. Hundreds of legal petitions to the Virginia governor asked for exceptions from this law. Because cases like these were unwinnable without the support of white acquaintances willing to pledge for them, those who dared to submit a petition presented only a small fraction of illegal free blacks. Granted petitions were the exception. Legislative Petitions, LVA.

18. Officially, any person with at least one quarter of African blood was considered to be black. However, since genealogy and physical appearance often do not overlap, the legal definition of slavery stumbled. Thomas Morris, *Southern Slavery and the Law, 1619–1860* (Chapel Hill: University of North Carolina Press, 1996), 22; and Ira Berlin, *Slaves without Masters: The Free Negro in the Antebellum South* (New York: Pantheon Books, 1974), 97.

19. Carey H. Latimore IV, "A Step Closer to Slavery? Free African Americans, Industrialization, Social Control and Residency in Richmond City, 1850–1860," *Slavery & Abolition* 33, no. 1 (2012): 124–25.

20. Ended Chancery Court Cases, June 10, 1847, LVA, in Race and Slavery Petitions Project, Series 2, County Court Petitions, University of North Carolina at Greensboro.

21. Berlin, *Slaves without Masters*, 93–94.

22. House of Delegates, Senate & Virginia State Papers, Calendar of Virginia State Papers and Other Manuscripts from January 1, 1799, to December 31, 1807; Preserved in the Capitol, at Richmond, ed. H. W. Flournoy, vol. 9 (Richmond, 1890), October 1800, 162, LVA.

23. Calvin Schermerhorn, *Money over Mastery, Family over Freedom. Slavery in the Antebellum Upper South* (Baltimore: Johns Hopkins University Press, 2011),

207–8. Other severe legislative intensifications followed after David Walker's *Appeal to the Coloured Citizens*, a pamphlet distributed throughout the American North and South in 1829, and after the Nat Turner rebellion in 1831.

24. Solomon Bayley, *A Narrative of Some Remarkable Incidents in the Life of Solomon Bayley, Formerly a Slave in the State of Delaware, North America; Written by Himself, and Published for His Benefit; to Which Are Prefixed, a Few Remarks by Robert Hurnard* (London: Harvey and Darton, 1825), 4.

25. General Assembly, Session Records, Miscellaneous Petitions, November 1825–January 1826; House Committee Reports, Propositions and Grievances, Miscellaneous, North Carolina Department of Archives and History, Raleigh, North Carolina, in Race and Slavery Petitions Project, Series 1, Legislative Petitions.

26. Daniel Blake Smith, "Family Dynasties," in *The New Encyclopedia of Southern Culture*, vol. 13, ed. Nancy Bercaw and Ted Ownby (Chapel Hill: University of North Carolina Press, 2009), 103.

27. Slavery became increasingly integrated into the capitalist market and came to work hand in hand with industrial production. As opposed to the "first slavery," when colonialism and slavery were interdependent and the latter only took place at the margins of the empire, now it moved into the core of society. Dale W. Tomich, *Through the Prism of Slavery: Labor, Capital, and World Economy* (Lanham, Md.: Rowman & Littlefield, 2004), 57–61.

28. John J. Zaborney, *Slaves for Hire: Renting Enslaved Laborers in Antebellum Virginia* (Baton Rouge: Louisiana State University Press, 2012), 11–14; and Morris, *Slavery and Law*, 132.

29. Calvin Schermerhorn demurred that slave hiring usually meant dislocation, attributing the often positively depicted image a second face. Schermerhorn, *Money over Mastery*, 107.

30. Leni Ashmore Sorensen, "Absconded: Fugitive Slaves in the Daybook of the Richmond Police Guard, 1834–1844" (Ph.D. diss., College of William and Mary, 2005), 20; and Elisa Barkley Brown and Gregg Kimball, "Mapping the Terrain of Black Richmond," *Journal of Urban History* 21, no. 3 (1995): 297.

31. Daybook of the Richmond Police Guard, 1834–1844, April 30, 1840, UVA.

32. Daybook of the Richmond, Virginia Police Guard, 1834–1844, April 22, 1839, UVA.

33. Goldfield, "Black Life," 125; and Barbara Fields, *Slavery and Freedom on the Middle Ground: Maryland During the Nineteenth Century* (New Haven, Conn.: Yale University Press, 1985), 35.

34. See Latimore, "Closer to Slavery."

35. Sidney Chalhoub, *Visões da Liberdade: Uma história das últimas décadas da escravidão na Corte* (Sao Paulo: Companhia das Letras, 2011), 29; and Sidney Chalhoub, "The Precariousness of Freedom in a Slave Society (Brazil in the Nineteenth Century)," *International Review of Social History* 56, no. 3 (2011): 409.

36. This is the reverse interpretation of Chalhoub's claim that, in nineteenth-century Brazil, slavery did offer opportunities for social mobility, which had

negative effects on horizontal solidarities due to its competitive nature. Chalhoub, "Precariousness of Freedom," 412.

37. David Walker, *Walker's Appeal, in Four Articles; Together with a Preamble, to the Coloured Citizens of the World, but in Particular, and Very Expressly, to Those of the United States of America, Written in Boston, State of Massachusetts, September 28, 1829* (Boston: Revised and Published by David Walker, 1830).

38. Marie Tyler-McGraw and Gregg D Kimball, *In Bondage and Freedom: Antebellum Black Life in Richmond, Virginia* (Richmond, Va.: Valentine Museum, 1988), 12.

39. Brown and Kimball, "Mapping the Terrain," 302.

40. Takagi, *Rearing Wolves*, 96–97; Schermerhorn, *Money over Mastery*, 135, 147; and Kimball, *American City*, 74–75.

41. Kimball, *American City*, 28, 126; and Albert J. Raboteau, *Slave Religion: The "Invisible Institution" in the Antebellum South* (New York: Oxford University Press, 1978), 197. Despite of the remarkable autonomy, it was not until 1866 that the FABC was led by a black pastor.

42. House of Delegates, Senate & Virginia State Papers, Annual Messages, Journal of the House of Delegates of Virginia, Session 1846–47 (Richmond: Manuel Shepherd, 1846), Speech by W. M. Smith, LVA; and Hustings Court Suit Papers, Ended Causes, City Jail-Report Concerning, August 15, 1850, LVA.

43. Raboteau, *Slave Religion*, 197.

44. In the row behind the name, the church clerk would note whether a member was free; when a member was enslaved, the clerk would write the name of the owner. In surprisingly many cases, the row behind the name was either left blank or doubts were made visible by a question mark. First African Baptist Church (Richmond, Virginia) Minute Books, 1841–1930, July 2, 1848; May 12, 1849, LVA. Many thanks to Gregg Kimball for making these sources available to me.

45. Kimball, *American City*, 120.

46. Goldfield, "Black Life," 133; and Berlin, *Slaves without Masters*, 238.

47. Daybook of the Richmond Police Guard, 1834–1844, August 16, 1836, UVA.

48. S. Sidney Bradford, "The Negro Ironworker in Ante Bellum Virginia," in *The Making of Black America*, vol. I: *The Origins of Black Americans*, ed. August Meier and Elliott Rudwick (New York: Atheneum, 1971), 139.

49. Daybook of the Richmond Police Guard, 1834–1844, January 28, 1835, UVA.

50. Berlin, *Slaves without Masters*, 219; Takagi, *Rearing Wolves*, 11, 26; and Suzanne Gehring Schnittman, "Slavery in Virginia's Urban Tobacco Industry-1840–1860" (Ph.D. diss., University of Rochester, 1986), v.

51. Berlin, *Slaves without Masters*, 219.

52. *Daily Dispatch*, November 28, 1860.

53. County Court Chancery Papers, February 19, 1855, LVA, in Race and Slavery Petitions Project, Series 2, County Court Petitions, University of North Carolina at Greensboro.

54. Seth Rockman, *Scraping By: Wage Labor, Slavery, and Survival in Early Baltimore* (Baltimore: Johns Hopkins University Press, 2009), 140.

55. *Charleston Courier*, January 4, 1830.

56. Schermerhorn, *Money over Mastery*, 139, 147.

57. Rockman, *Scraping By*, 140; and Michael Douglas Naragon, "Ballots, Bullets, and Blood: The Political Transformation of Richmond, Virginia, 1850–1874" (Ph.D. diss., University of Pittsburgh, 1996), 48.

58. Curry, *Free Black in Urban America*, 12; Tera W. Hunter, "The 'Brotherly Love' for which This City is Proverbial Should Extend to All," in *The African American Urban Experience: Perspectives from the Colonial Period to the Present*, ed. Joe W. Trotter, Earl Lewis and Tera W. Hunter (New York: Palgrave MacMillan, 2004), 80; and Naragon, "Ballots, Bullets, and Blood," 48.

59. Daybook of the Richmond Police Guard, 1834–1844, May 22, 1838, UVA.

60. Kimball, *American City*, 29–30, 165. The famous Tredegar Iron Works was not an option in this context because enterpriser Joseph Anderson meticulously monitored his staff. Even in times when he experimented with enslaved employees, Anderson opposed boarding out.

61. David R. Goldfield, *Urban Growth in the Age of Sectionalism: Virginia, 1847–1861* (Baton Rouge: Louisiana State University Press, 1977), 34; Naragon, "Ballots, Bullets, and Blood," 3, 11; and Steven J. Hoffman, *Race, Class and Power in the Building of Richmond, 1870–1820* (Jefferson, N.C.: McFarland, 2004), 18–21.

62. "'An Ordinance Concerning Negroes': The Richmond Black Code (1859)," in *A Richmond Reader*, ed. Maurice Duke and Daniel P. Jordan (n.p., 1974), 107–13; and Joshua D. Rothman, *Notorious in the Neighborhood: Sex and Families across the Color Line in Virginia, 1787–1861* (Chapel Hill: University of North Carolina Press, 2003), 120.

63. Exceptions are the disputes about the fugitive slaves being harbored and employed on board of ships and vessels. This reflects the concern about slaves attempting to flee to the northern states.

64. Loren Schweninger, "The Underside of Slavery: The Internal Economy, Self-Hire, and Quasi-Freedom in Virginia, 1780–1865," *Slavery and Abolition* 12 (1991): 3.

65. Peter Linebaugh and Markus Rediker, *Many-Headed Hydra: Sailors, Slaves, Commoners, and the Hidden History of the Revolutionary Atlantic* (Boston: Beacon, 2000), 319.

66. "'An Ordinance Concerning Negroes,'" 107–13; and Rothman, *Notorious in the Neighborhood*, 120.

67. Thomas Mann Randolph, The Speaker of the House of Delegates, Executive Communications, December 4, 1820, LVA.

68. Legislative Petitions, Petition by Citizens from Buckingham County, December 13, 1831, LVA.

69. Latimore, "Closer to Slavery."

70. Legislative Petitions, Petition by Society of Friends, December 31, 1844, LVA.

71. Latimore, "Closer to Slavery," 121.

72. Olmsted, *Seaboard Slave States*, 52.

73. First African Baptist Church (Richmond, Virginia) Minute Books, 1841–1930, December 1857, LVA.

74. Daybook of the Richmond Police Guard, 1834–1844, November 10, 1843, UVA.

75. Latimore, "Closer to Slavery," 128.

76. Daybook of the Richmond Police Guard, 1834–1844, February 15, 1844, UVA.

77. William Cobbs Letters, 1827–1841, Personal Papers Collection, August 15, 1827, LVA.

78. Society for the Prevention of the Absconding and Abduction of Slaves, Minutes 1833–49, Manuscripts, VHS.

79. Daybook of the Richmond Police Guard, 1834–1844, June 29, 1836; July 23, 1836; February 13, 1837; May 11, 1841; August 11, 1841; June 16, 1843, UVA.

7

Borderland Maroons

SYLVIANE A. DIOUF

John Sally "runned away an' didn' never come back. Didn' go no place either. Stayed right 'roun' de plantation."[1] Like Sally, most maroons did not look for freedom in remote locations; instead they settled in the borderlands of farms and plantations. If not caught by men and dogs, and depending on their health, survival skills, and their families' and friends' level of involvement, they could live there for years. These men and women have become the most invisible maroons although their (white and black) contemporaries were well aware of their existence. As is true for most maroons, their lives have remained partially unknown, but several individuals who later got out of the South or had loved ones who went to the woods described their experiences in autobiographies and memoirs. In addition, detailed and intimate information about their existence can be found in the recollections of the formerly enslaved men and women gathered by the Works Progress Administration. Some were former maroons themselves, others were their kin, acquaintances, and protectors.

Pieced together, these stories offer a striking portrait of a unique population and delineate how and why one became a borderland maroon; who the men, women, and children who settled by the plantations were; and what skills they needed to master in order to survive in the woods.

FAMILY CONNECTIONS

South, North, Indian territories, the periphery or the hearts of cities, remote swamps, or the edges of their own habitations—it was not always immediately apparent to slaveholders where their escaped workers were headed or whether they planned on being away for a few days, a few weeks, or hoped to remain at large forever. In other words, it was difficult to tell whether the absconders were truants, maroons, or runaways. Unless one was confronted with a habitual fugitive whose routine was known, or someone whose tentative destination could be guessed, it was often assumed that the escapee would go to the woods and stay there for a short time. Absconders were thus often treated as truants before some were reclassified as runaways headed for a southern city or a free state. However, when the absence continued, the individual would be labeled an outlier (or still referred to as a runaway) if known to be "lurking about" or "skulking" in the neighborhood.

It goes without saying that the people who chose to settle close to the farms and plantations had crucial reasons for doing so. Frederick Law Olmsted's conversation with an overseer indicates one of their major motivations. The overseer said of the runaways he knew, "They almost always kept in the neighborhood, because they did not like to go where they could not sometimes get back and see their families."[2] When people left—for Spanish Florida, Texas, Mexico, or the North, depending on geography and time—they did so with little hope of seeing their loved ones again. The latter, in turn, could spend a lifetime wondering if their relative had made it to safety or died trying. To sever the relations that sustained an otherwise dreadful life was a difficult, heart-wrenching decision both for those who remained and for those who left. Runaways accepted this as the unavoidable price of their desire to be free, but for others the priorities were reversed. They escaped to avoid being separated from their relatives or to reconstitute their families.

Newspaper ads are a good tool to map this geography of love, migration, and defiance, but they must be treated with care. When a slaveholder wrote that he "suspected" or "believed" that someone was going back to a relative or spouse, he made it clear that he was not fully certain this was the case. That some people had other plans in mind is a given; still, slaveholders made sure they kept track of family connections as best they could because they knew that reunification was a strong motivating factor in desertions. In colonial South Carolina, apparently four times as many escapees were said to have been looking for relations rather than trying to pass for free; 66 percent of the male runaways and 80 percent of the females were thought to have run off to relatives or spouses.[3] In colonial Chesapeake, between 29 percent (Virginia) and 54 percent (Southern Maryland) of the runaways were expected to be heading to their relatives or acquaintances.[4] In North Carolina (1775–1840), 57 percent of 1,380 advertised individuals for whom a destination was provided were believed to be attempting reunification while only 7 percent were thought to be going to a free state.[5] Reflecting on these numbers, historian Philip Morgan has concluded, "A considerable number of advertised runaways were said to be visiting acquaintances, friends, or relatives."[6] In reality, they were not "said" to be "visiting" because that terminology was not used. Among the thousands of notices gathered from New York, New Jersey, Pennsylvania, Georgia, Virginia, Maryland, and South Carolina newspapers, the word "visit" appears only five times.[7]

Morgan equates what he considers visits with petit marronage: people went to see a loved one in the neighborhood and came back after a few days. These activities, illegal as they were, were expected and did not translate into manhunts and notices. However, when slaveholders posted ads stressing that runaways were thought to be going to relatives, especially in distant places, not only did they not use the term "visit" but the mere fact of advertising for their capture shows that they did not expect them to come back quickly and voluntarily. To be sure, occasionally someone would go see a spouse faraway, as did a man from Virginia who visited his wife in Alabama and returned, a transgression for which he received two hundred blows with a paddle.[8] But was a family visit Lucy's objective when she left Saint Thomas Parish in South Carolina with her four children, the older aged eight, to join her sisters in Georgia?[9] Or the goal of a man, his pregnant wife, and their two sons, aged five and two and a half, when they departed from Georgia supposedly headed for "Carolina neighboring plantations," where the man had "a great number of relations and acquaintances"?[10] The parents took enormous risks—including being sold separately if caught—with two small children in tow and one on the way. They went away equipped with clothes, provisions, and blankets for what could only be a long stay. The stakes were just too high for them to envision a simple visit to relatives, followed by a return home. There were, indeed, visits meant to be just that: brief encounters, and there were reunifications—or attempts at reunification—that took place at the borderlands because, once successfully reunited with their families, runaways had few options. The only places that were close to their loved ones and also relatively safe were the forests and swamps that bordered the plantations.

Men, mostly, and some women attempted to permanently reunite with relatives following the dislocation of families that was all too common in slavery. When a slaveholder migrated, he sometimes sold some individuals to help finance the move and took along the rest; but even when everyone was part of the journey the separation of some families was inevitable because husbands and wives often resided in different places. They were said to have "broad" husbands or wives, as in "abroad." It was especially frequent when they belonged to small farms and plantations where prospective mates were in short supply. These "broad marriages" were often judged problematic, at least by the males' owners.[11] "When a man and his wife belong to different persons," warned an 1833 essay on the management of slaves, "they are liable to be separated from each other, as well as their children, either by the caprice of either of the parties, or where there is a sale of property. This keeps up an unsettled state of things, and gives rise to repeated new connections." What was at issue was not the agony of dislocation but its potential harm to the slave system. Men, out of the "control of their master for a time" as they visited their wives, got a dangerous "feeling of independence." But even worse, "wherever their wives live, they consider their homes."[12] And this was exactly what precipitated a large number of men's escapes: they wanted to stay with their wife and children.

Couples or families who decided to stay together permanently when one person was slated for sale or migration essentially used two strategies to achieve their goal. In the first case, the spouse who was to move away escaped and hid in the woods, like a North Carolina woman did when she learned that her owner was migrating west with his workforce. Because she had a broad marriage and was determined to prevent a separation, she took her infant girl with her and settled in the swamps close to her husband.[13] Some families chose to stay where they were, with all their relatives. When Samuel Andrews moved to Camden, South Carolina, sometime in 1777, eleven men, women, and children failed to follow. Andrews believed they had stayed behind in the neighborhood of his old plantation.[14]

The second strategy was the opposite of the first: the spouse who was to stay followed the departing one to new and unknown territory. Such was the decision made by Randol, who ended up being wanted in four states. Randol was believed to have "marks of shot about his hips, thighs, neck and face, as he has been shot at several times." He was fired at as he was escaping from a plantation in Franklin County, North Carolina, in January 1817. The wounded young man likely stayed in the woods near his wife, who lived on another plantation. In February 1818, a year after Randol had absconded, his spouse was taken to the Deep South. What Randol did was expected: his owner was certain he would follow his wife. To thwart this project, the planter put up ads in North Carolina, South Carolina, Tennessee, and Georgia newspapers.[15]

To follow his family was also the choice made by Will, a man who had "the incisions of the whip on his back," an indication that he had run away before or stood up to authority. He was believed to be heading for a plantation by the Coosawhatchie River in South Carolina. Just a week before, his wife and five children had been sold to a planter living there.[16] Other examples help reveal the profound attachment that bonded spouses and led them to become maroons. Strongly suspected of migrating South was Tom from Virginia. "I have reason to believe, from what he told my overseer a little before he went off, that he intends for South Carolina, as his wife was sold to a gentleman there a few months ago," wrote his owner.[17] Will ran away for the same reason. Embarking on a six-hundred-mile trip, he absconded from Maryland "in pursuit of his wife, who was purchased in Somerset by a Mr. Lewis, from Georgia."[18] Another poignant case that reveals strong spousal devotion is the trek on which Sip embarked. He was fifty years old and—proof of an "intractable character"—had bullet scars on his back and shoulders. Sip left Bertie County, North Carolina, intent on reuniting with his wife en route to Alabama.[19] The decision to go on these hazardous journeys was all the more courageous given that people were moving deeper into the South, which made the prospect of escaping to a free state more remote than ever before. What they expected, at the end of their journey, was a reunion, which they knew would be complicated and could only be half-realized.

While some people left the Upper South for the Deep South in pursuit of a spouse or relative, others, also in search of loved ones, made the voyage in the opposite direction. With the development of the domestic slave trade, men, women, and children sold down the river had gone on forced journeys to Georgia, Alabama, Mississippi, Louisiana, Florida, and Texas. In an effort to reconnect with their families, they began walking back to Virginia, Tennessee, Maryland, and the Carolinas. Their reverse journeys of several hundred miles via discreet paths and through forests, swamps, and deserted fields were long and perilous. Two men who escaped from northern Alabama walked for three months to reach New Bern, North Carolina.[20] Ned, of Nash County, North Carolina, was sold to an owner in Georgia in 1816; he returned and was a maroon in Nash and neighboring counties for nine years before being captured in 1825.[21] Sylvester, from Maryland and sold down to Alabama, was caught in North Carolina after hiding for five years, and George came back from Kentucky to Virginia, "skulked" for three years, and finally took away his wife and young daughter.[22]

Determined to reunite with her loved ones, Tamar, of North Carolina, walked for three weeks. Her tragic life story was far from atypical. She had seen five of her children put up for sale before she too, along with her sixth child, was finally sold to slave traders. On her way to the Deep South she managed to escape, without her infant, after trekking more than a hundred miles in the speculators' coffle or slave caravan. Traveling at night and hiding in the woods during the day, she made her way back to her family and settled in the woods nearby.[23] William Kinnegy's saga paralleled Tamar's. A native of Jones County, North Carolina, he was sent to Richmond, Virginia, to be sold, leaving behind his wife and four children who lived on another plantation. From the slave pen in Richmond, Kinnegy was auctioned off to an Alabama planter who put him, along with another hundred people, on a train to Wilmington, whence they were to board a ship to the Gulf of Mexico. Kinnegy jumped off the train and settled in the woods near his wife.[24]

When people tried to reach loved ones, the first difficulty in locating them stemmed from a simple question: which relative were they looking for? Unlike any other community, the family networks of enslaved people were extremely far-flung. Families were broken up and scattered in all directions—even before the onslaught of the domestic slave trade, as some of the following examples show—because of a slaveholder's debt, relocation, bankruptcy, marriage, gift to a relative, divorce, or death. Enslaved men and women's large sets of widespread connections reflect the scope of the community's dislocation. But they also offered the maroons a choice of destinations. For instance, where was twenty-four-year-old Hagar, a mulatto with "a sulky impudent look," heading? She had left her South Carolina plantation with her blanket and bedding, and it was thought that she was being harbored either on a James Island plantation or in White Point, where she had a husband, or then again at another place where her mother lived.[25] As for Aaron in North Carolina, he could have been with the "notorious Jonathan Rector," a white man who was "lurking in the woods [of Iredell County] for a year . . . [with] runaway negroes"; or perhaps he was in Lincoln County near his wife; or close to a plantation near Salisbury, Rowan County, where he had a brother; or in Mecklenburg County, where another brother stayed.[26] Ben had an even more extended network of disrupted relations. He lived in Wilmington, North Carolina, but he had had three previous owners in different counties and a fourth residing in Virginia. It was thought that he had gone to any of these places or that he was being harbored near Cape Fear or on the Sound, where he probably had relatives as well.[27]

As they reunited with their families, the runaways became de facto maroons, living secretly in the woods by the plantations and farms, close to the world of slavery but free from white control.

Following his getaway, John Little first stayed near his mother: he lived "in the bush," as he put it, for two years.[28] Suck, a young woman who escaped from Edenton, North Carolina, in 1778, was believed to be staying near her husband "in the woods between the creek and the plantation of her late master's."[29] After she came back to her homeplace, Tamar lived for several years in the woods close to her mother and brother, giving birth to three children. Kinnegy settled "in a close jungle, so thick that you could not penetrate it, except with the axe." He stayed there for five years.[30] Andrew Johnson of Virginia ran away in October 1809 and was advertised the very next day, a hint that his absence was not expected to be a simple visit. His wife lived on a farm five miles from Alexandria, and his owner conjectured he might be "harbored by her at night, and skulk[ing] about the neighboring woods through the day."[31]

Unlike "visit," the word "harbored" (or "harboured" and sometimes "entertained") can be found in countless newspaper ads. To understand the borderland maroons' specific experience, it is essential to appreciate what harboring meant. Enslaved people were not able to conceal anyone clandestinely—except for brief moments—in their cabins as these could (and legally had to) be searched any time by overseers, militia, and patrollers. Freedman William H. Singleton noted, "Nights they [the patrollers] would go around to the houses where the slaves lived and go in the houses to see if there was anybody there who had no right to be there. If they found any slaves in a house where they had no right to be, or where they did not have a permit to be, they would ask the reasons why and likely arrest them and whip them."³² Naturally, slave quarters were the first places to be checked when a runaway was advertised; this was why "Ben dare[d] not stay very long at a time in his wife's cabin, as a strict watch was constantly kept, that the runaway might be apprehended."³³ William Kinnegy concurred, "I never dared to stay at my wife's cabin more than a few minutes at a time, although it was always night when I visited her."³⁴

Still, Isaac Jones of South Alabama took the risk. He "dodged about for sixteen months, sleepin' in de woods when it were warm, an' when it were cold hidin' in a cabin."³⁵ When Riley, of Kentucky, returned to his homeplace, he first hid in his mother's cabin but was sent to the barn as a precaution because of the owner's anticipated search. His next destination was a hole under his mother's house, where he stayed for a year and a half.³⁶ Like Riley, William Singleton succeeded in spending three years in a potato cellar below his mother's cabin until he was tricked out of the house. After he was captured he escaped again, but this time he was more cautious: he only went to the cabin at night and left before sunrise to spend his days in the woods.³⁷

The danger inherent in remaining too long on plantation grounds is illustrated by what happened to Tom, a maroon known to have committed robberies in the vicinity of Fishing Creek, North Carolina. His owner's son, William Mace, finally decided to put an end to his activities. He scoured the swamps and the woods for five days but, discouraged by his failure to find any trace of Tom, went back home. Stopping on the way to visit a farmer, he approached the quarters and became suspicious when a light was immediately put out. When he entered the cabin, he found Tom, shot him—he stated that he had only wanted to frighten him—and killed him.³⁸

To avoid detection, borderland maroons sometimes hid in outbuildings, and some were even smuggled into the main house rather than the quarters because it was safer. For instance, Maria and Betsy escaped from Charles Manigault's Gowrie Plantation in South Carolina and stayed near a neighbor's place. They "often hid in the kitchen as it is known that search would only be made for them in the negro houses."[39] Landon Carter was incensed when he learned that Johnny, his gardener, "had harboured Bart & Simon all the while they were out, sometimes in his inner room and sometimes in my Kitchen Vault." Of course, they "were placed in the Vault in particular the day my Militia were hunting for them."[40]

A remarkable case of harboring that unfolded in South Carolina in the summer of 1853 illustrates the subterfuges, solidarity, secrecy, and widespread complicity that often went into harboring borderland maroons. At an unknown date, Alfred, of Alabama, ran away and made his way to Anderson County, South Carolina. On the plantation of Hugh Gantt, he benefited from the active or tacit solidarity of several people. He lived at Bob's and then at Dina and Mahalah's. Throughout his stay, Alfred, a tall man, passed as a woman, wearing a white and blue dress. Everyone in the quarters and at least three people from other plantations saw him and knew who he was. Alfred did not stay in the cabins for long because of safety issues; he was soon transferred to one of Gantt's cellars. When slave hunters came by, Bob contacted Harriett on another plantation, asking her to conceal Alfred, whose odyssey took him from the woods to the quarters to a planter's cellar and on to another plantation.[41]

To harbor was to give food and assistance as well as occasional refuge; or, as the law defined it in South Carolina, it meant knowingly entertaining and giving victuals to runaways.[42] It was of course illegal and resulted in trials and punishments. Harry, of South Carolina, was tried for harboring Sylvia who left on January 1, 1838, with several possessions, such as baskets, clothes, and her bedding. Harry concealed her belongings in the planter's kitchen and brought her food when she stayed in someone else's barn, and he hid some of her clothes, wrapped in a blanket, under the floor of his cabin.[43] In Anderson County, South Carolina, Mary went on trial on March 9, 1843. She was accused of harboring Simon, who had lived in the woods from November 1842 to February 1843. She knew he was a maroon, but she did "harbour said Simon a Slave, by carrying to him victuals, and spirits and by sleeping with him the said Simon in a camp in the woods not far from the house of the said O. R. Broyles."[44]

Free blacks were also harborers. In many cases, the people they helped were their enslaved relatives.[45] But others were friends, acquaintances, and strangers. There was enough complicity between free blacks and runaways and maroons that it had to be controlled by law.[46] As early as 1740, South Carolina decreed that free blacks "harbouring" could be fined ten pounds for the first day, and twenty shillings for every succeeding day. If unable to pay, they were to be sold at public auction. Because there was sometimes insufficient evidence to punish the free individuals who harbored, entertained, and concealed, the act specified that any free Indian or slave could testify without oath against "any free negroes, Indians (free Indians in amity with this government, only excepted,) mulattoe or mustizoe."[47] A new law passed in 1821 condemned free harborers to corporal punishment only; nevertheless, in August 1827 Hannah Elliott, her daughter, and her son were sold into slavery in Charleston for harboring a fugitive. In the nineteenth century throughout the South, free and enslaved blacks guilty of harboring were liable to corporal punishment, short of mutilation and death.[48]

"Serial harboring" was one of the problems slaveholders confronted when trying to catch borderland maroons, who could be as itinerant as their networks and sense of safety allowed them to be. This was true mostly of people not encumbered with children, like Amy of Jones County, North Carolina. First harbored by Sam, she was then "entertained" on a second plantation. She crossed the Neuse River and found refuge and help on two other estates before being captured on a third. Less than three months later she disappeared again. She moved between five places.[49] Also quite mobile was Harry, about twenty-four, of Dinwiddie County, Virginia. He ran away in 1765 and was caught near Williamsburg in May 1767. In a matter of hours, he escaped once more. A year later, in March 1768, Henry Brodnax advertised for him and believed he was "lying lurking" in the neighborhood of Indianfield, York County, where he had previously lived. Harry was finally caught six months later and brought to prison in James City. He escaped and was brought back to the same jail on April 13, 1769.[50] On and off, Harry succeeded in remaining free for five years, harbored in three counties in a radius of about one hundred miles.

While maroons hoped to remain unseen via harboring, numerous notices reveal that many were spotted in the vicinity of various plantations. Abram, a middle-aged sawyer absent for two years, was known to be "harbored sometimes about Four Hole Swamp, sometimes about Mr. Baccots at Goose Creek, and sometimes on the Town Neck, he having been frequently seen about them Places, and not long since on the latter."[51] Bella was seen on the Augusta road "in company with some Negroes of Major Douglas's, on their way to their master's plantation . . . those negroes will probably endeavour to conceal her on the plantation."[52] A group of seven men, four women, and their five children living in the woods near their former South Carolina plantation was noticed in broad daylight in the quarters. When not around, they were "near Mr. Rowland's Mowberry Plantation or Mr. Dawson's with whom negroes they are also connected." Their owners even laid a plan for slave catchers to follow, as they offered two hundred dollars for their capture. They indicated the four points—two plantations, a boat landing "where they constantly cross and re-cross Wappoo Cut," and a store—that "if watched will insure success. . . . And if one is taken, he may be induced by reward, or constrained by punishment," they ominously announced, "to show where the rest are."[53]

Harboring and sightings expose the extent and the depth of the complicity many maroons enjoyed. There is no question that once someone was spotted, the entire community was questioned, often fruitlessly, as the repetition of ads attests. Moreover, the hiding places must have been well-chosen as, despite obvious clues as to their whereabouts, some maroons were able to stay hidden in the borderlands for years.

* * *

The maroons who settled close to the plantations where loved ones were enslaved lived in a paradoxical situation. While their objective was to reunite with their families, they remained separated from them. But by keeping members on the plantation, the family optimized the chance for the maroon(s) to remain at large—hence, to keep the family together—because the enslaved relatives could provide food, clothes, and precious intelligence. That it was the best solution dislocated families were able to find to stay together speaks volumes not only about the system they lived under but even more importantly about their willingness to make extraordinary sacrifices to circumvent it.

No one went to the woods mentally unprepared. Most runaways and maroons were caught and subjected to barbaric punishments administered in public as a deterrent, so absconders were well aware of what awaited them were they to become maroons. They exposed themselves to a hard life if successful and to ghastly reprisals if they failed, all in the hope of keeping their families together. These maroons delivered three blows to the slave system. They denied slaveholders the legal ownership of their bodies, they deprived them of the product of their labor, and they refused them the authority to manage and control what they considered their personal sphere: their families. Even though, by law, they did not have authority over their own bodies and movements—let alone those of their spouses, children, and relatives—they took that power knowing full well what this particular type of opposition to the institution of slavery could cost them.

VIOLENCE AND MARRONAGE

If the preservation of families was a significant objective that led men and women to become borderland maroons, severe whippings and other cruel treatments were a frequent catalyst to escape. "De slaves used to be badly treated, so dey would run off de woods and hide for a long time," recalled Sally Snowden, of Louisiana.[54] However, it was rare for a slaveholder to attribute an escape directly to a whipping or the promise of one. Charles Yates' notice in the *Virginia Gazette and Weekly Advertiser* of September 20, 1783, was one such anomaly. Anthony, he explained in a rambling ad, had run away three months earlier: "He hath formerly had two or three severe whippings (which his back will show) for his obstinacy and bad behaviour to his overseers, and his consciousness of deserving further correction, probably made him abscond." Also exposing a direct link between brutality and running away was a notice in the *Virginia Gazette* of August 6, 1772, for a twenty-two-year-old "Mulatto Wench named PHEBE": "A Propensity for Pleasure in the Night brought a little Punishment from the Overseer, which I suppose made her run off." Moses, who ran away on May 1, 1823, had been flogged a week before, and his owner expected that the mark of the whip would remain for some days, and Reuben had many scars on his back "from flogging ... which he justly merited."[55] The overwhelming majority of wanted notices, though, did not mention violence, other than to imply that the scarred backs, broken limbs, and severed ears and toes were relics of the past. If one is to believe slaveholders, no one ever escaped because of their brutality. While most people who left for violence-related reasons did return after they had healed or recuperated, others intended their departure to be permanent.

The men and women who fled because they had decided not to submit to an impending beating or had just received one did so on the spur of the moment. Nonetheless, lack of planning in the breakout did not inevitably mean failure. Harry Grimes of North Carolina went to the woods after being threatened with a hundred lashes and even death because he had gone without a pass to visit his wife five miles away. Although he left unprepared, Grimes was a successful maroon for twenty-seven months.[56] When S. Coutrell, of St. James Parish, Louisiana, struck Octave Johnson with a big stick and ordered him to be whipped, Johnson dashed for the swamp located a mile behind the plantation sugarhouse. He outran his pursuers and lived in hiding for eighteen months until he enrolled in one of the Corps d'Afrique regiments during the Civil War.[57]

The story of the Heard family illustrates the failures and successes of people who took refuge in the woods to escape violence.[58] Sylvia Heard's owner, Peter Heard, a rich planter near LaGrange in Troup County, Georgia, was reputed to be mean and cruel. He whipped and beat his workers without mercy, and Sylvia, a midwife, endured lashings on a regular basis. According to her family, the main reason for Heard's brutality was that Sylvia used to pray every morning. Heard forbade any expression of faith by his bondspeople because he believed that they prayed for freedom. Despite the beatings, Sylvia kept on praying. But one day "the master heard her and became so angry he came to her cabin seized and pulled her clothes from her body and tied her to a young sapling. He whipped her so brutally that her body was raw all over." All day long, Sylvia, who was reaching the end of a pregnancy, remained tied to the tree. At night her husband, Anthony, released her. Too weak to walk, Sylvia crawled to the woods. After she found a place to hide, Anthony greased her back to ease her pain and hasten healing. Then he went back to their cabin. The very next day, Peter Heard started to hunt Sylvia down. When he finally caught up with her, she had given birth to twins. Because she was captured, there is no way of knowing what her long-term strategy could have been. She may have planned to settle in the woods for good and raise her children there, as other women did. If this was her intention, Peter Heard and his dogs put an end to it. But the story of the runaway Heards continued with Sylvia and Anthony's son, William.

One night, patrollers caught William Heard off the plantation without a pass. After he was seized, the patrollers, as was their duty, beat William, who then ran off to the woods. His plan was not to nurse himself back to health only to go back to another whipping or worse. He decided to make his escape permanent and came to the conclusion that his family had to join him. To that end, he built a home in the woods and when it was finished, he returned at night to his cabin. It was a perilous move that could have ended his attempt at living free, but he succeeded in taking his wife and two children. The family made it safely to their new home. No patrollers, hunters, dogs, or passersby ever found them; several years later, in 1865, they emerged from the woods. By then William's family counted two more children, born free in the forest that bordered Peter Heard's plantation.[59] William had gone to the woods on the spur of the moment, in the middle of the night, empty-handed, wounded, and full of frustration and rage. But he quickly planned an alternative life for his family, complete with a secret home and a means of procuring food and of evading slave catchers and bloodhounds.

It was not the fear of violence that motivated people like Grimes and Heard. Bishop William H. Heard, a former runaway himself, understood that going to the woods under those circumstances was not a sign of defeat: "The blood would run from their heads to their heels," he wrote, "yet many of them were never conquered. They would go to the woods and stay there for months, yes, some of them years."[60] The maroons' determination to take control of their lives reflects the confidence they had in themselves and in their ability to create new lives even when physically diminished by the torture they had endured. Overtly disallowing anyone the right to assault them, they "would not yield to punishment of any kind," wrote former runaway from Virginia Henry Clay Bruce (brother of the first black U.S. senator, Blanche K. Bruce), "but would fight until overcome by numbers, and in most cases be severely whipped; [they] would then go to the woods or swamps, and [were] hard to capture, being usually armed."[61]

Violence cut both ways, and the woods were also the refuge of men and women who had attacked whites or were about to do so. Elizabeth Ross Hite of Louisiana joked in the 1930s, "We used to hear about de slaves beatin' up dere master and runnin' away. I wished I had de dollars for de slaves dat beat up dere masters, I would be rich."[62] Actually, records show that slaves were prosecuted for killing whites in about every state and every year.[63] William Ballard of South Carolina remembered how a man had whipped the overseer and "had to run away in the woods and live so he wouldn't get caught."[64] Men and women who assaulted or killed whites had few options other than to remove themselves from society and disappear into the woods, as William Robinson did after he knocked down his owner with an ax handle because he had cursed and kicked his mother. He made it to the swamps, where he knew he could join a group of maroons.[65]

FAMILIES AT THE BORDERLANDS

In addition to people who lived in the borderlands near their loved ones, families also settled there. Naturalist John James Audubon came across such a family in a Louisiana swamp in the 1820s. Eighteen months earlier, the man—whose name Audubon did not give—his wife, and their three children were sold at auction, and all ended up with different owners. With great optimism and resolve, the father devised an audacious plan to free his kinfolk. He settled in the swamps and made methodical and daring excursions at night to the plantations where his wife and children now resided. One after the other he "stole" them. The family lived close to their first homeplace.[66] In the fall of 1831 Henry fled from Little Rock, Arkansas. He remained in hiding in the area and in January 1832 was joined by his wife and their three children, who lived on a plantation north of the city. They took a bed with them, indicating that they did not expect to be on the move but rather planned to settle down in a place where they would not find furniture.[67] Ned, his wife, Bella, and their three children escaped in February 1827 and settled near a plantation in Christ Church Parish, South Carolina. More than a year later they were still being looked for.[68] Families started in the woods too: Pattin and his wife had fifteen children in the fifteen years they stayed in hiding. They left their refuge only after the end of the Civil War.[69]

The borderlands also sheltered groups consisting of several families. Perhaps the best example of such a community began its journey on February 21, 1825, after escaping from Kershaw and Lewis, one of the most prominent business houses in Charleston. Three months later, they were known to be living together in the woods near The Oaks Plantation, from where they had been bought a year earlier.[70] Among the seven men and four women there may have been up to four couples.

Children taken to the woods and the swamps near the plantations as well as those who were born there were spared the brutality and oppression of slavery, but they still led a dangerous, restrictive, and stressful life. Although nominally free, they were virtual prisoners, their movements restricted to a small perimeter mostly accessible at night and condemned to a life of whispers. The children of a woman from North Carolina experienced severe constraints: "by the strictest discipline, she prevented them ever crying aloud, she compelled them to stifle their little cries and complaints, though urged to it, by pinching hunger, or the severest cold. She prohibited them from speaking louder than a whisper."[71]

Yet the parents, to whom family was so precious that they went to the greatest lengths to keep it together, were willing to maintain these young children and adolescents in a state of social deprivation, a decision that illustrates how much they found the alternative—servitude or life in a Southern or Northern city under white hegemony—incomparably worse. What they could have envisioned as a long-term future for their children can only be conjectured, but they doubtless had to contemplate their forced reentry or entry into the world of slavery. Parents knew that this highly traumatic experience could be compounded by the possibility of the family being broken up by sale.

Family life had its obvious advantages but was also taxing: a family demanded more food and other necessities as well as bigger accommodations. This could have two negative consequences: in some cases it pushed the maroons to take more risks to provide for their loved ones, leading them to lose the very freedom they diligently sought for them. For others the challenge became too hard to face, and they had to give up, turning themselves in.

THE WOMEN'S EXPERIENCE

Gender—to which were linked violence and family—was an important variable that predicted who would most likely get away. "The women are always beat worse than the men. The more they whip the men, the more likely they are to run into the swamp, but the women don't run away so much," a former borderland maroon explained.[72] He was certainly right, as the overwhelming majority, up to 81 percent of runaways, were young men.[73] In the workplace, whether they were young, old, single, or married, females did not enjoy the same limited ability to move around that some males did. Their tasks rarely took them outside the plantation: they did not go on errands, drive the coach that took the slaveholders here and there or the cart that transported goods, or row the canoes or man the boats. In the personal sphere, they were not the ones going out at night to see a spouse or fiancé. Although they were familiar with parts of the borderlands—where some had gardens or had gathered medicinal plants—and the neighboring plantations, their knowledge of the outside world was more limited than that of men, as were their networks. Their presence on the roads was more conspicuous and more readily questioned than men's.[74]

Children also prevented women from escaping as often as men. James Curry, a runaway who reached Canada, recalled how his mother had escaped at fifteen and again sometime later. She was captured both times and before long had children. "This ended my mother's running away," he concluded. "Having young children soon, it tied her to slavery."[75] The alternative for women was to leave their children behind, as did Anney of Virginia, who escaped with a quantity of clothes but left her still-suckling infant behind.[76] For personal or social reasons, this was a choice few women made.

Although the number of female runaways was low, a new picture emerges when harboring is taken into account. In colonial South Carolina, where 17 to 21 percent of those who ran away were women, 80 percent of them were suspected of having gone to stay with relatives or spouses.[77] In Georgia (1783–95), about 44 percent of the females whose destination was mentioned were believed to be harbored or to have gone to family and friends.[78] Also in Georgia, between 1822 and 1829 close to 60 percent of all female runaways were thought to be harbored.[79] They were harbored either in town or at the plantations' margins. Some were undeniably visiting or were out for other reasons and expected to return after a few days or weeks. But others had gone to stay.

There was little doubt as to where a Georgia woman and her two children could be when they were sold in absentia "for ready money": they were "supposed to be in the woods."[80] Another Georgia woman, Sally, escaped in May 1764 with her "two mulatto children" a few days after they were all bought. Their former owner had died, and they had been auctioned off to Alexander Wylly, a justice of the peace in Christ Church Parish. Wylly believed the family had "run away into the woods," and he was so anxious to get them back that he placed twenty-two ads for their return. At least ten months after they had escaped Sally and her children were still at large.[81] Haly and Amy Tyler, who escaped from Moseley Hall at Bear Creek, North Carolina, in July 1838 were "supposed to be lurking about George Garne's in Craven County near Newbern."[82] They likely had relatives or friends there. Their "lurking" seemed to have been quite successful, as their owner was still running his notice two years later.

For some women determined to escape slavery, even pregnancy was not a deterrent. Moll, eighteen and "very big with child," ran away with her Angola-born husband.[83] Because it was more difficult for Africans to pass for free in a city, it is reasonable to infer that the couple chose the woods instead, perhaps staying close to Moll's relatives since she was born in Virginia. In Georgia, Betty, "big with child," was believed to be "harboured at some plantation."[84] Expecting a child may actually have been the reason why some women escaped in the first place, hoping to reunite with a husband or relative who would provide them and their child with support and love.

In some crucial respects, isolated women were at a clear disadvantage. To sustain themselves and their children in the woods, they needed to build shelters, fish, hunt, and trap. Few were familiar with—let alone proficient in—these activities. They had to learn how to do these things as they went along, and some never did. The young North Carolina woman was not good at hunting and fishing, and when her husband did not bring them food, she fed her children frogs, terrapins, snakes, and mice. When, as in her case, a woman was staying near her husband's farm or plantation, he played the traditional role of provider that slavery denied him. He became the supplier of food and other necessities and her link with the outside world; but therein lay an inherent danger. Maroons, whatever their gender but especially those who did not hunt, could not rely exclusively on a spouse. When her husband "deserted" her—the circumstances remain unknown, he may have been sold, fallen sick, or died—she was no longer able to feed her family and after seven years she surrendered.[85]

However, few women on the borderlands seem to have been on their own. The available evidence indicates that most of them lived as couples, in families, or in mixed groups where they benefited from a support network of husband and relatives. Tamar, cited earlier in this chapter, relied on her mother, brother (the memoirist Moses Grandy), and husband; she delivered three babies as a maroon. She lost one, but even in her difficult circumstances, her children's survival rate was better than that on any average plantation. Nonetheless, pregnancy and delivery were times of particular vulnerability; tellingly, Tamar was captured before she had time to recover from the birth of her youngest child.[86]

Caring for infants in the wilds was a challenge, as attested by the experience of Hannah, a habitual runaway from Virginia, who escaped repeatedly with her two children. She lost one, and when she was captured, the other was, according to her owner, "lingering from the effects of . . . exposure." In 1855, pregnant again, Hannah remained in hiding most of the year and lost her third child "from neglect and exposure."[87] In the woods, exposure to the elements and lack of adequate food and clothing compounded the health issues that originated on the plantations.

AD HOC GROUPS

Many borderland maroons lived in nonkin groups. The interrogation records of a group of six arrested in the fields in Attakapas County, Louisiana, in July 1771 sheds light on the composition of these ad hoc groups. One of its members, Mariana, was looking for food when she was caught in the dairy of the prominent Mr. de Saint Denis. She said she had come from New Orleans and had been away for eight months in the company of another woman, a man, and a young child. She stayed briefly on Louis Harang's plantation before meeting Louis, a maroon of two years, who took her and the other woman to the woods. Joining them were Charlot, who had run away from New Orleans and was absent for fourteen or fifteen months; Gil, also from New Orleans and a fugitive for two years; and Miguel, who had left the city three months earlier and spent most of his time in the woods. Jean-Baptiste Raoul had been away from New Orleans for seven months and had lived in various places together with other maroons.[88] The six members of the group, formerly held by different planters over 130 miles away, had gathered at different times and pooled their resources together in order to survive.

Another Louisiana group of twelve arrested by the slave patrol in October 1805 in St. Charles Parish was international, an apt reflection of the diversity of the enslaved community of the time that counted men and women born in Africa, Louisiana, and the Caribbean.[89] Celeste, aged forty, was born in the Congo and lived in New Orleans before she ran off. Her husband, James, was Creole. Augustin Kernion, a mulatto, was part of the group, as was John, a nineteen-year-old from Jamaica who had escaped from New Orleans. Other members were Marie, Charles, and Lucie, enslaved by a man named Joachim; Senegaux and Etienne, from different plantations; and two individuals whose gender was not specified. They all lived in the cypress swamp near the Labarre Plantation, but when they saw Joachim searching for his three escapees, they thought it more prudent to split up. Eight people hid near a Ms. Pain's place while four remained at Labarre. Celeste revealed that she and three others lived for two weeks with other maroons, whose leader was a man named François from New Orleans, and that she knew of still another group "hiding in the swamps along the shore of Lake Pontchartrain." The group was disparate, made up of small subunits (Marie, Charles, and Lucie; Celeste and James; and the two anonymous members) having come together as circumstances dictated. It was also mobile, moving from borderland to borderland, and fluid, associating with and separating from other groups. Its regrouping was opportunistic, based on need and efficiency, as was its dismantling in response to circumstance.

The comings and goings of three men arrested in the spring of 1808 in St. Charles Parish offers further details on the wandering life of some of these groups and the temporary nature of their relations. Honoré, one of the members of the trio, ran away from François Piseros, captain of the Hussards and chief of the slave patrol, and hid in the swamp behind his farm. There he came across Gabriel and Lindor, who had two guns. The three decided to move back of the Delhomme farm.

They built a shack and got food at the slave quarters. They also hunted near two other farms. They then proceeded to the Cabaret farm, where Louis and Celestin, who, like Honoré, had escaped from Piseros' estate, joined them. Honoré, Lindor, and Gabriel then settled behind Pierre Renine's farm for two weeks and later established a camp between the Fortier and Saint Martin farms. They later stayed for two months with a band of maroons living in the cypress swamps by the Destréhan Plantation. After this, Lindor spent a week in Ceba's cabin on the Fortier Plantation. A free black man—and slaveholder—Charles Paquet housed him and Gabriel for five or six nights while Honoré remained close to the Fortier farm, where he was ultimately discovered.[90] Honoré thus moved around between eight farms and three maroon groups in a matter of months. Closeness to friends, safety, the possibility of procuring better or more food, the risk of being hunted down after too much plunder, and immediate danger dictated his and other maroons' wanderings.

THE MAROONS' SKILLS AND PROTECTIVE STRATEGIES

To live successfully at the margins of plantations and towns, maroons had to develop a number of new skills and devise protective measures that would increase their chances of remaining undetected. Staying close to inhabited areas, they were vulnerable at all times. For example, contrary to runaways to the North or to the southern cities who, when successful, rarely had to confront dogs again, maroons were constantly at the mercy of dogs. Not only were dogs unleashed after them when they escaped but they could also be sent to search for the people who lived in the woods at any time. For that reason, the maroons' methods of evading dogs were varied, had various purposes, and were used at different stages. Over time, people concocted, experimented with, discarded, talked about, shared, celebrated, or cursed a number of strategies designed to neutralize or annihilate the bloodhounds.

The simplest and most common tactic was to use a kind of dog repellent, most often made of pepper, black or Cayenne. Texas freedman Walter Rimm explained that all people had to do was to "take black pepper and put it in your socks and run without your shoes. It make de hounds sneeze." Another method was to make a deep impression in the ground with one's heel and sprinkle the hole with pepper. Some people added ingredients such as saltpeter or turpentine. They put the mixture in their shoes and rubbed their soles with pine tops as an extra precaution, hoping to repel the dogs and mask their own odor. Trying to cover up one's scent was a prevalent tactic. Borderland maroons would run amid the people working in the fields, attempting to make their scent disappear in the midst of everybody else's. Sometimes they exchanged their shoes with a friend, expecting that the ruse would throw the dogs off track.[91]

According to Albert Patterson, of Louisiana, the people who lived in the "great big woods in de back where de niggers would hide when they run away" could not be caught because "they put Bay Leaves on de bottom o' their feet an' shoes, then they go an' walk in fresh manure an' a dog can't track them."[92] Charles Thompson, from Attala County, Mississippi, escaped after taking his precautions: "I had provided myself a preparation called 'smut' among the negroes, which, when spread thinly on the soles of the shoes or feet, destroyed that peculiar scent by which blood-hounds are enabled to follow the trail of a man or beast."[93] This smut could be composed of snuff mixed with hog lard or rabbit grease. Likewise, Octave Johnson and the ten women and nineteen men who lived with him "carefully rubbed the soles of their feet with the feet of rabbits, with which they had previously supplied themselves for this purpose, and dragging these after them to deceive the scent of the hounds."[94] Water was considered an almost infallible ally in the battle against canines. Maroons crisscrossed creeks, springs, rivers, and bayous because dogs could not pick up a scent in the water. That ploy could be supplemented by tree climbing, as a man who was hunted by dogs several times testified: "The only way to do when I heard them coming, was to go across water, and put them off the scent, and then climb a high tree in the thickest part of the swamp where the overseer can't come."[95] Knowing how to swim was often a prerequisite to escape, if not to distract the dogs, at least until one reached a safer place. Essex, a maroon for three years, "wanted no better sport than to slip into the river and kiss good-by to hound and hunter. When necessary, he could remain in the river as long as an otter."[96]

Another of the maroons' survival skills was the ability to devise strategies that enabled them to make a quick getaway at any given moment. Jim Bow-Legs, who dwelled in a cave, always meticulously observed the surroundings when he wanted to take a nap: "he took care, first, to decide upon the posture he must take, so that if come upon unexpectedly by the hounds and slave hunters, he might know, in an instant, which way to steer to defeat them."[97] When living in a family or group unit, people created codes to announce their approach. The maroon Audubon met in the Louisiana woods "emitted a loud shriek, not unlike that of an owl," when he came close to home, to inform his wife and children of his arrival. "A tremulous answer of the same nature gently echoed through the treetops," his wife's signal that everything was clear.[98]

* * *

To be a borderland maroon could appear to be a half failure, a consolation prize for someone too scared to join a community in the hinterland or to cross the Mason–Dixon line. But it took as much courage to stay South as to go North. Henry Gorham, who lived in hiding for eleven months, was ready to "die in the woods, live in a cave, or sacrifice himself in some way . . . rather than remain a slave."[99] The borderlands were home to people who, like him, exiled themselves for reasons linked fundamentally to integrity and free will: the exact opposite of what slavery was about.

Maroon life on the borderlands was full of diversity. The woods and swamps hid a range of people whose experiences varied widely: from isolated individuals, families, clusters of strangers, itinerant and settled groups, to people who had moved just a few yards away from their cabins and others who had walked hundreds of miles to unfamiliar locations. The borderlands were places of creativity, innovation, exchange, and transformation; they were also places of anxiety and struggle. Borderland maroons knew they were in for a tough time. They could be discovered and suffer extreme punishment, shot, injured, or killed by wild animals, poisoned by unknown plants, or debilitated by diseases they could not treat. They endured because they found support in the borderlands, autonomy, a free life outside white control and a particular kind of security that only they could cherish. Reflecting on his life in the woods, Tom Wilson could say, "I felt safer among the alligators than among the white men."[100]

* * *

This chapter originally appeared as Sylviane A. Diouf, "Borderland Maroons," in *Slavery's Exiles: The Story of the American Maroons* (New York: New York University Press, 2014), 72–96.

NOTES

1. Charles L. Perdue Jr., Thomas E. Barden and Robert L. Philips, eds., *Weevils in the Wheat: Interviews with Virginia Ex-Slaves* (Charlottesville, University of Virginia Press, 1991), 117.
2. Frederick Law Olmsted, *A Journey in the Back Country* (New York: Mason Brothers, 1860), 48.
3. Philip D. Morgan, "Colonial South Carolina Runaways: Their Significance for Slave Culture," in *Out of the House of Bondage: Runaways, Resistance and Marronage in Africa and the New World*, ed. Gad Heuman, 57–78 (London: Frank Cass, 1986), 67.
4. Allan Kulikoff, *Tobacco and Slaves: The Development of Southern Cultures in the Chesapeake* (Columbia: University of South Carolina Press, 1986), 344–45; and Gerald W. Mullin, *Flight and Rebellion: Slave Resistance in Eighteenth-Century Virginia*, (New York: Oxford University Press, 1974), 108–9.
5. Freddie L. Parker, *Running for Freedom: Slave Runaways in North Carolina 1775–1840* (New York: Garland, 1993), 175, 180.
6. Philip D. Morgan, *Slave Counterpoint: Black Culture in the Eighteenth-Century Chesapeake and Low Country* (Chapel Hill: University of North Carolina Press, 1999), 525–26.
7. Daniel Meaders, *Advertisements for Runaway Slaves in Virginia, 1801–1820* (New York: Garland, 1997), 21, 35; Billy G. Smith and Richard Wojtowicz, eds., *Blacks Who Stole Themselves: Advertisements for Runaways in the Pennsylvania Gazette, 1728–1790* (Philadelphia: University of Pennsylvania Press, 1989), 107, 122; and "Run Away," *American Gazette and Norfolk and Portsmouth Public Advertiser*, March 4, 1796.
8. Benjamin Drew, *A North-Side View of Slavery* (Boston: J. Jewett & Co., 1856), 225.
9. *South Carolina Gazette and American General Gazette*, August 16, 1780.
10. *Columbian Museum & Savannah Advertiser*, March 23, 1798.
11. "Abroad marriages" were welcomed by females' owners, especially on small farms, because they resulted in the increase of their enslaved property.
12. Anonymous, "On the Management of Slaves," *Southern Agriculturist and Register of Rural Affairs* 6, no. 6 (June 1833): 285.
13. "Singular Relation from the Petersburg Republican," *American Masonic Register and Ladies and Gentlemen's Magazine* 1, no. 3 (November 1820): 196.
14. "The Subscriber Having Removed," *South-Carolina and American General Gazette*, April 17, 1777.

15. "Fifty Dollars Reward," *Reflector*, February 10, 1818; and *Register*, February 10, 1818.

16. John Davis, *Travels of Four Years and a Half in the United States of America during 1798, 1799, 1800, 1801, and 1802* (London: T. Ostell, 1803), 92–93.

17. *Virginia Gazette*, August 21, 1778.

18. *Norfolk Herald*, July 14, 1801.

19. "$10 Reward for Negro Sip," *Raleigh Register and North Carolina Weekly Advertiser*, July 24, 1818.

20. Vincent Colyer, *Report of the Services Rendered by the Freed People to the United States Army in North Carolina, in the Spring of 1862* (New York: V. Colyer, 1864), 22.

21. "Taken Up," *Raleigh Register*, February 17, 1826.

22. "Taken Up," *Carolina Sentinel*, April 8, 1826; and "Twenty-Five Dollars Reward," *Alexandria Daily Advertiser*, September 15, 1814.

23. Moses Grandy, *Narrative of the Life of Moses Grandy, Late a Slave in the United States of America* (London: C. Gilpin, 1843), 53–54.

24. Colyer, *Report*, 18–19.

25. "Run Away on Monday," *Gazette of the State of South Carolina*, October 7, 1778.

26. "Twenty Dollars Reward," *Western Carolinian*, June 20, 1826.

27. "New Bern," *North Carolina Gazette*, June 23, 1777.

28. Drew, *A North-Side View*, 205.

29. *North Carolina Gazette*, July 31, 1778.

30. Colyer, *Report*, 19.

31. "Fifteen Dollars Reward," *Alexandria Daily Advertiser*, October 16, 1809.

32. William Henry Singleton, *Recollections of My Slavery Days* (Peekskill, N.Y.: Highland Democrat, 1922), 4.

33. Charles Thompson, *Biography of a Slave* (Dayton, Ohio: United Brethren Publishing House, 1875), 24.

34. Colyer, *Report*, 21.

35. *Independent*, LXVIII (May 26, 1910), in *Slave Testimony: Two Centuries of Letters, Speeches, Interviews, and Autobiographies*, ed. John W. Blassingame (Baton Rouge: Louisiana State University Press, 2002), 536. See also Grandy, *Narrative*, 54.

36. William Lynwood Montell, *The Saga of Coe Ridge: A Study in Oral History* (Knoxville: University of Tennessee Press, 1970), 55–56.

37. Singleton, *Recollections*, 4–5.

38. Joseph Kelly Turner, *History of Edgecombe County, North Carolina* (Raleigh, N.C.: Edwards & Broughton, 1920), 177.

39. William Dusinberre, *Them Dark Days: Slavery in the American Rice Swamps* (New York: Oxford University Press, 1995), 145.

40. Rhys Isaac, *Landon Carter's Uneasy Kingdom: Revolution and Rebellion on a Virginia Plantation* (New York: Oxford University Press, 2004), 201.

41. *The State vs. Harriett*, Harboring a Fugitive Slave, Anderson District Court of Magistrates & Freeholders, L04190, Trial Papers #271, South Carolina Department of Archives and History. Bob was condemned to receive twenty-five lashes, to be jailed for two weeks, and to receive another twenty-five lashes when he got out. Harriett was condemned to forty lashes, and Dina, because she was quite old, was not punished.

42. David J. McCord, ed., *The Statutes at Large of South Carolina*, vol. 10 (Columbia, S.C.: A. S. Johnston, 1841), 280.

43. *The State vs. Harry*, Harboring a Fugitive Slave, Anderson District Court of Magistrates & Freeholders, L04190, Trial Papers #136, South Carolina Department of Archives and History.

44. *The State vs. Mary, Harboring a Fugitive Slave*, Anderson District Court of Magistrates & Freeholders, L04190, Trial Papers #139, South Carolina Department of Archives and History.

45. See, for example, "Forty Dollars Reward," *Alexandria Daily Advertiser*, January 24, 1804; "100 Dollars Reward," *Alexandria Daily Advertiser*, April 13, 1813; "Forty Dollars Reward," *Richmond Enquirer*, May 31, 1807; "Ranaway," *Richmond Enquirer*, December 3, 1813; and "15 Dollars Reward," *Richmond Enquirer*, May 11, 1814.

46. For relations between free blacks and runaways, see, in particular, Morgan, *Slave Counterpoint*, 493–96; and John Hope Franklin and Loren Schweninger, *Runaway Slaves: Rebels on the Plantation* (New York: Oxford University Press, 1999), 109–11.

47. Thomas Cooper, ed., *The Statutes at Large of South Carolina*, vol. 7 (Columbia, S.C.: A. S. Johnston, 1840), 402.

48. See George McDowell Stroud, *A Sketch of the Laws relating to Slavery in the Several States of the United States of America* (Philadelphia: Kinder & Sharpless, 1827), 16–18; North Carolina 1741 Act, *Laws of North Carolina*, 89; "An Act to Provide More Effectually against the Offense of Harbouring Negro or Other Slaves," *City Gazette*, January 5, 1822; McCord, ed. *Statutes*, 10:280; Oliver H. Prince, *A Digest of the Laws of the State of Georgia* (Milledgeville, Ga.: Grantland and Orme, 1822), 452; and William Goodell, *The American Slave Code in Theory and Practice* (New York: American and Foreign Anti-Slavery Society, 1853), 232–33.

49. "Ran-Away," *Carolina Federal Republican*, March 18, 1818.

50. *Virginia Gazette* (Rind), March 24, 1768; and *Virginia Gazette* (Purdie & Dixon), September 29, 1768, and May 11, 1769.

51. "Run Away from Roger Saunders," *South Carolina Gazette*, April 27, 1738.

52. "Two Guineas Reward," *Georgia State Gazette*, January 12, 1788.

53. *Charleston Daily Courier*, May 28, 1825.

54. Ronnie W. Clayton, ed., *Mother Wit: The Ex-Slave Narratives of the Louisiana Writers' Project* (New York: Peter Lang, 1990), 194.

55. "Twenty Dollars Reward," *Alexandria Advertiser and Commercial Intelligencer*, May 4, 1803; and "Ran-Away," *Richmond Enquirer*, June 13, 1807.

56. James Williams, *Life and Adventures of James Williams, a Fugitive Slave, with a Full Description of the Underground Railroad* (San Francisco: Women's Union Print, 1873), 75.

57. James McKaye, *The Mastership and Its Fruits: The Emancipated Slave Face to Face with His Old Master* (New York: W. C. Bryant & Co., 1864), 8–11.

58. George P. Rawick, ed., *The American Slave: A Composite Autobiography*, vol. 4, *Texas Narratives*, pt. 1 (Westwood, Conn.: Greenwood, 1979), 22–27.

59. United States Federal Census, Troup, Georgia, 438; 1880 United States Federal Census, La Grange, Troup, Georgia, 722.

60. William H. Heard, *From Slavery to the Bishopric in the A.M.E. Church: An Autobiography* (Philadelphia: A.M.E. Book Concern, 1928), 27.

61. Henry Clay Bruce, *The New Man: Twenty-Nine Years a Slave, Twenty-Nine Years a Free Man* (York, Pa.: P. Anstadt & Sons, 1895), 36.

62. Clayton, *Mother Wit*, 107.

63. Franklin and Schweninger, *Runaway Slaves*, 78. See also Philip J. Schwarz, *Twice Condemned: Slaves and the Criminal Laws of Virginia, 1705–1865* (Baton Rouge: Louisiana State University Press, 1988), 144.

64. George P. Rawick, ed., *The American Slave: A Composite Autobiography*, vol. 14, *North Carolina Narratives*, pt. 1 (Westport, Conn.: Greenwood, 1972), 27.

65. William H. Robinson, *From Log Cabin to the Pulpit or Fifteen Years in Slavery* (Eau Claire, Wis.: James H. Tifft, 1913), 29–30.

66. John James Audubon, *Ornithological Biography, or an Account of the Habits of the Birds of the United States of America*, vol. 2 (Edinburgh: Adam Black, 1835), 27–32.

67. *Arkansas Gazette*, February 1, 1832, in Orville W. Taylor, *Negro Slavery in Arkansas* (Durham, N.C.: Duke University Press, 1958), 216.

68. *Charleston Mercury*, March 26, 1828.

69. Perdue, Barden, and Philips, *Weevils*, 125.

70. *Charleston Daily Courier*, May 8, 1825.

71. "Singular Relation," *Petersburg Republican*, 196.

72. "Recollections of Slavery by a Runaway Slave," *Emancipator*, September 20, 1838. John Homes, who lived as a maroon before running away to Canada concurred. The overseer "whipped the women, but he did not whip the men, for fear they would run away." Drew, *A North-Side View*, 168.

73. See Franklin and Schweninger, *Runaway Slaves*, 211–12.

74. Anthony E. Kaye, *Joining Places: Slave Neighborhoods in the Old South* (Chapel Hill: University of North Carolina Press, 2007), 146–47; Stephanie M. H. Camp, *Closer to Freedom: Enslaved Women & Everyday Resistance in the Plantation South* (Chapel Hill: University of North Carolina Press, 2004), 38; and Wilma A. Dunaway, *The African-American Family in Slavery and Emancipation* (New York: Cambridge University Press, 2003), 193.

75. "Narrative of James Curry," *Liberator*, January 10, 1840.
76. "Ten Dollars Reward," *Alexandria Daily Advertiser*, May 28, 1807.
77. Morgan, "Colonial South Carolina," 67.
78. Betty Wood, "Some Aspects of Female Resistance to Chattel Slavery in Low Country Georgia, 1763–1815," *Historical Journal*, 30, no. 3 (September 1987): 614.
79. Timothy James Lockley, *Lines in the Sand: Race and Class in Lowcountry Georgia, 1750–1860* (Athens: University of Georgia Press, 2001), 119.
80. "To Be Sold for Ready Money," *Georgia Gazette*, April 19, 1764.
81. *Georgia Gazette*, May 17, 1764.
82. *New Bern Spectator*, August 30, 1838.
83. *Virginia Gazette* (Parks), October 26 to November 2, 1739.
84. *Georgia Gazette*, December 24, 1788.
85. "Singular Relation," 196.
86. Grandy, *Narrative*, 54.
87. Petition of R. L. T. Beall to the County Court of Westmoreland, Virginia, February 1856, Library of Virginia, in *Digital Library on American Slavery*, PAR 21685603.
88. "Records of the Superior Council of Louisiana," *Louisiana Historical Quarterly* 8, no. 3 (July 1925): 527–28.
89. Glenn R. Conrad, *The German Coast: Abstracts of the Civil Records of St. Charles and St. John the Baptist Parishes, 1804–1812* (Lafayette: University of Louisiana at Lafayette Press, 1981), 21. For the slave trade to Louisiana, see Thomas N. Ingersoll, "The Slave Trade and the Ethnic Diversity of Louisiana's Slave Community," *Louisiana History* 37, no. 2 (Spring 1996): 133–61.
90. Conrad, *German Coast*, 65–66.
91. George P. Rawick, ed., *The American Slave: A Composite Biography*, vol. 16, *Kansas, Kentucky, Maryland, Ohio, Virginia, and Tennessee*, pt. 3 (Westwood, Conn.: Greenwood, 1972), 248–49; John Hill Aughey, *Tupelo* (Lincoln, Nebr.: State Journal Company, 1888), 250; James W. C. Pennington, *A Narrative of Events in the Life of J. H. Banks, an Escaped Slave from the Cotton State, Alabama, in America* (Liverpool: M. Rourke, 1861), 65; George P. Rawick, ed., *The American Slave: A Composite Biography*, vol. 12, *Georgia Narratives*, pt. 3, (Westwood, Conn.: Greenwood, 1972), 94; and F. D. Srygley, *Seventy Years in Dixie: Recollections and Sayings of T. W. Caskey and Others* (Nashville: Gospel Advocate Publishing, 1893), 278.
92. Clayton, *Mother Wit*, 179.
93. Thompson, *Biography*, 97.
94. McKaye, *The Mastership*, 11. See also George P. Rawick, ed., *The American Slave: A Composite Autobiography*, vol. 11, *Arkansas and Missouri Narratives* (Westwood, Conn.: Greenwood, 1977), pt. 1, 163; and Octavia V. Rogers Albert, *The House of Bondage* (New York: Hunt & Eaton, 1890), 22.
95. "Recollections," *Emancipator*, September 13, 1838.
96. John George Clinkscales, *On the Old Plantation: Reminiscences of His Childhood* (Spartanburg, S.C., Band & White, 1916), 12.

97. William Still, *The Underground Railroad* (Philadelphia: Porter & Coates, 1872), 242.

98. Audubon, *Ornithological Biography*, 2:29.

99. Still, *Underground Railroad*, 381.

100. Liverpool *Albion*, February 20, 1858, in Blassingame, *Slave Testimony*, 340.

8

Advertising Maranda

Runaway Slaves in Texas, 1835–1865

KYLE AINSWORTH

At first glance the advertisement of Nacogdoches, Texas, slave owner Robert F. Millard for the return of his slave girl Maranda in 1838 seems rather unremarkable. He describes Maranda as being of "dark complection, rather low, and heavy built." She was nineteen and likely a house slave, taking with her two everyday "domestic" dresses as well as "one black silk dress [and] one black muslin dress."[1] The advertisement ran in two Houston newspapers, probably because that is where Millard thought Maranda was headed. He wanted fifty dollars for the capture of his property, which again was an average reward amount. And that was it. Millard did not give an elaborate story of Maranda's escape or substantive details about her appearance, personality, or education. Maranda, by all appearances, was just another fugitive slave.

There are tens of thousands of runaway slave advertisements like this one in newspapers throughout North America and the Caribbean. Often slaves like Maranda end up as statistics in large scholarly runaway slave projects or databases because their advertisements seem to lack the storytelling power that connects historians and readers alike to these remarkable individuals. This chapter suggests that runaway slaves like Maranda in generic advertisements actually do have an amazing story to tell. Their narrative is not located in the advertisement text but in the metadata of the newspapers from which those advertisements were published.

> **$50 REWARD**—Ranaway from the subscriber, a negro girl Maranda, of dark complection, rather low, and heavy built, about nineteeen years old, formerly the property of Lewis Knight, of this county; said girl carried off, when she left, two domestic dresses, one plaid blue and red domestic dress, one black silk dress, one black muslin dress.
>
> The above reward of Fifty Dollars will be paid to the person who may detain said girl, so I can obtain her.
>
> ROBERT F. MILLARD.
>
> *Nacogdoches,* nov2 272–tf

Figure 8.1. Newspaper advertisement submitted by Robert F. Millard of Nacogdoches, Texas, to two Houston newspapers for the capture of his runaway slave woman named Maranda, 1838–40. Source: *Telegraph and Texas Register*, November 28, 1838, pg. 3, col. 5; *Morning Star*, July 2, 1840, pg. 4, col. 2.

Repetition and time between submission and publication are two metadata-based variables that make Maranda's story substantially more interesting. The *Telegraph and Texas Register* published Millard's advertisement on November 28, 1838, twenty-six days after he wrote the submission. She had almost a month's head start before other Texans even knew they should be watching out for her. What did she do, where did she go, and how did she get there? Maranda's advertisement does not answer these questions, but the metadata creates intrigue and interest. The newspaper also reprinted Maranda's advertisement in eighty-one issues over the course of the next two years. Millard additionally submitted Maranda's advertisement to another Houston newspaper, the *Morning Star*, where it was published twenty-one times between July and August 1840. Who was Maranda and why did Millard apparently want her back so desperately?[2]

This chapter draws from the Texas Runaway Slave Project dataset to examine the profiles and experiences of runaway slaves in Texas, in spaces of both formal and informal freedom, usually Mexico and urban areas within Texas, respectively.[3] Employing a metadata approach, it uncovers many of the hidden stories behind runaway slave ads throughout that state, offering historians a new tool for research fugitive slaves in the antebellum South. While it includes many comparisons and percentages to make broad conclusions, it is important to remember that every runaway slave in those figures is more than just a statistic. Each, like Maranda, is a person with a unique and interesting history waiting to be unveiled.

RESEARCH METHODS

The Texas Runaway Slave Project dataset allows historians to extrapolate a diverse array of new information about the fugitives and their owners. There is an order and specific terminology to the research that is very important for the reader to understand the information they are seeing. The terms "entry," "iteration," "attempt," and "runaway" are used throughout the essay, but each means something very different than the other.

An *entry* is each distinct advertisement, article, or capture notice. In the case of an advertisement that describes three fugitive slaves, the entry considers all three runaways as one record. There is not much utility in the entry except for analyzing aspects of how newspapers published about runaway slaves: content placement, repetition, and word choice.

Iterations in the Texas dataset are any documentary source of information about an individual fugitive slave. The majority of research in this chapter comes from newspaper articles, advertisements, and capture notices, but there are also a handful of court records and materials from manuscript collections. Slave owners frequently modified their newspaper advertisements, especially when their first iteration was not successful or new information came to light. They might add more details about a runaway's physical description or the things they carried, change the reward amount, change the slave's presumed destination, or report on the capture of a companion. Slave owners would also publish their advertisements in multiple newspapers. In addition to what each different iteration might say about a slave's circumstances, they also contain information about the newspaper (its name, editor, volume and issue numbers, page and column numbers, and date).

The Texas dataset is organized around the individual, so advertisements and capture notices with multiple runaway slaves are counted not as a single entry but as an iteration for each fugitive in the text. For example, J. H. Robinson's two-hundred-dollar-reward advertisement for James, Sidney, William, and John appeared in four Houston, Austin and San Antonio newspapers in 1851.[4] This single advertisement is counted as sixteen iterations (four slaves multiplied by four newspaper entries).

Most statistics in the Texas dataset are measured by *attempts*, the number of times runaway slaves attempted to run away. Josephus

Brooks' overseers account book for Franklin B. Sublett's plantation in Trinity County, Texas, documents nine slaves that made twenty-one combined attempts between January 1859 and September 1860. The account book records the capture and return of the runaways on nineteen occasions. Rens led the way with four escapes, followed by Gus and Alfred with three apiece. All told there are forty-four iterations in the account book. Gus had two iterations each for his first attempt and four iterations for his third.[5] It is important to be able to document separate attempts because the circumstances for each could be different. Even with Gus, whose three escapes span less than six months, each varies in duration, destination, and companionship.

Two of the best examples from newspaper advertisements are Commodore and Cain, who each have documented attempts separated by more than a decade. Commodore ran away from Jesse Burditt at Hornsby's Bend outside Austin in 1854, was caught and sold to J. H. Simpson of Colorado County at some point, then was sold to J. E. White near Navasota, Grimes County. In 1864 White advertised for Commodore, suspecting him to be near Austin and using a forged travel pass to move about the city.[6] Cain escaped first in 1839 at age thirteen with his mother and another slave from the plantation of P. Bertrand. Eighteen years later, Emily A. Bertrand advertised for his return along with two others.[7]

The idea for including attempts in the dataset was a product of trying and failing to create a composite record for individual runaways with multiple escapes. Take Frank, for instance. He ran away from H. G. Johnson of Montgomery County in July 1839 and again almost a decade later in March 1849. In 1839 Frank was described as "stout, well made, complexion light yellow, quick speech, [and] 22 years old," running away with a man and two women, and thought to be headed for the United States. Ten years later, Johnson described Frank as literate, thirty years old, copper colored, running away by himself, "heavy built and very stout," and likely making for Mexico or California.[8] Every detail of the two escapes is different (decade of escape, age, complexion, education, destination, and escaping party size). It makes sense to still record total number of *runaways* but analyze the research by each attempt and not try to make decisions (and inevitably compromises) about how to combine this information.

The statistics are ordinated on the largest data subsets. When there is overlap (such as a slave that has an advertisement and a capture notice), the runaway is enumerated as a distinct individual in the following order:

Advertisement + Notice + Article = enumerated by Advertisement
Advertisement + Notice = enumerated by Advertisement
Advertisement + Article = enumerated by Advertisement
Notice + Article = enumerated by Notice

While complicated, this methodology is employed to prevent duplication in the counting of individual runaway slaves. If there is any duplication in the dataset, it comes from the articles, where often there is little more information than the number and location of a large group of runaways. In 1854 an editorial mentioned that "within the last few weeks, twenty-odd runaway negroes have passed at no great distance from Austin."[9] These fugitives are counted as twenty iterations but with such a vague description that there is no way to connect any of them to contemporary advertisements or capture notices.

RESEARCH

The data documents 2,053 individual runaway slaves from Texas, 1835–65. There are 985 runaways enumerated in advertisements, 443 documented in capture notices, 574 described in articles, 25 listed in estray notices, and 26 documented in manuscript collections.[10]

John Hope Franklin and Loren Schweninger, in their groundbreaking study, suggest a timeline for how slaveholders decided to submit a newspaper advertisement for a runaway slave.[11] An advertisement was often the last resort for slave owners and overseers with runaway slaves. They would first hunt for the runaway themselves, hoping to capture the fugitive while they were still close to home. Some would alternatively give runaways a day or two to return of their volition, figuring that the slave had gone to visit a friend or family member on a neighboring farm or plantation.[12] All the while, a vigilant master would notify neighbors and scan capture notices in local newspapers. The next recourse available was to hire a slave catcher or team of slave dogs to professionally seek out and capture the slave. If all else failed, then

> **NOTICE.**
>
> TAKEN away on Tuesday night the 2d of October 1860, from a runaway negro, one chestnut sorrel American Mare, blaze in the face, about 15 years old. The owner is requested to pay charges and take her away, or I shall proceed according to law.
>
>   S. LOCKWOOD.
>
> Webberville, Oct. 3, 1860.   v12n9-3w

Figure 8.2. Newspaper notice for a horse captured from a runaway slave by S. Lockwood near Austin, Texas, 1860. Source: *State Gazette*, October 6, 1860, pg. 3, col. 5.

the slave owner would spend the money to place an advertisement in the newspaper.[13]

It is not hard to imagine Millard following a similar course leading up to Maranda's advertisement (unfortunately there is no indication of when she escaped, only when Millard made his submission). Knowing from the repetition of metadata how much Millard wanted Maranda back, however, the Franklin and Schweninger model seems too cold and calculated. Writing a newspaper advertisement had to be emotional because the act of running away challenged a slave owner's control of the household—their patriarchy and paternalism.[14] Perhaps it was these things that really drove the Franklin and Schweninger model.

Maintaining the household was a central tenet to southern social order. A planter who could not maintain the rigid etiquette, both public and private, for his family and property would be negatively perceived by society.[15] The procedure of placing a runaway slave advertisement was at its core the capitulation of a slave owner's desire to protect their honor to market forces, with the capture of the slave and their value (as a commodity and a laborer) outweighing the need to present a unified and cohesive vision of the home.

The personal search for a fugitive kept the incident private, but with each notification, first to family, then to neighbors, and finally to the community, the escape of a runaway slave became more public. There was a progression with each subsequent notice, but even at this point the escape was localized to the slave owners' inner circles. The decision to publish a runaway slave advertisement then was a major escalation. The runaway went from being neighborhood news to published local,

Table 8.1. Runaway slave content in Texas documents, 1835–1865

	Entries	Iterations	Runaways	Attempts
NEWSPAPER ADVERTISEMENTS				
For slaves from Texas	941	1,374	985	1,016
For slaves from Louisiana	47	82	68	68
For slaves from Arkansas and Indian Territory	21	30	24	24
For slaves from other locations	31	20	19	19
Subtotal	1,040	1,506	1,096	1,127
NEWSPAPER CAPTURE NOTICES				
For slaves from Texas	415	556	443	446
For slaves from Louisiana	115	137	100	102
For slaves from Arkansas and Indian Territory	28	38	33	33
For slaves from Mississippi and Alabama	25	52	36	40
slaves from other locations	16	19	17	18
Slave owner location not indicated	54	71	54	56
Subtotal	653	873	683	695
NEWSPAPER ESTRAY NOTICES				
Horses caught from Texas runaways	28	34	25	25
NEWSPAPER ARTICLES				
Texas (about ads, captures, etc.)	498	1,287	574	576
Texas (legal and legislative)	67	67	0	0
Louisiana (pertaining to Texas)	10	25	28	28
Arkansas (pertaining to Texas)	3	7	3	3
Mexico (pertaining to Texas)	58	58	0	0
Subtotal	636	1,444	605	607
ARCHIVAL DOCUMENTS				
Texas (escapes)	20	36	24	31
Texas (captures)	15	26	2	7
Louisiana (captures)	4	3	3	2
Subtotal	39	65	29	40
Total	2,396	3,922	2,438	2,494

regional, state, or interstate news, depending on the newspaper and how the advertisement was circulated. The proliferation of runaway slave advertisements in southern newspapers suggests just how important, or unimportant, patriarchy and paternalism was to profit-minded slaveholders.

The majority of Texas slaveholders (76.5 percent) who advertised for their fugitive slaves a total of five times or fewer (a month in most weekly publications). There was pragmatism at work here, and most

Table 8.2. Newspaper repetitions of Texas runaway slave advertisements

Repetitions[a]	Entries
1	275
2	151
3	146
4	85
5	63
6–10	127
11–20	58
21–40	24
41–153	12
Total	941

Note: a. Includes the first appearance.

slaveholders recognized that if the slave was not recovered after a month of advertisements, the announcement had been ineffective, and it was time to discontinue publication. The advertisements by some masters persisted, however.

In these cases, the slaveholder demonstrated that the capture of the runaway slave or slaves was more than business; it was personal. One wonders if Maranda was a mistress or something more to Robert F. Millard.[16] In 1837–38, Edwin Waller increased the reward amount for Gumby and Zow from fifty dollars to one hundred dollars, to two hundred dollars, and to five hundred dollars over the course of a year and a half. It is not clear why Joseph W. Pilant, who lived somewhere on the Brazos River in 1840, was so persistent. He described Dill as "one of the likeliest negro men in the republic" and authorized 162 advertisements for him over a nine-month span in Houston newspapers.[17]

Editors made their own commentary on the likelihood of capturing a runaway slave by where they placed an advertisement in the newspaper. Texas newspapers, generally, were four pages long and four to six columns wide. Fictional stories and other miscellaneous news items were on page 1, domestic and national news were on pages 2 and 3, and commercial and legal advertisements on page 4. The first appearance of advertisements for runaway slaves from Texas were usually on pages 2 (338 times, 35.7 percent) or 3 (409 times, 43.1 percent), where the information subscribers were most interested in reading appeared. Less common were advertisements that started on pages 1 (75 times), 4 (85 times), and 5 through 7 (41 times).[18] Advertisements with repetition beyond the first appearance generally migrated further back into the newspaper the longer they ran. Sometimes, right before the advertisement was scheduled to end, the editor would bump the advertisement back up to page 1 as a last futile reminder that the fugitive was still at large. Maranda's advertisement was quickly and permanently relegated to page 4. After first appearing on page 3, 78 of the remaining 81 repetitions were on page 4. Robert F. Millard might have still thought there was hope, but the editor evidently did not.

If a runaway slave advertisement was expected to have any luck, the slaveholder had to write their announcement with a certain amount of urgency. Franklin and Schweninger found that 33 percent of slave owners waited at least a month and 10 percent at least four months in the 1840s and 1850s.[19] While these numbers are more or less accurate for the Texas dataset, they were calculated without a crucial element to the equation. The time between when a runaway escaped and when a slave owner wrote an advertisement is important, but so is when that advertisement actually appeared in the newspaper. Just because the slave owner wrote the advertisement did not guarantee timely placement in the newspaper. This was especially the case if they sent their advertisement to other newspapers at places where they thought their fugitive slave might go. Ben, Arch, Frank, and Harrison ran away from the salt works of H. B. Jones in Brazoria County on September 6, 1862. Jones posted an advertisement nine days later (September 15) in the Houston *Tri-Weekly Telegraph*, which asked the "Marshall Republican, Alexandria Democrat, Austin Gazette and San Antonio Herald [to] copy 3 weeks and send bill to this office." The Austin *State Gazette* published the advertisement on September 17 (eleven days after the escape) and the *San Antonio Weekly Herald* on September 20 (fourteen days after the escape). Wherever the slaves went, the time between escape and publication in each place could have made the difference between freedom and capture.[20]

Table 8.3 illustrates that many owners were vigilant when they noticed or were informed of a runaway slave from their property. Within two weeks, 58.4 percent of masters had prepared a description, and by the end of a month, that number rose to 76 percent. That so many slaveholders advertised so quickly suggests that recovery of the fugitive slave far outweighed concerns about societal perceptions. Critically for slave owners, however, table 8.4 demonstrates that newspaper editors,

Table 8.3. Days between when a runaway escaped and when the slave owner wrote the advertisement

	Days between Escape and Ad Written	Percent
Same day	106	7.7
Within a week	442	32.1
1–2 weeks	256	18.6
2 weeks to a month	242	17.6
1–2 months	114	8.3
2–6 months	110	8.0
More than 6 months	46	3.3
Does not say	59	4.3
Total	1,375	

Table 8.4. Days between when a runaway escaped and when the advertisement was published in a newspaper

	Days between Escape and Ad Published	Percent
Same day	95	6.9
Within a week	267	19.4
1–2 weeks	284	20.7
2 weeks to a month	275	20.0
1–2 months	170	12.4
2–6 months	167	12.1
More than 6 months	64	4.7
Does not say	53	3.9
Total	1,375	

most likely because they managed weekly publications, were not able to print the notice with the same timeliness that slaveholders wrote their advertisements.[21] There is a noticeable 13.5 percent difference between the submission and publication dates for advertisements one to seven days after an escape.[22] The longer periods of time at the bottoms of the tables skew the averages in that direction, so the median is more representative of the trend in the dataset.[23] The median is ten days for table 8.3 and fifteen days for table 8.4. Almost 50 percent of runaway slaves in Texas could expect to have two weeks or more before an advertisement would appear in the newspaper.

Fugitive slaves were never "safe" considering all the aforementioned actions a slave owner might take before submitting an advertisement, but ten to fifteen days is a long time nevertheless. Contemplate the opportunities that this time lag would create. Slaves were likely aware of their owner's tendencies when it came to capturing and punishing runaway slaves. A slave with an advantage of two weeks could have had a walking radius of 30–40 miles or more (2,800–5,000 square miles) if they wished to move about their neighborhood and return home, and twice as far if they sought permanent freedom.[24] Millard suspected Maranda to be in Houston, 135 miles from Nacogdoches, but he offered no reasoning for this supposition. Maranda could have been anywhere, with a twenty-six-day head start. With each example or statistic that follows, imagine the psychological and geographic spaces that this kind of time could create for prospective and in-flight runaways like Maranda.

RUNAWAY SLAVES

The average runaway slave from Texas was a twenty-eight-year old man who had escaped by himself, departed from either Brazoria or Harris County, and was most likely headed making his way to an urban area or Mexico. Most runaways from Texas were men (91 percent), but not insignificant numbers of women were fugitive slaves.[25] Female runaways were very independent, escaping as individuals in 53 out of their 132 advertisement and capture notice attempts.

Texas runaway slaves escaped at all ages, with women ranging from little Eliza, age eight, to the sprightly octogenarian Kitty.[26] Female runaway slaves were by average and median two to three years younger than male fugitives.[27] A limited sample size for women creates measurable fluctuation from decade to decade that is not evident with the information on male runaway slaves. It is worth pointing out that the age of a runaway slave could be highly subjective. Edwin Waller advertised for Gumby and Zow in July 1837 as being twenty to twenty-five years old, only to suggest two months later in a new advertisement that they were each thirty years old.[28]

The frequency of runaway slaves traveling alone, in pairs, or in groups changed over time in Texas. The percentage of single runaways increased every decade, steadily increasing from about 46 percent in the 1830s and 1840s to 50 percent in the 1850s and 60 percent for the 1860s. There were likely a number of factors contributing to this shift, including the increased population of the state, the wider geographic

Table 8.5. Frequency of slave flight attempts from Texas counties, 1835–1865

Region (total # Attempts)	County (# Attempts)
Brazos-Colorado Region (503 attempts)	Washington Co. (102), Travis Co. (69), Bastrop Co. (67), Fayette Co. (47), Wharton Co. (46), Austin Co. (44), Colorado Co. (42), Milam Co. (34), Matagorda Co. (28), Burleson Co. (24)
Brazos-Trinity Region (492 attempts)	Harris Co. (120), Brazoria Co. (92), Fort Bend Co. (83), Robertson Co. (46), Montgomery Co. (44), Walker Co. (37), Grimes Co. (28), Galveston Co. (22), Freestone Co. (20)
East of the Trinity (219 attempts)	Harrison Co. (61), San Augustine Co. (43), Houston Co. (26), Nacogdoches Co. (25), Red River Co. (22), Smith Co. (22), Anderson Co. (20)

distribution of that population, stronger anti-runaway slave laws, and more vigilant enforcement of those laws.[29] With these countermeasures in place, running away in pairs or groups probably seemed like a less secure option for would be fugitives.[30]

The departure point for runaway slaves in Texas closely correlates to the plantation and farming districts along major rivers. Slaves escaped from all over Texas (there were specific locations for 1,646 attempts from ninety-two counties), but 73.8 percent of runaways left from just twenty-six counties. Each of these twenty-six counties had 20 or more escapes between 1835 and 1865 and can be divided into three general areas: ten counties between the Brazos and Colorado Rivers, nine counties between the Brazos and Trinity Rivers, and seven counties east of the Trinity River along the Angelina, Neches, Red, and Sabine Rivers.[31]

Slave owners and newspaper editors gave 783 possible destinations for runaway slaves. Most often they assumed fugitives were headed for free soil in Mexico (54.9 percent) or some place within Texas (22.9 percent).[32] In an important nuance however, slave owners, who had a financial stake in giving an accurate location, were much more liable to give a variety of destinations. All the possible destinations for Arkansas and Mississippi, as well as the majority for the Indian Territory (34 of 41) and Texas (163 of 179), come from slave-owner-written advertisements. In contrast, newspaper editors, who wrote the articles and might have been interested in making a sociopolitical statement about

Table 8.6. Presumed destination of fugitive slaves in Texas, 1835–1865

Presumed Destination	1830s Ads	1830s Arts	1840s Ads	1840s Arts	1850s Ads	1850s Arts	1860s Ads	1860s Arts	Total
Mexico	1	0	27	72	75	177	28	18	398
"West"	4	0	7	0	19	0	2	0	32
Texas	12	0	30	9	84	4	37	3	179
Louisiana	4	0	2	1	12	1	33	0	53
Indian territory	0	0	3	0	31	4	0	3	41
Arkansas/Mississippi	3	0	4	0	9	0	7	0	23
North / Union lines	4	0	2	0	1	2	9	9	27
Other	1	0	4	7	11	3	4	0	30
Not indicated	39	9	106	18	257	190	228	49	896
Total	68	9	185	107	499	381	348	82	1,679

Notes: 470 in advertisements ([312×1] + [65×2] + [8×3] + [1×4]) + 630 Not indicated = 1,100 (1,016 Attempts).
313 in Articles ([307×1] + [3×2]) + 266 Not indicated = 579 (576 Attempts).

Mexico, overwhelmingly identified that country as the destination of Texas' runaway slaves (267 of 313).

Slave owners sometimes had an idea where their slave might be going. In more than twenty attempts, it was specifically indicated that the runaway might be found visiting a family member. Other slaveholders were certain, especially with recently arrived slaves, that they were headed back to their old plantations or owners. Planters and farmers suspected their slaves would make for cities, where they could blend in with the free black and slave populations. Houston was the speculated destination for thirty-three attempts and Austin, fifteen. Cities are also mentioned as "by way" points to more distant destinations. The slave Anderson was thought to be going to Mexico from Velasco "by way of San Antonio or La Bahia" while John Henry Brown of Belton speculated John to "doubtless[ly] aim for Mexico, by way of Austin and San Antonio, or possibly by San Saba."[33]

Sometimes it was clear that slave owners had no clue about where their bondsmen were headed because they provided destinations in different cardinal directions. The owners of sixteen fugitives speculated that their slaves could be headed to either Mexico or Indian Territory. One exasperated master in Anderson County summed it up best when he wrote about the likelihood of either place for finding a group of five runaways, saying, "It is not known which, as one of the boys has been to Mexico, and another has been about the Indians."[34]

The story of Brad brings all of these potentialities together. He ran away from Jane Bagby, administrator of James B. Shanahan's Clarksville estate, in October 1858. The first advertisement was in January 1859, and Bagby did not know where Brad was going. In April she wrote a revision stating that Brad was making his way to Mexico after stopping in Washington County around New Year's. Bagby wrote a second revision in June 1859 relating that Brad had actually been living in Washington County all along, hiring his time, preaching, and visiting with his mother, who lived in Independence. Bagby still thought he was on his way to Mexico. This advertisement evidently succeeded, and she was able to capture Brad and sell him to William Hart of Clarksville. Hart referenced Bagby's experience when he wrote his own advertisement for Brad in March 1860, speculating that his newly acquired slave was either back in Washington County, making his way to Mexico, or going to Kansas.[35]

Many masters could not believe that their bondsmen would willingly leave them. T. M. Rector wrote honestly in his advertisement for Henry, "He is a boy of good countenance, and . . . I believe said negro was decoyed from my house by some white man or run away negro, as there was no cause for his leaving, that I am aware of."[36] The terminology varies—assisted, deceived, enticed, induced, tampered with—from person to person, but 20.6 percent of fugitive slave advertisement and articles include some inference of outside assistance in the escape attempt (328 runaways out of 1,592).[37]

In the eyes of many Texans, there were three main culprits to blame when it came to the disappearance of slaves: Mexican laborers, white negro thieves, and abolitionists. The vilification of Tejanos was ironic because it was their efforts in the 1820s and early 1830s that allowed Anglo-American immigrants and their slaves to establish a foothold in Texas. The Texas Revolution, the abbreviated Mexican invasion of 1842, and the Mexican-American War, combined with an influx of Anglo-American immigrants after each conflict unfamiliar with earlier Tejano sacrifices, reversed the perception of Tejanos in the state.[38] Mexico had outlawed slavery and refused to sign an extradition treaty for runaway slaves, so it seemed completely logical to many Texans that Mexicans living in Texas might have an ulterior motive.[39] Mexican peons in Texas were regarded as almost worse than slaves—"a lazy, thievish horde of lazaroni, who in many instances are fugitives from justice in Mexico, highway robbers, horse and cattle thieves, and idle vagabonds, who prowl about our western country with but little visible occupation or pursuit."[40] Their interactions with slaves unnerved slaveholders. Newspaper headlines like "Mexicans Aiding Negroes" and "More Slaves Piloted to Mexico by Mexican Peons" reinforced negative perceptions of Mexican immigrants.[41] Colorado and Matagorda Counties even expelled all Mexicans from their boundaries in 1856.[42] It was easier to scapegoat Mexico and its citizens than to accept the systemic reasons for flight.[43]

Slave theft was a problem in Texas, especially as the market value of bondsmen increased across the South throughout the 1840s and 1850s. Slave owners often attributed attempts to steal slaves to networks of thieves. Editor R. W. Loughery, summarizing the failure of one such plot, wrote: "Those who were captured stated that they had been induced to run away by several white men who told them they should be taken through Arkansas into Missouri to a free state. It is believed that there is an organized gang of negro thieves that has its station extended from the Colorado to Missouri."[44]

There were abolitionists or "free-soilers" in Texas working an "Underground Railroad" to Mexico and the northern United States, and they did succeed in helping some slaves escape.[45] A. B. Chamberlain, who married into a "respectable" Fayette County family, was caught there with a slave stolen from neighboring Burleson County. Chamberlain professed himself to be an abolitionist and that he "intended to free the negro, after hiring him for a time, or selling and stealing him again, to raise money to carry him to a free State."[46] Abolitionism was an ideological assault on Texas' slave society, and Texans lashed out with fear and violence against it. Texans were paranoid about the "evil emissaries," concerned that "in no portion of the Union is there a more inviting field for the emissaries of abolition than in Western Texas. We should watch with sleepless vigilance every step calculated to disturb the quiet and faithfulness of the slave population."[47] Slaveholders attributed the organization and fomenting of slave insurrections in the state, culminating with the "Texas Troubles" of 1860, as being the work of revolution-minded abolitionists.[48] In the face of action and rhetoric such as this, Chamberlain was fortunate to escape with a few years at the state prison in Huntsville.

The Texas dataset classifies slaves "stolen" by Mexicans, slave-stealers, or abolitionists as fugitive slaves. It is hard to read between the lines and discern whether these "thefts" occurred or whether the slaveholder just needed a convenient explanation to write off the uncomfortable truth of a runaway slave. Perhaps S. C. T. Ford said it best about his runaway, Joe Jackson: "I suppose he is either stolen by a free-soiler or an abolitionist or a negro thief; it all amounts to the same."[49]

Other ethnic groups were sometimes scapegoats of aggrieved and suspicious slaveholders. Charles De Morse, editor of the Clarksville *Northern Standard*, wrote two withering editorials about the Choctaw Nation in Indian Territory, accusing it of allowing "avowed abolitionists" in the form of northern missionaries on their lands. It was, De Morse writes, "a well known fact that all the runaway negroes from this part of Texas always fly to the Nation, and it is equally well known that they receive encouragement and are harbored by reason of the influence of the sentiments propagated by these Reverend Northern gentlemen."[50] J. P. Kingsbury, editor of the Doaksville, Oklahoma, *Choctaw Intelligencer*, responded in-kind:

> Some who have avowed themselves as abolitionists after their arrival here have remained but a short time, believing that this people were giving over to hardness of heart. . . . This people do not harbor runaway slaves and I defy anyone to prove to the contrary.—Runaway negroes are not such comfortable neighbors as to receive encouragement in lying out. Empty smokehouses and impoverished granaries would be the consequence. [We presume that it is very easy to get possession of slaves who escape to the Comanche and Mexican country where the Northern Missionaries have not yet gone!][51]

De Morse claimed victory with his rebuttal, quoting Kingsbury's first sentence, and some additional evidence, as proof that "Abolition Missionaries are there and exert the same influence as if they had been sent out by some plan." He rejected an offer by Kingsbury to inspect the Choctaw missions because "we can hear better preaching nearer home" and also cancelled the two newspapers' issue exchange.[52] De Morse's accusations against the Choctaw Nation belie the general lack of education Texas slaveholders had about their Native American neighbors' attitudes toward slavery.

Indian Territory was generally not a welcome destination for runaway slaves as many Texas slaveholders surmised. Although attitudes about slavery were not homogenous among the Cherokees, Chickasaws, Choctaws, Creeks, and Seminoles living in Indian Territory, and there were even significant divisions within the ethnic groups, citizens from all five tribes owned slaves. The "Lower Town" Creeks along the Arkansas River operated southern-style plantations and owned more than 1,800 slaves by 1860, more than 10 percent of the population for the entire Creek Nation in Indian Territory.[53] The Cherokee Nation created a slave code between 1839 and 1841 that outlawed literacy, possession of weapons, and intermarriage, and that organized a slave patrol.[54] There are many examples in the Arkansas and Mississippi datasets of slaves running away from masters in the Indian Territory.[55]

At the other end of the slaveholding spectrum, many Seminoles gave their slaves almost complete autonomy, requiring only an annual tribute or tithe. These Seminoles and their slaves lived separately but were close allies economically and militarily. The Seminoles were moved to Indian Territory from Florida by a treaty they signed with the United States and expected to assimilate into the Creek Nation, but the incongruous slave systems contributed to conflict between the "Lower Town" Creeks and a Seminole faction opposed to integration. Ultimately, about four hundred Seminoles, along with runaway slaves from Cherokee, Creek, and Seminole slave owners, immigrated to Mexico in 1850.[56] This migration created hysteria in Texas among slaveholders worried about the supposed lure of Wild Cat, leader of the Seminole dissidents, and his band of runaway slaves to their own bondsmen.[57] David Wall, from Grayson County on the Red River, advertised for two runaway slaves in December 1850, nine months after their disappearance. He was certain that Toney, who "was raised (in Mississippi) among the Chickasaw Indians," and his younger brother Sam, who was owned by George Wall across the river in the Choctaw Nation, were "in Texas with Wild Cat."[58]

Some slaveholding Texans also had an adverse view of German and Czech immigrants, conflating their minimal slaveholdings with abolitionism sentiments. When a small group of Germans from Kendall County labeled slavery as "evil" in an 1854 manifesto, and the editor of the San Antonio *Zeitung* doubled down in support, Germans from around central Texas vocally denounced the agitators and reaffirmed their support for slavery.[59] One German from Colorado County wrote the local editor to reassure him that "Germans are not opposed to slavery, but on the contrary, would own slaves themselves generally were they able to buy them." The same article also informed readers that in the first eight months of 1858, the sheriff of Gillespie County captured "twenty-three negroes who were attempting to make their escape into Mexico," with "the Germans of that section us[ing] every exertion to arrest [runaway] negroes making attempts."[60]

The preponderance of advertisement for attempts from the Colorado-Brazos-Trinity River regions noted earlier in the chapter is important context to understanding the locations of capture attempts (appendix table 8A.2). There are 976 documented capture locations for runaway slaves in Texas from 104 counties and five frontier forts. Between appendix table 8A.2 and the presumed destinations of fugitives in table 8.5, it is clear that there was a pronounced outward movement of runaway slaves from Texas' river plantation districts toward its borders with Mexico, Louisiana, and Indian Territory. The counties on Texas' western margins—Bexar (126), Travis (47), Gillespie (38), and Williamson (24)—had the most fugitive slaves captured. The residents of Fannin County caught 24 runaway slaves likely trying to make their way to Indian Territory. Runaway slaves headed east toward central and northern Louisiana were frequently jailed in Harrison (19), Nacogdoches (24), and San Augustine (19) Counties. Slaves trying to make their way into southeastern Louisiana were caught in Harris (39) and Galveston (22) Counties.

Despite the opportunities these places afforded runaway slaves, the statistics demonstrate the significant risk of capture a runaway slave faced by going to a city or town. More than 25 percent of capture attempts in the Texas dataset are from the six counties containing San Antonio, Austin, Houston, Galveston, Marshall, and Nacogdoches.

Cities and towns were important crossroads for slave owners and slave catchers. The latter came to population centers to search for runaway slaves, bring captured slaves to jail and collect the reward for their work. Slave owners came to personally look for runaways, post rewards, or collect bondsmen from jail. Runaway slave advertisements were often submitted to the Austin and Houston newspapers because their wide local and regional distribution increased the likelihood a subscriber would recognize and detain escaped slaves. Austin's main antebellum newspaper, the *Texas State Gazette*, published more runaway slave–related content than any other Texas newspaper.[61]

It is very likely that there were many more runaway slaves captured in Texas than reported. Lawmen, although required by republic and then state statutes, often did not publish notices for captured fugitive slaves. Many runaways were caught by their master or returned of their own accord, precluding the need for a capture notice. Even though the sheriff of Gillespie County "committed and delivered to their owners" twenty-three escaped slaves, there is not one documented newspaper capture notice for 1858 from Gillespie County yet in the Texas dataset.

Considering how often Texans presumed Mexico as the destination for their slaves, it is surprising that there were only eight runaways recorded in the dataset with a point of capture from across the Rio Grande. One reason might be that several articles illustrated to Texas subscribers that the capture of runaway slaves across the Rio Grande might encounter deadly resistance from the runaway slave and Mexicans. In November 1860 a slave convinced the ferryman at Laredo that he was a freeman and secured passage across the Rio Grande. Laredo resident Santos Benavides learned of the action and even gathered a posse of ten men to capture the fugitive, who "in the face of the entire population of the place, seized the negro, and succeeded in making good their retreat to the boat." Benavides and his group succeeded even though one man was severely injured from the "heavy fire" the Mexican citizenry laid on the boat "the moment they pushed out into the stream."[62]

This apprehension, as well as much less successful adventures like the 1855 Callahan "Indian hunting" expedition, illustrate the extreme risks Texans were willing to take to recover fugitive slaves and the lengths some would go to defend them. Eleven percent (175 of 1,592) of Texas fugitives described in advertisements and article attempts took a knife, pistol, rifle, or shotgun along with them. Even those without weapons could be dangerous. Captain J. Dellaney caught two runaways along the San Bernard River in 1852, but in the process of getting down an embankment to get them back to his boat, "Mr. Mills' negro sprang forward and seized hold of the gun and cried out to the other negro to strike [Dellaney] with a club . . . [and] when I raised my arm

Table 8.7. Escape attempts where the runaway slave stole a horse or mule

Dataset	State or Territory of Origin	Attempts with Equine	Total Attempts	Percentage
Texas[a]	Louisiana	10	200	5.0
	Texas	390	2,101	18.6
Arkansas[b]	Arkansas	20	403	5.0
	Louisiana	2	88	2.3
	Mississippi	1	86	1.2
	Texas	6	30	20.0
Mississippi[c]	Louisiana	3	500	0.6
	Mississippi	18	1,628	0.1

Notes: a. There are mounted escape attempts for 19.7 percent of advertisements (200/1,015), 11 percent of capture notices (49/446), all the estray notices (25/25), 19.8 percent of articles (114/577), and a few archival documents (2/38).
b. S. Charles Bolton, "Arkansas Runaway Slaves: 1820–1865" (unpublished manuscript, in the author's possession, February 2013).
c. Douglas B. Chambers and Max Grivno, "Runaway Slaves in Mississippi (1800–1860): Series I" (unpublished manuscript, in the author's possession, February 2013).

to ward off another blow aimed at me by the other negro, Mills' negro then got full possession of the gun." The slave fired and missed the captain, who now had to make his own escape.[63] Randolph Campbell wrote that "runaways, although they often were armed, generally did not use violence against their pursuers." Perhaps, but that might also be because the slaves who were caught infrequently had weapons. In a stark contrast to advertisements and articles, only 9 slaves out of 695 capture notice attempts had a knife or a gun.[64]

Another deterrent to capture was transportation. Fugitive slaves in Texas traveled by boat and, in at least one instance, escaped by rail, but the preferred conveyances were horses and mules.[65] There are 390 documented attempts of Texas runaway slaves using horses or mules to aid in their escape (18.6 percent of all attempts).[66] This is a substantially higher percentage than slaves from neighboring Arkansas and Louisiana documented in the Texas, Arkansas, and Mississippi datasets. Even with only 30 attempts, the percentage of slaves from Texas in the Arkansas dataset closely mirrors the Texas dataset. The quantity of escapes also counters recent historiography that horses had minimal utility to fugitive slaves.[67]

CONCLUSION

The nuances of entry, iteration, attempt, and runaway are banal to think about and seemingly divert attention from the amazing stories runaway slave advertisements can tell. It is this metadata-centric methodology, however, that draws out and provides new details about forgotten fugitive slaves like Maranda, who are no longer condemned to being statistics supporting runaway slaves with more descriptive textual evidence. By analyzing her advertisement's repetition, submission versus publication times, page placement, and so forth in concert with other archival sources, Maranda's humanity is acknowledged in ways that it might not have been previously. She has a voice, a story, "personality and personhood."[68] Metadata can help us to remember a runaway like Maranda, especially when her master's description was so minimal.

The focal point of runaway slave historiography in Texas may be the Mexican borderlands, but this was not the only place where slavery was contested in Texas. Indeed, if there is anything that the available research demonstrates, it is that fugitive slaves were ubiquitous in antebellum Texas itself, treading spaces from El Paso to Marshall and from the Red River to the Rio Grande. The number of runaways climbed every decade, increasing by 420 percent in the 1840s (92 to 400) and 279 percent in the 1850s (400 to 1,115). Even in the Civil War–shortened 1860s, the number of runaway slaves was on pace to exceed the 1850s.[69] There is little indication that the risks of running away—bodily harm, theft, capture, confinement, resale, death—outweighed the opportunity for freedom, be it temporary, long term, or permanent.

APPENDIX

Table 8A.1. Departure locations for fugitive slave escapes in Texas, 1835–1865

County (year created)	1830s	1840s	1850s	1860s	Total
Anderson (1846)	—	0	16	4	20
Angelina (1846)	—	0	1	0	1
Austin (1837)	5	4	21	14	44
Bandera (1856)	—	—	0	1	1
Bastrop (1837)	1	30	26	10	67
Bell (1850)	—	—	7	3	10
Bexar (1837)	0	3	15	5	23
Blanco (1858)	—	—	0	2	2
Bosque (1854)	—	—	—	1	1
Bowie (1841)	—	6	5	0	11
Brazoria (1837)	23	12	32	25	92
Brazos (1843)	—	0	1	2	3
Burleson (1846)	—	1	10	13	24
Burnet (1854)	—	0	4	0	4
Caldwell (1848)	—	0	2	1	3
Calhoun (1846)	—	0	3	1	4
Cass (1846)	—	0	10	2	12
Chambers (1858)	—	—	1	0	1
Cherokee (1846)	—	0	7	1	8
Collin (1846)	—	1	3	0	4
Colorado (1837)	1	4	21	16	42
Coryell (1854)	—	—	2	1	3
Dallas (1846)	—	0	2	4	6
DeWitt (1846)	—	0	12	3	15
Denton (1846)	—	0	1	1	2
Ellis (1850)	—	—	0	4	4
Falls (1850)	—	—	6	3	9
Fannin (1838)	0	0	4	1	5
Fayette (1838)	1	15	21	10	47
Fort Bend (1838)	5	7	50	21	83
Freestone (1851)	—	—	15	5	20
Galveston (1839)	0	3	11	8	22
Goliad (1837)	0	0	2	0	2
Gonzales (1837)	0	0	11	7	18
Grayson (1846)	—	0	1	0	1
Grimes (1846)	—	0	15	13	28
Guadalupe (1846)	—	0	10	3	13
Hardin (1858)	—	—	0	1	1
Harris (1837)	10	31	23	56	120
Harrison (1839)	0	4	37	20	61

County (year created)	1830s	1840s	1850s	1860s	Total
Hays (1843)	—	0	8	7	15
Henderson (1846)	—	0	1	2	3
Hopkins (1846)	—	0	1	1	2
Houston (1837)	1	7	10	8	26
Hunt (1846)	—	0	1	0	1
Jackson (1837)	0	1	1	0	2
Jasper (1837)	0	3	0	1	4
Jefferson (1836)	0	0	2	5	7
Johnson (1854)	—	—	1	1	2
Karnes (1854)	—	—	2	0	2
Kaufman (1848)	—	0	1	5	6
Lamar (1841)	—	3	4	0	7
Lampasas (1856)	—	—	0	1	1
Lavaca (1846)	—	0	3	11	14
Leon (1846)	—	2	7	3	12
Liberty (1837)	0	6	8	0	14
Limestone (1846)	—	0	15	4	19
Live Oak (1856)	—	—	1	0	1
Madison (1854)	—	—	3	5	8
Matagorda (1837)	3	3	18	4	28
McLennan (1850)	—	—	11	6	17
Milam (1837)	0	10	15	9	34
Montgomery (1837)	4	13	9	18	44
Nacogdoches (1837)	5	8	8	4	25
Navarro (1846)	—	1	7	1	9
Nueces (1846)	—	0	0	4	4
Panola (1846)	—	0	3	1	4
Parker (1855)	—	—	3	0	3
Polk (1846)	—	2	8	9	19
Red River (1837)	0	9	11	2	22
Robertson (1838)	0	19	16	11	46
Rusk (1843)	—	1	9	7	17
Sabine (1837)	0	6	3	0	9
San Augustine (1837)	6	8	23	6	43
San Saba (1856)	—	—	0	2	2
Shelby (1837)	0	3	2	0	5
Smith (1846)	—	0	13	9	22
Tarrant (1850)	—	—	0	3	3
Titus (1846)	—	2	2	0	4
Travis (1840)	2	8	35	24	69
Trinity (1850)	—	—	0	1	1
Tyler (1846)	—	0	3	2	5
Upshur (1846)	—	0	9	1	10
Uvalde (1856)	—	—	0	1	1

(continued)

Table 8A.1—*Continued*

County (year created)	1830s	1840s	1850s	1860s	Total
Van Zandt (1848)	—	0	0	5	5
Victoria (1837)	0	0	5	3	8
Walker (1846)	—	14	14	9	37
Washington (1837)	3	25	54	20	102
Wharton (1846)	—	0	24	22	46
Williamson (1848)	—	0	11	6	17
Wood (1850)	—	—	1	0	1
Young (1856)	—	—	1	0	1
Texas (General)	7	68	62	38	175
Does not say	8	24	217	87	336
Total	85	367	1,074	631	2,157

Note: Data compiled from 1,016 attempts in advertisements, 527 attempts in capture and estray notices, 576 attempts in articles, and 38 attempts in archival documents.

Table 8A.2. Capture locations for fugitive slave captures in Texas, 1835–1865

County (year created)	1830s	1840s	1850s	1860s	Total
Anderson (1846)	—	1	2	0	3
Atascosa (1856)	—	—	1	0	1
Austin (1837)	0	3	0	15	18
Bandera (1856)	—	—	0	2	2
Bastrop (1837)	0	3	15	0	18
Bell (1850)	—	—	3	0	3
Bexar (1837)	1	14	47	64	126
Blanco (1858)	—	—	0	1	1
Bowie (1841)	—	3	0	0	3
Brazoria (1837)	2	5	4	3	14
Brazos (1843)	—	0	5	0	5
Burleson (1846)	—	0	2	0	2
Burnet (1854)	—	2	3	2	7
Caldwell (1848)	—	0	4	3	7
Calhoun (1846)	—	1	0	0	1
Cameron (1846)	—	0	2	3	5
Cass (1846)	—	0	1	0	1
Cherokee (1846)	—	0	1	0	1
Coleman (1858)	—	—	1	0	1
Collin (1846)	—	0	2	0	2
Colorado (1837)	2	0	5	2	9
Comal (1846)	—	0	1	3	4
Comanche (1856)	—	—	5	0	5
Coryell (1854)	—	—	4	2	6

County (year created)	1830s	1840s	1850s	1860s	Total
Dallas (1846)	—	1	10	2	13
DeWitt (1846)	—	0	2	1	3
Denton (1846)	—	0	0	1	1
El Paso (1850)	—	—	1	0	1
Ellis (1850)	—	—	7	1	8
Erath (1856)	—	—	1	0	1
Falls (1850)	—	—	1	1	2
Fannin (1838)	0	10	9	5	24
Fayette (1838)	0	2	3	7	12
Fort Bend (1838)	1	10	6	1	18
Galveston (1839)	0	1	9	12	22
Gillespie (1848)	—	0	33	5	38
Goliad (1837)	0	0	2	0	2
Gonzales (1837)	0	1	3	4	8
Grayson (1846)	—	0	4	0	4
Grimes (1846)	—	0	4	5	9
Guadalupe (1846)	—	0	1	2	3
Hamilton (1858)	—	—	3	0	3
Harris (1837)	8	18	3	10	39
Harrison (1839)	0	3	4	12	19
Hays (1843)	—	0	6	3	9
Henderson (1846)	—	0	2	0	2
Hill (1853)	—	—	—	2	2
Hopkins (1846)	—	0	1	0	1
Houston (1837)	0	4	7	0	11
Hunt (1846)	—	0	3	0	3
Jackson (1837)	1	1	2	0	4
Jasper (1837)	0	1	0	2	3
Jefferson (1837)	1	1	0	0	2
Johnson (1854)	—	—	0	1	1
Kerr (1856)	—	—	3	0	3
Kinney (1850)	—	—	1	0	1
Lamar (1841)	—	0	2	6	8
Lampasas (1856)	—	—	2	4	6
Lavaca (1846)	—	0	8	0	8
Leon (1846)	—	0	3	0	3
Liberty (1837)	0	3	9	2	14
Limestone (1846)	—	0	10	4	14
Live Oak (1856)	—	—	0	1	1
Llano (1856)	—	—	1	1	2
Madison (1854)	—	—	2	2	4
Marion (1860)	—	—	—	3	3
Matagorda (1837)	0	1	3	2	6
Maverick (1856)	—	—	5	0	5

(continued)

Table 8A.2—*Continued*

County (year created)	1830s	1840s	1850s	1860s	Total
McLennan (1850)	—	—	0	1	1
Medina (1848)	—	0	2	0	2
Milam (1837)	0	6	1	0	7
Montgomery (1837)	0	2	2	9	13
Nacogdoches (1837)	6	6	8	4	24
Navarro (1846)	—	1	2	1	4
Nueces (1846)	—	0	1	3	4
Orange (1852)	—	—	0	7	7
Panola (1846)	—	0	1	1	2
Parker (1855)	—	—	0	1	1
Polk (1846)	—	2	0	1	3
Presidio (1857)	—	—	1	0	1
Red River (1837)	0	6	7	3	16
Robertson (1838)	0	16	5	0	21
Rusk (1843)	—	2	3	13	18
Sabine (1837)	0	7	0	0	7
San Augustine (1837)	0	8	10	1	19
San Patricio (1837)	0	0	6	0	6
Shelby (1837)	0	1	1	1	3
Smith (1846)	—	0	1	0	1
Starr (1848)	—	0	0	2	2
Tarrant (1850)	—	—	0	1	1
Travis (1840)	0	2	28	17	47
Trinity (1850)	—	—	2	1	3
Tyler (1846)	—	0	1	3	4
Upshur (1846)	—	0	0	2	2
Uvalde (1856)	—	—	4	2	6
Van Zandt (1848)	—	—	0	2	2
Victoria (1837)	1	2	7	2	12
Walker (1846)	—	0	6	8	14
Washington (1837)	2	0	11	0	13
Webb (1848)	—	0	10	5	15
Wharton (1846)	—	0	2	0	2
Williamson (1848)	—	0	16	8	24
Wood (1850)	—	—	0	1	1
Young (1856)	—	—	2	0	2
Ft. Chadbourne (1852)	—	—	2	1	3
Ft. Graham (1849)	—	0	2	—	2
Ft. Lancaster (1855)	—	—	1	0	1
Ft. McKavett (1852)	—	—	6	0	6
Ft. Phantom Hill (1851)	—	—	0	1	1
USS Morning Light (1863)	—	—	—	21	21

County (year created)	1830s	1840s	1850s	1860s	Total
Texas (General)	1	1	31	8	41
Mexico	0	0	7	1	8
Indian Territory	0	1	5	1	7
Other states (La./Mo.)	0	0	5	1	6
Does not say	2	6	53	26	87
Total	28	158	536	362	1084

Note: Data compiled from 695 attempts in capture and estray notices, 305 attempts from articles, and 20 attempts from archival documents. The appendix also includes 39 instances when there was an advertisement and a capture notice for the same individual. These were indexed in table 8A.1 as advertisements.

NOTES

1. *Telegraph and Texas Register*, November 28, 1838, pg. 3, col. 5; and *Morning Star*, July 2 1840, pg. 4, col. 2.

2. Maranda was in the *Telegraph and Texas Register* eighty-two times, between November 28, 1838, and October 7, 1840, and *Morning Star* twenty-one times between July 2, 1840, and August 25, 1840.

3. The basis for this chapter is research from the Texas Runaway Slave Project (TRSP) http://digital.sfasu.edu/cdm/landingpage/collection/RSP. The author is project manager and principle researcher. TRSP research commenced in December 2012 and is ongoing. The project documents over 17,430 extant antebellum Texas newspaper issues and has reviewed nearly 15,600 of them. All data presented in the chapter is current as of September 2017. Many thanks to Dr. Douglas B. Chambers, Linda Reynolds, and Hayley Hasik for proofreading chapter drafts; the Summerlee Foundation and Stephen F. Austin State University for financially supporting the project; Dillon Wackerman for creating the project website and managing the initial contents uploads; and all the project researchers—Patricio DeJesus, Hayley Ellisor, Nydia Hernandez, Joanna Lovejoy, Mark Musquiz, Michael Smith, and Darah Vann.

4. *Democratic Telegraph and Texas Register*, February 21, 1851, pg. 3, col. 4; *Texas State Gazette*, February 24, 1851, pg. 5, co1.3; *San Antonio Ledger*, March 6, 1851, pg. 3, col. 3; and *South-Western American*, May 28, 1851, pg. 4, col. 1. Robinson asked in his first advertisement for newspapers in Brownsville, San Antonio and Austin to republish the notice. Armed with three guns, including two double-barreled shotguns, these were a potentially dangerous group of runaway slaves.

5. "Account of the Farm," Josephus Brooks, 1859–1860, Box 1, Folder 1, A102, *Josephus Brooks Account of Franklin B. Sublett Plantation, Trinity County, Texas, 1859–1891*, East Texas Research Center, Stephen F. Austin State University, Nacogdoches, Texas.

6. *Texas State Gazette*, February 21, 1854, pg. 6, col. 2; and *Weekly State Gazette*, August 31, 1864, pg. 1, col. 5.

7. *Telegraph and Texas Register*, October 9, 1839, pg. 3 col. 3; and *Galveston News (Tri-Weekly)*, September 26, 1857, pg. 2, col. 4. Cain is described as being thirteen in 1839 and twenty-six in 1857. Likely his owner did not know Cain's real age and made an educated guess.

8. *Telegraph and Texas Register*, July 31, 1839, pg. 3, col. 3; and *Democratic Telegraph and Texas Register*, March 1, 1849, pg. 3, col. 4.

9. *Texas State Times*, July 28, 1855, pg. 2, col. 1.

10. Table 8.1 breaks down the Texas dataset for each of the four measurements. "Advertisements" data in the chapter should sum up to 1,016, the number of attempts from Texas. There are 446 "capture notice" attempts for slaves from Texas. The data point for "articles" is 576 attempts. There are 25 attempts in "estray notices," which generally describes situations where someone confronted a mounted runaway slave but chose to capture the horse and let the fugitive go. The Texas dataset is just beginning to incorporate archival documents, so there are only 38 attempts. Jail breaks (25 entries, 38 iterations, 27 runaways, 27 attempts) are found in advertisements, capture notices, and articles. The TRSP includes fugitive slave content (more than four hundred article iterations) about other states. Table 8.1 does not include this material because it does not pertain to Texas. There are a far higher number of runaway slaves from Texas in the Texas dataset (84.2 percent) than from Arkansas in the Arkansas dataset (53 percent—326 of 615). Arkansas' position on the Mississippi River and border with five slave states and Indian Territory might be the reason. See S. Charles Bolton, *Fugitives from Injustice: Freedom-Seeking Slaves in Arkansas, 1800–1860: Historic Resource Study* (Philadelphia: National Underground Railroad Network to Freedom, 2006), 24.

11. See John Hope Franklin and Loren Schweninger, *Runaway Slaves: Rebels on the Plantation* (New York: Oxford University Press, 1999), 282. Franklin and Schweninger made understandable and strategic choices in largely omitting borderland states like Arkansas, Missouri, and Texas from their monograph. These states were on the margins, adopted large-scale plantation slavery much later that southeastern states, and thus had smaller slave populations.

12. Sterling Robertson had three slaves run away, "who, in a few days concluded that 'there is no place like home' and returned, but not until he had been at some considerable expense in having them posted." *Belton Independent*, June 19, 1858, pg. 2, col. 4. Franklin and Schweninger contend that "most runaways remained out only a few weeks or months." Franklin and Schweninger, *Runaway Slaves*, 282.

13. Texas newspapers frequently mention slave owners and others going into Mexico to capture runaway slaves but rarely in a professional capacity. Fredric Law Olmsted encountered "a considerable number of men making a business hunting" fugitives. See Fredric Law Olmsted, *A Journey through Texas, Or a Saddle-Trip on the Southwestern Frontier* (1857; repr., Lincoln: University of Nebraska Press, 2004), 313–14, 327. Slaveholders like C. H. Taylor of Fayette County were willing to pay a lot of money for runaway slaves caught in Mexico. Taylor offered three hundred dollars if his slave Gin, a blacksmith, was caught west of the Rio

Grande and two hundred dollars if he was caught west of the San Antonio River. See *Texas Monument*, January 29, 1851, pg. 3, col. 4. A network for bonding and transporting captured runaway slaves in Texas did exist. In the published "Proceedings of Bexar County in regard to Runaway Slaves," the last sentence reads "The sheriff is recommended to discountenance the practice of officers or others purchasing rewards to which others are entitled, and the executive committee are not to give the purchaser more than the actual cash which he paid for the claim." *Texas State Gazette*, September 16, 1854, pg. 4, col. 3. Three examples of Texans with slave dogs for hire: *Bastrop Advertiser*, March 14, 1857, pg. 3, col. 4; *Democrat and Planter*, July 8, 1856, pg. 4, col. 3; and *Huntsville Item*, March 16, 1860, pg. 3, col. 3.

14. For slaveholders, "paternalism defined the involuntary labor of the slaves as a legitimate return to their masters for protection and direction." See Eugene D. Genovese, *Roll Jordan Roll: The World the Slaves Made* (New York: Vintage Books, 1976), 5. Sean M. Kelley writes that paternalism negotiated the "middle ground, or borderland" of master–slave relationships. He suggests that early Texas slaveholders thus carved their farms and plantations out of the frontier with a "borderland paternalism" in which their slaves were "partners" cultivating and civilizing the wilderness. See Sean M. Kelley, *A Plantation Society in the Texas Borderlands, 1821–1865* (Baton Rouge: Louisiana State University Press, 2010), 93–98.

15. Bertram Wyatt-Brown, *Southern Honor: Ethics and Behavior in the Old South* (Oxford: Oxford University Press, 2007).

16. Robert F. Millard and his young daughter, Mary Anna Frances Isabella, moved to Nacogdoches County sometime before 1835. "Merinda," eighteen years old and of good health, was purchased in Mary's name from Lewis Knight on February 12, 1838 for eight hundred dollars. Maranda was the Millard's only slave from 1837 to 1840. She had a child named Phebe in 1842, so she was apparently returned or was captured between sometime between 1840 and 1842. Millard married Massie W. Sparks in December 1843. Maranda had two more children before Millard died in 1847. The 1849 probate guardianship record for Mary lists "Marinda," age thirty to thirty-five, and three children—Phebe, seven; Harriet, three; and Helen, eighteen months. Was Millard the father of Maranda's children? It is impossible to say either way. See Nacogdoches County Deed Book B, p.349; "Probate Guardianship of Mary A. F. I. Millard," Nacogdoches County Probate Case Files, box 10, folder 43; and 1837–48 tax records for Robert F. Millard in Nacogdoches County Tax Rolls, 1837–1880, microfilm. These records are all at the East Texas Research Center, Ralph W. Steen Library, Stephen F. Austin State University, Nacogdoches, Texas. See also "Millard, Robert F.," Nacogdoches County Genealogical Society, *Nacogdoches County Families* (Dallas, Curtis Media Corp., 1985), 467–68.

17. See the progression for Gumby and Zow in the *Telegraph and Texas Register*. They were advertised for from June 8–24, 1837 ($50, 3 times), July 22–August 5, 1837 ($100, 3 times), December 16, 1837–December 5, 1838 ($200, 20 times), May 19–May 26, 1838 ($200, 3 times), May 30–November 17, 1838 ($500, 17

times), and November 24, 1838–January 26, 1839 ($500, 19 times). Dill was in *Morning Star* 153 times (January 29, 1840–August 4, 1840) and *Telegraph and Texas Register* (July 8, 1840–October 7, 1840) 9 times.

18. The first appearance sums to 947 entries instead of 941 entries because in six cases the advertisement appears on multiple pages. The most common locations for runaway slave advertisements in Texas newspapers are on page 3, columns 2–4 (260 times) or page 2, columns 4–6 (211 times).

19. Franklin and Schweninger, *Runaway Slaves*, 238–39.

20. *Tri-Weekly Telegraph*, September 15, 1862, pg. 1, col. 4; *State Gazette*, September 17, 1862, pg. 1, col. 5; and *San Antonio Weekly Herald*, September 20, 1862, pg. 2, col. 5.

21. Slave owners might have to travel a fair distance to get their advertisement to the closest town with a newspaper. Delays or omissions also occurred when newspapers editors also ran out of paper (for example, the *Belton Independent*, December 1858–February 1859), rationed their print paper by publishing half-sheets (such as during the Civil War), cut back in anticipation of going out of business, or took vacations.

22. There are 1,374 iterations in table 8.1 but 1,375 in tables 8.3 and 8.4. The advertisement that lawman W. B. Reeves of Houston placed for the slave Sam uniquely has five associated dates (Sam's departure from the plantation of Charles Lastrapes about August 3, 1850; Lastrapes' advertisement, August 17; no date of capture; Sam's escape from jail in October 1850; Reeves' advertisement December 12; and the publication of the and advertisement in the *Democratic Telegraph and Texas Register*, December 13, 1850, pg. 3, col. 3). In instances where only the month of escape is provided, the author used the midpoint of that month (the fifteenth) as the basis for calculations. Sam is entered twice in table 8.3 (August 3–17 [fourteen days] and October 15–December 12 [fifty-eight days]) and table 8.4 (August 3–17 [fourteen days] and October 15–December 13 [fifty-nine days]).

23. B. W. Rentfrow of Milam County submitted an advertisement for Henry and Bob, who ran away in the summer of 1861, roughly 600–650 days after they escaped. *San Antonio Herald*, April 4, 1863, pg. 2, col. 4.

24. For slave neighborhoods, see Anthony E. Kaye, *Joining Places: Slave Neighborhoods in the Old South* (Chapel Hill: University of North Carolina Press, 2007). There are several tangential lines of thought on runaway slave mobility. One perspective can be generalized as the "absentees": that slaves had only "an elementary knowledge of geography and had no means of transportation at their command," which supports the argument that most fugitives were "lying out" locally as "truants" or "lurkers" for a few days before returning home. See Genovese, *Roll, Jordan, Roll*, 650; Franklin and Schweninger, *Runaway Slaves*, 97–109; and Larry Eugene Rivers, *Rebels and Runaways: Slave Resistance in 19th Century Florida* (Urbana: University of Illinois Press, 2013), 40, 68. Historians also make distinctions about the nature of fugitive slaves, suggesting behavioral differences between African-born and mulatto, and skilled and unskilled bondsmen. See

Gerald W. Mullin, *Flight and Rebellion: Slave Resistance in Eighteenth-Century Virginia* (New York: Oxford University Press, 1972), 34–37. Other scholars, while not dismissing absenteeism, note that many slaves in the Lower South, and in particular those in frontier states like Texas, were well traveled. These bondsmen and women were walked, carted, or boated either with their masters as they and their families immigrated westward or transported from the Upper South to hubs like New Orleans as part of the interstate slave trade. S. Charles Bolton writes that the slaves acquired knowledge, experience, and a "worldliness that when beyond that of slaves who lived on the plantation where they had grown up." See Walter Johnson, *Soul by Soul: Life Inside the Antebellum Slave Market* (Cambridge, Mass.: Harvard University Press, 1999), 5–7; and Bolton, *Fugitives from Injustice*, 4–5. Outside San Antonio, Olmsted interviewed a slave who was raised on Maryland's Eastern Shore, bought from a coffle marched to South Carolina, moved to Tennessee with his master, sold to Arkansas, and then sold to a man immigrating to Texas. The slave had been in the state four years, including three years hiring his time out in San Antonio. See Olmsted, *A Journey through Texas*, 230. Slaveholders ascribed a trade skill to only 93 of 1,711 runaway slaves in Texas advertisement and capture notice attempts.

25. There are 152 female and 1,533 male runaway slaves documented from advertisements and capture notice attempts. Age-based statistics exclude children aged eleven and under (9 female, 21 male) and runaways with no age given (12 women, 247 men).

26. See iterations for Eliza in the *Morning Star*, August 31, 1844, pg. 3, col. 3; *Telegraph and Texas Register*, September 11, 1844, pg. 3, col. 3; and *Telegraph and Texas Register*, January 8, 1845, pg. 4, col. 2. See the advertisement for Kitty in the *Goliad Express*, September 5, 1857, pg. 3, col. 1.

27. The sample consists of 131 women (mean age of 25.5 and median age of 23.3) and 1,264 men (mean age of 28 and median age of 26).

28. *Telegraph and Texas Register*, July 22, 1837, pg. 3, col. 1; and *Matagorda Bulletin*, September 27, 1837, pg. 3, col. 1.

29. In 1846 the Texas Legislature created the formal slave patrol system and in 1858 passed An Act to Encourage the Reclamation of Slaves Escaping Beyond the Limits of the Slave Territories of the United States to legalize the capture of runaways in Mexico. See Randolph B. Campbell, William S. Pugsley, and Marilyn P. Duncan, *The Laws of Slavery in Texas* (Austin: University of Texas Press, 2010), 65–66.

30. Historians should consider better periodization (by the decade or less) if they are going to use the number of runaway slaves as a statistic. The Arkansas dataset for 1820–36 (49.3 percent of fugitive slaves escaped alone) and 1836–61 (70.7 percent escaped alone); the Kentucky dataset from 1788–1849 (78.4 percent escaped alone) and 1850–63 (64 percent escaped alone); and The Runaway Slave Database: 1790–1816 (60 percent escaped alone) and 1838–1860 (72 percent escaped alone) are too open to false positives on this count. Measured the same way, the data (1835–65) from Texas misleadingly suggests that the number

of individual escapes (1,201 total—51.9 percent) and pairs/group escapes (1,041 total—45 percent) were fairly balanced over time. See Bolton, *Fugitives from Injustice*, 21; J. Blaine Hudson, *Fugitive Slaves and the Underground Railroad in the Kentucky Borderland* (Jefferson, N.C.: McFarland, 2002), 33; and Franklin and Schweninger, *Runaway Slaves*, 229.

31. See appendix table 8A.1 at the end of the chapter for the full distribution of escape attempts.

32. In the descriptions of thirty-two advertisements, slaveholders simply state that their slave or slaves are making their way "West." This was likely synonymous with Mexico, as cardinal west for most antebellum Texans put runaway slaves in the heart of Comanche territory, where they were as unwelcome as their masters. Fugitive slaves that were captured by the Comanche might be killed and tortured, assimilated into the tribe, ransomed back to U.S. or Texan officials, or sold to other Native Americans. See Pekka Hämäläinen, *The Comanche Empire* (New Haven, Conn.: Yale University Press, 2008), 153–54, 213–19.

33. *Brazos Courier*, July 14, 1840, pg. 3, col. 2; and *State Gazette*, June 19, 1858, pg. 3, col. 7.

34. *Galveston News (Tri-Weekly)*, September 5, 1857, pg. 2, col. 4.

35. *Standard*, January 22, 1859, pg. 2, col. 7; *State Gazette*, April 2, 1859, pg. 3, col. 4; *State Gazette*, June 25, 1859, pg. 3, col. 4; and *Standard*, March 3, 1860, pg. 3, col. 5.

36. *Weekly State Gazette*, March 9, 1864, pg. 2, col. 5.

37. Slaveholders in Kentucky suspected outside assistance for 30.9 percent of escapes between 1850 and 1863. By comparison, Texans indicated the same concerns in about 18.2 percent of runaways escaping between 1850 and 1865. See Hudson, *Fugitive Slaves*, 39. Bondsmen may have used slaveholders' own fears against them by claiming, when they were finally captured, to have been stolen. Kevin Grubbs suggests this played into slave owners' paternalism, the runaway slaves casting themselves as unwitting victims and as still "loyal" servants in the hopes of receiving a reduced punishment for their escape. See Kevin Grubbs, "Pathways of Escape: The Interstate Slave Trade and Runaway Slaves in Mississippi," *Journal of Mississippi History* 75 (Summer 2013): 159–60.

38. Andrew Torget, *Seeds of Empire: Cotton, Slavery, and the Transformation of the Texas Borderlands, 1800–1850* (Chapel Hill: University of North Carolina Press, 2015), 220–22, 256–57.

39. James David Nichols argues that there was actually a much more complex cross migration in play as poor Mexicans immigrated north to Texas looking for work at the same time slaves sought freedom by crossing the Rio Grande from Texas. For research on their intersection, see James David Nichols, "The Line of Liberty: Runaway Slaves and Fugitive Peons in the Texas-Mexico Borderlands," *Western Historical Quarterly* 44 (Winter 2013): 413–33.

40. "Public Meeting at Seguin—Vagrant Mexicans," *Texas State Gazette*, September 9, 1854, pg. 5, col. 2.

41. "Mexicans Aiding Negroes," *Texas State Times*, October 7, 1854, pg. 2, col.

6; and "More Slaves Piloted to Mexico by Mexican Peons," *Indianola Bulletin,* May 31, 1855, pg. 2, col. 5.

42. Randolph B. Campbell, *An Empire for Slavery: The Peculiar Institution in Texas, 1821–1865* (Baton Rouge: Louisiana State University Press, 1989), 219.

43. Rosalie Schwartz, "Runaway Negroes: Mexico as an Alternative for United States Blacks (1825–1860)" (M.A. thesis, San Diego State University, 1974), 56–57.

44. "Negro Thieves," *Texas Republican,* July 13, 1849, pg. 2, col. 5.

45. Sol Childress captured a slave in Mexico who told his jailers in San Antonio that he "went to Chihuahua over the Memphis and El Paso Mail route, and that he was assisted and fed at the stations all along the road by the employees of the line. After crossing the Rio Grande, he was employed by the Company as station keeper for them at $20 per month." *Civilian and Gazette (Weekly),* December 21, 1858, pg. 1, col. 1. An editorial by "Vijante" questions the veracity of this narrative, however. See "Mistakes—Unwelcome Visitors—Troops returning Home—Spiritual Rappings—Negro Falsehoods concerning Overland Mail Company, &c., &c.," *Southern Intelligencer,* February 9, 1859, pg. 1, cols. 5–6.

46. "Negro Thief," *True Issue,* February 23, 1856, pg. 2, col. 4.

47. "Runaway Negroes," *Indianola Bulletin,* May 24, 1853, pg. 2, col. 3.

48. For an early insurrection scares, see *Telegraph and Texas Register,* September 15, 1841, pg. 2, col. 4. For the 1850s and 1860, see Donald E. Reynolds, *Texas Terror: The Slave Insurrection Panic of 1860 and the Secession of the Lower South* (Baton Rouge: Louisiana State University Press, 2007). See also, "Sentiments of the Press and People," *State Gazette,* August 4, 1860, pg. 2, cols. 6–7.

49. *Texas Republican,* May 31, 1851, pg. 3, col. 2.

50. Charles De Morse, "Choctaw Missionaries," *Northern Standard,* June 15, 1850, pg. 2, col. 4.

51. Brackets in the original. J. P. Kingsbury, "Decidely Rich!" *Choctaw Intelligencer,* June 27, 1850, pg. 2, cols. 2–3.

52. De Morse, "Choctaw Intelligencer Missionaries &c," *Northern Standard,* July 6, 1850, pg. 2, col. 4.

53. See David A. Chang, *The Color of the Land: Race, Nation, and the Politics of Landownership in Oklahoma, 1832–1929* (Chapel Hill: University of North Carolina Press, 2010), 29. In contrast to the "Lower Town" Creeks, the "Upper Town" Creeks owned very few slaves.

54. See Celia E. Naylor-Ojurongbe, *"More at Home with the Indians": African-American Slaves and Freedpeople in the Cherokee Nation, Indian Territory, 1838–1907* (Ph.D. diss., Duke University, 2001), 3–5, 76–82.

55. Alice Ivas analyzes all seventy-seven in her article "Claims to Freedom: Slave Resistance and Southern Indian Identity, 1820–1850," *Journal of Mississippi History* 75 (Summer 2013): 173–91.

56. See Kevin Mulroy, *Freedom on the Border: The Seminole Maroons in Florida, the Indian Territory, Coahuila, and Texas* (Lubbock: Texas Tech University Press, 1993).

57. The Seminole immigration is accurately described in an article from the *Texas State Gazette*, November 16, 1850, pg. 2 col. 1. In contrast, W. Secrest suggests "there are not less than eighteen hundred runaways at the town that has lately been built by Wild Cat near the mouth of Los Moras. The greater part of these runaways have escaped from Arkansas, but at least five hundred are, it is said, fugitives from Texas." *Telegraph & Texas Register*, August 29, 1851, pg. 2 col. 4.

58. *Texas State Gazette*, December 21, 1850, pg. 7, col. 1.

59. Campbell, *Empire for Slavery*, 215–17.

60. *Colorado Citizen*, August 14, 1858, pg. 2, col. 4.

61. The Texas dataset contains 564 iterations from 769 issues of the *Texas State Gazette* (1849–65). Despite having been published for fourteen more years and having 450 more issues, there are only 388 iterations from the newspaper with the second most runaway slave content, Houston's *Telegraph and Texas Register* (1835–64).

62. "Capture of Runaway Negroes," *Ranchero*, December 29, 1860, pg. 2, col. 5; and "A Speck of War," *The Civilian and Gazette (Weekly)*, November 27, 1860, pg. 3, col. 1.

63. *Texas State Gazette*, July 10, 1852, pg. 4, col. 3.

64. Campbell, *Empire for Slavery*, 183.

65. Slaves in Galveston on at least two occasions stole boats from Galveston to try to reach the Union blockade during the Civil War. See "Affairs in Galveston," *Tri-Weekly Telegraph*, October 20, 1862, pg. 1, cols. 4–5. The best example of boat travel in the dataset are eight slaves owned by the Louisiana Pilot's Association who stole a boat from the mouth of the Mississippi River and were thought to be sailing down the coast for Texas or Mexico. See *Civilian and Galveston City Gazette*, June 8, 1844, pg. 3, col. 3. An example of rail travel is Abe, whose owner, John Ewing, wrote that Abe had been sighted at "Millican's depot June 25th trying to make his escape to Galveston with my other negroes.—If he did not get on the cars there, he will try other depots." *Tri-Weekly Telegraph*, July 15, 1863, pg. 2, col. 6.

66. Slaves were adept at stealing horses. One observer in Columbus, Texas, noted after Indians were blamed for stealing horses and the culprits turned out to be runaway slaves that "no doubt half the cattle and horses that are stolen and charged upon the Indians are taken either by white men . . . or negroes." *Morning Star*, December 10, 1840, pg. 2, cols. 1–2. Olmsted, in describing how a runaway slave in Texas escaped, said they traveled by dark and "follow[ed] the roads upon any horse he can lay his hands upon." See *A Journey Through Texas*, 327–28. Hudson gives several examples of Kentucky fugitive slaves stealing horses and mentions their importance in the introduction of a short analysis entitled "By Road, River and Rail," but then fails to follow-up, focusing exclusively on steamboat and train travel. See Hudson, *Fugitive Slaves*, 60–61, 65.

67. Only maroons, Sylviane A. Diouf suggests, had any real use for horses. See

Slavery's Exiles: The Story of the American Maroons (New York: New York University Press, 2014), 231–34.

68. Paraphrased from Douglas B. Chambers, "I Was an Estray," *Journal of Mississippi History* 75 (Summer 2013): 90.

69. The number of runaways from 1860 to 1865 (705) divided by 55 percent (5.5 years into the decade in June 1865).

9

"Design His Course to Mexico"

The Fugitive Slave Experience in the Texas–Mexico Borderlands, 1850–1853

MEKALA AUDAIN

Henry hoped that November 12, 1853, would be the last day he used an anvil as an enslaved man. After careful planning, he escaped from Port Lavaca, Texas, located about eighty miles north of Corpus Christi. He was between thirty and thirty-five years old—neither he nor his owner were certain of his actual age—and fit into the typical fugitive slave profile: a male between sixteen and thirty-five years old. (Family obligations and childrearing responsibilities often prevented most enslaved women from escaping at the same rates as their male counterparts.) Like most Texas slaveholders in the 1850s, his owner, John Irwin, was certain that Henry had escaped to Mexico because the nation's proximity to Texas made it a suitable option for runaways. He believed Henry used the road leading to Lockhart, Texas, to escape north, then traveled west to San Antonio, and finally traversed south Texas until he crossed the Rio Grande. Henry's familiarity with this road to Lockhart likely stemmed from being hired out for blacksmith work on several occasions. Besides being well traveled for an enslaved person, Henry had also become very comfortable speaking to white people. Irwin warned that he was "very smart and when interrogated [would] tell a very plausible story."[1] If questioned during his escape, he could mislead others about his intentions by telling them that he was traveling for work. His frequent travels on this road and access to a travel badge would easily corroborate his story.[2]

Henry could have reduced the length of his journey to Mexico by traveling south directly toward Matamoros, a northeastern Mexican port city just south of Brownsville, Texas, instead of escaping west to San Antonio and then southwest or southeast to a Mexican border town. It is possible that he wanted to visit family and friends or earn money before he reached freedom. The most probable reason for Henry's travels in this direction was that he had to use his limited geographic knowledge to abscond, regardless of how far this information detoured him away from his intended destination. If Henry had traveled south, tall prairie grass, scattered oak trees, and mesquite and acacias trees would not have camouflaged him from slave catchers. If he became lost and ventured too far east, he would have encountered marshes filled with mosquitoes, alligators, and snakes. Despite the animal predators and insects, escaping along the Texas Gulf Coast provided fish (Spanish mackerel, sea trout, and red fish among others), oysters, and turtle to supplement a runaway's meager diet. Although Henry was fortunate enough to be well traveled, he still did not adequately comprehend how to arrive to Mexico using the fastest and most direct route while still avoiding detection.[3]

Henry's trek through Texas to reach freedom across the Rio Grande deviates from typical narratives about fugitive slave escapes during the 1850s. As slavery expanded farther south and eventually west to Texas, enslaved Texans did not escape to the northern United States or Canada but instead sought refuge in Mexico. Their process of planning to escape—such as deciding to abscond and gathering information and supplies—shared similarities with the experiences of those who fled north. Linking these flight strategies highlights the continuities in which slaves throughout the South thought about escape and executed their intentions for freedom, despite absconding in opposite directions. Yet the Texas landscape and social, political, and spatial ramifications of U.S. expansion were unique factors that shaped runaways' escapes to Mexico. Texas's vast, changing topography; the threat of capture by Texas Rangers and members of the U.S. military; and the likelihood of encountering treacherous Comanche Indians were dangers that Texas fugitive slaves faced because of their location on the Texas–Mexico borderlands. Thus, fugitive slaves had to calculate how to overcome natural and man-made obstacles while devising a series of new stratagems that they often had to modify as they absconded to Mexico.

The experiences of Henry and other fugitive slaves from Texas who escaped to Mexico have received limited scholarly attention in comparison to those who escaped north. In the 1970s Ronnie C. Tyler's "Fugitive Slaves in Mexico" (1972) and Rosalie Schwartz's *Across the Rio to Freedom* (1975) first challenged the dominant narrative of runaway slave escapes to the North by recovering the history of fugitive slave escapes to Mexico. More recent scholarship builds on Tyler's and Schwartz's works by detailing that enslaved Texans who escaped to Mexico were a part of the black American quest for freedom during the antebellum era and contending that runaway slaves who sought refuge in Mexico were among a number of people who crossed the U.S.–Mexico border legally and illegally in the 1850s. While these works discuss the important role of Mexico as a site for African American freedom in the nineteenth century, they do not explain the process in which Texas runaways reached Mexico. Tracing the ways in which enslaved Texans planned their escapes captures the intellectual scope of their resistance efforts. The inclusion of what they believed made a successful escape and the obstacles they anticipated and overcame on their journeys to freedom centers their efforts to self-emancipate with no aid or limited assistance from poor whites and local Mexicans in the absence of a well-developed abolitionist network in Texas. The experiences of Texas runaways in the 1850s revise ideas about antebellum escape routes to include pathways to freedom that ushered fugitive slaves to different sites throughout North America.[4]

By the 1850s most enslaved Texans knew about Mexico as a destination for freedom. In the 1930s Texas resident Felix Haywood participated in a Works Progress Administration interview. The ninety-two-year-old Haywood discussed his years as an enslaved person in Texas. During the interview, he recalled, "Sometimes someone would come 'long and try to get us to run up North and be free. We used to laugh at that. There wasn't no reason to *run* up North. All we had to do was to *walk*, but walk *South*. And we'd be free as soon as we crossed the Rio Grande. In Mexico, you could be free. They didn't care if you was black, white, yellow or blue. Hundreds of slaves did go to Mexico and got on all right."[5]

Haywood's interview documents the existence of an informal communication network that spread information about options for freedom to Texas plantations and ranches. This network not only provided information about Mexico as a haven but also made clear that escaping there from Texas was a shorter distance than absconding to the northern United States or Canada. Moreover, reports about fugitive slaves' lives in Mexico relayed that there were economic opportunities and a greater degree of social acceptance for African Americans if they lived south of the border. This knowledge helped cement Mexico as a space for freedom in the minds of many enslaved Texans. Local Tejanos (Mexicans residing in Texas), who sometimes worked alongside enslaved black people on Texas plantations and ranches, and enslaved communities helped sustain the circulation of information about freedom in Mexico. Despite this assistance, however, the burdens of planning the escapes and successfully doing so largely remained on the enslaved people intending to run away.[6]

Although information about Mexico and confirmation of its proximity to Texas was helpful, for enslaved African Americans who had never traveled outside of their plantations or ranches, or who had only traveled a few miles outside of their prescribed boundaries, the distance to freedom seemed insurmountable. Most runaways who planned to escape—regardless of direction—were unable to successfully gauge distances and had difficulty learning about the best way to reach freedom. Creating an enslaved labor force with a limited knowledge of direction was a manufactured consequence of slavery. Slaveholders used this tactic to discourage escape and center labor and the spatial parameters of a plantation or ranch as the focal points in enslaved black people's lives. Consequently, distorted ideas about space reinforced the fear of escape as enslaved people remained uncertain about the perceived and actual distances to free territory.[7]

To learn more about the distance to freedom and the surrounding area, enslaved people planning to escape tried to secure as much information as they could. Enslaved men who had gained the trust or favor of their owners often had the opportunity to run errands or travel with them. Traveling outside of the plantation or ranch, even for a few miles, familiarized some men in bondage with the neighboring community. If these trips became more frequent, houses, barns, fences, forks in the road, and other landmarks represented distances away from the plantation or toward a river or town that made sense to members of enslaved communities.[8]

Some enslaved Texans learned about Texas geography when traveling long distances with an owner. Ben Kinchlow, a former slave originally from Wharton County, Texas, recalled that in the 1850s enslaved men often accompanied their owners to sell cotton at the Texas–Mexico border. Upon removing cotton from the wagon, "they would then be persuaded to go across the border by Meskins [sic], and then they would never return to their master."[9] For those who did not flee while unloading cotton, these trips not only allowed them to gather valuable information about Texas roads beyond their limited travel radius but also verified that there were some Mexicans at the Rio Grande willing to assist runaways.

In addition to securing information on their own or with the unwitting assistance of their owners, enslaved men could also acquire information from a limited number of local, sympathetic white people. On July 16, 1853, twenty-three-year-old Julius escaped from Columbia, Texas, about fifty-five miles southwest of Houston. His owner, Henry Dance, suspected that a "vagabond white man" had helped him escape because he saw them speaking on at least one occasion before Julius absconded.[10] White men like the one who allegedly assisted Julius in escaping were rare. Slaveholders from Missouri, Louisiana, Virginia, Georgia, and Tennessee, among other slave states, moved to Texas throughout the antebellum era believing that the institution of slavery would be safe and protected there. By the 1850s Texas had over forty-eight thousand slaves, an increase of over thirty thousand slaves since 1840. This growing proslavery population did not allow a strong abolitionist movement to develop in the state. Thus, runaways or those who planned to abscond could not depend on most white residents to assist them.[11]

Tejanos also assisted fugitive slaves by sometimes accompanying them during their escapes. In July 1853 twenty-three-year-old Nacogdoches slave Isham escaped from his owner, S. M. Orton. Isham was nearly six feet tall and "fond of showing his strength and activity by vaulting [and] doing half summersets [sic]." His talents helped spare him from many whippings. He only had a few lash marks, indicating that he was generally a well-behaved or favored slave. Orton offered a one-hundred-dollar reward to anyone who captured him and delivered "the person who decoyed [Isham] off." He suspected that Isham would "design his course to Mexico" and was in the company of a "large Mexican, rather white."[12] Unlike Isham, his Mexican travel companion traveled more freely throughout the state and was likely more familiar with the surrounding area and the routes leading to Mexico. He also may have had better knowledge of the locations in Mexico where runaways should seek refuge. Unlike the Underground Railroad in the North, where there were more established routes for runaways by the 1850s, enslaved Texans like Isham and the Tejano who aided him determined pathways to Mexico based on where they believed spaces of freedom might exist for fugitive slaves. However, reaching one of these destinations required Isham to navigate a variety of landscapes.[13]

When Isham began his escape from Nacogdoches in eastern Texas, he encountered a landscape made up of piney woods with rolling hills. There were also oak, hickory, and maple trees. Once he exited the piney woods region of Texas, he could reach Mexico by traveling south along the coast of Texas or in a southwest direction, escaping near Austin and San Antonio. If traveling south, he would traverse the same grassland marshes that Henry, at the beginning of this chapter, encountered. The southwest direction would lead him into a region described as post-oak savannah in some areas and blackland prairies in others. Characterized by scattered oak trees and tall prairie grass, there was limited shelter for Isham against the hot July sun and inadequate cover for him to avoid slave catchers or others who aimed to return him to slavery. By July the sun had dried out small sources of water such as creeks and streams. Thus, an additional challenge for Isham and other fugitive slaves who escaped through this region was finding a water source to avoid dehydration. If his food supply ended, there were pecans, if he could open their shells. Corn would not be a part of Isham's diet at the beginning of his escape because corn-planting season began in mid-February and the harvest would not begin until late July or early August. He could fish in the Brazos River to supplement his diet once he reached it, but the river was over one hundred miles away from Nacogdoches.[14]

As Isham escaped through Travis County (where present-day Austin is located), the landscape shifting from rolling to sharp hills added more physical difficulty to his escape. The steep hills slowed his pace. If he had any injuries or suffered from hunger or thirst, navigating this landscape became even more arduous. If he continued to escape in the area west of Austin, rolling hills and rough and rocky terrain described the landscape, which was also known as Hill Country. Prone to droughts, man-made water wells and the Colorado River helped white,

Tejano, and enslaved residents secure water. In contrast, fugitive slaves were not able to safely access these water sources. Riverbanks and areas near wells were not safe for runaways to approach as white residents and others who might be sympathetic to slavery could capture fugitive slaves and return them to slavery. For food around the Austin area, Isham could hunt for possum and rabbit, if he could steal a gun. Eight miles south of Austin, runaways could find wild lettuce, mustard greens, and watercress.[15]

The changing topographies that fugitive slaves from eastern Texas encountered in the first two hundred miles of their journeys were obstacles to their success in addition to slave catchers, slave patrols, and others who wished to capture them. The landscapes that Isham traversed while on his route to freedom shifted in ways that he and most other fugitive slaves could not anticipate. While the first part of his route directed him south to freedom, it also contained barriers that made the escape more difficult and dangerous. Beyond ensuring that he traveled in the correct direction and had enough food, he had to successfully navigate each landscape as it arose, forcing him to quickly adapt. In regions where grassy plains were the dominant landscape, this exposure required more stealth or even traveling at night to avoid apprehension. Farther southwest, runaways needed stamina and a degree of physical fitness to climb the steep hills in Travis County. Most importantly, Isham still had to avoid capture, which became more challenging as even obtaining water from a well or a river could mark the premature end of a runaway's journey. To better negotiate these conditions, runaways attempted to better prepare for their escapes by collecting more information about the nearby landscapes and stealing items to assist them during their escapes.

Originally from Tennessee, Abraham arrived near Egypt, Texas, in the winter of 1851 when Joel H. Hudgeons purchased him. Abraham had a penchant for escaping. In June 1852 he absconded, but someone captured him in Seguin, Texas, nearly forty miles east of San Antonio. As punishment, he wore "a clog of iron" around his leg. On July 3, 1852, he escaped again. Hudgeons described the twenty-three- or twenty-four-year-old as "very talkative when alarmed" and believed that Abraham was "on his way to Mexico."[16]

During his first escape attempt in summer 1852, Abraham was ill prepared for the landscape and the region's growing population, both of which likely aided in his capture near Seguin. A German traveler in the 1840s described Seguin as only having six houses hidden by live oaks and located on the edge of a highland. The edge of this highland was a bare and treeless prairie where "suddenly the plain [gave] way and offer[ed] an unobstructed view of a beautiful and broad valley below."[17] Seguin's population had increased when Abraham arrived in the area in the early 1850s—tax collectors in 1858 counted 792 white residents. This growing population heightened his chance of discovery while the plains landscape and unobstructed views allowed slave catchers to observe him from a significant distance.[18] Abraham had only been enslaved in Texas for a few months before his first escape. Because he was not yet familiar with this region and the ways in which Texas runaways' experiences differed from those in Tennessee, his escape ended in re-enslavement instead of freedom.

However, failed escape attempts became opportunities for runaways to gather information about the landscape and slave catching systems. By the 1850s an expansive system had developed throughout the South and in parts of the North to ensure that runaways were not successful. Slave catchers, slave patrols, white residents, and even free black people purporting to sympathize with those who absconded were among the people who apprehended fugitive slaves. Additionally, some enslaved men and women who escaped returned to their owners if they became unsure about how to continue their journeys and were too fearful to seek assistance. These layers of support for the institution of slavery in conjunction with efforts to keep enslaved black people unfamiliar with their surroundings discouraged many of those in bondage from fleeing. Yet once habitual runaways like Abraham had a better understanding of the ways in which these systems operated, they could better plan their escapes instead of abandoning the idea of freedom altogether.

Determined to successfully abscond, Abraham stole a mackinaw blanket, which was waterproof, and a "large sorrel American horse" for his second escape. Whether from his personal experience or through a communication network among enslaved Texans, Abraham stole items that reflected what he had learned about the Texas landscape and local geography. In preparation for this escape, Abraham gathered more information and used his horseback riding skills to improve his chances of success. He stole this blanket because he anticipated rain, damp conditions, or cool weather. A horse allowed him to travel faster and farther and was a better way to evade slave catchers than on foot. Moreover, the iron clod on his leg would have slowed his pace if he elected to escape on foot. Despite these initial plans, however, Abraham still faced uncertainty as he fled his plantation and had to navigate the unfamiliar region as best he could.[19]

The Guadalupe River played an important role in directing Abraham to San Antonio during the early stages of his escape. He likely fled from a sugar plantation as Egypt, Texas, was in Wharton County, a sugar-growing region of the state. Beginning in the gulf and marshes region of Texas, Abraham traveled west toward Bexar County where present-day San Antonio is located. The Guadalupe River runs through Wharton County, and it is likely that he followed the river until he reached Opelousas Road, a trading route connecting San Antonio to New Orleans. Trees or bushes along the riverbanks provided shelter from the hot July sun and camouflage from slave catchers. More importantly, the river's fish provided food. The landscape in this area was a combination of post-oak savannah and blackland prairies, where there were scattered oak trees and tall grass. Cotton and sugar plantations near the river and the use of the Opelousas Road for trade required Abraham to move quickly because there were increased chances of apprehension. Because he escaped by horse, the horse hoofs made a significant amount of noise. Thus, fugitive slaves like Abraham aimed to avoid capture, not detection, as they believed that traveling by horse created a significant advantage for them.[20]

Abraham developed a rival geography by incorporating what he learned during his first escape into his plans for his second attempt. In establishing the importance of landmarks in the surrounding area, he repurposed the Guadalupe River and the Opelousas Road to aid him in his quest for freedom. In contrast to Isham's experience and perhaps Abraham's first attempt, Abraham used the river and other aspects of the landscape to his advantage. In some regions of the state, the landscape in Texas aided runaways while other routes added difficulty to the escape or hindered fugitive slaves' progress altogether. Thus, the ways in which a potential runaway selected a route and the existing terrain were essential parts of the Texas runaway experience as they could determine whether or not a fugitive slave would reach Mexico successfully.

Both Henry, from the beginning of the chapter, and Abraham used San Antonio as a point of reference to help guide them to freedom in Mexico. With a population of nearly 3,500 residents in 1850, it was one of Texas' larger towns and most likely known among enslaved communities. For runaways, reaching the town marked a degree of success in their journeys. The town's location assured them that they were escaping southward, and the San Antonio River was a source of fresh water, if they could avoid discovery. However, Texas slaveholders viewed the town as a critical turning point in fugitive slaves' paths to freedom. In 1844 the Texas legislature passed a law that allowed anyone who captured a runaway slave west of the San Antonio River (the side closest to the Rio Grande) to charge fifty dollars per runaway for the reward. Additionally, a slave catcher who traveled beyond San Antonio was able to charge two extra dollars per every thirty miles he traveled to return the runaway to his owner. The increased reward money indicates the difficulty slaveholders anticipated in apprehending fugitive slaves after they crossed the San Antonio River. Thus, this law confirmed not only fugitive slaves' ideas about San Antonio but also the town's importance to runaways' escapes. For fugitive slaves, San Antonio could reorient lost runaways, supply them with fresh water, and provide food to steal as they continued to traverse Texas.[21]

While reaching San Antonio represented a triumph on runaways' journeys to Mexico, traveling through regions south of San Antonio presented less forgiving landscapes. Upon exiting San Antonio's blackland prairies with tall grass and scattered oak trees, the landscape became more level but with higher temperatures. Animal predators such as coyotes, wolves, snakes, and foxes in the area added more peril to the journey. Similar to Abraham when he approached Seguin, the south Texas grassy plains with post and live oak trees offered few opportunities for fugitive slaves to conceal themselves. The closer runaways escaped to the Rio Grande, the more man-made and natural obstacles that awaited them to hinder their progress.[22]

As runaways escaped farther south, they entered a region formerly known as the Nueces Strip, a region of south Texas that had loosely enforced laws. Once disputed territory between the United States and Mexico, this area of land that was adjacent to the U.S.–Mexico border and located between the Rio Nueces and the Rio Grande, had attracted illegal activity and residents who were often on the wrong side of the law. A number of the residents there were prostitutes, bounty hunters, mercenaries, and army deserters. Because of its isolation and the absence of more law-abiding citizens in the region, one U.S. boundary commissioner who surveyed the land in 1850 reported that "murders were common" and "the guilty escaped justice" often.[23] Runaways could not avoid traveling through this area to reach Mexico. This region offered limited access to water, and there was the possibility that they would have to defend themselves against people suspicious of their recent arrival and who would welcome the reward money that accompanied capturing a runaway. While some South Texas residents represented barriers to fugitive slaves' success, the region also contained state-supported officials tasked with capturing Texas runaways before they reached Mexico.[24]

In addition to traveling through the former Nueces Strip, fugitive slaves had to avoid encountering Texas Rangers. A state law enforcement agency formed in the early 1820s, Texas Rangers defended the state against Native American raids. Tasked with pursuing Native Americans who raided Texas ranches and fled into northeastern Mexico, white Texas residents recruited Texas Rangers in the mid-1850s to also apprehend and deliver fugitive slaves to their owners. This expansion of the Rangers' job description was a critique of the federal government's policy toward runaways. The Fugitive Slave Law of 1850 compelled residents of free states, particularly in the northern United States, to report and detain African Americans suspected of being formerly enslaved. Under this law, the North was no longer a space where some fugitive slaves, and even some free black people, believed that they could live without compromising their safety and freedom. Because the law did not allow for the recapture of runaways who had reached foreign soil, some fugitive slaves and free black people living in the North immigrated to Canada or England to secure a more stable freedom. However, in Texas, Rangers made escapes to Mexico more difficult and dangerous as they worked to capture runaways before they crossed the Rio Grande. The insertion of Texas Rangers into the existing slave catching system became part of the increasing role of both state and federal government entities on the Texas–Mexico borderlands that attempted to thwart runaways' plans to enter Mexico.[25]

The looming presence of the U.S. military added another obstacle near the end of fugitive slaves' journeys to freedom. Constructed as safety measures against Native American raids, more U.S. military forts peppered the Texas borderlands region upon the signing of the Treaty of Guadalupe Hidalgo (1848). Fort Duncan, founded in 1849 at Eagle Pass, and Fort Clark, established in 1852 approximately forty-five miles north of Eagle Pass, were reminders of the United States' physical and military expansion onto the U.S.–Mexico borderlands. The expansion of the U.S. military in Texas was another way in which the federal government could encumber fugitive slave escapes beyond legislation. As Frederick Law Olmstead described, Fort Duncan was "situated upon a broad and elevated plateau on the banks of the Rio Grande."[26] This strategic positioning allowed for patrols, surveyors, and other military-affiliated personnel to obtain a clear sense of border activity, while also allowing them to function alongside local and state mechanisms to detain fugitive slaves. Ultimately, members of Fort Duncan and Fort Clark could protect U.S. property interests by preventing fugitive slaves from escaping closer to Mexico while also protecting south Texas residents against Native American violence.[27]

Because U.S. settlement and slavery in Texas disrupted indigenous communities, fugitive slaves had to be wary of encountering some groups of Native Americans. Unwilling to distinguish between white and black Americans, some Comanche Indians captured, tortured, and killed members of both races. In 1850 a group of Comanches captured two enslaved girls. When a Delaware-based slave trader traveling in Texas located the girls and brought them to a military camp, he noticed that the Comanche had "scraped through their skin into the flesh" because they believed that "beneath the cuticle the flesh was black like" the color of the girls' skin. The Comanche had also "burned them with live coals to ascertain whether fire produced the same sensations of pain as with their own people."[28] According to Randolph B. Marcy, a U.S. Army officer traveling in Texas in the 1850s, the Comanche were hostile to enslaved Texans because of their status as unfree people, which placed them at the bottom of Texas' existing racial hierarchy. Additionally, Marcy claimed that the Comanche killed enslaved black people to reduce the number of fugitive slaves who reached Mexico, believing that successful runaways' willingness to defend the border towns to which they fled interfered with Indian raids. On the Texas–Mexico borderlands, enslaved Texans' quests for freedom in Mexico not only threatened the institution of slavery but also disrupted Native American raiding patterns. News and rumors about Comanche and Indian violence traveled throughout Texas and in enslaved communities, likely warning potential fugitive slaves that they could not rely on this group of people for assistance to freedom. While runaways continued to negotiate a variety of physical threats in South Texas, the arduous landscape and terrain still required careful navigation.[29]

The closer fugitive slaves traveled to the Rio Grande, the less accommodating the environment. Texas' southern plains had a hot, dry climate; high grass; and prickly shrubs such as prickly pear cacti and mesquite. The prickly pear from the cacti could provide food, but rattlesnakes were among the animal predators that runaways had to avoid. If traveling in a southwest direction, fugitive slaves would reach the town of Eagle Pass, Texas, if not discovered near Fort Duncan. Captain Abner Doubleday, a veteran of the Mexican–American War, who traveled to the Texas border town in 1854, described the town as a place without laws except "that of the Bowie knife and pistol." The town also had a reputation of being a gateway for fugitive slaves into the neighboring Mexican border town Piedras Negras (Black Stones). As a result, slave catchers and kidnappers gathered in Eagle Pass hoping to detain runaways before they entered Mexico. During the antebellum era, borders separating slavery and freedom in the United States were inherently dangerous because slave catchers knew that runaways would cross these boundaries to reach freedom. However, unlike escape to the North, where freedom existed across imaginary state borders and the Mason–Dixon line, the freedom fugitive slaves from Texas sought in Mexico required them to escape across a physical border that added one final hurdle to their journeys.[30]

Approaching and crossing the Rio Grande was the last physical barrier for Texas runaways. Thorny, dry chaparral grew on the banks of the river. This thicket of vegetation provided the last opportunity to shield runaways from exposure. Besides slave catchers who awaited runaways, there were also slaveholders at the border. The border was more than a separation between U.S. slavery and Mexican freedom. It was also a site of economic exchange where Texas slaveholders sold bales of cotton to Mexicans and received goods from them as well. These transactions threatened fugitive slaves' attempts to cross the Rio

Grande undetected. Additionally, based on the time of year, the river's depth could be low enough for it to be forded or swam across to arrive to the Mexican side, if the runaway knew how to swim. However, at other times during the year, the river could be too high, and runaways would have to pay for a ferry or find a sympathetic border resident to take them across by boat. Like much of their escapes while traversing Texas, the final part required fugitive slaves to calculate how to best cross the river and enter Mexico with or without the assistance of others.[31]

The process of escape on the Texas–Mexico borderlands in the 1850s outlines the intellectual work of being a fugitive slave. Potential runaways gathered information from an informal communication network that spread information about the surrounding area and about the African American experience in Mexico. They discerned this information's veracity to craft a semblance of a route to arrive to specific destinations of freedom. An additional part of this planning process included learning from past failures and stealing items they deemed necessary for their escapes. Because most runaways were unfamiliar with the extensive changes in Texas landscapes that awaited them, they had to adapt to these conditions to progress in their journeys southward. These calculations, navigation of a multitude of terrains, and subsequent immigration to Mexico should be included into the study of nineteenth-century African American thought. By planning escapes to Mexico, Texas runaways rejected notions of black progress and equality within the United States by seeking freedom elsewhere.

The experiences of fugitive slaves from Texas to Mexico alters the current understanding of escapes to freedom. The role of the environment and terrain had central roles in Texas runaways' experiences that is often not present in the representation of escapes to the North. For runaways in Texas, the difficulty of the terrain added to the already demanding task of escaping. Another element that made escape more arduous was the lack of a well-developed abolitionist network within Texas to help guide runaways to the Rio Grande and assist them in entering Mexico. Instead, members of marginalized groups in Texas helped in sometimes very limited ways that ultimately required runaways to use more improvisation during their escapes as there were not many places in which to seek temporary refuge.

NOTES

1. "25 Dollars Reward," The *San Antonio Ledger*, January 5, 1854.
2. Deborah Gray White, *A'r'nt I a Woman? Female Slaves in the Plantation South*, rev. ed. (New York: W. W. Norton, 1999), 70. Mexico abolished slavery in 1829. See David Waldstreicher's "Reading the Runaways: Self-Fashioning, Print Culture, and Confidence in Slavery in the Eighteenth-Century Mid-Atlantic," *The William and Mary Quarterly* 56, no. 2, (April 1999): 243–72, for more about how fugitive slaves remade themselves while absconding.
3. Frank W. Gould, *Texas Plants: A Checklist and Ecological Summary* (College Station: Texas A & M Press, 1962), 8–9; and Richard P. Schaedel, "The Karankawa of the Texas Gulf Coast," *Southwestern Journal of Anthropology* 5, no. 2 (Summer 1949): 120–21.
4. Ronnie C. Tyler, "Fugitive Slaves in Mexico," *Journal of Negro History* 57, no. 1 (January 1972): 1–12; Rosalie Schwartz, *Across the Rio to Freedom: U.S. Negroes in Mexico* (El Paso: Texas Western Press of the University of Texas at El Paso, 1975). The following all expand Tyler's and Schwartz's work: Sean Kelley, "Mexico in His Head: Slavery and the Texas–Mexico Border, 1810–1860," *Journal of Social History* 37, no. 3 (2004): 709–23; Sarah Cornell, "Citizens of Nowhere: Fugitive Slaves and Free African Americans in Mexico, 1833–1857," *Journal of American History* 100, no. 2 (2013): 351–74; and James David Nichols, "The Liberty Line: Runaway Slaves and Fugitive Peons in the Texas–Mexico Borderlands" *Western Historical Quarterly* 44, no. 4 (November 2013): 413–33. The Spanish-speaking world provided a haven for fugitive slaves as early as the late 1600s, when slaves in colonial South Carolina escaped to Spanish Florida for freedom. See Jane Landers, *Black Society in Spanish Florida* (Champaign: University of Illinois Press, 1999). Recovering enslaved African Americans' experiences on the U.S.–Mexico borderlands also makes significant interventions in borderlands history. In the late 1990s and early 2000s, borderlands historians suggested new approaches to borderlands history. See Jeremy Adelman and Stephen Aron, "From Borderlands to Borders: Empires, Nation-States, and the Peoples in Between North American History," *American Historical Review* 104, no. 3 (June 1999): 814–41; Samuel Truett and Elliot Young, *Continental Crossroads: Remapping U.S.–Mexico Borderlands History* (Durham, N.C.: Duke University Press, 2004); and Pekka Hämäläinen and Samuel Truett, "On Borderlands," *Journal of American History* 98, no. 2 (September 2011): 338–61. Examples of recent scholarship about the abolitionist movement in the northern United States and fugitive slave escapes to the North include Eric Foner, *Gateway to Freedom: The Hidden History of the Underground Railroad* (New York: W. W. Norton, 2015); and Manisha Sinha, *A Slave's Cause: A History of Abolition* (New Haven, Conn.: Yale University Press, 2016).
5. George P. Rawick, ed., *The American Slave–Texas Narratives*, vol. 4, pt. 2, (Westport, Conn.: Greenwood Press, 1972), 132; emphasis in the original narrative.

6. Mekala Audain, *Mexican Canaan: Fugitive Slaves and Free Blacks on the American Frontier* (Ph.D. diss., Rutgers University, 2014), 132. Some runaways also practiced marronage, a permanent escape to nearby woods or swamps. See Sylviane Diouf, *Slavery's Exiles: The Story of American Maroons* (New York: New York University Press, 2014). Enslaved women typically used truancy because childrearing and familial obligations prevented them from escaping the plantation at the same rates as men. Women in bondage also did not have the same opportunities to travel outside of the plantation as enslaved men. See also Deborah Gray White's *A'r'nt I a Woman?* and Stephanie Camp's *Closer to Freedom*: *Enslaved Women and Everyday Resistance in the Plantation South* (Chapel Hill: University of North Carolina Press, 2004). For more about slaves working on Texas ranches, see Randolph B. Campbell, *An Empire for Slavery: The Peculiar Institution in Texas, 1821–1865* (Baton Rouge: Louisiana State University Press, 1989), ch. 6; Sara R. Massey, ed. *Black Cowboys of Texas* (College Station: Texas A & M Press, 2004), ch. 1; and Carey Davenport's (part 1) and William Moore's (part 3) WPA narratives in Rawick, *American Slave–Texas Narratives*.

7. For example, an enslaved man named John Brown decided to escape to England from Georgia. He determined that if he continued traveling on his town's main road, it would eventually lead him to the island nation. John Brown, *Slave Life in Georgia: A Narrative of the Life, Sufferings, and Escape of John Brown, a Fugitive Slave Now in England* (London: W. M. Watts, 1855); 72. John Hope Franklin and Loren Schweninger discuss how runaways decided where to escape in their book *Runaway Slaves: Rebels on the Plantation* (New York: Oxford University Press, 2000), 109–10, 116.

8. Stephanie Camp's *Closer to Freedom* applies Edward Said's theory of rival geographies to truancy and slave escape in the slave South. Camp defines rival geography as "the movement of bodies, objects, and information within and outside of the plantation space." Camp, *Closer to Freedom*, 7–9.

9. Rawick, *American Slave–Texas Narratives*, vol. 4, pt. 2, 265.

10. "One Hundred Dollar Reward," *San Antonio Ledger*, September 15, 1853.

11. Fears of antislavery sentiment and slave rebellion infiltrating Texas were significant concerns for Texas residents in the late 1850s and throughout the 1860s. For more about the fear of abolition in Texas, see Wesley Norton, "The Methodist Episcopal Church and the Civil Disturbances in North Texas in 1859 and 1860," *Southwestern Historical Quarterly* 68, no. 3 (January 1965): 317–41; and Frank H. Smyrl, "Unionism, Abolitionism, and Vigilantism in Texas, 1856–1865" (M.A. thesis, University of Texas, 1961). For fear of slave uprisings in 1860s Texas, see Donald C. Reynolds, *Texas Terror: The Slave Insurrection Panic of 1860 and the Secession of the Lower South* (Baton Rouge: Louisiana State University Press, 2007); and Campbell, *An Empire for Slavery*, 55–56. In 1840 there were 12,570 slaves in twenty-six of Texas's then thirty-two counties. Campbell notes that tax assessors did not always count all of a slaveholder's slaves, believing that infants and elders slaves had minimal value. Additionally, slaveholders omitted slaves

from their roster in order to reduce their annual tax burdens. Campbell, *An Empire for Slavery*, 54.

12. "100 Dollars Reward," *Nacogdoches Chronicle*, July 12, 1853. It is unclear how long the Tejano man accompanied Isham during his escape.

13. Many white Texas slaveholders accused Tejanos of helping enslaved men abscond. As a result, in October 1854, Austin, Texas, residents passed a law that ordered Tejano residents to leave town. See Cornell, "Citizens of Nowhere," 360; and *Texas Monument*, "The Austin Resolutions," October 17, 1854, Microfilm Reel July 20, 1850–November 7, 1854, Dolph Briscoe Center for American History, University of Texas at Austin. For more about the Tejano experience in antebellum Texas, see Arnoldo de Leon, *They Called Them Greasers: Anglo Attitudes toward Mexicans in Texas, 1821–1900* (Austin: University of Texas Press, 1983); David Montejano, *Anglos and Mexicans in the Making of Texas, 1836–1986* (Austin: University of Texas Press, 1987); and William D. Carrigan and Clive Webb, *Forgotten Dead: Mob Violence Against Mexicans in the United States, 1848–1928* (New York: Oxford University Press, 2013).

14. Gould, *Texas Plants*, 8–10; Elizabeth Silverthorne, *Plantation Life in Texas* (College Station: Texas A & M University Press, 1986), 106; and Elizabeth Cruce Alvarez and Robert Plocheck, eds., *Texas Almanac, 2014–2015* (Denton: Texas State Historical Association, 2014), 115.

15. Gould, *Texas Plants*, 9–12; Gary Clayton Anderson, *The Conquest of Texas: Ethnic Cleansing in the Promised Land, 1820–1875* (Norman: University of Oklahoma Press, 2005), 214; and Rawick, *American Slave–Texas Narratives*, vol. 4, pt. 4, 48.

16. "$25 Reward," *Texas Monument*, July 3, 1852, Texas Runaway Slave Project http://digital.sfasu.edu/cdm/compoundobject/collection/RSP/id/8082/rec/1.

17. Alwin H. Sorgel, *A Sojourn in Texas, 1846–47*, trans. from German and ed. by W. M. Von-Maszewski (San Marcos, Tex.: Southwest State University, 1992), 48.

18. See Henry Bibb's slave narrative where he says, "I learned the art of running away to perfection. I made a regular business of it, and never gave it up, until I had broken the bands of slavery." Henry Bibb, *Narrative of the Life and Adventures of Henry Bibb* (New York: Henry Bibb, 1849), 15; and see Sorgel, *A Sojourn in Texas, 1846–47*, 48. In the 1860 U.S. Census, Seguin reported 792 residents, a figure collected during an 1858 tax collection. There are no population numbers for the 1850 U.S. Census. *Texas Almanac*, Texas State Historical Association, http://texasalmanac.com/topics/population, accessed June 18, 2016.

19. "$25 Reward," *Texas Monument*, July 3, 1852, Texas Runaway Slave Project http://digital.sfasu.edu/cdm/compoundobject/collection/RSP/id/8082/rec/1. Abraham's runaway advertisement does not include whether he used a horse during his first escape attempt in summer 1852.

20. Silverthorne, *Plantation Life in Texas*, 109; Raúl A. Ramos, *Beyond the Alamo: Forging Mexican Ethnicity in San Antonio, 1821–1861* (Chapel Hill: University

of North Carolina Press, 2008), 16; and Alvarez and Plocheck, *Texas Almanac, 2014–2015*, 115.

21. Randolph B. Campbell, ed., *The Laws of Slavery in Texas: Historical Documents and Essays* (Austin: University of Texas Press, 2010), 65; and Campbell, *An Empire for Slavery*, 62–63.

22. Gould, *Texas Plants*, 10; and Jean Louis Berlandier, *Journey to Mexico during the Years 1826 to 1834*, vol. 1, trans. by Sheila M. Ohlendorf, Josette M. Bigelow, and Mary M. Standifer, with an introduction by C. H. Muller (Austin: Center for Studies in Texas History, 1980), 271–72. In 1828 Jean Louis Berlandier, a French naturalist, botanist, and physician, traveled between San Antonio and Laredo. He reported that the landscape comprised vast plains, and there were streams and small ponds that supplied fresh water. Berlandier deemed the route between Laredo and San Antonio unsafe during his travels because of the prospect of encountering Comanche and Lipan Indians. Berlandier, *Journey to Mexico during the Years 1826 to 1834*, 1:272.

23. Mekala Audain, *Mexican Canaan: Fugitive Slaves and Free Blacks on the American Frontier* (Ph.D. diss., Rutgers University, 2014), 137.

24. Audain, *Mexican Canaan*, 137.

25. John Salmon Ford, *Rip Ford's Texas*, edited by Stephen B. Oates (Austin: University of Texas Press, 1987), 215; and Seymour V. Connor, "Ford, John Salmon [RIP]," *Handbook of Texas Online*, http://www.tshaonline.org/handbook/online/articles/ffo11, January 15, 2014, published by the Texas State Historical Association. For more about Texas Rangers, see Walter Prescott Webb, *The Texas Rangers: A Century of Frontier Defense* (Austin: University of Texas Press, 1965); Robert M. Utley, *Lone Star Justice: The First Century of the Texas Rangers* (New York: Oxford University Press, 2002); Michael L. Collins, *Texas Devils: Rangers and Regulars on the Lower Rio Grande, 1846–1861* (Norman, Okla.: University of Oklahoma Press, 2008); and Frederick Law Olmsted, *A Journey through Texas Or, A Saddle-trip on the Southwestern Frontier with a Statistical Appendix* (1857; repr., New York: Burt Franklin, 1969), 300–302. In May 1846 Texas state legislature created a formal slave patrol system. The creation of a formal system to recapture runaways signaled a persistent problem of fugitive slave escapes from Texas into Mexico, especially at the beginning of the Mexican-American War, which began in April 1846. Campbell, *Laws of Slavery in Texas*, 66. Historically, enslaved populations have used the chaos of war to escape to enemy lines in search of freedom. See Gary B. Nash, *The Forgotten Fifth: African Americans in the Age of Revolution* (Cambridge, Mass.: Harvard University Press, 2006); Alan Taylor, *The Internal Enemy: Slavery and War in Virginia, 1772–1832* (New York: W. W. Norton, 2013); and Gene Allen Smith, *The Slaves' Gamble: Choosing Sides in the War of 1812* (New York: St. Martin's Press, 2013).

26. Olmsted, *A Journey through Texas*, 314.

27. Ben E. Pingenot, "Fort Clark," in *Handbook of Texas Online*, Texas State Historical Association, accessed June 29, 2016, http://www.tshaonline.org/handbook

/online/articles/qbf10.; "Fort Duncan," in *Handbook of Texas Online*, accessed June 29, 2016, http://www.tshaonline.org/handbook/online/articles/qbf17.

28. Randolph B. Marcy, *Thirty Years of Army Life on the Border* (New York: Harper and Brothers, 1866), 35–36.

29. Marcy, *Thirty Years of Army Life*, 14–15, 35. Marcy believed that the two young girls were a part of a group of black Seminole Indians traveling to Wild Cat's newly established community in northeastern Mexico. For more about this settlement, see Kevin Mulroy, *Freedom on the Border: The Seminole Maroons in Florida, Indian Territory, Coahuila, and Texas* (Lubbock: Texas Tech University Press, 2003). Since the early 1820s white American settlers who immigrated to Mexican Texas feared hostile Native Americans. However, by the 1850s Texas's new settlers established communities farther westward, including on Comanche land between the Trinity and San Antonio Rivers because they were convinced that Texas Rangers and newly built U.S. military forts would protect them. The Comanche attacked and raided not only these settlements but also others throughout Texas. In addition to the Comanche, the Kiowas, Lipan Apache, and to a lesser degree the Kickapoos also attacked Texas military forts. See David J. Weber, *The Mexican Frontier: The American Southwest Under Mexico* (Albuquerque: University of New Mexico Press, 1982), 162; and Pekka Hämäläinen, *Comanche Empire* (New Haven, Conn.: Yale University Press, 2008), 305–6. For more about Native Americans in Texas during the antebellum period, see Anderson, *Conquest of Texas*; Brian DeLay, *War of a Thousand Deserts: Indian Raids and the U.S.–Mexican War* (New Haven, Conn.: Yale University Press, 2008); David La Vere, *The Texas Indians* (College Station: Texas A & M University Press, 2004); and Sherry Robinson, *I Fought a Good Fight: A History of the Lipan Apaches* (Denton: University of North Texas Press, 2013).

30. Collins, *Texas Devils*, 54–55; Audain, *Mexican Canaan*, 137; Mulroy, *Freedom on the Border*, 57; and Olmsted, *A Journey through Texas*, 314. Slave catchers and slavery sympathizers in the North eagerly awaited fugitive slaves on Pennsylvania's and Ohio's southern borders ready to capture them for reward money and return them to slavery. For more about slave catchers on slavery's borderlands in the North, see Stanley Harrold, *Border War: Fighting over Slavery before the Civil War* (Chapel Hill: University of North Carolina Press, 2010); Matthew Salafia, *Slavery's Borderland: Freedom and Bondage along the Ohio River* (Philadelphia: University of Pennsylvania Press, 2013); and James J. Gigantino, *The Ragged Road to Abolition* (Philadelphia: University of Pennsylvania Press, 2014).

31. J. Fred Rippy, "Border Troubles along the Rio Grande, 1848–1860," *Southwestern Historical Quarterly* 23, no.2 (October 1919): 91.

10

Freedom Interrupted

Runaway Slaves and Insecure Borders in the Mexican Northeast

JAMES DAVID NICHOLS

> Gonna come a time
> There's gonna come a time when
> I can go to Mexico
> CASSANDRA WILSON[1]

In January of 1850 three black men crossed over the Rio Grande to reach Nuevo Laredo. Like so many millions who would come after them, they crossed the border hoping for a better life on the other side, but they did not go in the direction we are most accustomed to hearing about. Rather than making a furtive night crossing to get into the United States, they went the other way. They crossed over into Mexico because it was a site of formal—legal—freedom. Upon arriving on the other side of the border, the three black men immediately sought out the *alcalde* (mayor) who headed up Nuevo Laredo's governing body, or *ayuntamiento*, for protection. After meeting with the men and hearing their plight, the alcalde granted them their request for freedom. He also gave them the *amparo* (refuge) offered by Mexican law that they so desired. When the alcalde followed this course of action, he confirmed that Mexico was a site of freedom, even at its most distant northern frontier and in a town sitting just across the river from Texas.[2]

But there is much more to the story than this. This chapter complicates the idea that enslaved black men and women could be truly free merely by setting foot on Mexican soil. It argues that Mexican law and even the loftiest of principles espoused by the independent government of that country could be abjured through simple force majeure. Texan pirates could easily cross the border to recapture their so-called property and interrupt the freedom that runaways found on the Mexican side of the border under the supposedly ample protection of the law. The fluidity of the borderlands worked not only to the advantage of runaway slaves looking to cross an artificial line drawn across the sand (or in the case across the channel of a river) to freedom. It abetted their pursuers as well. They could just as easily cross that line to interrupt the freedom that African Americans so desperately sought. As a result, Mexico never really transformed into an uncomplicated zone of freedom, whatever the status of runaway slaves was on paper there.

It was not for a lack of trying. Mexico started outlawing slavery explicitly in 1829, and in subsequent decades Mexicans grew increasingly intransigent on the issue of runaways, putting teeth into new laws guaranteeing the freedom of runaway slaves. By the 1850s at the latest, they established the practice of granting freedom to runaway enslaved people who escaped and set foot on Mexican soil. Hundreds, if not thousands, of slaves ran away and hoped that the border would close up behind them like a steel trap. In crossing over, they also forced the Mexican state to take on their cause. Mexico might have returned the occasional runaway slave in the early years of the nineteenth century, but in the wake of the Texas Revolution (1836) and the U.S.-Mexico War (1846–48), resistance to returning runaway slaves stiffened. During these years, the country passed several statutes in the states and at the federal level, including antislavery colonization laws in 1836 and 1848. Then, in the new federal constitution of 1857, the country outlawed slavery in all forms and officially enshrined the policy of granting freedom to runaways in national law. Enslaved people in Texas were not unaware of these developments, and many had "Mexico in their heads" from the earliest days of Texan independence.[3] The fact that runaway slaves could go "across the river to freedom" (as one early scholar of this subject put it) and escape slavery is now well known to historians.[4] The border region that lay along the south side of the eastern terminus of the Rio Grande, and which comprises the geographic scope of this study, was a legal site of freedom in the years before the American Civil War—and one that greatly irked slaveholders in Texas. Hence, when these black men and women crossed into Mexico, they did not just cross a border between the United States and Mexico. They also crossed a border between slavery and freedom.

Sources from both Mexico and Texas confirm that a large number of African Americans escaped slavery by going across the new border drawn up by the Treaty of Guadalupe Hidalgo. Some people in Texas projected the number of runaways to be upward of two thousand. But guesstimates made by figures like Frederick Law Olmsted and John S. Ford—both of whom had a stake in the antislavery argument—varied wildly. The anxieties of Texan slaveholders probably account for the rather high estimate of two thousand runaways proposed by "Rip" Ford. (One historian has recently done him one better and estimated four thousand runaways).[5] Whatever the ultimate number turns out to be, the fear of runaways loomed large and threatened the institution of slavery in Texas. One petitioner from that state even referred to the "insecurity of property" in the region around San Antonio when he voiced his deep concerns to the Texas legislature. He was certain that Mexico and Mexicans were at the root of the many attempts by slaves to run away across the border.[6] Still, the numbers we have are fuzzy. To determine the number of runaways more scientifically will probably involve many visits to municipal archives in the states of Tamaulipas and Coahuila and a lot of counting.[7]

Yet the freedom of formerly enslaved people in Mexico was hardly complete. Thanks to scholars doing research on both sides of the border, we now know, for instance, that when runaways exited Texas and went into Mexico, they did not enter a social vacuum. They found all sorts of new requirements and expectations that hampered their independence. Not only did they find their lives intricately intertwined with the state, they also found themselves drawn into relations with their new neighbors in Mexico as well. As I have written in another context, blacks could hardly hope for an area where, as one Mexican official astutely put it toward the end of the 1850s, "their liberty was absolute."[8] Not even in Mexico, a country that outlawed slavery, could blacks hope to plot out their own life courses completely independently. The official quoted above referred to the several demands that Mexicans put on blacks who immigrated into their country in exchange for "amparo." Mexicans often demanded military service of black immigrants, and they also expected them to carry on good relations with their neighbors and stay out of trouble. If they did not do what they were told, and especially if they did not leave on expeditions against the Comanches and Apaches willingly, Mexicans might threaten to send them back to Texas and slavery.[9]

Beyond the ties of reciprocity with the state and with their neighbors, there were other limits to the liberty of black people in Mexico. Work conditions for blacks in Mexico did not always differ all that markedly from debt peonage. In Mexico, blacks found other unfree systems of labor that all too often rested upon the implied threat of violence or imprisonment. "When the negro gets to Mexico, he . . . finds nothing but the most squalid wretchedness, poverty, and starvation for his lot. Some become peons as a matter of self preservation," wrote the *Texas State Gazette*. Certainly we need to read statements such as these with a grain of salt, but Mexican sources do confirm that many blacks who escaped Texas ended up as servants in Mexico having traded "one master for another."[10] One scholar has taken a particularly dim view of freedom in Mexico, writing that blacks could not expect fair treatment in their adopted country since they were hostages of the state and "citizens of nowhere."[11] Undoubtedly, freedom could be a fleeting prospect for runaways.

There was another reason why liberty eluded blacks in Mexico. They could expect freedom when they crossed the border, but they were able to cross the border so easily precisely because there was very little in the way of institutions or men regulating the line. Invaders and pirates could cross the lawless borderlands just as easily. Worse yet, once invaders reached the other side, they could summon the border against their victims and drag them back across the river to slavery. Nuevo Laredo perfectly exemplified this problem. Its location so close to the border meant that it was a transnational space of refuge, but its proximity also invited trouble from the other side. Soon after the black men in the vignette that opened this chapter escaped to Nuevo Laredo, several men arrived from Texas to challenge the alcalde's decision to grant them amparo. By extension, they challenged Mexico's right to grant freedom to refugees. By actually seeking out the alcalde, they lent meaning and credence to this border fiction—that a hard and fast line legally and politically separated two regimes from one another. But the alcalde stood his ground, and he regretfully informed the men that enslaved people became free through the mere act of setting foot on Mexican soil and that there was nothing that he could do to help the Texans recover the men they considered their property. Geography—not the past condition of servitude and not race—determined the men's free or unfree status. On the other side of the river from Texas, Mexican soil made enslaved people free.

But the fluidity and lawlessness of the borderlands encouraged the transgression of the line between freedom and slavery—especially if posses of armed Texans did not care to recognize the border. Once the black men escaped to Nuevo Laredo and earned the alcalde's protection, the Texans hatched a plan to remove them from Mexican soil and interrupt their freedom since they could not convince the alcalde in Nuevo Laredo to return them to their power. A few days after the disappointing meeting with the alcalde, two of the men ignored his decision and illegally crossed the river. They intended to kidnap the black men, take them across the Rio Grande to the Texas side, and transform them back into slaves. They only managed to capture one of the runaways in the end, but the alcalde of the town bemoaned the fact that he could do nothing to stop them. Disheartened, he said that these "North Americans," even after learning that the black men were free on the other side of the river had nevertheless "scorn[ed] Mexican law" and kidnapped one of the runaways back, stealing him away from his newly won freedom.[12]

Despite the best efforts of the alcalde, a group of Texan filibusters had interrupted Mexican freedom by simply removing the runaway from Nuevo Laredo. Further, these "pirates"—as others would refer to international slave hunters—had scorned Mexican law, desecrated the new international border, and insulted the nation.[13] Attacks like these tied together the issues of Mexican legal sovereignty over its territory and freedom for runaway slaves. If Mexicans could not fully protect the refugees who streamed into their country, then their sovereignty was incomplete and the border was not very meaningful. The border registered a number of important contradictions. The border signified a line of liberty between freedom and slavery. It also drew a boundary between two very different legal regimes, two highly contrasting racial milieus, and two independent political systems. But due to the fluidity of the borderlands, this border remained all too easy to transgress.

Unfortunately for Mexican national pride and legal integrity, as significant as this line may have been on paper, it was really only a barrier in the minds of its authors. In its earliest days (after 1848), the border was fairly easy to traverse—there were no guard towers and no twenty-first-century gatekeeping technology for the state to deploy. Hence, people crossed in large numbers. Runaway slaves were perhaps the most significant cross-border migrants of the 1850s to summon the border, drawn across by the irresistible promise of freedom on Mexican soil. But the border was a swinging gate for runaway slaves. It refused to stay closed once they made it to safety. The conflict between enslaver and enslaved spilled over into Mexican space precisely because the border failed to contain this violence in discreet national containers. Mexican officials recognized the gravity of this problem of border insecurity. In fact, some of the earliest efforts to secure the border came from the Mexican side—to keep Texans out. Filibusterers, slave raiders, and "pirates" pushed Mexicans into a concerted response in defense of their country's sovereignty, security, and freedom when they found their territory threatened from abroad.

Filibusterers, including slave hunters, were among the first to inspire gatekeeping on the Mexican side of the border. Filibusterers were Americans who invaded foreign territories in pursuit of their own national or even private goals, especially once Manifest Destiny stalled out following the U.S.-Mexico War. The most notable filibusters in the 1850s were Narciso López's invasion of Cuba and William Walker's overthrow of the Nicaraguan government. In both cases, the filibusterers set out to accomplish the national expansion that their federal government could not, and they justified their actions by pointing to the derelict state of the governments they sought to overthrow.

Mexico was not immune to the threat of filibusterers. John S. Ford, who we met above, also edited the *Southwestern American*. In his newspaper he fanned the flames, undermining any claims that Mexico had on sovereignty in its own territory. Mexico's weak hold on the frontier was a justification for illegal raids, according to Ford, since Mexico was not "in possession of the real attributes of a sovereignty."[14] At other times, Ford vindicated filibustering and raiding since Mexicans would not return Texan slaves and had "so little respect for themselves or any other country."[15] Several popular movements overtly disrespected Mexican sovereignty over its territory, usually mocking Mexico's claims to be a self-governing republic. The so-called Republic of the Sierra

Madre movement, which sought to carve out a new republic in the Mexican North, was a filibuster that involved many white Texans as well as Tejanos. In their manifesto—notably written and published in English—they called openly for the return of runaway slaves from the Mexican states east of the Sierra Madre. One anonymous U.S. senator protested against these movements, sure that they were efforts to expand slavery into Mexico. But the borderlands all too often represented a wide open and generally lawless space.[16]

Most often filibusters-cum-slave hunts involved private citizens, but there were rare occasions where people on the federal payroll crossed over illegally into Mexico. In February of 1850 four soldiers left Fort Duncan to speculate in runaway slaves on the other side of the border. These enlisted men learned about a runaway who took up shelter on a local ranch named Sanguijuela, just outside of Guerrero, and they left their posts to cross the river and find him. Once they reached their destination with the help of a couple of Mexican guides, they held the inhabitants of the ranch hostage and demanded that they turn over the African American who worked there. Fearful for their lives and unable to resist, the *vecinos* (neighbors) stood by as the soldiers turned slave hunters abducted the black man. The violence did not stop after they had achieved this end, however. The soldiers then turned their considerable fury against the vecinos themselves, and they badly beat Ramón Gonzales, the man who owned the ranch. Gonzales' son and wife came in for similar treatment, suffering mightily from the physical blows that the soldiers dealt to them before they slipped back across the river with the newly re-enslaved black man in tow. These soldiers deeply implicated the local federal officials, and their raid would have surely aroused howls of protest in the American North—had anyone ever learned about it.[17]

State and municipal authorities in Texas lent support to slave-hunting filibusterers as well. Both Texas governor Peter Bell and the sheriff of Bexar County deputized all citizens in South Texas to lend help to slave hunters like Warren Adams in search of runaway slaves along the border in the autumn of 1851.[18] Adams had already earned a reputation as a slave hunter in the Mexican borderlands after he kidnapped a family from Músquiz in 1850.[19] The next year he hoped to abduct the chief of the black Indians in Mexico, John Horse of the Mascogos

(Black Creeks), and ultimately succeeded. Then, when the chief won his freedom, the mail carrier from San Antonio sought again to abduct him.[20]

John Horse was a particularly high-profile case, and he might have provoked Texans far up the chain of command into a concerted response. The majority of slave hunters in Mexico seem to have been private citizens, however—men who were either trying to return their own runaways or bounty hunters deputized to do their dirty work for them. Slave hunters ranged throughout the southernmost extremities of the state and even crossed the border into Mexico to impart through force what they could not achieve through more regular means. It was an open secret that some masters encouraged slave hunters to cross the border and go into Mexico. At least one master advertised a scaled reward for the capture of a runaway, offering a larger sum the closer to Mexico he was taken up. He offered a greater reward still if the slave hunter illegally went into Mexico to reclaim the runaway. If captured in Mexico, the former master of Gib would reward the slave hunter with three hundred dollars, a hundred dollars more than if he was taken up west of the San Antonio River. This was a huge portion of an average annual salary, if not an even greater sum, and the equivalent to nearly ten thousand dollars in today's money.[21]

Such an enticement was nearly irresistible, and masters got good results from deputizing private citizens to go into Mexico to kidnap African Americans, even once Texas seceded from the Union. In June 1861, for example, the *Nueces Valley Weekly* carried an advertisement from a Major S. Peters from Padre Island who wanted a man, a woman, and four children who ran away from slavery to Mexico recovered. "Boys on the Rio Grande," he wrote, "times are hard, and now you have a chance to get a large reward."[22] Thus, even in the ink-spilled public forum of Texas weeklies, slaveholders openly encouraged traffickers to go into Mexico, which was both an illegal and immoral act as soon as the slave hunter crossed the border.

Given the tremendous rewards that could result, most towns along the Rio Grande suffered at least one notable slave raid during this decade. Matamoros, long known as a destination for runaway slaves, witnessed a frightening attack in 1850. Two armed American men crossed over the river from Brownsville and assaulted the house of Luís del Fierro on the night of August 20. The Texan William Cheney orchestrated the invasion, hopeful of capturing a woman named Matilda Haynes and a young "creature of color" in her care, both of whom he claimed had once belonged to him. But del Fierro had probably already suspected something was amiss that night, especially when some foreigners addressed him suspiciously, inviting him to hear the music of a band playing in the town square. Del Fierro did not really know the men and he declined, choosing instead to go to bed. As he prepared to turn himself in, he heard his servant Haynes shriek for his wife to come and help her. When del Fierro descended the stairs with a gun in his hand, he saw that Cheney and another man had broken into the house through a back door. They were busily engaged in the act of tying the woman up when del Fierro surprised them, gun in hand. Cheney's wife lit out upon the balcony to call for the militia's auxiliary while del Fierro held the men captive. They refused to answer del Fierro's questions, however, and, growing desperate, Cheney's assistant grabbed the young girl who was with Haynes and ran out the door. But as soon as he realized he was being pursued, he let the child go, and he probably did not stop running until he reached the other side of the river.[23]

Cheney would not be so lucky. Questioned by the police, he insisted that he just hoped to come to terms with Haynes. He wanted her to pay for her emancipation or return to Brownsville when she finished working for del Fierro. But other witnesses described a much more terrifying version of events and testified that Cheney had clearly intended to use force. Cheney had even hoped to enlist and pay additional auxiliaries besides the foreigners who lived in del Fierro's house to help him achieve his objective. One man, Richard Ford (or Enrique Fority, as the documents record his name) claimed that Cheney had offered him a hundred dollars for his assistance, a sum that he had the wherewithal to refuse. Despite his protests, Cheney ended up imprisoned at the end of the night, demonstrating ably how Mexican soil could reverse the order of things. Black people went free even as whites languished in jail just across the border.[24]

Yet sometimes the borderlands were more fluid than this, and the border did not have the power to halt international pirates. Mexicans were not always successful in enforcing their laws protecting freedom and lending meaning to the border as a line of liberty. Some blacks had their freedom interrupted permanently. One particularly violent episode of this sort occurred at Mier, Tamaulipas, in 1851. A free African

American named Melchor Valenzuela lived and worked in Mier, employed by Bernardo Baker, a shipbuilder. In many ways, Valenzuela lived a typical life for an African American in the borderlands, scraping to get by in both the formal and informal economy. Many knew Valenzuela as the fiddler who performed at fandangos thrown by merchants and officers in the borderlands. He also may have dabbled in cattle rustling, and he may have even stolen a Mexican barge on one occasion, putting it up for sale on the Texas side in Roma. One night, while performing at a fandango thrown by his employer, two Texans—a Captain Jack and a man known as "Dickson" (Dixon)—approached him, shoved a gun into his chest, and crossed him over in a boat to the Texas side. Wanted for crimes in Texas, Valenzuela ultimately lost his freedom to the arbitrary and illegal power of slave hunters in Mexico.[25]

The raiders justified the kidnapping. They said that Valenzuela's employer, Baker, owed a debt to a merchant in Roma. Thus, even once he found freedom in Mexico, an African American could still be transformed at the point of a gun into chattel. On the other side of the border, African Americans could not completely escape the violent reduction of blackness to servility—despite the best intentions of the law to protect them. The borderlands were just too lawless to grant Mexicans and blacks the sort of security for which they so desperately hoped. When the kidnappers secured Valenzuela as payment on a debt, they stripped him of his personhood and transformed him into a commodity. Flaunting the laws of Mexico, they overpowered Valenzuela and reduced him to slavery with no greater justification than their own might, removing him from his social milieu and his Mexican wife (a servant of Baker's). Undoubtedly the Texans sold him into slavery to repay the Roma merchant's debt and received handsome rewards for doing so. Slavery reached Valenzuela across the border—even after he had found safety and refuge under the theoretically ample protection of Mexican law.[26]

This episode threw into sharp contrast the distinction between a lawful border and a fluid, unregulated, and insecure borderland. Both things could exist at the same time. Even if slavery was illegal in Mexico, the Texans had still achieved their objective. Baker tried to recover Valenzuela and consulted a lawyer in Starr County, but he had no success. The *Jefe Político* of Mier had the final word on the raid, and the damage these slave hunters had caused to his national pride colored the terms he used to describe what happened. Texan "pirates" had not only abducted an African American. They had also "violate[d] Mexican territory" and cast indignity upon Mexico's "national honor"—yet again.[27] Diplomatic pressure and measured responses could not ensure the freedom of African Americans on the Mexican side of the border.

Despite the incredible damage that slave hunts did to Mexican sovereignty, they continued unabated. Slave hunts continually undid the effort to make a meaningful and distinct line between Mexico and the United States. Anastacio Aguado was another black man who found himself victim of the arbitrary and illegal violence visited upon Mexico and its inhabitants by filibusterers. Aguado had integrated into Mexican society during the 1850s, if not even earlier. He had married a Mexican woman, and he worked for a relative, most likely his brother-in-law. Then one day, while toiling away for his relation, two Mexican kidnappers surprised him. They then carried him off toward the banks of the river with the help of a Texan named Francisco Camargo (which was perhaps a Hispanicization of an Anglo name). The men crossed Aguado to the left bank—the Texas side of the river—in a ferry commanded by a local Mexican man by the name of Timoteo Cabos to where two men waited on the other side. These two men—their identities are unknown—promptly stripped Aguado of his clothing, tied him to a stake they had pounded into the ground for this purpose, and then proceeded to whip him ferociously. As they abused the naked, bleeding, captive black man, they accused him of stealing cattle from the Texas side. The two Texans then dragged Aguado off to Brownsville on horseback and left him there in prison, where he languished for three days.[28]

Then something extraordinary happened. The day after the kidnapping, Aguado's brother-in-law, Juan Cos, began investigating the situation, and he reported the kidnapping to the regional *juzgado* (magistrate). Camargo, who had likely deputized the Cabos brothers to capture Aguado, accused the captive man of being a runaway slave, but there was no proof of this. For the Texans, the man's blackness allowed his reduction to slavery, even if Cos pleaded that Aguado was free. Whether he had been free before, or whether Mexican soil had transformed Aguado from an enslaved man into a free man, he nevertheless regained his liberty after his brother-in-law's intervention. At last, the border mattered. Not only that, upon returning to Mexico, Aguado himself testified before the regional magistrate, which was a mighty testament to the startlingly real legal personhood of this black man in Mexico, just across the border form the United States of America's newest and fastest-growing slave state.[29]

Despite the happy ending that Aguado found, however, we should be careful in ascribing too much significance to the international line. As the vignette above clearly demonstrates, Aguado had his freedom abruptly interrupted, and this was not an uncommon occurrence. Others similarly had their freedom taken away, and for most it was permanent. In 1859, for example, the entire Henderson family—who were probably refugees from slavery—went missing from the right bank (Mexican side) of the river never to return. Perhaps their fate would have escaped the historical record if not for another "woman of color," named Merley, who crossed the border from Texas to alert the alcalde of the ayuntamiento of Reynosa that the Hendersons had disappeared. Merley informed the alcalde that the family, which included a black man, his wife Anna, and their four children, had gone missing from the ranch of Juan Longoria Tijerina. She said that some men had violently captured them and sent them back to slavery on the other side of the river, and they were now in the hands of their old master.[30]

A short while later, the alcalde began an investigation into the disappearance. He discovered that five Americans had recently crossed the border to visit various ranches on the other side, raising some suspicions among the vecinos who inhabited it. The Americans claimed that they wanted to purchase *ganado menor* (sheep and cattle) from the Mexican side, and they were merely looking for the best prices. A Mexican named Manuel Muñoz who accompanied them probably did the talking for them. But then, just a few days later, the same group of men crossed the river, kidnapped the Henderson family, and trafficked them to the other side in a ferry belonging to Salvador Cavazos. For his assistance, Cavazos allegedly received a reward. The Hendersons undoubtedly ended up back in their old master's power. One witness called before the alcalde claimed that he had seen the mother of the family at work in his friend Tomás' house in Brownsville, probably lent out as a domestic servant by her master.[31]

With Texans so willing to break the law to achieve their own ends, Mexicans took it upon themselves to try to transform the lawless borderlands into a lawful bordered land. At last, they began to make a concerted effort to assert legal sovereignty over their territory, bring security to the border, and expel unwanted and illicit foreigners from their territory. Mexican diplomats bristled that they could get no satisfaction from the American government for crimes committed by Texans on their side of the border, and Luís de la Rosa in particular waged an intensive letter-writing campaign to resolve border issues. De la Rosa, the hapless foreign minister to the United States, made many complaints to the U.S. government for a variety of misdeeds committed by private Texan citizens during the 1850s.[32] But, unable to convince Americans to respect their sovereignty, Mexicans were left to come up with their own solutions in the absence of treaties or impressive national authority. Tremendous conflict and violence resulted as Texans and Mexicans battled it out in a borderland that refused to heed to law and governance.

In Tamaulipas, resistance to American slave raiders most often took the form of imprisonment for the treacherous Mexicans who helped them. In an effort to make some order out of the chaos and punish those who ran afoul of the laws, Mexican officials punished their own citizens who assisted slave raiders for pay. The authorities could not reach across the border and extricate those who organized the slave hunts, so instead they found the traitors in their own midst and held them responsible. In the case of the attack made on Rancho Sanguijuela by the troops from Fort Duncan, the authorities on the Mexican side of the river eventually identified the two vecinos who had assisted the invaders and led them to the ranch that employed the black man: José María Nuncio and Marcos Mariscal.[33] Exercising the right to punish their own citizens, the authorities imprisoned them for violating the antislavery laws of 1837 and 1846.[34] The attack on Anastacio Aguado also involved help from several local vecinos who lived on the right bank of the river, including Manuel Hernandez, Luís and Timoteo Cabos, and their servant Pedro Cadena. The Cabos brothers received four-year sentences and were put to work for violating the law (Hernandez had disappeared).[35] If the Mexican authorities could capture American kidnappers while they were on their side of the river, they punished them as well. As a result of the botched kidnapping of Matilda Haynes, the black woman's erstwhile master went to prison. Haynes remained free even as her former master, William Cheney, languished in a Matamoros calaboose for weeks. A month after the attempted kidnapping, when Cheney petitioned the local judge for his release owing to his own "grave internal injuries" and the infirmity of his wife in Texas, he could only hope that he might at last regain his freedom.[36] Punishments such as these lent meaning to the international border as a gateway to liberty.

But given the large cash rewards offered to those who helped slave hunters, the Mexican authorities could not entirely stamp out the illegal assistance that some vecinos lent to filibusterers. Further, some probably had more enticement than cash rewards to help kidnappers. Some vecinos had ties that reached across the border and that were more meaningful to them than any decrees issued by the local authorities against slavery and slave hunting. In November of 1860 a group of "Americans" captured a couple of blacks heading toward Laredo on the San Antonio road. Then, a couple of days later, Santos Benavides of Laredo and a number of white Americans and Hispanics from the Texas side of the border carried out a transnational slave abduction. Perhaps as many as fifteen people participated in this kidnapping of a black man who had arrived at Laredo with two horses and a stallion a few days earlier. The ferryman who crossed the black man and his (likely stolen) animals over must have alerted Santos Benavides. Hopeful to defend "the laws and institutions of Texas," Benavides gathered a posse and crossed the river at eight o'clock that same night. As many of the startled citizens of Nuevo Laredo looked on, Benavides and his men went straight to the house of Francisco Ciprian, where the black man had holed up. They rousted him out of the house, tied him up so he would not scream, and dragged him back to the boat and, almost inevitably, slavery. As these invaders pushed out into the water for the Texas side, they met some resistance and several Mexicans began firing upon their boat. Benavides and his friends returned the fire, and one white man was hurt badly—shot through the jaw. But the men escaped this cavalcade of fire, made it to Texas, and deposited the black man in the city jail of Laredo where he awaited his "owner." According to the *Corpus Christi Ranchero*, Benavides was a friend to the Texans, and he had done his race proud. He helped correct an "erroneous impressions" of many Texans regarding their "fellow-citizens of Mexican origin." Benavides had already distinguished himself by "restoring runaway slaves to their owners; always with the same indifference to danger, the same prudence and foresight in forming his plans, and complete disinterestedness, as he has invariably refused to receive any recompense for his exertions."[37]

But *mexicanos* on the other side of the border, the ones who had shot at Benavides and his men as they escaped across the river, did not feel the same way. The following day the alcalde of Laredo began his investigation into the situation. He discovered that among the surnames of the abductors were both Anglo and Hispanic names—indeed, the newspapers were right in characterizing this slave hunt as an interethnic one. Hence, it would do us well to remember that the Hispanic community was very divided on this issue. Lower-class Mexicans and Mexican nationals likely sided with the runaway slaves. Elite Tejanos—especially around Laredo—probably did not. Ultimately the investigation came to very little. The authorities found the blood-stained boat resting at the ford, but they could find no one to punish.[38] Enforcing antislavery edicts and protecting Mexican jurisprudence from only one side of the river did little to discourage future slave hunts. They continued to occur throughout the Civil War in the environs of the lower Rio Grande, sullying Mexico's reputation as a site of legal freedom.

Further up the river, at the border between Coahuila and Texas, Mexican authorities took a more active approach than their countrymen in Tamaulipas. In Coahuila, some Mexicans threatened to "meet force with force" if slave hunters and filibusterers dared to spoil their sovereignty, cross the border, and return runaway slaves.[39] As a result of threats to their legal sovereignty, vecinos mustered into militia units under the charge of patriotic officers time and time again to protect their own law and order. On occasion they did indeed meet force with force to mete out exemplary punishment to filibusterers-cum-slave hunters in the name of territorial sovereignty and legal integrity.

A raid that took place outside of Guerrero in 1851 served as a particularly gruesome warning to would-be slave hunters, alerting them to the growing Mexican resolve to halt illegal and illicit kidnappings in their territory. The incident began innocently enough when a Mexican man approached an African American to ask him if the ranch that employed him had any meat for sale. The African American replied in the affirmative, but upon returning with the goods, a hidden white man set upon him, tied him up, and began to fasten him to a horse. The black man struggled mightily, even managing to grab the American's pistol and to shoot his Mexican accomplice in the wrist. He nevertheless lost his freedom. The African American captive howled mightily as the men carried him away, protesting that he would rather be dead than captured in this way.[40]

Luckily for the captive, a Mexican youth soon spotted the trafficker and his captive en route back toward the border. The boy ran to alert the officer, Manuel Flores, who then set off with three other vecinos in pursuit of the slave hunter and his accomplice. Picking up the trail, they discovered the African American's hat on the ground. Then, a bit later, they happened upon the camp that the kidnapper had made. Flores and his deputies quietly approached the kidnapper, surrounded him, and surprised him. Flores demanded that the slave hunter surrender. Instead, the Texan looked up with "swiftness and resolve" and reached for his holster. Before he could reach his pistol, however, Flores and the vecinos who accompanied him fired upon the man, felling him from his horse. The Texan raider, lying on the ground, shot in the lung and the arm and bleeding out into the Coahuila desert sands, still managed to draw his weapon "with his last breath." Flores knocked it out of his hand. Soon, an American doctor living nearby came to investigate the scene and pronounced the slave raider dead. (According to his report, the man was neither breathing nor responding to his questions—and he evinced other "señales cadavericas," or corpse-like signs).[41] A small military party in Coahuila composed of three vecinos and a captain had arrested and executed a Texan slave hunter filibustering in Mexico, asserting their laws violently against those who would dare transgress them.

Statecraft in northern Nuevo León and Coahuila did not involve much out and out militarization of the physical border itself during this period (this probably would have been impossible anyway since they did not have the resources to create a "gatekeeper state").[42] Rather, the practice of sovereignty and securing the border involved keeping the Mexican hinterlands free from border transgressors with malicious intent through military forces made up almost exclusively of vecinos who were compelled to volunteer. These militias had two tasks: protect authorized border crossers and expel illegal and illicit ones. If they could not turn the borderlands into a bordered land, then they at least hoped to filter their territory from unwanted transgressors. Further, when the vecinos came to the defense of runaway slaves, the state appropriated this flow of human beings into Mexico, which it had very little control over, and used them to build sovereignty. By offering these mobile peoples refuge, the state made the line between Texas and Mexico more meaningful, and Mexico's own sovereign laws stood out in sharp contrast. Runaways became refugees through the magic of "setting foot" on the other side of the border, and vecino militias enforced this transition. Twice Manuel Maldonado, the subinspector of the western military colonies, referred to pirates as those who would assault "our laws and the cause of liberty which they protect." He perhaps more than anyone else at the time dreamed out loud of a meaningful border between the two nations.[43]

A few years later, hundreds of Texan volunteers who sought out the Lipan Apaches and probably runaway slaves perpetrated the Callahan Raid of 1855. The vecino militias and military colonists soundly defeated the filibusterers and Santiago Vidaurri, governor of Nuevo León, crowed proudly. The great northern caudillo praised his subordinates. He used the valor of the vecino militias to grandstand for the cause of national sovereignty and underscore his region's loyalty to Mexican ideals and laws. The "patriotism and valor" of the militias had achieved the most happy results and the frontier caudillo broadly praised the comportment of his subordinates, who had acted bravely "under the honorable name of *México*."[44] In a letter republished by the national newspaper *Siglo XIX*, Vidaurri wrote that it was because Mexico "professed the principal of liberty of the slaves and the abolition of slavery ever since it became independent" that filibusters had scorned its laws. In a twist of fate, the causes of anti-Americanism, border security, and liberty for African Americans became joined. Blacks may have been troublesome, but protecting them offered an opportunity for Vidaurri, his minions, and the vecinos of the frontier to prove their patriotism by rebuffing raiders, protecting Mexican soil, and ensuring legal integrity.[45]

Yet there were problems involved with this method of enforcing Mexican sovereignty over the frontier and securing the border. There was one group of people for whom the levée en masse was not entirely beneficial: the vecinos themselves. In March of 1859 yet another threat of filibusterers emerged. According to reports, nearly four hundred North Americans were readying themselves to cross the border, preparing to abduct African American refugees from Nacimiento de los

Negros, near the village of San Fernando de Rosas.[46] All the vecinos on haciendas and ranchos near Guerrero were commanded to abandon their work and take up arms. They were not allowed, under any conditions, to leave the jurisdiction's limits. Nor could the vecinos' property be spared in this effort, and they would have to lend up their horses, weapons, and munitions to the effort.[47] It was all for a good cause, however. The alcalde of Sabinas Hidalgo, who readied a list of all the citizens of his municipality capable of bearing arms from age sixteen to sixty, plainly stated "an exemplary punishment of the *osadía* [arrogance] of the Texans was the most just measure one could undertake."[48] Instead of turning over runaway slaves, the officers of the Mexican North and their minions planned to filter vigorously the borderlands against invaders. They expelled unwanted visitors upon their soil and defended it against illegal and illicit border crossings through employing the vecinos in defense of the national territory—and by coincidence, black refugees.

And yet, if seeking out common solutions in an official capacity somehow remained out of the question, there were other ways to make inroads toward international cooperation quietly. In the wake of yet another filibusterer threat in 1859, the authorities of Coahuila and Nuevo León removed all African Americans from the border region and internalized them deep within Coahuila, at Parras. A couple of years later, in 1861, a number of Mascogos petitioned the government of Nuevo León y Coahuila to allow them to return to Nacimiento, but Vidaurri's secretary wrote back that this would be impossible. They would surely invite the jealously or greed (*"codicia"*) of Texan adventurers. This would "alter the relations of both countries" and affect adversely "the peace along the frontier." Further, the vecinos would also have to remain in a state or war-like readiness.[49] There was even some headway on the issue of runaway slaves made between the two sides which deeply betrayed the reputation Mexico had worked so hard to assert for itself as a land of liberty.[50]

The last great mustering of vecinos against slave hunters in the West Texas borderlands occurred in late 1861 as a Texan force threatened the poor little settlement of Resurrección for harboring a runaway slave. The captain of the vecinos of this town—who were mostly Tejano immigrants from Bexar, settled only recently in this remote location—met the Texans and convinced them to ride off, but not before the invaders threatened to return with a hundred more men who were waiting for them at Moras. This was, in fact, the second attack on the town that year, the first having occurred at the hands of the Lipans back in February. All fifty of the families that remained in Resurrección after the February attack then packed up their things and left in the wake of the Texans' threat.[51]

Learning of the threat against the settlers at Resurrección, Captain Vicente Garza went through the usual drill, enlisting 176 men from nearby Rosas, Nava, and Allende. Once again, he swore to punish those who had compromised "the respectability, interests and credibility" of Mexico and rode roughshod over its "national integrity." Garza then wrote to Manuel Rejón, governor Santiago Vidaurri's secretary, in Monterrey. "We must," he insisted, "reorganize and establish in this frontier at least one hundred and fifty men to contain and punish the arrogance of the savages and the Texan volunteers who trespass the line of the Bravo without permission." Unfortunately, it would be impossible to maintain such a sizable force to secure the border given the frontier's absolute dearth of resources. Thus, it would fall upon patriotism that stirred in the breasts of the civilian "sons of the state" to muster into military service, hold the line, and defend national integrity.[52]

The efforts to assert Mexican liberty, to make that country stand out in sharp contrast against Texas, were very costly. But as the Civil War broke out in the United States and as the French occupied Mexico, it would seem that Mexicans largely deserted the attempts to mark their territory off from the United States as a land of liberty. Furthermore, great profits could be made through bootlegging cotton from Texas, and many did not dare risk alienating the Texans. By the time of the Civil War, many Mexicans had compromised their country's reputation as a guarantor of freedom.

Nevertheless, in the 1850s, Mexicans sought to express their sovereignty through the protection of runaway slaves. They sought to enforce a border that separated a land of liberty from a land of slavery and bring some stability to a borderland that failed to capitulate to law and order. Mexican officials sought to protect runaways and secure the border through diplomatic channels and through expelling foreign pirates from their soil. But their efforts to transform Mexico into a (bordered) land of freedom were greatly complicated by illegal transnational violence emanating from the United States. Mexicans responded to this pressure of course. The authorities arrested corroborators on their side of the border. Further west, in Coahuila, Mexicans charged vecino militias with clearing their territory of those who violated the laws and, particularly, "the liberty which they protected." Despite these efforts, the northern Mexican frontier merely comprised a highly contested site of legal freedom for runaway slaves. Insecure borders all too often allowed for the interruption of freedom. The bordered land of liberty that Mexican officers dreamed of continued to butt up against the reality of a lawless frontier. Mexican efforts to make their country's soil distinct and even deadly to those who transgressed its laws probably discouraged some filibustering. But they also greatly raised the stakes and turned a highly contradictory border into one that could be enforced only with great amounts of effort and blood.

* * *

This chapter includes excerpts from *The Limits of Liberty: Mobility and the Making of the Eastern U.S.–Mexico Border* (Lincoln: University of Nebraska Press, 2018).

NOTES

1. Cassandra Wilson et al., *"Go to Mexico,"* from *Thunderbird*, Cassandra Wilson, Blue Note 0946 3 55876 2 3, 2006, CD.

2. Alcalde Laredo to Governor of Tamaulipas, January 17, 1850 [Copy 1873], f. 239, Legajo Encuaderno [LE] 1595, Archivo de la Secretaría de Relaciones Exteriores [SRE]; and Governor of Tamaulipas to the alcalde of Laredo, March 2, 1850 [copies 1873], f. 239, LE 1595 SRE.

3. Manuel Maldonado to Galán Falcón, January 24, 1850, Ficha 392 C5 F2 E16 5F, Fondo Colonias Militares Orientales [FCMO], Archivo General del Estado de Coahuila [AGEC], refers to antislavery colonization laws. See title 1, section 1, article 2 of the 1857 Federal Constitution of the United States of Mexico translated in H. N. Branch and L. S. Rowe, "The Mexican Constitution of 1917 compared with the Constitution of 1857," *The Annals of the American Academy of Political and Social Science*, vol. 71 supplement, May 1917, 2. See also Sean Kelley, "Mexico in His Head: Slavery and the Texas–Mexico Border, 1810–1860," *Journal of Social History*, 37, no. 3 (2004): 709–23.

4. Rosalie Schwartz, *Across the Rio to Freedom: U.S. Negroes in Mexico* (El Paso, Tex.: *Southwestern Historical Quarterly* Monograph Series, 1974).

5. For various estimates, see "Mexican Affairs," *Southwestern American*, November 17, 1852; John Salmon Ford, *Rip Ford's Texas*, ed. Stephen B. Oates

(Austin: University of Texas Press, 1963), 250; and Omar S. Valerio-Jiménez, *River of Hope: Forging Identity and Nation in the Rio Grande Borderlands* (Durham, N.C.: Duke University Press, 2013), 185.

6. Petition to S. A. Maverick and the members of Bexar Delegation, December 20, 1851, Box 100–357, Texas State Archives [TSA], Austin, Texas.

7. I look forward to reading the research currently being conducted by Alice Baumgartner from Yale and Thomas Mareite from Leiden University on this subject.

8. Primero alcalde de Músquiz to secretario del gobierno, September 6, 1857, and September 28, 1857, LE 1596 [duplicated 1873] SRE.

9. My forthcoming work, *The Limits of Liberty: Mobility and the Making of the Eastern U.S.–Mexico Border* (Lincoln: University of Nebraska Press, 2018), addresses this problem. For one example, see Packet entitled Plaza de Monterrey, Causa instruida contra los capitanes de caballeria D. Tomás Santa Cruz y Don Jesús María Chisman, fs. 8–9, April 18, 1856, Caja 121, Militares Archivo General del Estado de Nuevo León [AGENL], Monterrey, Mexico. Exp. 1, fs. 430–32, Archivo de la Embajada de México en Estados Unidos de América [AEMEUA] SRE.

10. *Texas State Gazette*, September 30, 1854. When Governor Santiago Vidaurri collected together the African Americans in Coahuila to move them to Parras, several were employed at nearby ranches, some of whom were indeed employed as servants or peons. See 1 foja, Pablo Espinsoa to Alcalde de la Villa de Guerrero, April 18, 1859, C2 F10 E2, Fondo Siglo XIX [FSXIX], AGEC; Pablo Espinosa to the Alcalde of the Villa de Guerrero, Morelos, May 29, 1859, Caja 3 F4 E9 1 foja, FSXIX AGEC; Luís Villarreal to secretary of the governor, N. L. y Coahuila, Villa Aldama, August 18, 1858, Militares C133, AGENL.

11. Sarah E. Cornell, "Citizens of Nowhere: Fugitive Slaves and Free African Americans in Mexico, 1833–1857," *Journal of American History* 100, no. 2 (September 2013): 351–74.

12. Alcalde, Laredo, to Governor of Tamaulipas, January 17, 1850 [Copy 1873], f. 239, LE 1595 SRE; and Governor of Tamaulipas to the alcalde of Laredo, March 2, 1850 [copies 1873], f. 239, LE 1595 SRE.

13. For the term "pirate," see Joaquín J. de Castillo to Severiano Madrano, primero alcalde de San Antonio de Reynosa, fs. 6–7, 8, March 28, 1853, Catálogo del AEMEUA, Siglo XIX, 4-1-5489; and Gobierno, Saltillo, Coahuila, October 5, 1854, to Ministro de Gobierno, FSXIX, C8, F7, E9, 3F, AGEC, among others.

14. "Mexican Affairs," *Southwestern American*, November 17, 1852.

15. *Texas Ranger*, February 25, 1859.

16. *Southwestern American*, November 17, 1852; Ford, *Rip Ford's Texas*, 215; *Latigo de Tejas*, extra, June 26, 1849; Declaration of Independence, June 16, 1849, The Unanimous Declaration of the Seven Northern States of the Sierra Madre of Mexico, found in Leg. 3057 f. 13, Archivo Secretaría de Defensa Nacional [SEDNA]; An ex-member of the U.S. Senate to Luís de la Rosa, August 15, 1851,

Leg. 33, Exp. 1, fs. 29–30, AEMEUA SRE; and An ex-senator of the United States to Percy Doyle, Washington, copy dated and signed Luís de la Rosa, August 21, 1851, Leg. 33, Exp. 1, fs. 430–432, AEMEUA SRE.

17. Luís de la Rosa to John M. Clayton, March 1850, f. 43, Leg. 32, Exp. 2, AEMEUA SRE. On the assault on Sanguijuela, see José María Lacunza to the Luís de la Rosa, Minister Plenipotentiary of México in Washington, February 12, 1850, fs. 15–16, Leg. 28 Exp. 3, AEMEUA SRE; and Governor of the state of Coahuila, Santiago Rodriguez to the Minister of Foreign Relations, January 31, 1850 (copy), fs. 15–16, Leg. 28, Exp. 3, AEMEUA, SRE.

18. Directive from Peter Bell, September 17, 1851, Office of the Governor of Texas, Correspondence Concerning the Texas Rangers, vol. 2, 1851–1856, Walter Prescott Webb Papers, Briscoe Center for American History [WPW BCAH].

19. Emilio Langberg, *Itinerario de la Espedicion San Carlos a Monclova el Viejo Hecha por el Coronel D. Emilio Langberg*, (Monterrey, 1851), 35.

20. *Western Texian*, November 18, 1852. For attempts made on John Horse in Coahuila, see Manuel Flores to the Governor's Secretary, Coahuila, September 27, 1851, C9 E3 F5, FSIX, AGEC; Juan Manuel Maldonado, Rio Grande, to Ayuntamiento de la Villa de Guerrero, February 23, 1851, C9 E3 F5, FSIX AGEC; José Antonio Arredondo, Piedras Negras, to the Commander at Fort Duncan, September 20, 1851, (copy certified by Maldonado, Rosas), folder 25, September 1851, Governor's Papers, TSA; and Arredondo to Maldonado, September 21, 1851 (copy certified by Maldonado, Rosas), folder 25, September 1851, Governor's Papers, TSA.

21. *LaGrange Texas Monument*, January 29, 1851; for another example of a scaled reward, see *Texian Advocate*, Victoria, June 12, 1852.

22. *Nueces Valley Weekly*, July 17, 1861, cited in Paul Schuster Taylor, *An American-Mexican Frontier: Nueces County: Texas* (Chapel Hill: University of North Carolina Press, 1934), 35.

23. Investigation of the alcalde of Matamoros, August 1850 [copy 1873], fs. 1–3, Caja 3 Exp. 13, Fondo Comisión Pesquisidora del Norte [FCPDN], SRE.

24. Investigation of the alcalde of Matamoros, fs. 1–3.

25. Investigation of alcalde of Mier, July 7, 1851 [copy 1873], fs. 8–10, Caja 3 Exp. 13, FCPDN, SRE.

26. Investigation of alcalde of Mier, July 7, 1851.

27. Investigation of alcalde of Mier, July 7, 1851.

28. Justo Treviño, Investigation by juzgado del Primer Instancia del Distrito del Norte de Tamaulipas, January 1859 [1873], fs. 3–5, C3 E13, FCPDN, SRE.

29. Treviño, Investigation by juzgado.

30. Treviño, Investigation by juzgado.

31. Treviño, Investigation by juzgado.

32. See for instance, De la Rosas to Secretaría de Relaciones Exteriores, May 19, 1850, L32 E2 f. 112, AEMEUA, SRE; *El Constitutional* (Matamoros) September 16, 1850, and September 30, 1850 (found in Caja Hemeroteca AHMAT).

33. Juan Manuel Maldonado to Francisco Barela, January 24, 1850, Ficha 396, C5 F2 E20, FCMO AGEC.

34. Francisco Barela, Rio Grande, to Manuel Maldonado, January 24, 1850 (copy January 28, 1850), Ficha 392 C5 F2 E16 5F, FCMO AGEC; and Francisco Barela, Guerrero, to Manuel Maldonado, January 26, 1850 (copy 28 Jan. 1850), Ficha 392 C5 F2 E16 5F, FCMO AGEC.

35. Justo Treviño, Investigation by Juzgado del Primer Instancia del Distrito del Norte de Tamaulipas, January 1859 [1873], fs. 3–5, Caja 3 Expediente 13, FCPDN, SRE.

36. Leonardo Espinosa to Sr. Juez del Primer Instancia, Matamoros, September 14, 1850, Caja 35-A, Exp. 911, Justicia, Archivo Historico de Matamoros [AHMAT].

37. *Corpus Christi Ranchero*, November 17, 1860, pg. 2

38. Alcalde primero Laredo to Secretary of the Ayunamiento of Laredo, November 6, 1860 [copy 1873], f. 7, Caja 3 Expediente 13, FCPDN, SRE.

39. This phrase was used frequently in Coahuila and Nuevo León. See, for instance, Ignacio Galindo (secretary to Vidaurri) to Langberg, Monterrey, September 11, 1855, reprinted in *El Siglo XIX*, November 12, 1855.

40. Testimony of Benjamin Thomas, Jesús Rodríguez, Vicente Garza, and Pedro Guerrero, witnesses Jesús Flores, A. Luís Benavides, J. Juan de la Garza, March 18, 1851, C3 F8 E8 7F, FSXIX AGEC.

41. Testimony of Benjamin Thomas, Jesús Rodríguez, Vicente Garza, and Pedro Guerrero, witnesses Jesús Flores, A. Luís Benavides, J. Juan de la Garza, March 18, 1851, C3 F8 E8 7F, FSXIX AGEC.

42. On the gatekeeper state, see Willem Van Schendel, "Spaces of Engagement," in *Illicit Flows and Criminal Things: States, Borders, and the Other Side of Globalization* (Bloomington: University of Indiana Press, 2005), 55.

43. Maldonado to the Aytuntamiento of Guerrero, September 23, 1851, C14 F9 E131, FCMO AGEC; and Juan Manuel Maldonado to president of the Ayuntamiento of Guerrero, February 23, 1851, C9 F5 E3, FSXIX AGEC.

44. Vidaurri to Ignacio Galindo, secretaría al señor comandante de la plaza de Matamoros, October 6, 1855, fs. 11–12, C3 E5 Cuaderno 10, Sobre la Invasion de Piedras Negras, FCPDN, SRE; and Secretary of the governor, Monterrey, October 8, 1855, fs. 11–12, C3 E5 Cuaderno 10, Sobre la Invasion de Piedras Negras, FCPDN, SRE.

45. *El Siglo XIX*, November 12, 1855.

46. Miguel Blanco to Alcalde de Villa de Guerrero, March 16, 1859, C3, F3 E8, 2F, FSXIX, AGEC.

47. Pablo Espinosa to Sr. Alaclde de Guerrero, June 18, 1859, C3, F6, E2, 2F, FSXIX, AGEC; and Pablo Espinosa to Sr. Alcalde de Guerrero, June 3, 1859, C3, F5, E2, 2F.

48. Alcalde Sabinas Hidalgo, March 23, 1859, to secretary of governor Nuevo Leon y Coahuila, March 23, 1859, Militares C135, AGENL.

49. Pablo Espinosa to sr. alcalde primero de la villa de Guerrero, May 27, 1859, C3 F4 E7 F1, FSXIX AGEC; Pablo Espinosa to sr. alcalde primero de la villa de Guerrero, May 29, 1859, C3 F4 E9 1F, FSXIX AGEC; Pablo Espinosa, Morelos, to alcalde de la Villa de Guerrero, September 12, 1859, C4 F1 E13 1F, FSXIX AGEC; Alcalde, Músquiz, to prefect of Río Grande, March 10, 1859, LE 1595, SRE; and Secretaria del gobierno to sr. alcalde de Músquiz, July 6, 1861, box 10 folder 121, AGEC.

50. *Matagorda Gazette*, October 16, 1858; and Vidaurri to Ignacio Galindo, November 7, 1858, fs. 5080–5082, fondo Vidaurri, Correspondencia, Igancio Galindo-Santiago Vidaurri, AGENL.

51. On the founding of Ressurección, see SRE 29-15-46 fs. 160–63; *Boletín Oficial*, Monterrey, November 30, 1861, no. 77.

52. *Boletín Oficial*, Monterrey, November 30, 1861, no. 77.

11

The U.S. Coastal Passage and Caribbean Spaces of Freedom

JEFFREY R. KERR-RITCHIE

The Ocean, if not the land, is free.
FREDERICK DOUGLASS, *The Heroic Slave*, 1853

EMPIRES

During the late 1830s the British state finally terminated chattel slavery after benefiting from the lucrative colonial system for two centuries. Emancipation, however, was an evolutionary process rather than a revolutionary transformation. Wartime measures designed to maintain the empire in two Anglo-American conflagrations between 1776–81 and 1812–14 resulted in a small but not insignificant number of enslaved people seeking freedom within British territory. The prohibition of slave trading in the British Empire crept along, beginning with England in 1772, Scotland in 1778, and Upper Canada in 1793, and culminated in parliamentary legislation against British participation in the Atlantic slave trade passed on March 25, 1807 and coming into effect on May 1, 1807. London's legislation was momentous less because it reflected self-proclaimed national values of glorious liberty and more because it terminated the prodigious activities of the busiest transatlantic slave-trading nation globally.

The integrity of colonial plantation slavery in the British West Indies also became increasingly undermined during the early decades of the nineteenth century through increased intervention by the British state. Such actions included legislation for registering slaves, the passage of amelioration laws, and the combined might of military and naval power to defeat massive slave revolts in Barbados (1816), Demerara (1823), and Jamaica (1831–32). An Act for the Abolition of Slavery, passed on August 1, 1833, and implemented a year later in 1834, was the logical consequence of this expansive state power. Its passage was made possible by compensation of £20 million (about 1.7 billion pounds sterling today[1]) to former slave owners in the British West Indies, largely drawn from an increase in foreign sugar duties. It was prematurely terminated in 1838 because planters and apprentices opposed the new free-labor system. Planters thought the new system was too "free" and sought to control labor in old coercive ways. Apprentices demanded access to land and fair compensation for their labor. Consequently, an alternative labor system of recruiting and transporting indentured workers from British imperial India was organized and managed by the colonial authorities to run sugar plantations in Trinidad, Guiana, Jamaica, and elsewhere in the Caribbean.[2]

Moreover, this antislavery state had global tentacles.[3] After clamping down on the nation's slave-trading activities, the British government robustly pursued a diplomatic front against the continuation of the Atlantic slave trade through a series of treaties with several major slave-trading countries. These anti–slave trade treaties took several forms over several decades. Conventions for the mutual right of search over shipping were signed with Spain (1817, 1835), Portugal (1817, 1842), Netherlands (1818, 1822), Sweden (1824), Brazil (1826), Norway (1835), and Argentina, Uruguay, Bolivia, Chile, and Ecuador between 1839 and 1841. Additional treaties were agreed at 1831 and 1833 Anglo-French conventions and were subsequently ratified by other states including Denmark, Haiti, and the European provinces. By the 1840s anti–slave trade squadrons policed the West African coast: their combined force reached nearly sixty British, French, and American cruisers, while the Portuguese-Angolan squadron stationed four to five ships. Anti–slave trade treaties were also signed between Britain and the African states of Madagascar, Zanzibar, and Muscat.[4]

Eloquently presented as humanitarian philanthropy to address its powerful abolitionist lobby at home, London's key strategic aims included restricting foreign competition with its own sugar-producing colonies as well as the expansion and consolidation of its global power through the gunships of the Royal Navy. By the late 1830s most former slave-trading nations had signed anti–slave trade treaties with Great Britain, except the United States. Washington's refusal was driven by concerns with British interference with American commercial activity as well as fears of compromising its own national sovereignty. Consequently, numerous transatlantic slavers from Europe, Brazil, and elsewhere hoisted the American flag in the hope that this tactic would protect them from the prying eyes of the Royal Navy.[5]

Military power buttressed these numerous diplomatic protocols. By the mid-1840s, 15 percent of British warships and 10 percent of total naval power was allocated to anti–slave trade activities. By the 1850s transatlantic slavers were being pursued and intercepted by 26 ships and 2,000 personnel of the West African Squadron. Their impact can be partly measured by the fact that between 1807 and 1866 (Spanish law abolishing its Atlantic slave trade), some 160,000 Africans were liberated from the holds of more than 600 slave vessels that had broken treaties and agreements. Most ships were detained on British orders. Many were stopped outside British territorial waters, suggesting the warm enthusiasm with which London's Admiralty ignored international law. These antislavery actions were carried out by the world's mightiest maritime power. New Orleans editor James D. B. De Bow estimated that the British Navy consisted of 636 vessels with 17,681 guns operated by 40,000 seamen with 141 war steamers in 1848. The magnitude of this maritime might is illustrated by comparison with fifteen other naval powers with a combined total of 1,497 vessels bearing 28,802 guns with 122,098 men and 135 war steamers. To paraphrase the popular nationalist song, *Rule Britannia*, Britannia ruled the waves.[6]

While the British antislavery state was expanding, the American slaveholding republic was also on the move. The passage of the Missouri Compromise in 1820, together with the annexation of Florida and Texas and their admission to the Union in 1845, massively expanded the real estate of slave states and their political power in the U.S. republic. Slaveholders dominated federal government positions. Between 1788 and 1850, slaveholders controlled the U.S. presidency for five decades, the House Speaker's chair for four decades, and chairmanship of the powerful House Ways and Means Committee for four decades. Eighteen of thirty-one Supreme Court justices owned slaves.[7] John Tyler, the tenth president of the United States between 1841 and 1845, hailed from a traditional slaveholding Virginia family. Several electronic sources conveniently describe his political career, although the reader has to look closely for references to his propertied inheritance and ownership of slaves.[8] There is little doubt that this slaveholding heritage helped shape President Tyler's enmity toward the British over the *Creole* slave ship revolt in November 1841. In June 1842, British special envoy Lord Ashburton informed British Secretary Lord Aberdeen that the "President, as a Virginian, has a strong opinion about Creole cases, and is not a little disposed to be obstinate over the subject."[9] Virginia slaveholder Andrew Stevenson served as U.S. minister to Britain between 1836 and 1841. He was serving in London when the United States sought compensation for the liberation of slaves from the slave ships *Encomium* and *Enterprise* (discussed below). He reported British opposition, no doubt because of the recent passage of colonial abolition.[10] John Forsythe hailed from Georgia, where he owned slaves and supported American slavery. His reward for loyalty to President Andrew Jackson was the post of secretary of state from 1834 to 1841, a position from which he denied British claims to search U.S. vessels for slaves.[11] Although his successor, Daniel Webster, hailed from New England's abolitionist heartland, the new secretary of state repeatedly insisted on the maritime rights of American merchant ships, opposition toward interference with the coastwise slave trade, and the sanctity of property rights during his 1841–43 federal tenure.

Moreover, the slaveholding republic wielded substantial power beyond its national borders. In 1823 President James Monroe submitted his doctrine to Congress and the world. The Virginia slaveholder supported anticolonial movements in the hemisphere, pledged noninterference in European affairs in both old and new nations, and warned that European interference in the New World would be considered a threat to the national security of the United States.[12] The rapid expansion of the young republic's economy encouraged the establishment of a network of consular agents in seaports around the world. Their mission was to encourage trade opportunities for shippers as well as to deal with any problems that might emerge between merchants and the foreign nations in which they operated.[13] They also sought to expand U.S. interests globally. John Bacon in Nassau, Bahamas, was one such consul who had to deal with the fallout from the *Creole* rebellion, as we shall see in a moment. For sure, the U.S. Navy was much smaller than the Royal Navy, with only seventy-seven vessels carrying 2,345 guns, and with 8,724 seamen and five war steamers.[14] But canny southern editor De Bow already understood the key role maritime power played in empire building. The dress rehearsal would be the Union's successful naval blockade of the Confederate States of America during the early 1860s.[15] This understanding was fully implemented several decades later under the influence of naval strategist Alfred Thayer Mahan and the expansion of American naval power throughout the Caribbean and Pacific Oceans.[16]

While it is evident that the British anti–slavery state was the most powerful adversary faced by the U.S. slaveholding republic, it is important not to overlook other antislavery states. The Republic of Haiti also clashed with the United States. Traditional interpretations of Haiti's pariah status, uniqueness, and insignificance have been persuasively challenged by new research that firmly anchors the former French slave colony within the currents and eddies of the age of Atlantic revolutions.[17] The Haitian Revolution inspired slaves and disturbed slaveholders across the Americas.[18] Haiti's successful declaration of independence in 1804 and the writing and implementation of a new constitution in 1805 were followed by a bloody civil war that divided the second republic in the Americas until 1820.[19] Civil conflagration, however, did not stop Haiti's new rulers from asserting their autonomy. Henri Christophe—who presided over the State of Haiti, consisting of the northern and Arbonite departments, and crowned himself King Henry I in 1811—seized several American cargoes as reimbursement for previous acts of fraud committed against him in Baltimore, Maryland.[20] Alexander Pétion, who assumed the presidency of the west and south departments called the Republic of Haiti, was particularly dedicated to challenging slavery in the Americas. In January 1816 Pétion provided guns, munitions, supplies, ships, and money to Spanish American liberator Simón Bolívar in exchange for a promise to abolish slavery in the new independent nations of Latin America. In early 1817 slave pilots steered the schooner *Deep Nine* to Haiti from Jamaica looking for formal spaces of freedom. President Pétion refused all requests to return the former captives. The "moment they set foot in its territory," he explained, they were at liberty. Haiti's status as an antislavery state and site of formal freedom for runaway slaves continued after the death of Pétion and the termination of the civil war. In February 1822 President Jean-Pierre Boyer spearheaded an invasion of twelve thousand troops into neighboring Santo-Domingo (the Dominican Republic after 1844) leading to the liberation of four thousand slaves and the promise of land redistribution. Some six thousand African Americans—mostly free but some self-emancipators among them—ended up in Haiti during the 1820s. The Haitian Republic joined the Anglo-French anti–slave trade conventions of the early 1830s.[21] These expanding antislavery states clashed with America's burgeoning domestic slave trade, especially at sea.

COASTAL PASSAGE

America's coastwise slave trade began with port-to-port connections. The key trading ports in the Upper South from which enslaved people embarked were Baltimore, Maryland; Alexandria, D.C. (retroceded to Virginia in 1846); and Richmond and Norfolk in Virginia. Further south, captives were transported from the ports of Wilmington, North Carolina; Charleston, South Carolina; Savannah, Georgia; and St. Petersburg, Florida. The major disembarkation ports abutted the Gulf and Mississippi, and included Pensacola, Florida; Mobile, Alabama; and Galveston, Texas. The most important port was New Orleans, Louisiana, especially from the 1820s onward.[22] These ports linked merchants, captives, slaveholders, and capital over thousands of miles. The Coastal Passage essentially linked the ports and hinterlands of the nineteenth-century American South. The essential point is that these ports served as sinews of empire. The westward expansion of the United States during the first half of the nineteenth century was as much a maritime as a land-based endeavor.[23]

The coastwise trade route ran from the Chesapeake Bay's narrow shipping lanes and cleared the North Carolina capes at Hatteras, Lookout, and Fear. These shoals were maritime graveyards. The slavers then headed for the Florida peninsula. Rather than hug the coastline, they followed the most direct route through the Providence Channel and the "Hole-in-the-Wall" passage through the Bahamas to the northeast of Nassau. Once cleared of the Bahamas, the ships turned southwest by west to approach the south Florida coast. The gulf currents were quickest around the Florida peninsula, with reefs festooned with "carcasses of ships and men" from which wreckers earned a comfortable living.[24] This coastal trade crossed thousands of ocean miles sailing off coasts of islands in the northern Caribbean claimed by the British and Spanish before disembarking captives in unfamiliar territory along the gulf coast. This was the geography of the Coastal Passage.

Traders were the key operators of this coastwise commerce. They chose to transport their human cargo via sailing vessel rather than by coffle or rail overland. Although expensive, the maritime journey was quicker, thus better for preserving the human merchandise, and there was a fleet of ships ready for business. This maritime trade displayed some recognizable decennial patterns. The period immediately following the 1807 anti–slave trade legislation did not see much coastal activity, probably due to the War of 1812 and its aftermath.[25] During the 1820s, however, the maritime business took off as traders shipped captives from Baltimore to New Orleans. Abner Robinson shipped ninety captives from Baltimore to William Kenner & Co. in New Orleans in 1819. By 1832 Robinson had relocated to New Orleans.[26]

Austin Woolfolk, however, proved to be Baltimore's most prominent and successful trader in the Coastal Passage. Born in North Carolina, he spent his childhood in Tennessee where he also served in the state militia against British forces during the War of 1812. Within fifteen years, he had built the largest slave-trading firm in the slaveholding republic. The key to the firm's rise was its owner's mastering of a complex marketplace and competitive advantage. Headquartered on Pratt Street near the Three Ton tavern from 1821 through the early 1840s, the site is now buried under a four-lane highway. During the 1820s through the mid-1830s, Woolfolk dominated the coastwise trade from Baltimore, transporting some 2,288 slaves to Louisiana between 1819 and 1832. His industriousness earned him some reputation. Frederick Douglass later recalled that the Baltimore trader's "agents were sent into every town and county in Maryland, announcing their arrival through the papers, and on flaming hand-bills, headed, 'cash for negroes.'"[27] Eastern Maryland slaves reportedly spoke of sales to the Deep South as being "sold to Woldfolk [sic]."[28]

Traders like Woolfolk helped initiate a major southern commodity market in slave sales during the 1820s. In the following decade, traders in the Old Dominion began to assert control of the Coastal Passage for reasons that are not altogether clear. George Apperson, W. T. Foster, R. H. Banks, and R. L. Marsh were among the most prominent traders operating from Norfolk. Both Banks and Marsh mastered their own ships.[29] Merchants Bacon Tait, John and Sam Corby & Company, Lancaster Denby & Company, and Thomas McCargo all operated out of Richmond, Virginia.[30]

The leading firm, however, was Franklin & Armfield located on Duke Street in Alexandria, D.C. Born in 1789 in Tennessee, Isaac Franklin served in the state's cavalry against the British during the War of 1812. Engaged in commerce on the Mississippi, Franklin turned to trading slaves. From 1828 onward the firm used company ships to transport slaves from the Chesapeake to the lower Mississippi valley. Franklin was stationed in New Orleans and Natchez. John Armfield, his brother-in-law, ran the shipping center and jail in Alexandria, D.C. Rice C. Ballard ran the buying agency headquartered in Richmond and partnered with a trader in Fredericksburg. It was a massive and lucrative business. The jail at Natchez held between 600 and 800 slaves at any one time. They transported 1,000 slaves on the firm's ships in 1833 and expected more in 1834. According to one source, "they had agents in almost every large southern city, a fleet of ships, and earned more than $100,000 in profits annually through the sale of approximately 1,200 enslaved persons into the Southwest region."[31] This business proved so lucrative that when he retired, Franklin owned several plantations in Tennessee and Louisiana encompassing "8,500 acres and 550 slaves."[32]

Traders also worked the Coastal Passage from ports outside of the Upper South. Hugh Macdonald traded from Charleston, South Carolina. He shipped 145 slaves to New Orleans between December 13, 1834, and March 19, 1835. Major shippers in New Orleans included Isaac Franklin, Thomas Boudar, Edward Williams, Theophilus Freeman, R. W. Semington, Paul Pascal, Brander & McKenna, and Bullitt, Shipp, and Co. The year following the *Creole* revolt, Pitts & Clarke's directory for 1842 listed 49 brokers, 25 auctioneers, and 185 slave traders in the Crescent City. One of the latter was John Hagan, whose five male and four female captives aboard the *Creole* were now at liberty in the Caribbean as a consequence of a slave ship rebellion the previous November.[33]

The traders' initial task was to advertise their interest in buying Negroes for the purpose of selling them into Lower South markets to meet the insatiable demand for plantation labor in the sugar and cotton fields. Newspaper readers would have encountered countless advertisements from Maryland, Virginia, and Washington, D.C. "CASH FOR NEGROES." "*Two Hundred* NEGROES WANTED." "CASH FOR 200 NEGROES, Including both sexes, from 12 to 25 years of age." "CASH FOR 400 NEGROES." A "liberal price in cash" for a "few Negroes." "CASH WILL BE GIVEN for a few likely NEGROES." "Cash for negroes."[34] The cash nexus illustrated the profitability of trading slaves. The demand was great, as illustrated by the prolific number of these advertisements. Young men and women were preferred because they were in their prime working years and, if shipped, were likely to survive the journey much better. Readers would have noticed an advertisement placed by one Virginia trader in the final edition of the *Richmond Enquirer* in 1835:

> CASH FOR 200 NEGROES. We will give the highest market price, in cash,
> for two hundred like-Negroes, from 12 to 25 years of age. Every person who
> intends to sell, will do well to give us a call, Seabrook Warehouse, where we
> are prepared to keep them safe and comfortable, whether for sale or otherwise.
> THOS. M'CARGO & CO.[35]

This Richmond trader would relocate to New Orleans and transport thirty-nine captives aboard the *Creole* six years later.

After successful transactions, the recently purchased captives were moved to so-called holding pens. The most prominent of these were located in Baltimore, Alexandria, Richmond, and Norfolk, all of which provided easy access to the Coastal Passage. Both contemporaries and historians agree that these cells were invariably crowded, noxious, filthy, and disease-ridden.[36] Moreover, they were less pens, cells, or warehouses than secure prisons. Historian Winfield Collins referred to them as "slave prisons" of Alexandria and Washington, D.C.[37] Franklin & Armfield's place on Duke Street consisted of a solid phalanx of bolts, locks, doors, cells, and guards, illustrating the difficulty of breakouts. Visitor Ethan Andrews described it as a "penitentiary."[38] Kidnapped New Yorker Solomon Northup recalled William's slave pen in Washington, D.C., as being twelve feet square with walls of solid masonry, a heavy plank floor, and "one small window, crossed with great iron bars, with an outside shutter, securely fastened."[39] Mr. Goodwin's "slave pen" in Richmond was similar.[40]

The captives were then transferred from stationary to floating prisons.[41] Franklin & Armfield ran a flotilla of ships from Alexandria through Richmond and Norfolk to New Orleans. In 1828 the firm bought the *United States*, a brig with 158-ton burden and mastered by Captain Henry C. Bell. Those wishing to transport slaves southward would have been interested in the following advertisement in the *Phenix Alexandria Gazette* of late December 1829: "For New Orleans, To sail from this port, about the 15th of January the fast sailing packet brig UNITED STATES Henry C. Bell, Master Persons wishing to ship, will please make early application to Franklin & Armfield." The brig made regular trips from Alexandria to New Orleans.[42] Another one of the firm's prominent ships was the *Isaac Franklin*—no doubt named in recognition of the fifty-six-year-old founder's commercial success. Built in Baltimore shipyards in 1835, this 189-ton vessel measured eighty-nine feet five inches in length, twenty-three feet in width, and ten feet four inches in depth. It had a square stern, one deck, and two masts. On April 22, 1836, master William Smith of Alexandria signed a registry oath "that John Armfield of the town of Alexandria" was "the true and only owner of the Ship or Vessel called the Isaac Franklin."[43]

Another member of the firm's flotilla was the *Tribune*—the Latin name drawing either from champion of the people or a Roman legionary officer. A visitor described the vessel in early 1834: "The hold is appropriated to the slaves, and is divided into two apartments. The after-hold will carry about eighty women, and the other about one hundred men. On either side were *two platforms* running the whole length; one raised a few inches, and the other half way up to the deck. They were about five or six feet deep. On these the slaves lie, as close as they can stow away."[44] Later on that same year, this vessel and another were advertised as being ready for the season's business:

> Brig TRIBUNE, Captain Smith, and Brig UNCAS, Captain Boush,
> will resume their regular trips on the 20th of October: one of which

will leave this port every thirty days throughout the shipping season.

They are vessels of the first class, commanded by experienced officers,

and will at all times go up the Mississippi by steam, and every exertion

[will be] used to promote the interests of shippers and comfort of passengers.[45]

One year later, Captain Boush and Thomas McCargo signed the *Tribune*'s manifest swearing that the sixty-five captives embarking from Alexandria and destined for New Orleans were "held to serve or labor as Slaves" under the laws of Virginia and were not imported in contravention of the 1807 act.[46]

To prevent the continuation of transatlantic slave trading, the federal legislature passed laws requiring all coastal slave traders to be inspected at ports of embarkation and disembarkation. On March 2, 1807, the U.S. Congress passed An Act to Prohibit the Importation of Slaves into Any Port or Place Within the Jurisdiction of the United States. Section 9 stipulated that the ship's captain "sailing coastwise," with "any negro, mulatto, or person of color, for the purpose of transporting them to be sold or disposed of as slaves," was required to provide "duplicate manifests" of the human cargo to be delivered to the collector of the port who would, along with the captain, "severally swear or affirm" that the persons aboard "were not imported or brought into the United States" after January 1, 1808. The collector or inspector was a federal employee who was required to certify the manifest. A copy was to be carried by the captain, "authorizing him to proceed to his destination." Failure to comply with this federal law would result in the ship's confiscation and the captain's "forfeit" of one thousand dollars per "negro, mulatto, and person of color." Section 10 required the ship's captain to "deliver to the collector" of the port of entry "the manifest certified by the collector" from the port of embarkation, after which "a permit for unlading" the cargo would be granted. Failure to do so would result in a ten-thousand-dollar fine.[47]

A brief examination of four ship manifests reveals some of the spatial, temporal, and human dimensions of the Coastal Passage. The brig *Ajax*—probably named after the legendary Greek fighter who boasted about his independence—carried a burden of 147 tons and was mastered by William Smith. On February 13, 1832, the manifest was signed by the captain, shipper Tait, and the collector of the district and port of Norfolk and Portsmouth, with permission granted to proceed from Norfolk to New Orleans. The brig arrived on February 29, 1832, having been examined and found correct by the local inspector, who signed with an illegible name on the manifest. There were a total of four different manifests, suggesting four sets of captives by different shippers and buyers. Richmond trader Bacon Tait shipped twenty-year-old Adam, nineteen-year-old Lightfoot, and sixteen-year-old Duke to Thomas Sloo Jr. of New Orleans. Moses Payne shipped seventeen-year-old Emanuel and sixteen-year-old Caroline to W. B. Kenner and G. L. Duncan of New Orleans. B. Ballard, who traveled with the ship to New Orleans, shipped twenty-year-old Patsy, sixteen-year-old Louisa, nine-year-old Daniel, and ten-year-old Betsy. Thomas McCargo shipped twenty-one-year-old Maria, three-year-old Thomas, two-year-old Sam, twenty-one-year-old Cecilia, three-year-old Emily, and two-year-old Catherine to A[bner?] Robinson.[48]

On October 17, 1835, the schooner *Hunter* left Norfolk bound for New Orleans with a human cargo of five captives. Richmond trader Thomas McCargo was shipping fifteen-year-old James Page, sixteen-year-old George Christian, fifteen-year-old Noah Nelson, fifteen-year-old Jerry Page, and sixteen-year-old Oliver Peyton to J & S Crosby of Richmond and E. Archinark of New Orleans. Captain Robert Benthall, shipper McCargo, and the port collector signed off on the manifest. The 119-ton vessel sailed for three weeks before arriving at New Orleans on November 11, 1835, where it was examined, found in compliance, and signed over by the port collector.[49]

The *Caledonia*, captained by D. W. Slavey (?), embarked from Petersburg, Virginia, on June 23, 1840, laden with thirty-five captives. They consisted of twenty-five males and ten females, most of whom were under thirty years of age. The shippers included Harrison Cook, Thomas B. Jackson, William H. Betts, George W. Brown, and Mr. Davies. The consignees were Thomas McCargo, Richard H. Beazley, Theo Apperson, and Mark Davies. The vessel arrived in New Orleans a month later, on July 24, where it was examined and found correct by the port collector.[50]

The schooner *Josephine* weighed 190 tons and was skippered by Joseph Robinson. On December 23, 1841, the master and collector Thomas Nelson signed the manifest for transporting seventy slaves from Richmond to New Orleans. Forty-two were male and twenty-eight were female. It was a young group of captives, with only eight being older than twenty-five years. The shippers were George Kephart, George Rust, James F. Purvis, George W. Barnes, Andrew Grimm—a suitable surname for such business—John W. Coleman, and Shields L. Somerville. The consignees were Thomas Boudar, Theophilus Freeman, and Robert A. Gramman—all of whom resided in New Orleans. Coleman shipped twenty-one-year-old John Redman to Thomas McCargo of New Orleans. The vessel appears to have arrived on January 17, 1842, where the local inspector passed the vessel as satisfactory.[51]

Despite a rich historical literature on the domestic slave trade stretching back a century and increasing markedly over the past two decades, scholars are only recently beginning to closely examine the migratory experiences of American slaves.[52] What about the experiences of captives in ships in the Coastal Passage?

Most accounts are either by supporters of slavery or antislavery adherents and thus need to be used with caution. William H. Seward, New York abolitionist and future U.S. secretary of state under President Abraham Lincoln, described human cargoes being prepared for transportation from Virginia to New Orleans in 1846. A white man led seventy-five young men, women, and children to the steerage cabin. The children bore nothing, but the adults carried bags, bundles, and chests containing their earthly possessions. They "huddled together on the lower deck, [and] looked with puerile [why must adults look childish, Mr. Seward?] curiosity and gratification at all that surrounded them." They joined 125 slaves already aboard ship. (This was a large number of captives for the coastwise trade). As the ship undocked, the captain turned to a clearly disturbed Steward and said: "'Oh, sir, do not be concerned about them; they are the happiest people in the world!'" The New Yorker was skeptical. "I looked, and there they were—slaves, ill protected from the cold, fed, capriciously on the commonest food—going from all that was dear to all that was terrible, and still they wept not . . . And these were 'the happiest people in the world'!"[53] Their experiences of poor conditions, familial uprooting, and stoicism were no doubt shared by many thousands of coastwise captives over the antebellum decades.

Recollections by survivors of the Coastal Passage do exist, although these need to be treated guardedly. Interviewers controlled information through the questions they asked. Interviewees' memories were not infallible. Jim Crow and racial violence exerted powerful forms of control over black Southerners' freedom of expression. In 1902 and 1907, historian Fredrick Bancroft interviewed a number of former slaves near New Orleans. Nathan Ross recalled being sold to Richmond trader Daniel B. Budder:

> Budder brought 'bout 50 or 60 all de way by boat to New Orleans. We drifted down de Jeems to Po'tsmouth an' den we was put on de New Orleens ship. Dere was 30 or 40 uthahs owned by traders. On board de ship we was treated well; had plenty to eat. We was allowed to walk on deck. We was not in de hol' 'cep'n at night er when it sto'med. At New Orleans we was taken to a tradah's office. De yahd was walled up 13 er 14 feet high 'round to de front.

The original number of captives as well as those owned by traders is plausible. The route was a familiar one. The availability of food on this ship was not impossible. (Why would Ross embellish?) Daily deck walks and nocturnal confinement confirms established practice. The formidable walls were probably unforgettable to those like Ross who wanted liberty.

Washington Taylor was born in Gloucester County, Virginia. In 1853 he was sold to a trader, handcuffed, and then sold to another trader in Richmond. Taylor, along with eighty other slaves, was shipped to New Orleans. They were treated all right, except the food was not good. Frederick Bancroft thought this was "a doubtful criticism." Yet poor food on this ship was as likely as food aplenty on Ross' ship. Seward noted the "commonest food" on the trader that he witnessed.[54] Solomon Northup recalled being appointed steward of food and water aboard the *Orleans*. Jenny, one of his assistants, prepared "the coffee, which consisted of corn meal scorched in a kettle, boiled and sweetened with molasses." His other assistants, Jim and Cuffee, "baked the hoe-cake and boiled the bacon."[55] Madison Washington cooked for captives and seamen aboard the *Creole*.

Most of the sea journeys occurred during the winter months. The captives on the *Ajax*, for instance, had to endure a three-week passage in February 1832.[56] Such voyages could not have been pleasant with cold, fierce winds; tempestuous waves; and rolling, pitching ships. These harsh conditions brought on vomiting, human waste, and sickness, especially to the uninitiated. One former captive recalled being on the ship "for weeks an' days. It were dark an' I were feared an' homesick an' seasick."[57] Solomon Northup reported "sea-sickness rendered the place of our confinement [aboard the *Orleans*] loathsome and disgusting."[58] In addition, coastal slavers could be packed like Atlantic slavers. Captain Basil Hall compared a slaver with two hundred slaves in New Orleans to an Atlantic slaver he had seen in Rio de Janeiro. Antitrader Joseph Holt Ingraham quipped sarcastically that Virginia slaves "shipped for New Orleans, with as comfortable accommodations as can be expected, where one or two hundred are congregated in a single merchant vessel."[59] Moreover, forced removal from families, homes, and communities must have been heartfelt. And let us not forget that these awful journeys could last three to four weeks from Richmond and Norfolk to Mobile and New Orleans. The ship manifests record many such lengths of time between the two inspectors' signatures in the ports of embarkation and disembarkation.[60] The seasickness, separation, and poor conditions resembled the experiences of the Middle Passage. The shorter duration; relative freedom of the deck during the day; and preexisting knowledge of American slave society—all these made the experience different to the transatlantic crossing.

Much like the Middle Passage, the Coastal Passage claimed lives. Twenty-five-year-old Jesse Botts died en route to New Orleans aboard the *Lafayette*. Twenty-two-year-old Rachel died on the *Tribune* voyaging from Alexandria to Natchez in January 1833. Youngsters Henry and Simon both perished while in transit.[61] Robert Jones died of smallpox aboard the *Orleans*. Tom died ten days into his journey aboard the *Clio*. Four of Baltimore trader Woolfolk's original thirty-two captives died aboard a merchant sloop in 1831.[62] This does not include deaths resulting from shipboard revolts. Historian Eric Taylor estimates an average number of slave deaths in 170 transatlantic uprisings to be about 32 per rebellion.[63] Numerous rebels also lost their lives during ship revolts in the Coastal Passage. It will be a while before we can generalize about death rates on the Coastal Passage with the same degree of exactitude as the Voyages Database for the Atlantic slave trade. But at this stage, it is clear that claims for low mortality rates are inaccurate.[64]

How many captives were moved as a consequence of the Coastal Passage? Drawing upon a detailed investigation of inward-bound ship manifests into New Orleans from Baltimore and other Maryland ports between 1818 and 1856, local historian Ralph Clayton counts 11,550 slaves shipped by water.[65] Historian Ulrich B. Phillips provides total maritime transports ranging between 2,000 to 5,000 slaves per annum between 1815 and 1860.[66] This spectrum seems remarkably high. Not only would it mean that the total number of captives varied from 90,000 to 225,000 over a forty-five-year period, but these totals would range from 9 to 25 percent of the entire domestic slave trade of 1 million transported captives from the Upper to Lower South. Both the secondary literature on the domestic slave trade as well as preliminary investigations of ship manifests do not suggest in any way that around 1 in 4 slaves were transported by ship during the antebellum years. Historian Charles Wesley's pioneering examination of ship manifests provides a more modest total of 31,854 slaves transported in the coastwise trade between 1817 and 1852. He also suggests persuasively that this was a minimum because of lost manifests and press reports of coastal trading during years with no extant manifests.[67] Ancestry.com—the dues-paying genealogical website—has digitalized a number of these ship manifests. It totals 50,638 slaves shipped between 1790 and 1860.[68] This represents about 5 percent of all captives moved during the domestic slave trade. Only detailed investigation of thousands of ship manifests deposited at several National Archives and Record Administration repositories will provide us with a more accurate number of maritime captives, together with their comparative significance. What is already clear is that the existing historical scholarship on the domestic slave trade has paid inadequate attention to the magnitude of this maritime business.

But these statistics should not blow the historian away. It is impossible to determine exactly how many captives were moved in the Coastal Passage compared to riverine journeys or overland routes via coffle or railroad. Moreover, numbers reveal little about the ebbs and flows of maritime movements. In addition, the quantification of different methods of transportation is mute on the lived struggle of enslaved human beings and the consequences. As one trenchant critic of historians' preoccupation with counting once put it, "the complexities of personal relationships are especially resistant to this exercise" because quantification "press[es] the evidence into rude classifications."[69] One can be forgiven for sometimes thinking that slave trade enumerators are among the least polite of our colleagues! Indeed, the numbers game in older studies of the Middle Passage, and its rejection by some recent scholars, should serve as a cautionary tale of trying to reduce complex human experiences to manageable statistical analysis.[70]

In sum, the Coastal Passage represented the massive relocation of captive people along the southeastern Atlantic seaboard and the Gulf coast for nearly two generations. It wrought extensive profits for traders, owners, users, financiers, as well as the nation as a whole. It linked ports from the East Coast to the southern coast to the Gulf coast expanding the American empire along the way. It consumed hundreds of lives. It also generated resistance and agency. Most important, its extensive practice demonstrates that the maritime dimensions of American slavery continued rather than halted after the abolition of transatlantic trading.

SEVERAL CASES

On August 1, 1842, U.S. secretary of state Daniel Webster wrote to British special envoy Lord Ashburton requesting improved security of American merchant vessels sailing through the Bahamas Channel. He drew attention to "several cases" in previous years of U.S. ships engaged in coastwise trading being forced off course and into British-controlled ports in the Caribbean due to bad weather. The issue was merchandise consisting of human cargo being liberated by local authorities. The British government, Secretary Webster noted, had provided compensation in some cases, "for interference of the local authorities with American vessels having slaves on board, by which interference these slaves were set free." In other cases, this compensation had been refused. Secretary Webster told envoy Ashburton that U.S. president John Tyler thought it in the best interest of the two nations that "recurrences" of such cases "should be prevented."[71]

On January 26, 1829, the *Comet* weighing 138 & 76/95 tons was cleared to sail from Alexandria to New Orleans under Captain Isaac

Staples. John Armfield of Alexandria shipped 57 captives to consignee partner Franklin in New Orleans. John W. Smith of Alexandria shipped 36 captives to J. B. Digg of New Orleans. John Meek of Georgetown shipped 15 captives to someone with an unclear name on the manifest in New Orleans. Its total human cargo consisted of 110 captives, of whom 75 were male and 35 were female. Only captive David Allen had a surname. Most were in their late teens and twenties. There were a significant number of child captives—21—including the youngest, Kitty, at 4 years old. The complexions were often in the eye of the beholder, although the 24 captives described as "brown," "yellow," "copper," and "mulatto" implies American provenance. All of these captives were successfully transported into the long night of the American slave empire.[72]

The ship's next voyage, however, was to have a very different outcome. In December 1830 the *Comet* embarked from Alexandria, D.C., en route to New Orleans, Louisiana, carrying 165 captives bound for the U.S. domestic market. Traders Franklin & Armfield owned most of the captives. Mrs. Mudd and Colonel Tutt owned 9 apiece. The ship's maritime path took it through the Bahamas Channel. On January 2, 1831, poor weather conditions drove the brig onto a reef near the island of Abaco in the Bahamas. Three small craft rescued the captives and took them to Nassau. The Bahamas House of Assembly submitted an address to Governor Sir John Carmichael Smythe "requesting of me to direct the slaves in question to be forthwith restored to their American owners." The governor contacted British colonial secretary Lord Viscount Goderich about the incident and requested advice. On one point, however, Governor Smythe was adamant: "Eleven of the slaves from the American Brig made their escape on shore and came to the Government House to claim protection."[73] Whatever the Admiralty decided about slaves in general, he would not "permit these eleven men to be taken away as slaves."[74]

The American vice president, Martin Van Buren, vigorously protested these actions, "urging upon His Majesty's Government the alleged claims of certain Persons, Citizens of the United States for injuries which M. Van Buren states that they have sustained in consequence of proceedings of the British Colonial Authorities of the Bahamas."[75] Since the local authorities had released the slaves and were not prepared to turn them over to "a Foreign Country for the purpose of being dealt with as Slaves," Vice President Van Buren "demands on the part of the United States Government that reparation may be made to the Citizens of the United States, for the injury thus done to their Property, either by the restoration of the Slaves, or by compensation for their loss."[76] British foreign secretary Lord Palmerston requested an opinion from the House of Lords on the actions of the local authorities and Vice President Van Buren's claim. The House of Lords—effectively the supreme court of the British Empire—informed Foreign Secretary Palmerston that Custom House officers in the Bahamas had "seized these Slaves upon a charge that the British Statute for the abolition of the Slave Trade, had been violated by their importation into New Providence."[77] The esteemed jurists also considered the vice president's charge "well founded." They believed that the "entire loss of the Slaves to their Owners cannot be ascribed to any improper conduct on the part of the Americans, but was occasioned by the Act of the English Custom House Officers, in seizing them." The "original illegal seizure," they concluded, was "sufficient ground for the demand of a compensation."[78] Meanwhile, former American slaves enjoyed liberty as new British subjects in the Bahamas.[79]

Nearly three years later, the *Encomium* embarked from Charleston, South Carolina, destined for New Orleans, Louisiana.[80] It grounded near Fish Key, Abaco, in the Bahamas due to poor weather conditions in early February 1834. Lieutenant Governor Balfour wrote London that "a party of 69 Americans landed here, having been taken from a Brig wrecked upon Abaco; among them were 45 slaves who were, by my desire, informed that they were free to stay here unmolested, or to depart at their pleasure—forty one or two have taken advantage of this and intend to remain."[81] In other words, this act of emancipation resulted from wreckers assisting the captives from the grounded vessel and a senior colonial official refusing to prevent their walking to liberty. Lieutenant Governor Balfour also provided rations to those rescued and housed them in the local barracks. This was done to prevent the possibility of the former captives from "getting into any scrapes with the troops or others"—a concern that remains unexplained. He further hoped that in a short while, "we shall be relieved from any trouble or expence [sic] by their finding means to provide themselves with a livelihood."[82] In other words, state support was only temporary. These latest colonial subjects were expected to achieve economic self-sufficiency quickly. Interestingly, three or four captives decided against freedom in the Bahamas. We can only speculate as to why they chose to remain in captivity: kin relations in New Orleans? Fear of retribution should the British return them to American slavery? The documentary record is mute on when and how these captives were moved from the Bahamas back to the United States since the *Encomium* was wrecked. The majority of captives, however, clearly took advantage of freedom's opportunity provided by the British colonial official and made their short walk to freedom.[83]

In early February 1835, another slaver named the *Enterprise* left Alexandria, Virginia, for Charleston, South Carolina. This 127-ton vessel under the captaincy of Elliot Smith transported seventy-eight captives. The gender ratio was fairly even, with forty-one females and thirty-seven males. One striking aspect of these captives was their relative youth compared to those on many other slavers. Some forty-four captives—or more than half—were twelve years or younger. Of these, four were infants, including three-week-old Richard Pinney. Furthermore, many of these captives were kin. Twenty-five-year-old Dinah Buckingham carried her infant. Eliza Butler, twenty, was transported with her two-year-old, Harriet Ann Butler. Dafney Gray, twenty, was with her six-month-old, Grace Gray. There were six captives with the last name of Pinney, headed by twenty-four-year-old Eliza and the rest between eight years old and three weeks suggesting family ties. Twenty-five-year-old Matilda Ridgley traveled with her five children—ten-year-old Martha, seven-year-old Helen, five-year-old Mahaley, three-year-old Betsy, and five-month-old Ann.[84] Five children with the surname of Warfield were also onboard. One author states these youngsters were kidnapped from the Warfield plantation in Maryland. One nine-year-old—Mary Warfield—recalled "her mother, an Indian squaw, wringing her hands and screaming for the children."[85] The owners of the ship's captives, including unidentified "widows and orphans," were John Strohecker and other South Carolina slave owners. They contracted with the Marine and Fire Insurance Company of Charleston to protect their investment against loss.[86] Rather than pioneer uncharted regions like its spaceship namesake on 1960s US television, the *Enterprise* pursued a common, popular, and lucrative business. Ordinary citizens invested in slave trading, protected their risk, and helped expand American slavery.

On February 11, 1835, the vessel was knocked off course by a hurricane and forced to seek shelter in Hamilton, Bermuda. Now one of the smallest capital cities in the world, it was the scene of an important maritime liberation during early 1835. British customs officers who boarded the ship reported very poor conditions. The ship's manifest recorded tobacco, bricks, and food but made no mention of the vessel's seventy-eight captives. The officials probably believed the *Enterprise* was an illegal transatlantic slaver like the *Comet* that had been knocked off course, although this is not mentioned in the documentary record. They informed Captain Smith that slavery was now illegal in the British colony, and the slaves were free to leave. He responded that the ship had been accidentally driven into Bermuda's waters, was en route between American ports, and that the British authorities had no right to interfere. The Royal Navy detained the vessel while West Indian troops boarded the ship.[87]

All the while the *Enterprise* was in the harbor, a local benevolent organization called the Colored Friendly Society was taking an interest in these captives and their possible liberation. After the captives were brought ashore, the society obtained a writ of habeas corpus from the chief justice of Bermuda to get the captives into court. The attorney general asked each captive individually if they wanted to continue on to Charleston as slaves or obtain their freedom in Hamilton. Seventy-two of the original seventy-eight captives chose freedom in Bermuda over slavery in South Carolina. The exception was Matilda Ridgley, who opted to return with her five children to American bondage. In the absence of Matilda's own explanation, we can only speculate on her decision: Family at the plantation of destination? Kind owner? Retribution should the Bermudian authorities return the captives to the United States? The attorney general voiced the new imperative of the British antislavery state: "a slave was as much free when he arrived in the Bahamas or at Bermuda as if he had reached Portsmouth or Plymouth [England]."[88] This was the culmination of the "several cases" in the context of imperial abolition during the 1830s. Hamilton's mayor found temporary accommodation in a storeroom while society members assisted with employment and took some of the youngsters into their homes.[89]

The American government protested British actions requesting either the return of the slaves or compensation to the slave owners. The red- and ermine-draped law lords ensconced in their exquisite aristocratic chamber in central London were once again consulted. They upheld U.S. claims in the case of the *Encomium*, ruling that "the Slave Owner is entitled to Compensation when he has been lawfully in possession of the Slaves within the English territory, and he has been disturbed in his possession of them by a functionary of the English Government."[90] In short, the "case of the *Encomium* does not substantially differ from that of the *Comet*." But, continued the law lords, U.S. claims for compensation were "not well founded with respect to the *Enterprize* [sic]."[91] The slave owner with property on this vessel "never was lawfully in possession of the slaves within the English territory." As soon as the ship "entered the port at Bermuda they were free, as slavery had been abolished throughout the British Empire." These slaves "had acquired rights which the Courts there were bound to recognize and protect."[92] Indeed, the law lords informed the British foreign secretary of their "great satisfaction" that the cases of the *Comet* and the *Encomium* were the last of their sort since, "Slavery being now abolished throughout the British Empire there can be no well founded Claim for Compensation in respect of Slaves."[93] This alternative ruling, promoted by legal passage of British colonial emancipation in 1833, was to play a pivotal role in contrasting American and British responses to the *Creole* revolt, as it delineated British colonial space as a site of formal freedom.

The U.S. schooner *Hermosa* weighed 133 & 66/95 tons and was captained by John L. Chattin.[94] On October 10, 1840, the master, port collector George Read, and several shippers signed the ship's manifest as required by federal law. The vessel's business was to transport forty-seven captives from Richmond to New Orleans. L. C. Read of Richmond shipped forty-five-year-old Lewis Johnson to one J. H. Daly. As the eldest, he might have been marketed for work beyond the plantation. Prominent Richmond trader Lancaster, Denby, & Company shipped five boys and four girls aged between eleven and sixteen to consignee A. Ledoux. H. N. Templeman of Richmond transported the bulk of the captives. Twenty-one were males ranging in age between the youngest, sixteen-year-old Reuben Francis, and the oldest, thirty-five-year-old Edward Parker. Sixteen were females ranging in age between ten-year-old Louisa Gibbs, Dicey Lumkin, France Toublin and thirty-year-old Betsy Green. The age and gender of these captives suggest they were destined for plantation production. The list of names does not reveal much about possible familial relations. Some were only listed by one name. Others, like Malinda and Louisa, shared the same surname of Gibbs while William and another were both Smith. This similarity suggests either the same former slaveholder or some form of kinship.[95]

Nine days later, the *Hermosa* wrecked on one of the Abaco Islands. Bahamas governor Francis Cockburn reported that "every slave would have perished but for the gallant exertions of the Boatmen of that place [who] rescued [them] from a watery grave."[96] After being towed to Nassau, Captain Chattin arranged with U.S. consul John Bacon to get another ship to take the captives to their destination in Louisiana. British magistrates, backed by armed soldiers from a British West India Regiment, boarded the *Hermosa* and removed the captives. A local magistrate set them free—presumably arguing that the slaves were at liberty once they entered a British jurisdiction in compliance with the reasoning of Britain's highest courts in the previous case of the *Enterprise*. The Americans protested this decision, arguing that they had broken no local laws and were just seeking aid for the protection of private property. The Colonial Office regretfully informed Cockburn that "no funds" were available from Her Majesty's government for "remuneration" to the boatmen of Abaco "in saving the slaves."[97] Bahamian boatmen were also to play a decisive role in the liberation of captives from the *Creole* thirteen months later.

All four of these incidents involving American coastal slavers bore striking similarities: poor weather conditions drove the vessels off course into British waters and ports where captives were largely liberated by the local authorities. In the first two cases, the British government subsequently compensated U.S. slaveholders because colonial slavery still operated in its territories. In the latter two cases, U.S. slaveholders failed to receive compensation because Great Britain had abolished colonial slavery. Any slave on either British soil or within British maritime borders was legally free due to the passage of colonial abolition in 1833, its implementation in 1834, and its final manifestation in 1838. Although U.S. slaveholders continued to press for compensation, these two latter cases remained unresolved until the final deliberations of the Anglo-American Commission during the early 1850s.[98]

In contrast, nineteen captives aboard the *Creole* had revolted, commandeered the ship, killed a guard, wounded the captain and several crew, and steered for the Bahamas in the hopes of obtaining their freedom in free waters. This vessel's history was markedly unlike that of the *Comet, Encomium, Enterprise,* and *Hermosa.* The *Creole* ended up in British waters as a consequence of a successful slave insurrection whereas the previous slavers had been forced into British ports by poor weather after which their human cargo either walked or were transported to freedom. This latter action, it should be noted, resulted from similar expressions of pan-African solidarity between Caribbean boatmen and American captives. Black consciousness across the water receives only fleeting comment in the documentary record but was significant in these maritime acts of liberation.

REVOLT

Historians agree that about one in ten slave ships experienced an attempted insurrection during the Atlantic slave trade.[99] This estimate corrects an older view that enslaved Africans rarely revolted at sea. This is undoubtedly an underestimate. Some ships illegally engaged in slave trading probably experienced attempted revolts that went unrecorded. Some captains might have failed to report an uprising that they successfully suppressed because such knowledge could compromise their chances of obtaining future commissions. Eric Taylor's important monograph—the first exclusively devoted to maritime revolts—estimates 493 cases of shipboard revolts against the transatlantic trade between 1509 and 1865.[100] He goes on to argue that those that occurred in the nineteenth century constituted a "second" and "new" wave of shipboard rebellion.[101] This is a debatable proposition. Most Middle Passage revolts occurred close to shore because of the proximity of land. The same was true for Coastal Passage revolts. (It is not always appreciated that the rebellion aboard the *Amistad* occurred along the northern shoreline of Cuba). Furthermore, captives protested removal from families and homes, whether on the African or American continents. Both African-born and American-born captives were forced from their homes, families, kin, and communities, resulting in the need to establish new relations and networks. Most important, captives transported in the Coastal Passage during the nineteenth century rose against their captors in ways similar to their cousins during the previous three centuries of the Middle Passage. This was less a chronological division than a rebellious tradition.

That being said, the Coastal Passage was not exactly awash with slave ship revolts. Insurrections aboard the *Amistad* in 1839 and the *Creole* in 1841 were unusual, successful, and consequently famous. But they were by no means isolated. We would do well to recall historian Frederick Bancroft's older view that "actual or attempted slave mutinies by sea or land" were "frequent."[102] His aim was to draw attention to the dangers posed to slave traders using ships to transport their human cargoes. Our concerns are a little different: how did captives use the sea to effect their escape, did they succeed, and what was the significance of Caribbean spaces of freedom?

In late April 1826 Maryland trader Woolfolk led thirty-one captives from their Baltimore prison and boarded them on the *Decatur* bound for New Orleans. Among them was twenty-four-year-old William Bowser, alias William Hill, born at West River, who had already attempted to escape from the Harrison plantation before he was caught and sold to Woolfolk. After four days at sea, on the morning of April 25 off the Georgia coast, Bowser led other captives in an attempt to seize the ship. The rebels grabbed Captain Walter R. Galloway and First Mate William Porter and tossed them overboard, where they apparently drowned. Having seized control of the vessel, the rebels ordered one sailor to take them to Haiti, where they expected liberty and its guarantee. The rebels tried to avoid all other vessels but were unsuccessful. (They had unfortunately thrown overboard the two best navigators). They encountered the U.S. whaler *Constitution*, which removed one sailor and about half of the captives before sailing away. On May 5, the *Rookes*, commanded by Captain Atwood seized fourteen of them and placed an officer on deck to take the ship into port. Once the ship moored, the fourteen captives escaped, except the rebel leader, Bowser, who was taken to New York City to face trial. After seven months of incarceration, Bowser was convicted for the murder of the drowned captain and mate of the *Decatur* and sentenced to hang. At his execution, Bowser reportedly forgave the slave trader who was present. Woolfolk, however, was unrelenting, reportedly telling the rebel leader that he was going to get what he deserved "and he was glad of it."[103] This hatred for the liberty seeker encouraged Benjamin Lundy, the abolitionist editor of the *Genius of Universal Emancipation*, to condemn the Baltimore slave trader and his iniquitous business. Some months later, Lundy was accosted by Woolfolk in the streets and beaten violently to the point of incapacitation. Charged with assault, the slave trader got off with a one-dollar fine and court costs largely as a consequence of a sympathetic judge. Meanwhile, the former captives were at liberty.[104]

Almost three years later, the captain and crew of the schooner *Lafayette* experienced their worst nightmare. This slaver was a regular transporter of captives in the Coastal Passage during the late 1820s. On October 4, 1828, it left Norfolk with 161 captives bound for New Orleans.[105] On December 26, 1828, the *Lafayette* transported 67 captives from Norfolk arriving eleven weeks later in the Crescent City.[106] A much more bloody journey, however, ensued twelve months later. The schooner left Norfolk, Virginia, with 197 slaves bound for the New Orleans market. On December 17, 1829, around 100 rebels rose with the intention of seizing the ship and steering for the free black Republic of Haiti. During the fight, several rebels were injured, and the captain's life was only saved by chance. The crew managed to suppress the revolt. Twenty-five of the rebels were manacled to the deck and the rest were incarcerated in the ships' hold. The rebels were arrested once the ship arrived in New Orleans, with four sentenced to ten years hard labor and three rebels to five years.[107]

The schooner *Orleans* was built in Baltimore, Maryland, and launched in 1838. The following year, Richard Haskins and Luther Libby's vessel transported 135 captives who ended up in the Crescent City. In the spring of 1841, recently kidnapped Solomon Northup was put aboard the *Orleans* under Master William Wickham. The ship manifest listed its slave cargo under false names. Solomon Northup was registered as Plat Hamilton. They sailed down the James River and anchored outside of Hampton Roads, where they picked up several more captives. One was Arthur Curtis. He stood five feet ten inches tall, was dark-skinned, and bore a swollen face. This local resident had been beaten while resisting capture by several men on a Norfolk street before he was forcibly delivered to the ship and transported by renowned Norfolk trader George Apperson. The *Orleans* was steered by a master, mate, and six seamen. It carried fifty captives who were unchained during the day and locked in the hold at night. When the schooner stalled in the Bahamas Channel, Curtis and Northup plotted to seize the ship and take it to New York City. This might seem like an odd decision given their proximity to free soil under British control. Why not just steer for Nassau port? Northup was probably determined to head northward to his home and family in Upstate New York.[108] The plot evaporated through an outbreak of smallpox that ended the life of one of the conspirators, Robert Jones, and blew the wind out of the sails of the plotters. In May 1841 the *Orleans* successfully unloaded its human cargo where most of its people ended up in the long night of slavery. Northup was eventually to gain his liberty after serving twelve years as a slave.[109]

In late October 1841 the U.S. coastal slaver *Creole* left Richmond, Virginia, for New Orleans, Louisiana, carrying a cargo of tobacco and at least 137 captives.[110] On November 7 the brig stopped just outside of Abaco Island in the northern Bahamas to rest for the night. Around nine o'clock that night, nineteen of the captives rebelled, led by Madison Washington, Elijah Morris, Benjamin Johnson, and Dr. Ruffin. They killed one of the guards, wounded the captain and several crewmen, and seized control of the vessel. The rebels forced the crew to steer the ship to nearby Nassau, the capital of the Bahamas archipelago. Governor Francis Cockburn arrested the nineteen rebels and informed the other slaves they were free to leave if they wished, against the protestations of local U.S. consul John Bacon. The former captives were happily ferried to the shore with great enthusiasm by local Bahamians in many boats, after which they were escorted to the local police station for registration. Over the next few days, between sixty to seventy of the newly freed embarked on the schooner *Francis Cockburn* for Jamaica. After being incarcerated by the British authorities in the Nassau jail, the rebels were freed in April 1842. Two had died in prison, one from wounds sustained during the revolt. Most of the former captives from the *Creole* settled in the villages and outer islands of the Bahamas, where they became farmers, fishermen, householders, and new colonial subjects.[111]

There were also less spectacular emancipations. In 1811 the *Cynthia* left New York City bound for New Orleans. After touching at an unnamed British port, captive Catherine Richardson "secured her freedom under the British law that prohibited the importation of slaves."[112] In August 1835 slaveholder Joel Lee of Conecuh County, Alabama, advertised for the capture of twenty-year-old fugitive Caswell, who Lee reported "will attempt to get on board some boat or vessel [from Pensacola] bound to some port as soon as possible."[113] In the summer of 1855 John Anderson was removed from the U.S. brig *Young America* at Savanna-la-Mar, Jamaica, by a crowd some three hundred strong. According to the official report, the former American slave was "set at large" by locals under the protection of British colonial law that supported abolition.[114]

And then there were those thrusts for Caribbean spaces of freedom that just simply ran out of luck. In the summer of 1844, several bondsmen sought liberty from Pensacola, Florida. Moses Johnson was a thirty-five-year-old "blacksmith, basket maker, and great chopper." His brothers, Charles, Phil, and Leonard Johnson, were "excellent laborers." Silas Scott was a twenty-five-year-old fisherman and waiter; his younger brother, Harry, was a drayman. Anthony Catlett was an "excellent laborer." These seven bondsmen approached Cape Cod–born ship captain Jonathan Walker seeking his help to steer for northern freedoms. He agreed but proposed steerage for the Bahamas instead. It was closer and free soil. Most important, the local authorities had an established reputation for supporting the emancipation of slaves from the United States who could reach its waters. On the evening of July 22, the seven escaped the U.S. Navy yard and boarded Walker's green- and gray-painted thirty-foot schooner. The small vessel headed for the southern tip of Florida. Master Walker became ill. Meanwhile, numerous handbills were posted in Pensacola offering a "$1,700 Reward" for "SEVEN NEGRO SLAVES" who had absconded. After several days at sea, Commander Farrand of the U.S. steamer *Gen. Taylor* intercepted the vessel, and the captives were returned to Pensacola. Six of the seven escapees eventually returned to slavery in Pensacola. Silas Scott slit his throat and belly, either due to personal issues with his wife or because he could not face being re-enslaved. Captain Walker was tried, found guilty, and served eleven months in jail before being eventually turned into an antislavery movement hero by northern abolitionists.[115]

In short, slaves transported in the nineteenth-century Coastal Passage rose against their captors in ways similar to their cousins during the previous three centuries of the Middle Passage. The key difference, of course, was that their actions were encouraged by the proximity of Caribbean spaces of freedom.

IMPACT

The *Creole* ship revolt had several well-known consequences. It fueled an international crisis between Washington and London over the clash between expanding slavery and antislavery empires.[116] It stoked sectional tensions between slaveholders with their sanctity for property rights and northern antislavery and abolitionist activists who declared the natural rights of freedom.[117] It revealed a revolutionary Atlantic that challenged slave powers as well as powerful empires.[118] But one argument that has not been made concerns the roles of liberation and revolt in the Caribbean undermining the maritime dimensions of the U.S. domestic slave trade. To what extent did the combination of Haitian independence, British colonial emancipation, and the well-publicized fallout from revolts aboard the *Amistad* and the *Creole* destabilize the Coastal Passage? This argument is suggested by several different bits of evidence, none of which are conclusive but collectively are intriguing.

Some contemporaries pointed to the danger of shipping slaves southward because of potential interference from British authorities. Recalling his Coastal Passage from Baltimore to New Orleans, captive William Grose observed nothing "especial occurred except on one occasion, when, after some thick weather, the ship came near an English island: the captain then hurried us all below and closed the hatches. After passing the island, we had liberty to come up again."[119] Visitor Ethan Andrews spoke with slave trader Joseph W. Neal, owner of slaves aboard the *Enterprise* that were liberated in Bermuda in 1835. The trader expected to recoup some of the loss through an insurance claim, but the rest was lost. "But why don't you go there and claim them?" asked a bystander. "Because," said Neal, "A NIGGER IS JUST AS FREE THERE, AND STANDS JUST AS GOOD A CHANCE IN THEIR COURTS AS A WHITE MAN."[120] Speaking on behalf of slaveholders, Kentucky congressman Henry Clay reported that the *Creole* had been carried to Nassau by "an act of mutiny and murder," and if the British authorities sanctioned "the enormity" of the crime, then "Americans would be virtually denied the benefits of the coastwise trade of their own country, because their vessels could not proceed in safety from one port to another *with slaves on board*."[121]

Moreover, an older historiography on the domestic slave trade hints at the decline of the maritime business by the 1850s. Ulrich Phillips suggests that one anonymous firm switched to overland trading because of the potential dangers at sea.[122] Frederick Bancroft estimates that a "greater portion of the interstate trade from the old States is supposed to have gone coastwise in the 'thirties than in the 'fifties."[123] Charles Wesley argues that the annexation of Texas, the discovery of gold in California, and the absence of ship manifests demonstrates the decline of the Coastal Passage by the early 1850s.[124]

The numerical reduction in slave ship voyages constitutes a third piece of evidence. In particular, there were fewer Coastal Passages during the 1840s compared to the 1830s, according to some ship manifest records. Between 1835 and 1845, twenty-five slave ships arrived in Mobile, Alabama, from Baltimore. Only eight came after 1841. Between 1837 and 1843, fourteen slave ships left Norfolk and Portsmouth for Mobile, of which only three departed after 1841. In other words, the *Creole* slave revolt, its success, and a history of British complicity in securing captives' liberty rendered the Coastal Passage an increasingly dangerous means of transporting human chattel.[125] Indeed, one reliable scholar finds "very few" coastwise manifests after 1852.[126] This was during the height of the domestic slave trade. It is not at all clear why this would have been the case, given the obvious advantages—shortness of passage, lower cost, survival rates—of coastwise transportation.

Let's not overdo it. There do not appear to have been increased preventative measures on coastal slavers during the 1840s. And the Coastal Passage continued. On March 29, 1842, the *Creole* embarked from Richmond with seventeen captives shipped by Robert Lumpkin of Richmond to John Mitchell of Alabama, arriving a month later, on April 25, 1842, in New Orleans. Thomas Nelson signed off in Richmond, and G. Brent Bayly passed the ship in New Orleans harbor. All looked the same. But the coastal slaver had a new skipper, Alexander Riddell. The number of captives was considerably reduced compared to previous slaving voyages.[127] According to the master abstract of registers, the final document was surrendered on October 26, 1842, at an undisclosed destination with the notation "Vessel wrecked."[128] Most important, the passage of British colonial emancipation during the mid-1830s increased the risk of American slavers being driven toward

British free soil, where captives could gain their liberty and traders and owners could lose their investments and profits in the Coastal Passage through the Bahamas Channel and Northern Caribbean. Moreover, successful slave ship revolts like the *Amistad* in 1839 and the *Creole* in 1841 raised the prospect of future maritime revolts. In short, the combination of antislavery practices in the Caribbean in proximity to American slave trading, together with ruinous real as well as potential slave ship revolts, impacted negatively the Coastal Passage.

CONCLUSION

Scores of thousands of enslaved men, women, and children were transported along the U.S. coastline from the Upper to Lower South as well as along the Gulf coast, especially from the 1820s through the 1850s. They were invariably separated from loved ones, homes, and communities. Some died. Others survived only to endure the harshness of the new exploitative regime in the cotton and sugar fields that expanded across the southwest United States. Meanwhile, traders and planters profited enormously from this lucrative system while the nation expanded territorially, demographically, and economically. Even a rough estimate of captives on select slave ships, however, suggests that nearly five hundred of them gained liberty in the Caribbean (see table 11.1). This was due to favorable winds, maritime rebellion, and the advent of a powerful antislavery state in proximity to the U.S. Coastal Passage. These small emancipations meant a great deal to the fortunate few.[129] The sea was a route to freedom, much like riverine crossing of the Ohio River into northern states, border crossings northward into British Canada, and cross-border movement southward across the Rio Grande into Mexico toward sites of formal freedom.[130] These former captives sought permanent freedom and had absolutely no intention of being returned to their former slaveholders. These maritime spaces of formal freedom deserve greater analysis than the fleeting attention they have thus far received in the scholarly literature.

Table 11.1. Liberated captives from select U.S. coastal slavers in the Caribbean, 1826–1841

Year	Ship	Total	Remain	Freed
1826	*Decatur*	31	18	13
1829	*Lafayette*	197	197	0
1831	*Comet*	165	0	165
1834	*Encomium*	45	4	41
1835	*Enterprise*	78	6	72
1840	*Hermosa*	47	0	47
1841	*Orleans*	135	134[a]	—
1841	*Creole*	137	5	130[b]
15 years	8 ships	835	364	468

[a] Rebel Robert Jones died.
[b] Rebels George Grandy and Adam Carnay died.

NOTES

1. All money conversions are calculated from MeasuringWorth.com, https://www.measuringworth.com/.

2. J. R. Kerr-Ritchie, *Rites of August First: Emancipation Day in the Black Atlantic World* (Baton Rouge: Louisiana State University Press, 2007), chaps. 1, 4; Richard Huzzey, *Freedom Burning: Anti-Slavery and Empire in Victorian Britain* (Ithaca, N.Y.: Cornell University Press, 2012), chap. 3; Michael Craton, *Testing the Chains: Resistance to Slavery in the British West Indies* (Ithaca, N.Y.: Cornell University Press, 1982), chaps. 20–22; Madhavi Kale, *Fragments of Empire: Capital, Slavery, and Indian Indentured Labor in the British Caribbean* (Philadelphia: University of Pennsylvania Press, 1998); and Legacies of British Slave-Ownership, University College London, Department of History, https://www.ucl.ac.uk/lbs/.

3. Chapter 3 of Huzzey's *Freedom Burning* outlines succinctly the global dimensions of the British antislavery state.

4. David Eltis, *Economic Growth and the Ending of the Transatlantic Slave Trade* (New York: Oxford University Press, 1987), 85–89; Keith Hamilton and Patrick Salmon, eds., *Slavery, Diplomacy and Empire: Britain and the Suppression of the Slave Trade, 1807–1975* (Eastbourne, U.K.: Sussex University Press, 2009), 1–10; and Mathew Mason, "Keeping Up Appearances: The International Politics of Slave Trade Abolition in the Nineteenth Century Atlantic World," *William and Mary Quarterly* 66, no. 4 (October 2009): 811–16.

5. Foreign Office (FO), October 2, 1855, *Slave Trade Ledger*, January–February 1855, vol. 16, FO 84/973, National Archives, Kew, London (TNA); FO, November 11, 1843, *Hayti Ledger*, FO 84/479, TNA; H. G. Soulsby, *The Right of Search and the Slave Trade in Anglo-American Relations, 1814–1862* (Baltimore: Johns Hopkins University Press, 1933); and Mason, "Keeping Up Appearances," 820–22.

6. Eltis, *Economic Growth*, 94–98; Huzzey, *Freedom Burning*, 42–51; Andrew Lambert, "Slavery, Free Trade and Naval Strategy, 1840–1860," in *Slavery, Diplomacy, Empire: Britain and the Suppression of the Slave Trade, 1807–1975*, ed. Keith Hamilton and Patrick Salmon (Eastbourne, U.K.: Sussex University Press, 2009); Huw Lewis Jones, "The Royal Navy and the Battle to End Slavery," BBC, http://www.bbc.co.uk/history/british/abolition/royal_navy_article_01.shtml; Rosanne Marion Adderley, *"New Negroes from Africa": Slave Trade Abolition and Free African Settlement in the Nineteenth-Century Caribbean* (Bloomington: Indiana University Press, 2006), 2–3; and James D. B. De Bow, "The Merchant Fleets and Navies of the World," *Debow's Review* 6, no. 4 (October–November 1848), 331. Linda Colley reports that the Royal Navy employed more than 140,000 sailors in 1812. See Linda Colley, *Britons: Forging the Nation 1707–1837* (New Haven, Conn.: Yale University Press, 1992), 287.

7. Leonard L. Richards, *The Slave Power: The Free North and Southern Domination, 1780–1860* (Baton Rouge: Louisiana State University Press, 2000), 9, 23–25; Leonard L. Richards, *Who Freed the Slaves? The Fight over the Thirteenth Amendment* (Chicago: University of Chicago Press, 2015), 12; and Sven Beckert, *Empire of Cotton: A Global History* (New York: Alfred A. Knopf, 2014), chap. 5, esp. 107–20.

8. "John Tyler Biography," Biography Channel, http://www.biography.com/people/john-tyler-9512796; "John Tyler," Totally History, http://totallyhistory.com/john-tyler/; and "John Tyler's Presidency," History Channel, http://www.history.com/topics/us-presidents/john-tyler.

9. Ashburton to Aberdeen, June 29, 1842, fol. 133–5, add. MS 43123, Aberdeen Papers, British Library (BL).

10. "Thomas McCargo v. The New Orleans Insurance Company," in Merritt M. Robinson, *Reports of Cases Argued and Determined in the Supreme Court of Louisiana*, vol. 10, March 1 to June 20, 1845 (New Orleans: Samuel M. Stewart, 1845), 281; Howard Jones, "The Peculiar Institution and National Honor: The Case of the *Creole* Slave Revolt," *Civil War History* 21, no. 1 (March 1975): 35; and Howard Jones, *Mutiny on the Amistad: The Saga of a Slave Revolt and Its Impact on American Abolition, Law, and Diplomacy* (New York: Oxford University Press, 1987), 53.

11. John Forsythe, Office of the Historian, U.S. Department of State, https://history.state.gov/departmenthistory/people/forsyth-john; Robert E. Luckett, "John Forsythe (1780–1841)," *New Georgia Encyclopedia*, http://www.georgiaencyclopedia.org/articles/government-politics/john-forsyth-1780-1841; and John Forsythe (Georgia), Wikipedia, https://en.wikipedia.org/wiki/John_Forsyth_(Georgia). Only the latter website refers to Forsythe as slaveholder.

12. John Mack Faragher, Mari Jo Buhle, Daniel Czitrom, and Susan H. Armitage, *Out of Many: A History of the American People*, vol. 1 (Upper Saddle River, N.J.: Prentice Hall, 2005), 265.

13. Charles Sellers, *The Market Revolution: Jacksonian America, 1815–1846* (New York: Oxford University Press, 1991), 81.

14. De Bow, "Merchant Fleets," 331.

15. According to a recent biography of Gideon Welles, secretary of the U.S. Navy from 1861 to 1869, the federal fleet increased from ninety ships, of which only forty-two were in commission, in 1861 to seven hundred vessels in 1865, only second to Britain. See Spencer Tucker, review of *The Civil War Diary of Gideon Welles, Lincoln's Secretary of the Navy*, ed., William E. Gienapp and Erica L. Gienapp (Urbana: University of Illinois Press, 2014), in *Journal of American History* 102, no. 2 (September 2015): 566.

16. For classic and recent statements respectively, see William Appleman Williams, *The Tragedy of American Diplomacy* (1959; repr. New York: Delta, 1962); and Gerald Horne, *Fighting in Paradise: Labor Unions, Racism, and Communists in the Making of Modern Hawai'i* (Hilo: University of Hawai'i Press, 2011).

17. David Barry Gaspar and David P. Geggus, eds., *A Turbulent Time: The French Revolution and the Greater Caribbean* (Bloomington: Indiana University Press, 1997); Laurent Dubois and John D. Garrigus, *Slave Revolution in the Caribbean, 1789–1804* (Boston: Bedford, 2006); Maurice Jackson and Jacqueline Bacon, eds., *African Americans and the Haitian Revolution: Selected Essays and Historical Documents* (New York: Routledge, 2010); Ashli White, *Encountering Revolution: Haiti and the Making of the Early Republic* (Baltimore: Johns Hopkins University Press, 2010); Jeremy D. Popkin, *You Are All Free: The Haitian Revolution and the Abolition of Slavery* (New York: Cambridge University Press, 2010); and Marcia Headley, *Imaging Haiti: Perceptions of Haiti in the Atlantic World, 1791–1875* (Ph.D. diss., Howard University, 2012).

18. Jeffrey R. Kerr-Ritchie, *Freedom's Seekers: Essays on Comparative Emancipation (Baton Rouge: Louisiana State University Press, 2014)*, 62–66.

19. Alex Dupuy, *Haiti in the World Economy: Class, Race, and Underdevelopment since 1700* (Boulder: Westview Press, 1979), chap. 4; and David Nicholls, *From Dessalines to Duvalier: Race, Color and National Independence in Haiti* (New Brunswick, N.J.: Rutgers University Press, 1979), chap. 2.

20. Dupuy, *Haiti in the World Economy*, 86; and Don E. Fehrenbacher, *The Slaveholding Republic: An Account of the United States Government's Relations to Slavery* (New York: Oxford University Press, 2005), 114.

21. Kerr-Ritchie, *Freedom's Seekers*, 62–71; Gerald Horne, *Confronting Black Jacobins: The United States, the Haitian Revolution and the Origins of the Dominican Republic* (New York: Monthly Review Press, 2015), chaps. 4 & 5; and Frank Moya Pons, *History of the Caribbean* (Princeton, N.J.: Markus Wiener, 2007), chap. 12.

22. Frederick Bancroft, *Slave Trading in the Old South* (Baltimore: J. H. Furst, 1931), 275; Ulrich B. Phillips, *American Negro Slavery: A Survey of the Supply, Employment and Control of Negro Labor as Determined by the Plantation Regime* (1918; repr. Baton Rouge: Louisiana State University Press, 1966), 196; and Walter Johnson, *Soul by Soul: Life Inside the Antebellum Slave Market* (Cambridge, Mass.: Harvard University Press, 1999).

23. For an influential account of the transatlantic functions of an African port, see Robin Law, *Ouidah: The Social History of a West African Slaving 'Port' 1792–1892* (Athens: Ohio University Press, 2004), 4–6.

24. Calvin Schermerhorn, *The Business of Slavery and the Rise of American Capitalism, 1815–1860* (New Haven, Conn.: Yale University Press, 2015), 48.

25. Charles H. Wesley, "Manifests of Slave Shipments along the Waterways, 1808–1864," *Journal of Negro History* 27, no. 2 (April 1942): 160.

26. Phillips, *American Negro Slavery*, 196.

27. Schermerhorn, *Business of Slavery*, chap. 2.

28. Robert H. Gudmestad, *A Troublesome Commerce: The Transformation of the Interstate Slave Trade* (Baton Rouge: Louisiana State University Press, 2003), 26; see also Barbara Jeanne Fields, *Slavery and Freedom on the Middle Ground: Maryland during the Nineteenth Century* (New Haven, Conn.: Yale University Press, 1985), 17.

29. Bancroft, *Slave Trading*, 276n25; and Troy Valos, Special Collections Librarian at Norfolk Public Library, email, July 19, 2017.

30. Bancroft, *Slave Trading*, 276n25; and Lancaster Denby & Company, Richmond City Personal Property Book, 1836, 1837, 1838, 1839, Reel 365, Virginia Library (VL).

31. "Isaac Franklin Plantation (Fairvue)," National Park Service, https://www.nps.gov/nhl/find/withdrawn/franklin.htm ("Southwest region").

32. Schermerhorn, *Business of Slavery*, 167; see also Schermerhorn, *Business of Slavery*, chap. 5; Gudmestad, *Troublesome Commerce*, 15–30; Bancroft, *Slave-Trading*, 276; and Wendell H. Stevenson, *Isaac Franklin: Slave Trader and Planter from the Old South* (Baton Rouge: Louisiana State University Press, 1938), chap. 4.

33. Bancroft, *Slave Trading*, 276n25, 315; and John Hagan, Bill of Lading, October 20, 1841, in "New-Orleans Directory for 1842: Comprising the Names, Residences and Occupations of the Merchants, Business Men, Professional Gentlemen and Citizens of New-Orleans, Lafayette, Algiers and Gretna" (New Orleans: Pitts & Clark, 1842), Box 106, Creole Affair Collection, 1854–1941, Amistad Research Center.

34. These advertisements were taken from the following sources: Bancroft, *Slave Trading*, 28; Wesley, "Manifests of Slave Shipments," 167–68; Schermerhorn, *Business of Slavery*, 36, 39, 165, 174–5; and Winfield H. Collins, *The Domestic Slave Trade of the Southern States* (New York: Broadway Publishing, 1904), 51.

35. *Richmond Enquirer*, December 31, 1835.

36. Ethan Andrews, *Slavery and the Domestic Slave Trade in the United States* (Boston: Light and Stearns, 1836), 80, 136–41, 164–65; Benjamin Drew, *A North-Side View of Slavery: The Refugee or the Narratives of Fugitive Slaves in Canada, Related by Themselves, with an Account of the History and Condition of the Colored Population of Upper Canada* (Boston: J. P. Jewett and Company, 1856), 82–84; Steven Deyle, *Carry Me Back: The Domestic Slave Trade in American Life* (New York: Oxford University Press, 2005), 115; Phillips, *American Negro Slavery*, 194; and Schermerhorn, *Business of Slavery*, 127, 130, 136, 146.

37. Collins, *Domestic Slave Trade*, 96–98.

38. Andrews, *Slavery and Domestic Slave Trade*, 80.

39. Solomon Northup, *Twelve Years a Slave: Narrative of Solomon Northup,*

a Citizen of New York, Kidnapped in Washington City in 1841, and Rescued in 1853 (New York: Norton, 2017), 28–32.

40. Northup, *Twelve Years a Slave*, 38.

41. For transatlantic slave ships as floating prisons, see chapter 2 of Marcus Rediker's *The Slave Ship: A Human History* (New York: Viking, 2007).

42. Stephenson, *Isaac Franklin*, 36.

43. Stephenson, *Isaac Franklin*, 38.

44. Stephenson, *Isaac Franklin*; original italics; and Bancroft, *Slave Trading*, 275–76.

45. Stevenson, *Isaac Franklin*, 37.

46. Manifest of Brig *Tribune*, January 18, 1836, *Slave Manifests of Coastwise Vessels Filed at New Orleans, Louisiana, 1807–1860*, Microfilm Serial: M1895, Microfilm Roll: 7, RG 36, NARA. The manifest states that the captives were slaves under the laws of Virginia even though Alexandria was in D.C. until its retrocession to Virginia in 1846.

47. "An Act to Prohibit the Importation of Slaves into Any Port or Place Within the Jurisdiction of the United States," in *Encyclopedia of Emancipation and Abolition in the Transatlantic World*, ed. Junius Rodriguez, vol. 3 (Armonk, N.Y.: Sharpe Reference, 2007), 686–89. See also Wesley, "Manifests of Slave Shipments," 157–59; John R. Spears, *The American Slave Trade: An Account of its Origin, Growth, and Suppression* (New York: Charles Scribner, 1900), 173–74; and Stevenson, *Isaac Franklin*, 39.

48. Manifest of *Ajax*, February 13 and 29, 1832, *Slave Manifests of Coastwise Vessels Filed at New Orleans, Louisiana, 1807–1860*, Microfilm Serial: M1895, Microfilm Roll: 7, RG 36, NARA.

49. Manifest of *Hunter*, October 17 and November 9, 1835, *Slave Manifests of Coastwise Vessels Filed at New Orleans, Louisiana, 1807–1860*, Microfilm Serial: M1895, Microfilm Roll: 7, RG 36, NARA.

50. Manifest of the *Caledonia*, June 23 and July 24, 1840, *Slave Manifests of Coastwise Vessels Filed at New Orleans, Louisiana, 1807–1860*, Microfilm Serial: M1895, Microfilm Roll: 7, RG 36, NARA.

51. Manifest of the *Josephine*, December 23, 1841, and January 17, 1842, *Slave Manifests of Coastwise Vessels Filed at New Orleans, Louisiana, 1807–1860*, Microfilm Serial: M1895, Microfilm Roll: 7, RG 36, NARA.

52. In *Slavery and Forced Migration in the Antebellum South* (New York: Cambridge University Press, 2015), Damian Alan Pargas draws on slave narratives, government interviews, interviews with refugee slaves in the North and Canada to reveal the different experiences of slave migrants, the ways they rebuilt their lives after being transported, and identity formation.

53. Bancroft, *Slave Trading*, 278.

54. Bancroft, *Slave Trading*, 279, 278.

55. Northup, *Twelve Years a Slave*, 42–43.

56. Manifest of the *Ajax*, February 13 and 29, 1832, *Slave Manifests of Coastwise*

Vessels Filed at New Orleans, Louisiana, 1807–1860, Microfilm Serial: M1895, Microfilm Roll: 7, RG 36, NARA.

57. Pargas, *Slavery and Forced Migration*, 117; see also Schermerhorn, *Business of Slavery*, 46–47, 58–59, 130.

58. Northup, *Twelve Years a Slave*, 43.

59. Pargas, *Slavery & Forced Migration*, 116–17.

60. Philip Troutman, "Grapevine in the Slave Market: African American Geopolitical Literacy and the 1841 *Creole* Revolt," in *The Chattel Principle: Internal Slave Trades in the Americas*, ed. Walter Johnson (New Haven, Conn.: Yale University Press, 2004), 229n22; and Johnson, *Soul by Soul*, 50.

61. Stevenson, *Isaac Franklin*, 117.

62. Schermerhorn, *Business of Slavery*, 187, 48, 66.

63. Eric Robert Taylor, *If We Must Die: A History of Shipboard Insurrections in the Era of the Atlantic Slave Trade* (Baton Rouge: Louisiana State University Press, 2009), 115–16.

64. Bancroft notes "only one death" aboard the *Uncas* in 1835 and "lively" arrivals in New Orleans a few years earlier clearly implying low mortality rates. Bancroft, *Slave Trading*, 279. Stephenson concludes that ship manifests "record very few deaths in transit." Stephenson, *Isaac Franklin*, 52.

65. Ralph Clayton, *Cash for Blood: The Baltimore to New Orleans Domestic Slave Trade* (Bowie, Md.: Heritage Books, 2002), 133–620. These 487 pages index all inward-bound ship manifests into New Orleans from Baltimore and other ports between 1818 and 1856 and are drawn from Record Group 36 in the U.S. National Archives.

66. Phillips, *American Negro Slavery*, 195.

67. Wesley, "Manifests of Slave Shipments," 172–73. To be exact, he recorded the total number of slaves reported in the manifests as 38,847, of which 6,993 were from internal manifests. The latter recorded the riverine not coastwise trade.

68. *U.S. Southeast Coastwise Inward and Outward Slave Manifests, 1790–1860*, Microfilm Serial: M1895, Microfilm Roll: 7, RG 36, NARA.

69. Edward P. Thompson, *Customs in Common: Studies in Traditional Popular Culture* (New York: New Press, 1993), 450.

70. The classic quantification studies in transatlantic trading are by Philip Curtin, Joseph Inikori, David Eltis, and contributors to the Transatlantic Slave Trade Database. Recent works by Markus Rediker, Stephanie Smallwood, Sylviane Diouf, Sowande' Mustakeem, and others focus on the horrors, losses, and survivors.

71. Daniel Webster to Lord Ashburton, August 1, 1842, Aberdeen Papers, BL.

72. Manifest of the *Comet*, Records of the U.S. Customs Service, 1745–1997, RG 36, https://catalog.archives.gov/id/17408488.

73. Governor Sir. John Carmichael Smythe to Lord Viscount Goderich, January 31, 1831, CO 23/84, TNA.

74. Smythe to Lord Viscount Goderich; see also Bancroft, *Slave Trading*, 277n29.

75. Herbert Jenner, J. Campbell, C. C. Pepys to Viscount Palmerston, April 9, 1834, in Baron Arnold Duncan McNair, "Slavery and the Slave Trade," in *International Law Opinions* (London: Cambridge University Press, 1956), 80.

76. Jenner, Campbell, Pepys to Viscount Palmerston, 80.

77. Jenner, Campbell, Pepys to Viscount Palmerston, 80.

78. Jenner, Campbell, Pepys to Viscount Palmerston, 81. See also W. E. B. Du Bois, *The Suppression of the African Slave-Trade to the United States of America, 1638–1870* (1896; repr. New York, Library of America, 1986), 309; Jones, *Mutiny on the Amistad*, 53; Arthur M. Schlesinger, ed., *The Almanac of American History* (New York: Barnes & Noble, 2004), 222; Gerald Horne, *Negro Comrades of the Crown: African Americans and the British Empire Fight the U.S. before Emancipation* (New York: New York University Press, 2012), 99–100; and Schermerhorn, *Business of Slavery*, 146–47. None of these sources mention the eleven captives' actions and Governor Smythe's determination illustrating the incompleteness of the documentary record.

79. According to federal records, the *Comet*'s last document was surrendered on February 24, 1831, and the "vessel lost." Documents Issued, Ship Registers and Enrollments of New Orleans, La, vol. II, NARA.

80. NARA archivist Mark Mollan kindly checked the Index to Enrolments for 1839 for Richmond through Charleston but could not find the *Encomium* nor *Hermosa*. Mollan, email, May 16, 2017.

81. Lt. Gvr. Balfour to Lord Stanley, February 18, 1834, CO 23/91/12, TNA.

82. Lt. Gvr. Balfour to Lord Stanley, February 18, 1834, CO 23/91/12, TNA.

83. Du Bois, *Suppression of the Slave Trade*, 309; Fehrenbacher, *Slaveholding Republic*, 104; and Arthur T. Downey, *Creole Affair: The Slave Rebellion that Led the U.S. and Great Britain to the Brink of War* (Lanham, Md.: Rowman & Littlefield, 2014), 63. The latter source states local authorities "liberated the slaves," which is inaccurate since the captives left unimpeded. But the interpretation was vital for contemporaries. American supporters of slavery protested what they saw as British interference. Captives on ships like the *Creole* were drawn to potentially liberating environments of free soil. Local authorities were serious about their jurisdiction: Bahamas' officials told the Americans on the *Comet* that the only thing against slave owners seeking to remove their erstwhile property was they were "liable to be hanged." Horne, *Negro Comrades of the Crown*, 110.

84. Nellie Eileen Musson, *Mind the Onion Seed: Black "Roots" Bermuda* (Hamilton, Bermuda: Musson's, 1979), 66–67; Du Bois, *Suppression of the Slave Trade*, 309; and Horne, *Negro Comrades of the Crown*, 108. The Adjustment Claims Commission, Sen. Doc. No. 103, 1856, 187, mistakenly states there were seventy-three slaves onboard. Bancroft, *Slave Trading*, 277, reports incorrectly seventy-five slaves.

85. Musson, *Mind the Onion Seed*, 66.

86. Petition by John Strohecker and others to South Carolina Senate, 1842, Petition 11384205, Race & Slavery Petitions Project (RSPP), http://library.uncg.edu/slavery/petitions/details.aspx?pid=1573. Bancroft lists Joseph W. Neal as one

of the slave owners although his name is missing from the petition. Bancroft, *Slave Trading*, 277.

87. Musson, *Onion Seed*, 65; Horne, *Negro Comrades of the Crown*, 107–108; Downey, *Creole Affair*, 63; and Adjustment Claims Commission, Sen. Doc. No. 103, 1856, 187.

88. Huzzey, *Freedom Burning*, 54.

89. Musson, *Onion Seed*, 66; and Horne, *Negro Comrades of the Crown*, 108; Downey, *Creole Affair*, 63.

90. J. Dodson, J. Campbell, R. M. Rolfe to Viscount Palmerston, October 31, 1836, in Baron Arnold Duncan McNair, "Slavery and the Slave Trade," in *International Law Opinions* (London: Cambridge University Press, 1956), 81.

91. Dodson, Campbell, Rolfe to Palmerston, 82.

92. Dodson, Campbell, Rolfe to Palmerston, 83–84.

93. Dodson, Campbell, Rolfe to Palmerston, 82. For the *Encomium* and *Enterprise*, see Keith Archibald Forbes, *Bermuda's History from 1800 to 1899*, Bermuda Online, http://www.bermuda-online.org/history1800-1899.htm; Jones, *Mutiny on Amistad*, 53–54; Jonathan Levy, *Freaks of Fortune: The Emerging World of Capitalism and Risk in America* (Cambridge, Mass.: Harvard University Press, 2012), 26–27; and Downey, *Creole Affair*, 64.

94. NARA archivist Mark Mollan checked the index to Enrolments for 1839 for Richmond through Charleston but could not find the *Hermosa*. Mollan, email, May 16, 2017.

95. Manifest of the *Hermosa*, October 10, 1840, in Bahamas 1840, vol. 1, January–December, Gvr. Cockburn, CO 23/107, National Archives, U.K.

96. Governor Sir Francis Cockburn to Lord ?, December 1, 1840, CO 23/107, TNA.

97. Colonial Office to Cockburn, February ? 1841, CO 23/107, TNA; see also Horne, *Negro Comrades of the Crown*, 133, 293. Both Downey, *Creole Affair*, 65, and Boyd Childress, "Hermosa Case (1840)," *Historical Encyclopedia of World Slavery*, ed., Junius P. Rodriguez., vol. 1 (Armonk, N.Y..: M. E. Sharpe, 2007), 340, inaccurately report thirty-eight slaves onboard. Howard Jones mistakenly refers to this vessel as the *Formosa*. Jones, "Peculiar Institution and National Honor," 35.

98. Jeffrey R. Kerr-Ritchie, *Rebellious Passage: The Creole Revolt and America's Coastal Slave Trade* (New York: Cambridge University Press, 2019), chap. 11.

99. Emory University, The Transatlantic Slave Trade Database, http://www.slavevoyages.org/voyage/; David Richardson, "Shipboard Revolts, African Authority, and the Transatlantic Slave Trade," in *Fighting the Slave Trade: West African Strategies*, ed. Sylviane A. Diouf (Athens: Ohio University Press, 2003), 201; Hugh Thomas, *The Slave Trade: The Story of the Atlantic Slave Trade* (New York: Simon & Schuster, 1997), 424; and Sowande' M. Mustakeem, *Slavery at Sea: Terror, Sex, and Sickness in the Middle Passage* (Urbana: University of Illinois Press, 2016), 4.

100. Taylor, *If We Must Die*, 3, 9, 139, 179–213.

101. Taylor, *If We Must Die*, 139–63.

102. Bancroft, *Slave Trading*, 277.

103. Schermerhorn, *Business of Slavery*, 60–62.

104. Gudmestad, *Troublesome Commerce*, 46; Clayton, *Cash for Blood*, 71–73; Taylor, *If We Must Die*, 147–49, 211; Deyle, *Carry Me Back*, 255; Anita Rupprecht, "'All We Have Done, We Have Done for Freedom': The *Creole* Slave-Ship Revolt (1841) and the Revolutionary Atlantic," *Internationaal Instituut voor Sociale Geschiedenis* 58 (2013): 263; Troutman, "Grapevine in the Slave Market," 209; and William Calderhead, "The Role of the Professional Slave Trader in a Slave Economy: Austin Woolfolk, A Case Study," *Civil War History* 23, no. 3 (September 1977): 205. The same year as the *Decatur* revolt, captives on board a flatboat on the Ohio River ninety miles west of Louisville, Kentucky, rebelled, killed the crew, sank the boat, and headed north for Indiana. Five slaves were killed, more than fifty were captured, but twenty-one eluded captivity. See Johannes Postma, *Slave Revolts* (Westport, Conn.: Greenwood Press, 2008), 83; and Taylor, *If We Must Die*, 211. In other words, self-emancipators also used rivers, streams, and internal waterways in search of semi-formal and informal spaces of freedom.

105. Wesley, "Manifests of Slave Shipments," 164.

106. Stevenson, *Isaac Franklin*, 35.

107. *Niles Register*, January 9, 1830; Taylor, *If We Must Die*, 150–51, 212; Stephenson, *Isaac Franklin*, 52n40; and Michael Tadman, *Speculators and Slaves: Masters, Traders, and Slaves in the Old South* (Madison: University of Wisconsin Press, 1996), 81.

108. Northup, *Twelve Years a Slave*, chap. 1.

109. Northup, *Twelve Years a Slave*, 67–76; and Schermerhorn, *Business of Slavery*, 182–88.

110. All of the scholarship on the 1841 *Creole* revolt—two books, five articles, and three book chapters—report 135 slaves. My research counts 137 captives. Kerr-Ritchie, *Rebellious Passage*, chap. 4.

111. Kerr-Ritchie, *Rebellious Passage*, chaps. 5–7.

112. *Niles Register*, September 30, 1815, in Spears, *American Slave Trade*, 174.

113. Matthew J. Clavin, *Aiming for Pensacola: Fugitive Slaves on the Atlantic and Southern Frontiers* (Cambridge, Mass.: Harvard University Press, 2015), 102. Our focus is on the coastwise trade and fugitives, but we need more research on riverine and coastal escapees. For an excellent study of the North Carolina coastline—which is also needed for Virginia, the Chesapeake Bay, and elsewhere—see David S. Cecelski, *The Waterman's Song: Slavery and Freedom in Maritime North Carolina* (Chapel Hill: University of North Carolina Press, 2001).

114. Henry Barkly to Lord John Russell, June 20, 1855, *Jamaica Ledger 1855*, pp. 530–31, CO 137/326, TNA; and Kerr-Ritchie, *Rebellious Passage*, epilogue.

115. Clavin, *Aiming for Pensacola*, 124–41. Dr. Clavin quotes an issue of the *Pensacola Gazette* in which Walker was accused of "the abduction of seven negro slaves" (129); elsewhere, he quotes slave owners whose advertisements for runaway slaves refer to them being "seduced away," or "went off with," or "enticed," and so forth (114). Such language exemplified slave owners' refusal to admit

slaves' own initiatives and was the logical consequence of a pro-slavery ideology of slaves' satisfaction with slavery.

116. Jones, "Peculiar Institution and National Honor"; Downey, *Creole Affair*; and Kerr-Ritchie, *Rebellious Passage*, chap. 8.

117. Jones, "Peculiar Institution and National Honor"; Downey, *Creole Affair*, chap. 5; and Kerr-Ritchie, *Rebellious Passage*, chap. 9.

118. Rupprecht, "'All We Have Done,'" is most eloquent here, although the author downplays the critical context of antislavery nation-states providing Caribbean spaces.

119. William Grose in Drew, *North-Side View of Slavery*, 84.

120. Andrews, *Slavery and Domestic Slave*, 278–79; see also Stevenson, *Isaac Franklin*, 52.

121. Spears, *American Slave Trade*, 181.

122. Phillips, *American Negro Slavery*, 195.

123. Bancroft, *Slave Trading*, 276–77.

124. Wesley, "Manifests of Slave Shipments," 172–73.

125. Finding Aid online, RG 36, U.S. Customs Service, Slave Manifests—Mobile, Alabama Inward (By Owner Name) National Archives at Atlanta, Georgia, https://www.archives.gov/atlanta/finding-aids/rg36_slave_mobileinw_owner.html.

126. Wesley, "Manifests of Slave Shipments," 173.

127. Robert Lumpkin (owner), Alexander Riddell (master), Thomas Nelson (collector), Manifest of the *Creole*, March 29, 1842, *Slave Manifests of Coastwise Vessels Filed at New Orleans, Louisiana, 1807–1860*, Microfilm Serial: M1895, Microfilm Roll: 9, NARA.

128. Brig *Creole*, Finding Aid, Bureau of Marine and Navigation, RG 41, NARA. My thanks to Mark Mollan for making a copy available.

129. David Turley suggests these slave escapes were "quantitatively insignificant." David M. Turley, "'Free Air' and Fugitive Slaves: British Abolitionists Versus Government Over American Fugitives, 1834–61," in *Anti-Slavery, Religion, and Reform: Essays in Memory of Roger Anstey*, ed. Christine Bolt and Seymour Drescher (Folkestone, Kent: Dawson, 1980), 177.

130. For southward flight as an alternative to the more familiar narrative of northern flight, see Clavin, *Aiming for Pensacola*; and Kerr-Ritchie, *Freedom's Seekers*, chap. 1, among others.

CONTRIBUTORS

Kyle Ainsworth is the creator and project manager of the Texas Runaway Slave Project as well as Special Collections librarian at the East Texas Research Center, Ralph W. Steen Library, Stephen F. Austin State University.

Mekala Audain is assistant professor of history at the College of New Jersey.

Gordon S. Barker is professor in the Department of History at Bishop's University in Canada. He has authored two books—*Fugitive Slaves and the Unfinished American Revolution, Eight Cases, 1848–1856* and *The Imperfect Revolution: Anthony Burns and the Landscape of Race in Antebellum America*—and numerous articles and reviews that have appeared in scholarly journals.

Sylviane A. Diouf is an award-winning historian of the African diaspora. She is a visiting scholar at Brown University's Center for the Study of Slavery and Social Justice and a member of the Scientific Committee of the International Coalition of Sites of Conscience Maison des Esclaves project on Goree Island, Senegal. She is the author or editor of several books, including *Dreams of Africa in Alabama: The Slave Ship Clotilda and the Story of the Last Africans Brought to America* which received the 2007 Wesley-Logan Prize of the American Historical Association and the 2009 Sulzby Award of the Alabama Historical Association.

Roy E. Finkenbine is professor of history and director of the Black Abolitionist Archive at the University of Detroit Mercy. While on the editorial staff of the Black Abolitionist Papers Project at Florida State University in the 1980s and 1990s, he coedited the five-volume *Black Abolitionist Papers, 1830–1865* and *Witness for Freedom: African American Voices on Race, Slavery, and Emancipation*. He is the author of *Sources of the African American Past*, as well as many articles and book chapters on black abolitionists and the Underground Railroad.

Graham Russell Gao Hodges is Langdon Professor of History and Africana & Latin American studies at Colgate University. Specialized in colonial and revolutionary American history, social history, labor and urban America, New York City history, and Asian American history, he has written and edited fourteen books and numerous articles.

Jeffrey R. Kerr-Ritchie is professor of history at Howard University. He is the author of several books, including *Freedom's Seekers: Essays on Comparative Emancipation* and *Rebellious Passage: The Creole Revolt and America's Coastal Slave Trade*.

Viola Franziska Müller received her PhD in history at Leiden University and currently holds a Max Weber Postdoctoral Fellowship at the European University Institute in Florence, Italy. She is an editorial assistant for the *Journal of Global Slavery*.

James David Nichols is assistant professor of history at CUNY Queensborough Community College. He is the author of an award-winning article, "The Line of Liberty: Runaway Slaves and Fugitive Peons in the Texas–Mexico Borderlands," which appeared in the *Western Historical Quarterly*.

Damian Alan Pargas is professor of the history and culture of North America at Leiden University. Specialized in North American slavery, he is the author of *The Quarters and the Fields: Slave Families in the Non-Cotton South*; *Slavery and Forced Migration in the Antebellum South*; and numerous articles for journals such as *Slavery & Abolition*, the *Journal of Early American History*, and *American Nineteenth Century History*. Pargas is also executive director of the Roosevelt Institute for American Studies in Middelburg, The Netherlands, and the founder and chief editor of the *Journal of Global Slavery*.

Matthew Pinsker holds the Brian Pohanka Chair of Civil War History at Dickinson College in Carlisle, Pennsylvania, and serves as director of the House Divided Project (http://housedivided.dickinson.edu/sites), an innovative effort to build digital resources on the Civil War era.

INDEX

Abolition (of the transatlantic slave trade), 3, 291, 293
Abolition (of slavery), 3, 5–7, 12, 21–22, 28–30, 35–38, 95, 97, 112, 267, 276, 278, 293, 297, 302
Abolitionists, 3, 6–7, 11, 14, 21–24, 30, 34–43, 93, 94, 105, 107–8, 110, 138, 160, 210–14, 236, 245, 246n4, 247n11, 276, 278, 287, 299–300, 302, 303
Alabama, 46, 47, 119, 123, 125, 170, 172, 173, 175, 176, 203, 280, 301–2, 304
American Revolution, 3, 8, 9, 10, 12, 15, 21–27, 76, 83, 143, 144
Amistad (ship), 298–99, 303–5
Arkansas, 65n45, 128, 182, 203, 208, 209, 211, 213, 216, 227n24, 230n57

Bahamas, 11, 12, 15, 43, 278, 280, 291, 293–98, 300–305
Baltimore (Md.), 7, 15n1, 45, 116, 118, 123, 279, 280, 281, 283, 284, 289–90, 299, 300, 303, 304
Bibb, Henry, 47, 50, 85
Black Loyalists, 13, 21–30
Boston (Mass.), 39, 99, 46, 50, 103–6, 109
Brazos (river), 204, 208, 214, 218, 220, 237
British Empire, 5, 11, 24, 275, 293, 296. *See also* Bahamas; Canada

California, 97, 101, 200, 304
Canada, xii, 4, 5, 6, 8, 11, 12, 13, 23, 28, 34–62, 74, 75, 77–82, 85–86, 109–10, 117, 123, 124, 137, 184, 233, 235, 242, 276, 305. *See also* Formal freedom
Caribbean, xii, 2, 11, 19n18, 24, 117, 118, 187, 197, 275, 276, 277, 281, 282, 291, 298, 299, 302–3, 305–6

Charleston (S.C.), 7, 121, 126–27, 130, 142, 177, 183, 280, 282, 293, 294–95
Cincinnati (Ohio), 34, 40, 45, 53–55, 80, 106–7, 123
Civil War (U.S.), xii, 3, 8, 12, 15, 22, 24–25, 34, 61, 94, 95, 101, 106, 109, 110, 124, 129, 137, 141, 149, 152, 180, 182, 217, 252, 265, 269
Coahuila (Mexico), 253, 265, 266, 268, 270
Comet (ship), 291–92, 295–98, 306, 312n83
Creole (ship), 14–15, 43, 278–305

Delany, Martin R., 40
Delaware (state), 26, 27, 102, 243
Detroit (Mich.), 40, 45, 46, 51, 70, 74–75, 77–78, 79, 81, 82, 84, 88
Detroit (river), 34, 40, 45–46, 51, 59, 70, 74, 75, 82–84
Dismal Swamp (Va.), xii, 8–9, 124
Douglass, Frederick, 95, 98, 275, 281
Dunmore, Earl of (Lord John Murray), 23, 25, 37

Encomium (ship), 278, 293–98, 306
Enterprise (ship), 278, 294–98, 303, 306

Florida, 9–10, 28, 117, 126, 137, 169, 173, 213, 280, 302
Formal freedom, 4, 5, 6, 8, 14, 15, 35, 38, 40, 118, 119, 123, 124, 131, 279, 296, 305
Free blacks, xi, 2, 3–4, 6–8, 9, 11, 14, 22, 24, 25, 26, 34–35, 43, 46, 47, 53, 62n3, 78–81, 84–85, 89, 95, 97–98, 102, 109, 110, 116–17, 121, 124–31, 138–61, 177, 188, 209, 239, 242, 300

Free soil, 2, 4, 5, 6, 13, 25, 49, 63n17, 95, 97, 103, 118, 138, 140–41, 160, 208, 211, 212, 301, 302, 305. *See also* Formal freedom; Semiformal freedom; *Somerset v. Stewart*
French Empire, 269, 276, 279, 280
Fugitive slave laws (U.S.), xi, 6, 13, 27, 29, 30, 74, 78, 80, 87, 93–112, 137, 156

Georgia, 45, 93, 122, 126, 129, 130, 170, 172, 173, 180, 184–85, 236, 247, 278, 280, 299
Great Black Swamp (Ohio), 71–77
Guerrero, Vicente, 5, 257, 265, 268

Haiti, 3, 4, 144, 148, 276, 279–80, 299, 300, 303
Hermosa (ship), 296–98, 306

Illinois, 97–98, 106, 108, 111
Indiana, 75, 79, 80, 81, 88, 97, 106, 108, 314n104
Informal freedom, 4, 6, 8, 9, 11, 12, 13–14, 116–31, 137–61, 168–90, 198
Iowa, 97, 108

Jefferson, Thomas, 25, 157
Judge, Ona, 30

Kansas, 73, 76, 86, 104, 210
Kentucky, 41, 45, 46, 70, 74–79, 81, 84–85, 106–7, 108, 123, 125, 127, 130, 173, 175, 228n37, 230n66, 303, 314n104

Lincoln, Abraham, 61, 94, 106, 111, 112, 287
Louisiana, 57, 119, 129–30, 173, 179, 180, 181–82, 186–87, 189–90, 203, 209, 214, 216, 236, 280, 281, 282, 292, 293, 297, 301. *See also* New Orleans (La.)

Manumission, 3, 6–8, 9, 22, 30, 143, 144, 156
Maroons, 8–9, 11, 14, 25, 84, 118, 123, 131, 168–91, 247n6
Marronage. *See* Maroons
Maryland, 1–2, 26, 27, 45, 98, 102–4, 116, 121–22, 123, 140, 170, 172, 173, 227n24, 279, 280–81, 283, 290, 294, 299, 300. *See also* Baltimore (Md.)
Massachusetts, 5, 22–23, 39, 99, 46, 50, 103–6, 109. *See also* Boston (Mass.)
Mexico, xii, 4–6, 8, 11, 14, 117, 137, 138, 169, 177, 198, 200, 203, 207–11, 213, 215, 223, 232–70, 305. *See also* Formal freedom
Michigan, 71, 78, 81, 83, 88, 40, 45, 46, 51, 59, 70, 74–79, 88. *See also* Detroit (river)
Mississippi (river), 73, 86, 88, 224n10, 280, 282, 285
Mississippi (state), 45, 126, 129, 173, 189, 203, 208, 209, 213, 216
Missouri, 106, 108, 211, 236

Nacogdoches (Tex.), 197–98, 207, 208, 214, 219, 222, 236, 237
Native Americans, xi, 9–10, 13, 23, 28, 70–89, 168, 210, 212, 213, 215, 230n66, 233, 242–44, 249n22, 250n29, 257–58, 294
New Jersey, 12, 22, 25–27, 28, 29–30, 102, 170
New Mexico, 129
New Orleans (La.), 7, 14–15, 43, 118, 120, 123, 124, 128, 142, 186–87, 240, 277, 280–304
New York (city), 25–27, 29, 30, 38, 39, 43, 45, 109, 110, 130, 299, 301
New York (state), 9, 18n14, 22, 25–30, 35, 38, 39, 43, 45, 46, 50, 54, 87, 103, 106, 109, 110, 130, 283, 287, 299, 301
North Carolina, 22, 45, 80–81, 120, 121, 122, 124, 125, 145, 171–75, 180, 183, 185, 280, 281
Northern U.S., xi–xii, 2–6, 8, 10–11, 12–13, 21–31, 34–62, 70–89, 93–112, 116–17, 124, 130, 137–38, 140, 141, 148, 160–61, 168–69, 183, 188, 190, 209, 211, 233–35, 237, 239, 242, 244, 245, 257, 301, 302, 303, 305. *See also* Free soil; Semiformal freedom; *individual states*
Northwest Territory, 5–6, 70–89
Nuevo León (Mexico), 266–68

Ohio (river), 5, 46, 74, 75, 77, 79, 81, 84, 87, 88, 106, 109, 305, 314n104
Ohio (state), 13, 34, 38, 40, 45, 55, 70–89, 106–11
Ontario (Canada), 4, 13, 34–69, 74, 75, 78, 79, 80–82, 85, 275

Pennsylvania, 2, 12, 27, 30, 38, 45, 46, 97–99, 101–4, 106, 109–10, 116, 141, 170, 250n30. *See also* Philadelphia (Penn.)
Personal liberty laws, xi, 6, 95–101, 103, 105
Philadelphia (Penn.), 22, 30, 38, 45, 101–2, 109–10

Quakers, 3, 22, 25, 80–81, 84, 88, 89, 108

Richmond (Va.), 7, 14, 34, 49, 121, 124, 125–26, 127, 130, 137–67, 173, 280, 282, 283–84, 286–89, 296, 301, 304
Rio Grande (river), 215, 217, 232–34, 236, 241–45, 251–52, 255, 258, 305
Ruggles, David, 39

Sabine (river), 208
San Antonio (Tex.), 199, 205, 209, 214, 232–33, 237, 238, 240, 241, 253, 258, 264
Second slavery, 4, 8, 11, 12–14, 119, 146
Semiformal freedom, 8, 9, 10–11, 13, 28, 84, 87, 93, 117
Seminoles, 213, 230n57, 250n29
Sierra Leone, 23–24, 28
Simcoe, John Graves, 35–36
Slave trade (domestic), 8, 11, 14, 119–23, 148, 173, 227, 243, 278, 280–305
Slave trade (transatlantic), 3, 24, 28, 38–39, 119, 275–80
Somerset v. Stewart, 25, 36–40, 97
South Carolina, 9–10, 23, 27, 96, 121, 122–23, 126, 127, 130, 169, 170, 171, 172, 174, 176–78, 182, 184, 280, 282, 293–95
Southern U.S. *See* Informal freedom; *individual states and cities*
Spanish Empire, 5, 9, 10, 28, 117, 137, 169, 233, 246n4, 277, 279, 281

Tamaulipas (Mexico), 14, 253, 259, 263, 265
Tennessee, 48, 172, 173, 227n24, 236, 238, 239, 281, 282
Texas, 5, 11, 14, 117, 137, 169, 173, 188, 197–223, 232–45, 251–70, 277, 280, 304
Treaty of Guadalupe Hidalgo, 243, 253
Tubman, Harriet, 49, 52
Tyler, John, 277–78, 291

Underground Railroad, xii, 14, 21, 24–28, 30, 39, 44, 51, 73, 75, 76, 80–81, 84, 86–87, 89, 95, 99, 107, 111, 138, 211, 237
Upper Canada. *See* Ontario (Canada)
U.S.-Mexican War, 252, 256

Vermont, 5, 22
Vigilance committees, 13, 95, 99, 102, 103, 105
Virginia, xi–xii, 1–2, 6–7, 8, 14, 23, 25–26, 27, 28, 30, 34, 37, 44–47, 49, 74, 75, 77, 78, 85, 98, 104, 118, 120, 122–23, 125–26, 128, 129, 130, 137–67, 170, 172, 173, 174, 177, 179, 181, 184, 185, 186, 236, 277, 278, 280, 282–89, 294, 300–301

Walker, David, 39, 49, 62, 148–49
War of 1812, 10, 27, 28, 35, 36, 53, 70–71, 75, 77–78, 82–83, 88, 118, 281, 282
Washington, D.C., 1–3, 7, 35, 41, 43, 107, 116–17, 122, 125, 129, 130, 277, 283–84, 303
Washington, George, 25
Wisconsin, 6, 105

SOUTHERN DISSENT

Edited by Stanley Harrold and Randall M. Miller

The Other South: Southern Dissenters in the Nineteenth Century, by Carl N. Degler, with a new preface (2000)
Crowds and Soldiers in Revolutionary North Carolina: The Culture of Violence in Riot and War, by Wayne E. Lee (2001)
"Lord, We're Just Trying to Save Your Water": Environmental Activism and Dissent in the Appalachian South, by Suzanne Marshall (2002)
The Changing South of Gene Patterson: Journalism and Civil Rights, 1960–1968, edited by Roy Peter Clark and Raymond Arsenault (2002; first paperback edition, 2020)
Gendered Freedoms: Race, Rights, and the Politics of Household in the Delta, 1861–1875, by Nancy D. Bercaw (2003)
Civil War on Race Street: The Civil Rights Movement in Cambridge, Maryland, by Peter B. Levy (2003)
South of the South: Jewish Activists and the Civil Rights Movement in Miami, 1945–1960, by Raymond A. Mohl, with contributions by Matilda "Bobbi" Graff and Shirley M. Zoloth (2004)
Throwing Off the Cloak of Privilege: White Southern Women Activists in the Civil Rights Era, edited by Gail S. Murray (2004)
The Atlanta Riot: Race, Class, and Violence in a New South City, by Gregory Mixon (2004)
Slavery and the Peculiar Solution: A History of the American Colonization Society, by Eric Burin (2005; first paperback edition, 2008)
"I Tremble for My Country": Thomas Jefferson and the Virginia Gentry, by Ronald L. Hatzenbuehler (2006; first paperback edition, 2009)
From Saint-Domingue to New Orleans: Migration and Influences, by Nathalie Dessens (2007)
Higher Education and the Civil Rights Movement: White Supremacy, Black Southerners, and College Campuses, edited by Peter Wallenstein (2008)
Burning Faith: Church Arson in the American South, by Christopher B. Strain (2008; first paperback edition, 2020)
Black Power in Dixie: A Political History of African Americans in Atlanta, by Alton Hornsby Jr. (2009; first paperback edition, 2016)
Looking South: Race, Gender, and the Transformation of Labor from Reconstruction to Globalization, by Mary E. Frederickson (2011; first paperback edition, 2012)
Southern Character: Essays in Honor of Bertram Wyatt-Brown, edited by Lisa Tendrich Frank and Daniel Kilbride (2011)
The Challenge of Blackness: The Institute of the Black World and Political Activism in the 1970s, by Derrick E. White (2011; first paperback edition, 2012)
Quakers Living in the Lion's Mouth: The Society of Friends in Northern Virginia, 1730–1865, by A. Glenn Crothers (2012; first paperback edition, 2013)
Unequal Freedoms: Ethnicity, Race, and White Supremacy in Civil War–Era Charleston, by Jeff Strickland (2015)
Show Thyself a Man: Georgia State Troops, Colored, 1865–1905, by Gregory Mixon (2016)
The Denmark Vesey Affair: A Documentary History, edited by Douglas R. Egerton and Robert L. Paquette (2017)
New Directions in the Study of African American Recolonization, edited by Beverly C. Tomek and Matthew J. Hetrick (2017)
Everybody's Problem: The War on Poverty in Eastern North Carolina, by Karen M. Hawkins (2017)
The Seedtime, the Work, and the Harvest: New Perspectives on the Black Freedom Struggle in America, edited by Jeffrey L. Littlejohn, Reginald K. Ellis, and Peter B. Levy (2018; first paperback edition, 2019)
Fugitive Slaves and Spaces of Freedom in North America, edited by Damian Alan Pargas (2018; first paperback edition, 2020)
Latino Orlando: Suburban Transformation and Racial Conflict, by Simone Delerme (2020)
Slavery and Freedom in the Shenandoah Valley during the Civil War Era, by Jonathan A. Noyalas (2021)

www.ingramcontent.com/pod-product-compliance
Lightning Source LLC
Chambersburg PA
CBHW031900220426
43663CB00006B/704